Capitalism and politics in Russia

Frontispiece. Top left: Andrei P. Shestov (1783–1847), who served as the mayor of Moscow from 1843 to 1846. Top right: Vasili A. Kokorev (1817–89), who was a liquor-tax concessionaire and the founder of railroad, steamship, and oil companies. Bottom left: Nikolai A. Naidenov (1834–1905), a cotton dyer, banker, Moscow Duma member, editor of historical records on Moscow and the merchants, and the president of the Moscow Stock Exchange Committee from 1877 to 1905. Bottom right: Grigori A. Krestovnikov (b. 1855), who was the son-in-law of Timofei S. Morozov, the leader of the Commercial-Industrial Party in 1905–6, and president of the Moscow Stock Exchange Committee from 1905 to 1915.

Capitalism and politics in Russia

A social history of the Moscow merchants, 1855–1905

Thomas C. Owen

Department of History
Louisiana State University

Cambridge University Press

Cambridge
London   New York   New Rochelle
Melbourne   Sydney

To Sue Ann

Published by the Press Syndicate of the University of Cambridge
The Pitt Building, Trumpington Street, Cambridge CB2 1RP
32 East 57th Street, New York, NY 10022, USA
296 Beaconsfield Parade, Middle Park, Melbourne 3206, Australia

First published 1981

Printed in the United States of America
Typeset by David E. Seham Associates Inc.,
Metuchen, N. J.
Printed and bound by The Murray Printing Co., Westford, Mass.

Library of Congress Cataloging in Publication Data
Owen, Thomas C
Capitalism and politics in Russia: A social history of the
Moscow merchants, 1855–1905
A revision of the author's thesis, Harvard, 1973,
Under title: The social and ideological evolution of
the Moscow merchants, 1840–1870.
Bibliography: p.
1. Merchants – Russia – History. 2. Merchants –
Russian Republic – Moscow – History. 3. Russia –
Social conditions. 4. Russia – Economic conditions.
I. Title.
HF3625.O93 1980 381'.0947 80–11279
ISBN 0 521 23173 6

Grateful acknowledgment is hereby made for permission to reprint several passages from the article "The Moscow Merchants and the Public Press, 1858–1868," *Jahrbüecher füer Geschichte Osteuropas*, N. S., vol. 23, no. 1 (March 1975), 26–38.

Sources for the photographs used in this book are as follows: Shestov and Naidenov portraits: Moscow, Birzha, *Moskovskaia birzha 1839–1889* (Moscow, 1889), portrait section; Kokorev and Krestovnikov portraits: P. Kh. Spasskii, ed., *Istoriia torgovli i promyshlennosti v Rossii*, vol. 1, 4 parts (St. Petersburg, 1910–11), part 2; Shchukin museum: Michael S. Ginsburg, "Art Collectors of Old Russia: The Morosovs and the Shchukins," *Apollo*, N. S., vol. 98, no. 142 (December 1973), p. 479; Tretiakov poorhouse chapel: Vasilii N. Storozhev, ed., *Istoriia Moskovskogo kupecheskogo obshchestva, 1836–1913*, 5 vols. (Moscow, 1913–16), vol. 5, part 1; Trimount factory: Akademiia nauk SSSR, institut istorii, *Istoriia Moskvy*, 7 vols. (Moscow, 1952–67), vol. 4 (1954), p. 105; and Moscow City Duma Building: *Istoriia Moskvy*, vol. 4 (1954), p. 499.

Contents

Preface

This study began as an inquiry into the social transformation of the Moscow guild merchants under the initial impact of industrialization. My doctoral dissertation, "The Social and Ideological Evolution of the Moscow Merchants, 1840–1870" (Harvard, 1973), sought to explain an apparent paradox of Russian social history: that the movement to foster local self-government, individual rights, and constitutional restraints on the state's autocratic power developed within the zemstvos under the leadership of the gentry, whose economic strength was gradually declining, while the increasingly wealthy industrialists remained largely indifferent to liberalism as a political creed. The present work traces the development of the merchants' ideology beyond 1870 to a crucial political watershed, the Revolution of 1905. This study describes the "prehistory" of the Russian industrialists' role in the struggle among autocracy, liberalism, and radicalism in the 1905–20 period and is offered as a contribution to the comparative social and political history of modern revolutions.

Moscow was chosen as the geographical setting of the study for several reasons. First, practical considerations made it necessary to limit the investigation to one major economic area – in this case, the Central Industrial Region of Russia, over five-eighths the size of France[1] – without considering in detail the peculiarities of such subsidiary areas as the Baltic cities, Russian Poland, the Ukraine and Black Sea littoral, the middle and lower Volga, the Ural region, and Siberia. Second, in the mid-nineteenth century, the ideological evolution of the industrialists proceeded further in Moscow than in any area other than St. Petersburg, and the industry of the Central Region was free from dependence on direct state purchases, unlike that of the northern capital. Therefore, the experience of Moscow promised to show best the political limits beyond which the Russian industrialists would not go. Finally, even as economic growth gradually enlarged the scope of possible political development, cultural traditions played a large role in determining the direction of that development. Moscow, "the heart of Russia," was the center of the country's native culture; and more merchants lived in Moscow province than in any other. This

vii

area therefore seemed the most logical setting for a study of the cultural and ideological changes that occurred within this social group.

The focus on the merchants cannot, of course, be justified in terms of their numerical importance, for they remained a small part of Russia's predominantly peasant society. Rather, it must be stressed that their limited numbers were no measure of the degree of their significance in public life. Elites, especially newly emerging ones with great wealth, have often played a crucial role in history, and the Moscow merchant leaders are best understood in this light. Within the merchant estate, moreover, the wealthiest families tended to take a more prominent place than the less affluent, so that the narrative at times reads like a collective biography of the twenty families whose extensive intermarriages are illustrated in the Genealogies in the Appendix. Several responses can be made to the objection that the cultural, economic, and political behavior of these leaders might somehow have been atypical of the Moscow merchant estate as a whole. First, the wealthy leaders were elected by their more humble fellows to important positions in the estate organization, the municipal government, and the stock exchange (see Appendix, Tables I and II), and they therefore deserve to be considered as spokesmen for the merchants as a group. Second, while it was generally the wealthy merchants who left what little documentary evidence there is, the available memoir literature, which is not contradicted by other sources, supports the hypothesis that the less affluent followed the lead of the rich in the affairs of the merchant estate in Moscow.

The question of the typicality of certain individuals and organizations within the Moscow merchant estate cannot be separated, therefore, from the problem of the reliability of existing source materials. A few voluminous works by Russian and Soviet authors do cast light on particular aspects of merchant life such as philanthropy, art patronage, and the labor question. However, merchants rarely committed their political opinions to paper, either in policy statements or in memoirs, and so the historian of this social group must use a variety of peripheral and obscure sources.[2] The present study draws on rare memoirs and family histories, some previously unavailable outside the Soviet Union. It is also based on evidence from selected Moscow archives, particularly those of industrial leaders and intellectuals who participated in what is called here *the merchant-Slavophile alliance*. As far as possible, the following narrative presents a balanced overview of the Moscow merchants' public activities in the half-century before 1905 and a general introduction to the role of capitalists in Russian political life.[3]

A tripartite terminology has been employed to represent the cultural, economic, and political evolution of the Moscow merchants in this period. The *traditional* merchant way of life persisted well into the nineteenth century. Only under the impact of West-European technological innovations in the 1840s did there emerge from the wealthiest traditional families a new group of merchant leaders, whose economic practices deserve the Weberian label of *capitalist*, and whose dynamic new view of the world is termed here *the merchant ideology*. Finally, after several decades of increasingly important activity by the capitalist merchants in the public life of the Russian Empire, leadership in Moscow passed to a younger group of merchants, who emerged from the Revolution of 1905 with a genuinely class-conscious ideology defined here as *bourgeois*. The rationale for these three terms is given at appropriate places in the narrative, and it is for the reader to decide whether they are useful or whether a different periodization and terminology should be sought. The major point made here is that the Moscow merchant estate was in fact neither a genuine class nor a bearer of liberalism before 1905, but achieved a rather comfortable place within the Russian old regime. Of the various theoretical conclusions that flow from this observation, the two most important are that the Marxist term *Russian bourgeoisie* appears to be a contradiction in terms for the nineteenth century, and that the theory of modernization, insofar as it posits a direct link between economic development and political liberalization, fits modern Russian history no better than does Marxian theory.

Except for a single digression in Chapter 2 into contrasts between the Moscow merchant ideology and that of the West-European bourgeoisie, the comparative aspects of this study remain implicit because of space constraints. However, the essential features of the Moscow merchants' economic role, social position, estate and class consciousness, and political activity are described here, so that the major contrasts between West-European and Russian patterns will become clear when this study is read in conjunction with works on the European bourgeoisie and liberalism.[4]

My debts to previous historians, both Russian and Western, are made clear in the notes. The pioneering work of several scholars, however, deserves special mention: the Menshevik writers Osip A. Ermansky (alias A. Gushka) and Pavel A. Berlin; the former merchants Pavel A. Buryshkin and Vladimir P. Riabushinsky; Roger Portal; and the Soviet historians Iosif F. Gindin, Ksana S. Kuibysheva, Vladimir Ia. Laverychev, and G. F. Semeniuk. I received valuable comments from Richard Pipes, my dissertation advisor, and from Edward Keenan, Charles Timberlake, Samuel Baron, and several anonymous readers. Special thanks are also due the International Research and Exchanges Board (IREX), under whose auspices I worked in Moscow archives and libraries in 1971–2; Nina S. Kiniapina, my advisor at Moscow State University; the Russian Research Center at Harvard; my department chairman at Louisiana State University, John L. Loos, and the LSU Council on Research; and the staff of Widener Library at Harvard and the Inter-Library Loan librarians at LSU, Janellyn Kleiner and Olar Bell. The late Ethel R. Derby kindly provided a secluded residence in the Vermont hills, where most of the study was written over several summers.

My wife, Sue Ann, provided endless encouragement throughout the slow and often difficult process of investigating and attempting to explain the curious behavior of the Moscow merchants. The book's thematic consistency owes much to her high standards of research and writing and her excellent critical sense.

Any errors of fact or interpretation remain, of course, my own responsibility.

The perennial problems that plague the Russian historian in transliteration and chronology have been dealt with in the following manner. All Russian words are transliterated according to the Library of Congress system, minus diacritical marks, with several minor exceptions: in the names of people and places, soft and hard signs are omitted; the final *i* in masculine names is dropped (e.g., Dmitri); and *-sky* and *-tiev* replace *-skii* and *-t'ev*. European names are given in the original Roman spelling whenever possible (e.g., Goujon, Heiden, Knoop, and Zindel – not Guzhon, Geiden, Knop, and Tsindel), but the names of all cited authors of books and articles in Russian (Witte excepted) are transliterated without modification for the sake of bibliographical accuracy (e.g., Katts, Kizevetter, Rozental, and Vistengof – not Katz, Kiesewetter, Rosenthal, and Wistenhoff). Dates are given according to the Julian or "old-style" Russian calendar, which lagged twelve days behind the Gregorian or "new-style" European calendar in the nineteenth century and thirteen days in the twentieth.

T. C. O.

Abbreviations of organizations

CTM   Council of Trade and Manufacturing *(Sovet torgovli i manufaktur)*, formed 1872 in St. Petersburg.

MIS   Moscow Industrial Society *(Obshchestvo dlia sodeistviia uluchsheniiu i razvitiiu manufakturnoi promyshlennosti)*, formed 1889 in Moscow.

MSCTM   Moscow Section *(Moskovskoe otdelenie)* of the CTM, formed 1872.

MSEC   Moscow Stock Exchange Committee *(Moskovskii birzhevoi komitet)*, formed 1839.

MSES   Moscow Stock Exchange Society *(Moskovskoe birzhevoe obshchestvo)*, formed 1870.

MSMC   Moscow Section of the Manufacturing Council *(Moskovskoe otdelenie manufakturnogo soveta)*, formed 1829.

MSRIS   Moscow Section of the Russian Industrial Society *(Moskovskoe otdelenie Obshchestva dlia sodeistviia russkoi promyshlennosti i torgovle)*, formed 1884.

PSM   Petersburg Society of Manufacturers *(Obshchestvo dlia sodeistviia uluchsheniiu i razvitiiu fabrichno-zavodskoi promyshlennosti)*, formed 1893 and chartered 1897 in St. Petersburg.

RIS   Russian Industrial Society *(Obshchestvo dlia sodeistviia russkoi promyshlennosti i torgovle)*, formed 1867 in St. Petersburg.

The Moscow merchant estate before 1855

The inferior position of merchants in Russian society

Bearded, patriarchal, semi-Asiatic in dress and manner, and fully versed in the arts of haggling and swindling, the Russian merchants in the early nineteenth century not only lacked the distinctive urban ethos of the West but also clung to their obscurantist cultural traditions. Historically, Russian merchants had been unable to accumulate large and stable fortunes, an important precondition for the formation of a self-reliant middle class. Russia lay outside the main world trade routes that enriched the Atlantic seafaring traders from the sixteenth century onward, and in the seventeenth and early eighteenth centuries the tsar monopolized several lucrative sectors of trade: salt, vodka, grain, caviar, and sable furs. While a few individuals and families became rich, often as contractors to the state, the tsars of the pre-Petrine period imposed on the merchant elite (*gosti*) a number of "decidedly onerous" duties. As customs collectors, as the supervisors of various state enterprises, and "as the sovereign's factors in a trade whose dimensions earned the tsar a reputation as Russia's first merchant," the *gosti* assumed heavy financial obligations toward the throne. Although endowed with various privileges and honors, they enjoyed their favored position only at the whim of the autocrat.[1] Furthermore, the lack of legal guarantees to protect private property from confiscation or outright theft by the state or by powerful noblemen prevented the growth of solid merchant fortunes and stifled entrepreneurial initiative.

Well into the nineteenth century, Russia lacked large commercial cities in which a bourgeois culture on the Western model could grow and flourish. In 1840, only St. Petersburg and Moscow contained more than 65,000 inhabitants, with 470,000 and 349,000, respectively; by 1863, Russia still had only three cities of over 100,000: the two capitals and the main Black Sea port, Odessa.[2] Between 1830 and 1858 the total male population of all

Russian cities, although it had grown from 1,182,500 to 2,089,100, represented only 6 to 7 percent of all males in the Russian Empire.[3]

Moreover, out of a population of 62 million persons in 1836, only 235,000 belonged to merchant families, or less than one-half of 1 percent of the empire's total population.[4] Merchants, whose numbers increased nearly threefold (from 72,700 to 215,200 males) between 1830 and 1858, still comprised only 6 to 10 percent of the total urban population.[5]

A similar pattern prevailed in Moscow, the center of native Russian merchant culture. In 1851, fully 22 percent of all the 180,000 Russian merchants, including their wives and children, lived in the provinces of the Central Industrial Region: Moscow, Vladimir, Kostroma, Iaroslavl, Tver, and Kaluga. Moscow led all the 67 provinces of the empire, excluding Finland and Poland, with 17,734 merchants, more than double the number in the province of St. Petersburg, the northern center of trade.[6] Yet even in their own stronghold, the very hub of Russian commerce and industry, the Moscow merchants accounted for only 4.8 to 6.0 percent of the city's population, in spite of an increase between 1835 and 1871 from 16,233 to 36,339.[7]

Had these men dominated Russian trade and industry as their legal title of *merchant* suggested, they might have offset their demographic disadvantage with economic power and influence. In fact, the guild merchants' demographic weakness resulted largely from their inability to dominate commercial and manufacturing activity. In the early nineteenth century, they shared the economic field with several other social groups who enjoyed superior economic power and numerical weight under the Russian government's system of social estates (singular, *soslovie*).[8]

City residents who were not in the gentry, clergy, or peasantry belonged to one of the three urban estates: the merchants *(kupechestvo)*, the petty townsmen *(meshchanstvo)*, or the artisans *(remeslenniki)*. The merchants owned the largest factories and managed wholesale and retail trading businesses. The urban residents known as *meshchane* engaged in petty retail trade, small-scale manufacturing, and sales activities for merchants. The artisans worked as skilled and unskilled laborers in craft guilds *(tsekhi)*. Income and occupation, far more than birth, determined a person's legal status in society. A free individual could leave one estate and join another in November and December of any year, provided he could pay an annual inscription fee.

A confusion of economic and legal categories pervaded the Russian system of estates. The word *trader (torgovets)*, a general economic term, designated any person who bought and sold goods in significant quantities. He might belong to the peasantry, the *meshchanstvo*, or the merchant estate. Only a small minority of traders in Russia were merchants *(kuptsy)* in the strict juridical sense; as members of the merchant estate, they received from the state specific privileges that distinguished them from the trading peasants, the *meshchane*, and the gentry. Unlike the *meshchane* and the artisans, the merchants were exempt from the soul tax, the military obligation, and (except for the third guild) corporal punishment. The most significant of the merchants' privileges was one they shared with the gentry: the right to engage in wholesale trade and to own a large factory. Thus, despite the narrowly commercial connotation of the term *merchant*, the merchant estate included industrialists as well as traders. To further complicate the situation, many petty traders and workmen who might have been expected to remain *meshchane* because of their small enterprises and incomes joined a merchant guild, not in order to expand their economic activities, but simply to avoid the obligation of military service.[9] Finally, manufacturers and traders from other estates – the gentry and "honorary citizens" (discussed later) – and merchants from other cities were entitled to register in a guild as "temporary merchants."

Within the City Society (*gorodskoe obshchestvo)* of every Russian city, the Merchant Section *(otdelenie)* was composed of three guilds (singular, *gildiia)*, in which merchants enrolled according to their declared wealth. All merchants were obligated to pay a yearly sum for a certificate that guaranteed their social privileges as well as their right to trade and to operate factories. Upon purchase of a first-guild certificate, costing 600 rubles after 1839, a merchant could engage in foreign or domestic commerce, own ships and factories, and perform banking functions, provided he declared at least 15,000 rubles in assets. Second-guild merchants could run factories and domestic wholesale or retail businesses worth at least 6,000 rubles upon purchase of a certificate for 264 rubles. Third-guild merchants could trade only as retailers in their own city or district *(uezd)*, but under the Guild Reform of 1824, they could operate small factories producing simple goods such as leather, candles, wax, timber, and bricks. From 1839 on, their certificates cost 30 to 66 rubles (1¼ percent of the declaration of worth), for assets ranging from 2,400 to 6,000 rubles.[10] Except for periodic changes in the certificate payments and the abolition of the third guild in 1863,[11] this formal structure persisted until 1917.

Despite the medieval West-European connotation of town self-government implicit in the word *guild*, the Merchant Section had no independent

role, but merely served the state by performing municipal police duties
and collecting local taxes. In addition, the merchants were required to
serve – without any remuneration from the city administration or the imperial government – when elected, by their assembled fellows, to such city
offices as mayor (*gorodskoi golova*), members (*poverennye*) of the House of
the City Society, Duma members, deputies of the City Assembly, judges,
police constables, and other posts.[12] Merchants also served, without pay,
as elected members of boards of various philanthropic and municipal institutions: the merchants' Practical Commercial Academy, the *meshchane*
school, commercial courts, and the Trade Deputation.

Not only were the merchants' privileges offset by the obligation of un-
paid city service; their entire social situation was precarious, since merchant status depended on the purchase of a guild certificate. If a merchant
and his sons failed to make the yearly certificate payment, all the members
of the family sank into the *meshchanstvo* and lost the right to continue their
usual business, by which they might raise the necessary funds to reenter
the merchant estate the following year. To compound this problem, merchants remained ineligible until 1861 to own populated land, a potential
source of additional income.[13] Peter III and Catherine II had deprived the
merchants of the right to obtain additional "possessional" serfs (those assigned by the state to a specific plant or factory); and in 1807, merchants
were barred from entrance into the "eminent citizen" (*imenitnyi
grazhdanin*) category, whose members were exempt from the yearly payment of merchant dues.

For these reasons, in the early nineteenth century, it became increasingly common for merchants to leave their estate as soon as they had accumulated a substantial amount of money. Many merchants trained their
most capable sons for military or bureaucratic service, which could lead to
a secure position outside the merchant estate. A merchant who became a
"cavalier" by receiving membership in an imperial honorary order from
the Governing Senate, or who was granted a ninth-class rank in recognition of his public service or charitable activities, automatically became a
member of the hereditary gentry.[14]

This process led one merchant in 1830 to claim that "the flow of the
leading factory owners" into the gentry was the main cause of Russia's
industrial backwardness in relation to Western Europe, inasmuch as it
deprived the empire of a sturdy entrepreneurial class.[15] The attainment of
gentry rank did not require a merchant to abandon his business, since he
could register in a guild as a "temporary merchant" from year to year for

an indefinite period. However, because of both the high social status of the gentry relative to the merchants and the gentry's privilege of collecting rents from serfs on landed estates without significant economic risk, ennoblement usually meant the end of a business career.[16]

Although limited and imprecise, the available statistical evidence illustrates the steady decline in the numbers of merchants in Moscow because of their insecure economic and juridical position. In 1747, there were 13,442 holders of merchant certificates; in 1765, 8,733; in 1812, 3,482; and in 1822, 1,695. To a certain extent, this decline is attributable to the consolidation of up to twenty relatives in a single "household." In this way, merchants could legally qualify for the right to trade under one certificate issued to the head of the household.[17] Still, these figures, when considered in conjunction with the foregoing observations, indicate that a small number of merchants from the first two guilds entered the gentry and military or bureaucratic service, while considerable numbers of third-guild merchants apparently slipped back into the *meshchanstvo.*

This outflow of persons from the merchant estate had such deleterious economic effects that the government created, in 1832, a new urban category to guarantee a degree of economic security for a few leading commercial and industrial figures in each Russian city. These merchants, who were granted the title of honorary citizen *(pochetnyi grazhdanin)*, received a lifetime exemption from the yearly certificate payment, and thus could freely engage in trade and industry as a member of one of the three guilds despite an occasional unprofitable year. "Hereditary honorary citizenship," which applied to the merchant, his family, and his heirs, could be attained after ten years in the first guild or twenty in the second, together with an unblemished court record. The Governing Senate also named as hereditary honorary citizens the recipients of the St. Stanislav medal and, after 1845, the order of St. Vladimir. A merchant might become a "personal honorary citizen" by receiving a gold or silver medal from the Ministry of Finance for exemplary conduct in trade or manufacturing.[18]

Yet the government was unable to strengthen the merchant estate by this simple modification of formal legal categories, since third-guild merchants, who suffered most from economic insecurity, had little hope of attaining honorary citizenship. After reaching its lowest point in 1822, the number of Moscow merchants grew to approximately 3,000 certificate-holders in 1835. However, a high degree of movement in and out of the Moscow estate is indicated by the fact that 2,489 merchant families sank into the *meshchanstvo* between 1835 and 1869.[19]

In 1841, the Third Section (secret police) warned that the new privileges created in 1832 had merely allowed a great many merchants to escape the yearly guild payment, to the detriment of the empire's economy and the city's finances. Although honorary citizens had the right to trade and manufacture, most did not, preferring to live off a fortune already accumulated.[20] Thus, in spite of the government's measures, merchant families rarely continued in the same business for more than two generations; some took up new enterprises, while most left the merchant estate entirely.[21]

Just as the government's regulation determined the juridical position of the merchant estate in Russian society, so the state, by sponsoring industry and trade in the second quarter of the nineteenth century, in effect controlled the entire economy of the Moscow region. Moscow served as the center of the wholesale trade of the Russian Empire. While St. Petersburg was the primary port for foreign trade, it was in the stalls of the Trading Rows *(riady)* in the Kitai-gorod area of Moscow that merchandise from all parts of the empire was bought and sold in vast quantities.[22]

Light industry – especially hand textile weaving, printing, and finishing – was also highly developed in the Central Industrial Region. The city of Moscow itself functioned as the commercial center for this textile production, but many of the largest factories were located in villages in the surrounding countryside. Rural manufacturing in the 1840s was based on a certain amount of hired labor in village factories; it also relied heavily on the "putting-out" system of cottage weaving and printing that employed serf families living at home during the fall, winter, and spring. Between 1840 and 1870, before mechanized weaving and printing destroyed these cottage industries, the modern factory and the cottage coexisted in a state of economic symbiosis: the yarn produced in the spinning mills went to the serf's simple handlooms and workshops for weaving, printing, and finishing.[23]

While the growth of industry and trade in the Moscow region reflected genuine economic potential in terms of propitious trade patterns, abundant fuel supplies, sufficient investment capital, and available labor, it was the state that provided an essential prerequisite for development – tariff protection.[24] The minister of finance from 1823 to 1844, Count E. F. Kankrin, established high tariffs to protect existing Russian industries from being ruined by increasingly cheap imported goods as industrial progress gathered momentum in Western Europe. The effect of the tariff was especially dramatic in the textile industry. Large spinning mills equipped with French and Belgian machines first appeared in small villages in the Moscow region in 1835: Lepeshkin's factory and that of Lukin and the Skuratovs.[25]

Many more factories sprang up after 1839, when Ludwig Knoop began importing French textile machines into Russia. After the British government formally abrogated its ban on exports of industrial machinery in 1842, Knoop established permanent offices in Britain and Moscow, through which all the major textile manufacturers in the Moscow area received the necessary spinning, weaving, and printing equipment for their rapidly developing factories.[26] Most of the textile industrialists whom Knoop supplied with machines were rich merchants recently emerged from serfdom.[27] They were typified by Savva V. Morozov (1770–1860), who purchased Knoop's first machines in 1839 and subsequently managed one of the largest rural textile complexes in Russia.[28]

The empire's cotton-spinning industry grew up rapidly under the extremely high tariff protection of 5 rubles on a pud of imported cotton yarn (6.5 after 1841). Between 1831 and 1860, Russian imports of raw cotton (mostly from the American South) rose from 149,000 to 2,622,000 puds a year, and Russia's annual yarn production increased from 690,000 to 2,511,000 puds. By 1861, the new, mechanized spinning mills supplied 91 percent of the yarn used in the Russian cotton-weaving industry, compared to 19 percent in 1831.[29] The high tariff wall against imported wool cloth also allowed Russian wool weaving to grow in quantity and technique between 1836 and 1860.

In addition to the tariff, the imperial government provided outright financial aid to industry such as loans and land grants to producers of coarse wool cloth (*sukno*) for the army. Other forms of subsidies included guaranteed state purchases of rails for the Moscow–St. Petersburg line from the iron plants in the Urals and special loans for textile manufacturers.[30]

In still another act of state initiative in industry, Count Kankrin established the Manufacturing and Commercial Councils (*Manufakturnyi sovet; Kommercheskii sovet*) in 1828 and 1829, respectively, as a source of economic data and as a forum for discussions among officials, merchants, and scholars.[31] State tutelage extended even to the appointment of the Manufacturing Council members by the minister of finance, subject to the approval of the emperor, and no substantial policy questions were ever raised for discussion. Manufacturers' requests for monopoly privileges on the use of new machines and techniques occupied most of the time and energy of the Moscow Section of the Manufacturing Council (MSMC).

Indeed, the council sections were permitted to submit statements on economic policy only in answer to specific questions from the Ministry of Finance.[32]

The state also regulated closely the most representative merchant organization, the Moscow Stock Exchange Committee (*birzhevoi komitet* – MSEC), established in 1839. From the eighteenth century until 1839, the Moscow Exchange had functioned mostly as a subsidiary office of the St. Petersburg Exchange, and the merchants in Moscow lacked a central institution and meeting place. Since 1812, they had gathered to discuss their business affairs, primarily wholesale trading in commodities, in the open area on the corner of Ilinka Street and Khrustalnyi Lane in Kitai-gorod (the commercial quarter) near the Kremlin. The only official act of the stock exchange was the election, by first-guild merchants, of a "court broker" (*gof-makler*) from among the registered brokers in Moscow, to supervise the setting of the rate of exchange (*veksel'nyi kurs*) – a crucial operation enabling the use of bills of exchange for commerce before modern banking facilities appeared in the 1860s.

From 1839 to 1870, the MSEC's four to eight members (*starshiny*) were elected every three years by the first-guild merchants of the city, except that the president's post was held ex officio by the Moscow mayor until 1859. Thus on the committee sat the most influential and respected personages in the Moscow merchant estate.[33] Upon moving into a new stock exchange building in the Merchants' Yard (*Gostinnyi dvor*), the committee assumed the court broker's function of establishing the rates for bills of exchange, and began to publish the commodity prices set by the court broker. It also regulated trade practices in Moscow, certified technical experts on legal questions, and supervised brokers and inspectors of commodities (*brakovshchiki*).

The committee had the legal right to discuss matters of state economic policy, "partly on the suggestion of the Ministry of Finance, partly on the statement of the stock exchange merchants"; but as late as the 1860s, its formal memoranda to the Ministry concerned only narrowly practical questions: problems of deliveries by the railroad, especially during the busy fair season in the fall; inconveniences of the Moscow customs office's procedures; and similar matters.[34] As the merchants were later to complain, the MSEC in no way functioned as a self-governing body of commercial and industrial leaders on the order of West-European chambers of commerce, but, like the Manufacturing and Commercial Councils, remained a consultative organization with no real influence on economic policy.

The leading role of the state in the Russian economy kept the merchants in a dependent relationship. They needed the protectionist tariffs, government subsidies, and loans; but at the same time, they were constrained by official regimentation of the councils and the MSEC. The Regulations on Trade specifically stated: "It is forbidden to speak in the stock exchange about political matters or military orders, and to repeat or spread rumors, under penalty of law."[35]

Social life and political attitudes in the 1840s

If state control hindered the development of a vigorous, self-confident merchant estate, of equal importance in this regard was the cultural traditionalism of the merchants themselves. Strong traditions of Asiatic dress, patriarchal family life, primitive business practices, and aversion to education still dominated the merchant culture in Moscow well into the nineteenth century. Despite the efforts of a small minority to adopt modern technology from the 1840s onward, the Moscow merchant leadership – meaning the most enterprising and the most outspoken in the political arena – was far less capable and less assertive than were European businessmen and the Russian gentry. The merchant way of life deserves the Weberian label "traditional," in the sense that the past provided legitimacy for behavior; in many ways, it resembled that of the Russian peasantry. Indeed, as one merchant leader later asserted, "We, the Moscow merchants, were essentially nothing but *trading muzhiks, the highest stratum of the thrifty Russian muzhiks.*"[36] The constant influx of enterprising peasants into the merchant estate naturally contributed to the persistence of many features of peasant life within the merchant milieu.

Subtle differences existed, however, between the culture of the peasant masses and that of the relatively affluent merchants. These were set forth in a slightly satirical way by Aleksandr S. Ushakov, an educated Moscow merchant well acquainted with the foibles of his comrades. In the introduction to his story entitled "The Big Shots" *(Tuzy)*, he traced the change of attitudes that often occurred when a peasant rose into the merchant estate.

[The] proximity of the city and especially of some great focal point of Russian life which lies not far off inspires him to bold thoughts that make his strong hands itch to go into business. First of all, he needs money – money for everything: to apply his hand to work, to carry on his business in a productive way, and finally to find a way out to a more open and a wider road: for the transition from the village way of life to that of the city, from peasant status to an estate title, to exchange the name of muzhik for a title: *meshchanin*, merchant, honorary citizen, manufacturing [or] commercial councilor, cavalier, etc. . . . This transition is not easy, however. Only those who are naturally talented and also lucky can achieve it. And in Russia one who becomes a rich big shot rarely remains a man. For the most part he becomes ugly and turns into a Russian merchant, a kulak, an oppressive factory owner, about whom there are so many stories in Rus'.[37]

Although Ushakov perhaps unfairly attributed to his fellow merchants the kulak vices of greed and cruelty, there is no doubt that the merchants' distinctive way of life showed little evidence of Peter the Great's attempt, more than a century before, to westernize Russian society. In old Muscovy, traditional business practices had proved quite useful, since obedience to habit and the avoidance of innovation had served to protect the merchants from sudden shifts in economic fortunes. The merchants had characteristically exercised extreme caution and defensiveness, fearing expropriation of their wealth by the tsar or powerful noblemen. As a result, they rarely risked their capital in long-term investments, preferring short-term economic gain and distrusting other estates and foreigners as dangerous competitors.

The merchants' defensive attitude toward the external world – *stepennost'* – revealed itself plainly in their old-fashioned way of life. The traditional merchant quarter of Moscow, Zamoskvoreche (literally, across the river, south of the Kremlin), was a tight mass of small, cloistered dwellings in firmly locked courtyards. Vissarion Belinsky once likened the houses there to tiny fortresses "preparing to endure a lengthy siege." "The windows there are hung with curtains, and the gates are under lock and key. A knock on them starts an expensive dog barking . . ."[38] A few merchants moved into other areas of Moscow, especially after the fire of 1812; by the early 1840s, many mansions formerly owned by prominent nobles had passed into the hands of wealthy traders and industrialists.[39]

Within these homes, whether poor or pretentious, the Moscow merchants dressed essentially like rich peasants, in long coats or Asiatic kaftans, wearing full beards and hair cut in a circle *(v skobku)* and parted in the middle. Their plump wives wore peasant scarves, heavily embroidered dresses, and ornate jewelry.[40] In keeping with their traditional culture, the father exercised absolute rule over the family. One merchant wrote that, "like everything in Russia at that time, the old family way of life [*byt*] was built on the principle of autocracy . . . Conscious of his power, father made absolutely sure that no one in the household would doubt it. He was the boss. He approved and condemned without appeal;

nothing, be it important or trifling, was done in the house without him."
The undisputed master kept the family's social contacts to a minimum.
"We led a sheltered life. We received only relatives and went visiting only
to see relatives. Father never let the sons go anywhere, even rarely to see
their married sisters." At ten o'clock, all guests left the house and it was
locked tightly for the night.[41] Wives and daughters were kept in submission, hidden from public view in the Asiatic manner. Contrary to the
Western bourgeois practice, they did not help run the family shop.[42]

Religion dominated merchant life as much as did the autocratic family
structure; indeed, the Old-Testament principle of patriarchal authority
buttressed the power of the father within the family.[43] Icons hung on the
walls of merchant dwellings, and rich patriarchs commonly built private
chapels in their homes. In keeping with this biblical outlook, Lepeshkin
named his cotton-spinning factory "Ascension," while Lukin and the
Skuratovs called theirs "Resurrection." Merchant life was particularly influenced by the fact that Schismatics (Old Believers), the religious fundamentalists whose strict asceticism underlay their great fortunes, primarily
in textiles, made up about half the population of Moscow, or 186,000
persons, in 1848.[44]

Among both Old-Believer and Orthodox merchants, religious rites and
holy days had a crucial social function. The privations of Lent (*velikii
post*), followed by the joyful celebration of Easter, marked the high point
of the annual cycle. Only on Christmas and Easter did the homes of traditional merchants remain open with warm hospitality to friends and relatives, who spent the whole day in a continual round of social visits. Then,
in keeping with the old Russian customs, merchants would serve tea from
a large brass samovar and offer the special token of hospitality: bread and
salt served on a silver platter (*khleb-sol'*).[45] The sacrament of matrimony
followed an elaborate ritual of matchmaking, including the annual "show
of eligible daughters" (*smotriny*) in May. "Loaded down with ornaments
and jewelry," they paraded silently before prospective in-laws, amid "a
great deal of haggling back and forth" over the dowry.[46] The wedding
itself cemented not only social but also business ties between merchant
families (see Appendix, Genealogies).

The grip of paternal domination and religious obscurantism remained
strong because of the lack of both practical and humanistic education in
the traditional merchant culture. A typical merchant's education consisted
of memorization of the Church-Slavonic alphabet and study of the prayer
book; "education ended with the book of Psalms."[47] So strong was the

influence of tradition that the merchants devoutly feared foreign and secular ideas as harbingers of "the violation of public order, atheism, and free-thinking." This superstitious attitude led directly to "the denial of the benefit of education in general . . ."[48]

A well-known anecdote about the mayor of Moscow from 1846 to 1849, Semen L. Lepeshkin (1785–1855), illustrated this interplay among religiosity, patriarchal rule, and fear of education. Riding with his adolescent son to the Nizhny Novgorod Fair during a severe thunderstorm, he crossed himself and muttered a prayer after every lightning bolt: "Holy, Holy, Lord God of Hosts." He looked at his son, who was smiling ironically. "Don't you see the powers and anger of God in the heavenly signs?" he demanded. "But that's only electricity, Papa, nothing more," answered the boy. After the storm had passed, the old man stopped the carriage and brutally whipped his son with a birch rod, saying over and over, "Here's for your electrics [*elektrizm*] and here's for you to know the reasons why you should cross yourself." Yet Lepeshkin "enjoyed universal respect" in the Moscow merchant society as a good and wise man.[49]

The merchants' low educational level, combined with their single-minded devotion to the fortunes of the family firm, created a vicious circle of cultural backwardness and commercial stagnation. Unlike the Western bourgeoisie, whose competitive spirit led to the adoption of efficient business practices, the Russian merchants shunned both commercial education and modern management techniques. This traditionalism was not wholly irrational, since innovation was financially dangerous and a single year of poor business could force a merchant and his family down into the *meshchanstvo*. The old habits thus persisted from generation to generation. As Haxthausen commented, "The merchants in the Russian towns constitute a virtually hereditary estate; the sons almost always become merchants. When they are twelve the father takes the sons into the business. Thus they receive no school education, only learning to read and write; but they all can calculate on the Russian abacus. It is axiomatic that the son should know no more than the father."[50]

The merchant Ushakov, one of the few who criticized the backwardness of his fellows, described this attitude of obscurantism in caustic terms.

The society of our rich merchants, whom the simple people have neatly called "big shots," constitutes its own special social group . . . Sham, deceit, short-sighted cunning, skill in arranging deals, doubtful honesty . . . – these make up a large part of their intellectual and moral capital. They make their poverty even greater by locking the door to genuine education and by treating coldly and unsympathetically those of their own people who develop a sincere desire to follow a trade other than their fathers'. Such individuals face an extremely dismal situation there. A living, free idea has up to now been stifled and confined in this society . . .[51]

Thus Russian commerce, as an astute though hostile Baltic German observed, continued to be merely "petty retailing on a large scale."[52] Most merchants, being illiterate, kept their complicated business figures in their heads, without any system of bookkeeping. Lacking written records of past transactions, they had no means of analyzing their businesses or improving their techniques. Only a few of the leading merchants maintained complete records of their commercial transactions, written mostly by hired clerks.[53] Yet even these were far from being modern European business journals. They ran from Easter to Easter, for example, reflecting the dominant influence of the religious calendar and the agricultural cycle. In some cases, they contained entries relating to both business and family expenditures.[54]

Commerce remained a precarious undertaking, even in the best of times, up to the 1860s, when a modern banking system appeared. In a bad year, the dearth of cash and credit made it impossible to meet previous commitments and often brought total ruin. Bills of exchange were used by some Moscow merchants as a means of payment, but only to a limited extent. The Nizhny Novgorod branch of the State Commercial Bank, which operated temporarily each summer during the huge fair there, noted that in the mid-1840s bills of exchange were used as payment for only about one-third of the total value of goods sold at the fair.[55] Account books of the Guchkov enterprises indicated that, for total sales of 3.7 million rubles between Easter of 1849 and Easter of 1850, the major forms of payment were "documents" (probably bills of exchange, 1,721,000 rubles); cash (1,230,000); "pending" (*neokoncheno*, apparently credit, 617,000); and goods (58,000).[56] Since Russia's primitive banking facilities limited the use of modern commercial devices such as the bill of exchange, most merchants, especially those with small firms, depended on cash deals and the word of their customers.

Thus what outsiders viewed as short-sighted greed was in fact a defensive urge toward immediate sales for cash. The structural deficiencies of the Russian economy impelled the merchants to rely on direct, personal business relations, often in taverns. They were accustomed to deal "in the course of conversation, in the form of requests, persuasion, consolation, flattery, compassion, refusal, and indulgence, in short, personal commerce. To most merchants, a bill of exchange represents something which *nemtsy vydumali*, that is, foreigners invented."[57]

Operating under serious deficiencies of cash and credit, the Moscow merchants perfected several means of surviving and prospering in trade. First, they cheated. Outright illegalities common to all modes of commerce in Moscow were cited in an official report in 1846: fraud, forgery, false measures, and false weights (*obman, podlog, obmer i obves*). The apparent contradiction between the merchants' virtuosity in cheating and their pretensions to strict religious faith can be explained without alleging hypocrisy or stupidity. There is ample evidence that toward wholesale suppliers, friends, and coreligionists (for example, Old Believers), they observed the Eighth Commandment scrupulously, if for no other reason than that ostracism on account of dishonesty might bring economic ruin. Cheating strangers, on the other hand, carried little moral censure among the traditional merchants.[58]

Second, in a special effort to win prospective buyers and to undercut their competition, they sold below cost to poor customers. Third, they gave personal credit, even to the point of extreme financial risk. Finally, they demanded high prices from rich customers and reduced them only after a long process of haggling.[59]

These same economic constraints reinforced the merchants' traditional caution and fear in manufacturing as well as trade. A civil engineer named Reinscher complained that most factory owners "are ignorant of even the simplest laws of nature, and . . . frequently do not know the mechanical aspects of their production, delegating its management to foreign (and sometimes Russian) foremen." He estimated that only five out of a hundred industrialists in Moscow understood the technical processes used in their factories, endeavored to improve their production, or cared about "the success and harmonious development of the country's industry . . ." A second category, comprised of technically competent factory owners and foremen (mainly foreigners), concentrated on "making a fortune as soon as possible and departing or living in luxury for the time being." The great majority of Russian merchant industrialists simply grew rich "selling the worst goods at a profitable price, being impeded neither by the means employed nor by the consequences of such dealings."[60]

The merchants' faith in the traditional ways of doing business could not be shaken by such palliative measures as the Manufacturing and Commercial Councils, Manufacturing Exhibitions, and commercial schools.[61] When the Ministry of Finance issued cheap journals to inform manufacturers of "new inventions and discoveries," the small number of subscribers indicated clearly the "indifference of factory and plant owners . . ."[62] Until they were shown the practical advantages of new European techniques, they would cling blindly to their old habits.

Two famous anecdotes revealed this distrust of innovation. Upon the completion of the new stock exchange building in November 1839, most merchants, as they traded, continued to stand outside in the snow. When the police forbade them to do business there in an effort to compel them to enter the stock exchange itself, the merchants moved to its terrace and steps, but not to the interior of the new building.[63] Likewise, the merchants shunned the new railroad built between St. Petersburg and Moscow (1842–51). Vladimir S. Alekseev (1795–1862) and several other prominent merchants were summoned to the capital to thank the tsar for constructing this marvel of modern communication. The tsar asked them how they enjoyed traveling to St. Petersburg in only fourteen hours, but they remained mute and embarrassed; after the irritated monarch left the room they confessed to an aide that out of fear of the train they had all traveled by stagecoach. He made them promise to return to Moscow by rail. Alekseev boarded the train alone the next day after seeing to some business affairs. In Bologoe station at midpoint, where the southbound and northbound trains stopped simultaneously to refuel, Alekseev alighted to take some refreshments. Tarrying too long at the buffet, he rushed out at the third bell, but used the wrong door and so boarded the northbound train by mistake. In conversation, he soon learned of his neighbor's destination. "How marvellous!" he exclaimed. "The same train that is taking you to Petersburg is taking me to Moscow. Devilishly clever, these Germans!" Confused and humiliated because of his blunder, Alekseev cursed the "gadget" (*zatei*), left the Petersburg railroad station, and rode back to Moscow on the stagecoach.[64]

Just as the traditional merchants clung to their old habits in religion, family life, and business, so their political attitudes remained quite primitive. The fragmentary evidence from the 1840s indicates the existence of a coherent political stance consisting of loyalty to Russia and the emperor, together with distrust and fear of the bureaucratic officialdom. The first Moscow merchant to dine with Nicholas I at the Winter Palace (1833) felt so honored that he left a written account of his conversation. I. N. Rybnikov, a devoutly patriotic industrialist, was overcome with awe in the presence of Nicholas and the finance minister, Kankrin. After every sentence he added the phrase "Your Imperial Highness." Fully conscious of the government's role in sponsoring Russian industry and trade, Rybnikov made clear his belief in the need for high tariffs against European competition. In response to suggestions that Russians improve their commercial and industrial capabilities, he submitted humbly, "Precisely, it is necessary to strive, Your Imperial Highness, but some time is still needed for this, for the foreigners are centuries ahead of us."[65]

Vishniakov also recalled that patriotism and total devotion to the tsar pervaded merchant life. His stern father "apparently believed that, in general, everything in our dear fatherland was all right. If there were some flaws, then where else did they not exist? . . . There is no doubt as to Petr Mikhailovich's loyalty to the emperor; the tsar personally, the tsar's family, and all events relating to him were always referred to with respect and interest."[66] However, his father hated the bureaucratic organs that affected him directly. They were "something evil and hostile to us, and also strong and merciless. The word 'bribe' became known to me very early."[67] Reinscher noted that Russians were accustomed to obey humbly "those whom they respect as having the right to command, and this right they recognize only by outward signs; that is, by a uniform, by medals, or also by a coach-and-four."[68]

In addition to this traditional Russian duality of attitudes toward the autocrat and the state officialdom, the merchants held a variety of views on their own obligation to serve as elected public officials. Most avoided election whenever possible. Some accepted the burden of public activity and made donations to the church in order to receive medals and even attain gentry status. Finally, a very small number dedicated themselves to public life in order to improve the lot of their fellow citizens.

A "negative attitude" toward service, wrote the foremost historian of the Russian city, "pervades the whole structure of city self-government up to the present time."[69] A position on the Commercial Court, the Trade Deputation, or the Board of the Practical Academy offered no opportunity for independent action. The city government, subject to the absolute rule of the provincial governor-general, lacked administrative and fiscal initiative. Furthermore, membership in an official body took a merchant away from his business for many hours, depriving him of personal contact with his customers and thereby causing financial losses for which there was no compensation. Finally, because of the low level of education among the merchants, almost every elected merchant was obliged to hire a clerk, at great personal expense, to handle the complicated mass of official documents.[70]

Vishniakov's memoirs again paint a vivid picture. Elective offices were "almost always financially ruinous" because they demanded a great amount of time. His father once wrote from the Nizhny Novgorod Fair that, despite his good health, "I am not at ease in spirit. I fear I will be elected director of the bank. The service is not important, just Fair business. Every day two hours of presence is necessary." Several days later he wrote with relief, "Thank God I was not made director."[71]

Merchants therefore went to extraordinary lengths to avoid public service. The textile manufacturer Petr K. Konovalov limited his public activity to substantial charity donations. He repeatedly refused to serve as mayor of Kineshma, and specified (upon giving 6,000 rubles to the town) "that neither he himself, nor his children, be designated for any municipal office before 1851."[72] Iakov V. Prokhorov, a leading cotton producer in Moscow, wrote to his brother Ivan in 1841 that he had left the city although "there is talk of electing me a member of the Meshchane School [Board] . . . . Let them do what they want without me."[73] Pavel Maliutin, an outstanding Moscow merchant and honorary citizen, for years avoided public service by acting as an elder of a church and by paying 500 rubles annually to it; his son requested and received a similar exemption in 1860 upon his father's death.[74]

Yet to the few merchants who willingly bore the financial burden, public service represented a means of acquiring personal status. A few examples will illustrate this common practice. The Ministry of Finance granted the title of "manufacturing councilor" *(Manufaktur-sovetnik)* to an industrialist who delivered over 100,000 *arshiny* (77,667 yards) of *sukno* cloth to the state each year from his own factory. A first-guild merchant who significantly expanded trade over a twelve-year period could became a "commercial councilor" *(Kommertsii-sovetnik)*.[75] The Ministry also granted medals inscribed "for service" *(za poleznoe)* and "for zeal" *(za userdie)* to reward public activity and technical improvements. Thus Mikhail I. Titov, a large-scale trader and silk factory owner, became a commercial councilor, a cavalier, and finally, with his two sons, a member of the gentry.[76] Fame came to the self-made cotton manufacturer Mikhail I. Krasheninnikov (1775–1849), who gave more than ten million rubles to charities.[77] The Kumanins produced more Moscow mayors than any other family and gradually rose into the hereditary gentry.[78] This striving for status stemmed directly from a static, hierarchal view of society. By building grand, stone mansions, riding in expensive carriages, and giving elaborate banquets, the wealthiest merchants simply aped the gentry's luxurious style of living and evinced only a desire for personal fame and recognition. In emulating the gentry, most merchants neglected the improvement of their own estate and its organizations.

Those few merchants who worked humbly in public service for its own sake exhibited no distinctive political attitudes. Andrei P. Shestov (1783–1847), a wholesale dealer in Chinese tea, was universally regarded as a "good mayor" of Moscow (1843–6). His business suffered as he devoted all his energy to city affairs. He appears to have earned the respect of all for reducing taxes, protecting the *meshchane* and artisans from abuse by the police, and settling disputes as Solomon did, "by a single word."[79] As Shestov's portrait suggests, however, he was essentially a traditional merchant who ruled like the firm but loving autocrat of a patriarchal family. He apparently had no political credo except fairness to all under the existing tsarist regime and, for this reason, was tolerated by the all-powerful governor-general, Prince D. V. Golitsyn.[80]

Similarly, Ivan F. Baranov (1807–48), a large-scale cotton textile manufacturer, honorary citizen, and mayor of his native Aleksandrovsk, became known for his generosity to the church and the poor. For his public service, he received the respect of his fellow merchants and the gratitude of the emperor. Twice elected mayor, Baranov received a gold medal inscribed "for service" in recognition of his economic achievements and another, in 1846, "for zeal" in constructing churches. In 1847, Nicholas I allowed him to use the imperial seal on his factory's cotton products.[81] Like Shestov, however, he displayed no political feelings other than devotion to his country, adoration of its sovereign, and dedication to the Orthodox church.

Yet as the merchants gained economic power in the first half of the nineteenth century, some began to feel the need for a new relationship with the gentry. To be sure, the assertion of merchant pride had a long history, dating back at least to Ivan Pososhkov, a merchant from serf origins whose major work, *The Book of Poverty and Wealth* (1725), had lauded the usefulness of trade and industry while alleging cowardice and lack of enterprise on the part of the gentry.[82] The merchants had also fought, unsuccessfully, in the Legislative Commission of 1767–8 to defend their economic privileges against the encroachment of the gentry and peasantry.[83] However, in the mid-nineteenth century, the Moscow merchants typically behaved in an obsequious and humble manner before officials and the gentry. Indeed, there exist almost no public policy statements by merchants on any aspect of Russian life, however noncontroversial, for the whole period of the reign of Nicholas I (1825–55).

The long speech delivered to the Practical Commercial Academy in 1832 by Nikolai A. Polevoi (1796–1842), a second-guild merchant, MSMC member, and editor of *Moskovskii telegraf* (*The Moscow Telegraph*, 1825–34), is thus of prime interest. The address commemorated the founding of the academy, a school for merchants' sons. In exalting the principles of estate pride, patriotism, and devotion to the tsar, Polevoi denied the possibility of a conflict of interest among different social groups. In his view, the purpose of the academy was "to increase even more in [the students'] hearts respect for themselves, love for the Fatherland, loyalty toward the throne, and faith in virtue." At the same time, Polevoi suggested that the growing economic importance of the merchants entitled them to challenge the gentry's claim to absolute preeminence. The very title "merchant" was worthy of respect by all. "Each of us, as a civic person [*grazhdanskii deiatel'*], is an official, and each official, as a producer, immaterial or material, is a merchant." Because the merchants had contributed "capital and life itself in the defense of the rights of the Fatherland," they deserved to be honored as the gentry were.[84]

Yet the aspirations of the merchant estate need not lead to "quarrels over the advantages of one estate before another"; the organic unity of all estates in Russian society permitted no real struggle for power. "As one broken link in an anchor chain exposes a ship to disaster, so the ship of state will perish from a break in the union among the estates." Within Polevoi's static ideal of Russian society, all estates performed essential roles: landlords, factory owners, and traders were responsible for the production and distribution of goods, while the clergy fulfilled a spiritual function and the bureaucracy a legal one. " . . . May the rights and distinctions of each estate be holy for us; may each of them be respected as it fulfills its duties and obligations placed upon it by the law of God and man."[85]

This remarkable address by a fully educated merchant apparently expressed much of the world view of his less articulate fellows. If we strip away Polevoi's artificial categorization of social roles,[86] we are left with three major sentiments: total devotion to Russian national greatness under autocracy; a striving toward increased social status for the whole merchant estate; and faith in gradual progress through commerce, industry, and agriculture.

Economic and cultural maturation, 1840–1855

The merchant ideology of the 1855–1900 period could not have developed without two prerequisites: a marked increase in wealth through economic modernization, and the raising of cultural standards. These two processes took place gradually among the leading Moscow merchant families in the two decades prior to the Crimean War. Protected from European competition by high tariffs (1822–50), Russian industrialists enjoyed increasing prosperity in the reign of Nicholas I. However, the introduction of steam-powered machinery in the 1840s also raised new economic problems for the merchants of the Central Region. First, the system of serfdom, by maintaining the peasantry's subordination to the landlord, prevented the formation of a skilled and dependable labor force. Despite a decree by Moscow Governor-General Golitsyn in 1835, which kept landlords from unexpectedly recalling hired serfs from the factory,[87] merchants often had to resort to illegal means, such as the hiring of runaway serfs, to meet their increasing need for labor.[88] Second, economists in the Ministry of Finance abruptly reduced the import tariff in 1850, causing the Russian textile industry to suffer severe economic hardships from European competition. The bureaucrats ignored the merchants' desperate pleas, which included an unusual petition affirming their "patriotism and humane feelings" toward factory workers who faced unemployment as a result of the tariff reduction.[89] Third, as the newly mechanized factories flooded the domestic market with mass-produced textiles, the persistence of the largely self-sufficient peasant economy under serfdom led to a problem of overproduction. Repeated attempts to dispose of the surplus in China, Central Asia, Transcaucasia, and Persia met with only limited success because of the Russian government's refusal to subsidize several expensive export schemes proposed by Moscow merchants.[90]

    Finally, the tsarist government avoided stimulation of industrial development out of a fear that an urban working class might emerge like that which had participated in revolutionary upheavals in Western Europe in 1830. Nicholas I and Count Kankrin shared the ideal of a strictly hierarchical society based on a predominantly agricultural economy. They believed that if the maintenance of Russia's military power necessitated a certain degree of industrial development, then inexpensive measures such as tariffs and manufacturing exhibitions would suffice to encourage it. Major innovations – the construction of a railroad network or the expansion of the tiny credit system of the state Commercial Bank – they regarded as unnecessary; and the abolition of serfdom or the fostering of a factory system they considered dangerous to the very foundations of the Russian autocracy.[91]

As the factory work force inevitably began to grow in the 1840s, the Ministry of Finance ordered the Manufacturing Council to placate disgruntled workers by hearing their complaints, and established "a semblance of government tutelage over the workers" after a protest at the Ascension cotton-spinning factory in 1844.[92] Following the urban riots of 1848 in Western Europe, Count Arseni A. Zakrevsky, the Moscow governor-general from 1846 to 1859, intensified the control of the police over the working population. He particularly feared the growing numbers of Moscow's factory labor force (36,000 full-time and 37,000 part-time workers). His decree banning the construction in Moscow of new cotton- and wool-spinning mills, pig iron foundries, and tallow and chemical plants provoked the opposition of industrialists in the MSMC but was approved by the Council of Ministers in June 1849. This measure also required that merchants receive the governor-general's permission before building any new weaving, printing, or other manufacturing enterprise in Moscow. Although it remained largely unenforced,[93] this law effectively placed the industrialists' economic fate under the arbitrary rule of the provincial authority. Similarly, to limit the establishment of new factories and thereby prevent an increase in the number of workers, Zakrevsky resurrected old ordinances against water and air pollution, including a forgotten law of 1840 ordering the substitution of peat for wood as fuel.[94]

If Zakrevsky, as one merchant wryly observed, viewed Moscow as "a sort of unpacified Caucasus,"[95] he claimed that his harsh rule "was the emperor's wish . . . and obviously I had no choice but to be stern."[96] Some merchants resorted to systematic bribery in order to evade Zakrevsky's bureaucratic hindrances, but most were helpless against his petty despotism. On one occasion, the governor-general so abused a factory owner following a worker's complaint that the merchant suffered a stroke on the way home and died.[97] The merchants rejoiced when Alexander II unexpectedly appointed S. G. Stroganov to replace Zakrevsky in February 1859.[98]

Although Zakrevsky's tyranny represented an extreme form of bureaucratic regimentation over the Russian economy, even his despotic rule and the policies of the Ministry of Finance could not restrain the expansion of the factory system. Instead, the development of industry in the Moscow region continued, and brought about an unprecedented cultural transformation within the Moscow merchant estate. The poorest merchants, particularly those who constituted the third guild until its abolition in 1863, continued their traditional way of life well into the twentieth century. From the wealthiest and most ambitious merchant families of the first and second guilds, however, came a number of individuals who deserve the name of "capitalist merchants." Their business activities corresponded closely to Max Weber's definition of the essential components of "modern capitalism": rational accounting within the firm, separately from the family's finances; competition in the free market, from which no individual was to be excluded because of social status; the employment of technologically advanced production techniques; the use of rational legal devices such as contracts within a system of firm protection for private property; the hiring of labor in the free market; and the public sale of shares in economic enterprises.[99] While the tsarist bureaucracy continued to block the full and free development of modern capitalist institutions in Russia, it was clearly toward this set of economic principles that the new Moscow merchant leadership was striving in the mid-nineteenth century.

Although the transition from traditional to modern ways occurred at different times in different families, it formed a general pattern of cultural change. The illiterate merchant or serf manufacturer who became rich between 1800 and 1840 passed a thriving business on to his sons. These young men, the first generation of capitalist merchants, introduced European machinery into the family's factory and provided their own sons with a substantial education. Thus in the middle of the nineteenth century, a profound transformation occurred within the leading merchant families of Moscow.[100]

The impetus for this cultural evolution derived from the urge to adopt Western (particularly English and German) technology, the desire for increased status in relation to the gentry, and the striving to escape the stereotyped role of the dishonest merchant, "the base, despicable, vulgar creature who serves Plutus [the god of riches] and Plutus alone."[101] In addition, the accumulated industrial wealth resulting from nearly three decades of high tariffs provided the opportunity for young merchant scions to become leading citizens of Moscow. Between 1840 and 1855, the wealthiest merchants gradually outgrew their traditional, patriarchal way of life and adopted the manners and dress of the Western bourgeoisie without, however, abandoning their old patriotic and religious attitudes toward politics.

The terminology used by Muscovites in the mid-nineteenth century reflected this cultural change. In accordance with age-old practice, anything from northern Europe was commonly labeled "German." At the same time, the foreigners in control of Russia's export trade and banking business, who appeared as the epitome of efficiency and thoroughness, were in fact German by culture and language. Two important aspects of modern business practice – the stock exchange and the bill of exchange – kept their German nomenclature in Russian: *birzha* and *veksel'*. Those who adopted modern clothes and looks – short frock coats, clean-shaven faces, and short hair parted on the side – were therefore known as "German-style" merchants. Their competence in business, their application of modern production techniques, and their outward resemblance to the westernized gentry earned them the respect of their peers and election to the most important city offices. Traditional, "Russian-style" merchants, while showing deference to their more modern fellows, continued to wear their hair cut in a circle and parted in the middle, together with full beards, long frock coats, and high boots. When one Russian-style merchant, K. K. Shaposhnikov, acceded to the mayor's post in 1841 on the death of the incumbent, many merchants objected to his mayoralty precisely because he lived in the traditional style.[102]

The capitalist merchants acquired a taste for balls, banquets, fine clothes, theater going, and art, and exhibited all the pompous ostentation of the *nouveau riche*. For example, Mikhail L. Korolev, the Moscow mayor from 1860 to 1863, often met to drink and do business in a tavern near the stock exchange with six important industrialists, including Aleksei I. Khludov. ". . . Korolev would set his silk top hat on the table, and then they would start drinking. They would drink until the hat was filled with corks from the champagne. Only then did they stop and disperse."[103] In his mansion in Zamoskvoreche, Korolev held "large social gatherings and receptions," at which he served Château Yquem. In this dining room, the host boasted, he had presented the traditional bread and salt offering to Emperor Alexander II. "Korolyoff loved reputation greatly. He wished to have a fame as wide as Russia. He desired first of all to be known as an honest man and a sound merchant; he wished to be esteemed also for his fortune and as a giver of splendid hospitality."[104]

While this new behavior appeared to be a direct imitation of Western bourgeois culture, in fact it represented just a further extension of the old merchant habit of aping the Russian gentry. One Russian nobleman de-

scribed how the wealthiest Moscow traders eagerly sought honor by asso-
ciating with high-ranking bureaucrats in the decades before Emancipation.

If a rich merchant of that time wished to give a dinner for some family occasion or
to celebrate receiving an honorable distinction granted him by the government, he
could find nothing more splendid to heighten the glitter of his table than the presence of a retired general or some actual state councilor whose breast was decorated
with a large ribbon. In Moscow especially, where the richest and most extravagant
of the Russian bourgeoisie lived, this mania for having a general among one's
guests became a *sine qua non* for a successful banquet.

Of course, the bureaucrats "were always remunerated richly and well" for
their "condescension."[105]

   The capitalist merchants acquired more than a taste for ostentatious
dress, manners, and luxuries. The central factor in the irrevocable adoption of modern ways was the provision of a good education. The views
articulated by Timofei V. Prokhorov (1797–1854) suggest that the first
generation of capitalist merchants defined a useful education as technical
training for factory management. Prokhorov, who had been quick to appreciate the advantages of European technology on his trips to St. Petersburg and abroad in 1832 and 1846, was known as "the German" for his
energy and his disdain for the "inertness" of the majority of merchants in
Moscow. He had introduced new techniques into his family's Trimount
factory and was a member of the MSMC in the 1840s.[106] International
competition required that young merchants master a variety of subjects,
he wrote. "How much knowledge a Russian needs in Hamburg in order to
be equal with foreigners: handling of merchandise, knowledge of the exchange rate, calculation, correspondence, languages, geography, mathematics . . . Merchants' children must henceforth be trained for constant
work, . . . for curiosity and love of learning . . ."[107]

   At the same time, moral indoctrination must accompany technical in-
struction; young merchants must be guarded against contamination by the
French language and secular ideas. To counter "sloth, falsehood, and care-
lessness" they must learn reverence for "prayer and everything religious."[108] Indeed, too much theoretical learning *(nauka)* was dangerous for
a merchant: "I am glad that I did not get to know astronomy, natural
history, and minerology; otherwise my head would be babbling . . . It is
good that as a child you diverted me from learning . . ."[109]

   Some younger merchants who received a Western education from tutors in Russia or in schools abroad imbibed approximately as much of

European culture as Prokhorov had recommended. Nikolai K. Krestovnikov (born 1831) went to England alone in 1850 to learn the language and modern business techniques. He remained a dutiful and pious son, and although he admired England as "such a cultured country!"[110] he returned to the family firm bearing only a thin veneer of modern European manners. Likewise, the factory owner, Vasili I. Iakunchikov (born 1839), "went off for a long time to England, perceived there only what was useful for Russia, and returned home, without having in the least lost Russian feelings and a Russian orientation . . . [He] continued [his] commercial way of life with dignity and honor for [his] country."[111]

However, in many cases the father's efforts to provide the best available education for his sons had unintended consequences. Two of the greatest art patrons of the second generation of capitalist merchants – Pavel M. Tretiakov (1832–98) and Dmitri P. Botkin (1829–89) – grew up in wealthy merchant homes in this period. They avoided moral degradation and frivolity, and continued to engage in linen and silk production and tea wholesaling, respectively; but the driving passion of their lives was culture.[112] This tension between the father's concern with technical education and the son's infatuation with culture for its own sake was best illustrated by the experience of Savva I. Mamontov (1841–1918), one of the leading patrons of Russian art and music in the late nineteenth century.[113]

However, the acquisition of Western ideas and manners could sometimes bring disaster, as in the case of Petr P. Kumanin, the heir to a large tea fortune. Possibly because one branch of his family had produced three Moscow mayors and eventually entered the gentry,[114] Petr Petrovich put on airs and "made himself into a luxurious gentleman." Having received a "poor education," he remained "essentially a very dull merchant's son," but acquired enough European tastes to ruin his family's reputation by his profligacy. Breaking free of the traditional subordination of a merchant son, Petr spent his 200,000-ruble dowry in one year on balls, parties, drinking bouts, and smart clothes. Dubbed "Pierre de Paris," he "cut a very ridiculous figure" as "a cross between a Frenchman and a Nizhnenovgorodian."[115] Kumanin's demise justified the merchants' worst fears of the disastrous consequences of exposure to European secular habits.

Thus many capitalist merchants of the first generation regarded a comprehensive Western education as "a gentleman's amusement" *(barskaia zabava)* that could contribute little to their sons' aptitude for industry and trade. Yet if many educated sons became "simply intellectuals who did nothing and spent the money accumulated by their forefathers,"[116] the old-fashioned traders who kept their "accustomed ways" often failed to adapt to new economic trends and went bankrupt suddenly.[117] The solution advocated by Ushakov – educational improvement among the entire merchant estate – proved elusive. The aversion of merchants, particularly those in the third guild, to any form of education beyond the elements of literacy persisted until 1874, when exemption from military service became contingent on a diploma or a degree.

By the Crimean War, then, gradual social changes had advanced so far that the leading merchant families in Moscow had adopted European economic techniques, modern dress, Western manners, and secular education. In their concept of the state, however, even these capitalist merchants had changed little. The limited available evidence suggests that the traditional views – adoration of the emperor, lack of enthusiasm for public service, and concern with raising the status of the merchant estate within a hierarchical society – underwent only slight modification.

The most notable change in political attitudes occurred among the Old Believers, many of whom gradually became loyal to the emperor. The disintegration of their egalitarian religious communities under the impact of westernization was hastened by a program of government repression.[118] Not only were the Preobrazhensk and Rogozhsk Communes deprived of their churches and philanthropic institutions; in 1854, Old Believers were prohibited from registering as merchants in the first and second guilds.[119] To escape this mortal blow to their livelihood, some devout Old Believers enrolled in the guilds of Eisk, a new Russian city on the Black Sea, until 1863, when this restriction was abrogated.[120] Others, more worldly, simply conformed to the standards of the Orthodox majority and abandoned the vestiges of political protest implicit in the Old-Believer doctrine equating the tsar with the Antichrist. In 1854, the Guchkov brothers, who had become rich textile industrialists in the 1840s, found it convenient to join *Edinoverie*, the "one faith" established by Catherine II as an intermediate religion to convert Old Believers to Orthodoxy.[121] The Guchkovs demonstrated their loyalty to the state by financing the construction of a *Edinoverie* church in the Preobrazhensk Commune in that year.[122]

The young generation of schismatic merchants who began praying for the emperor became more loyal to the Russian autocracy as their wealth and status grew. Efim Guchkov served as a docile mayor of Moscow in 1858–9 under the despotic Governor-General Zakrevsky. In the 1860s, one expert wrote that the Old Believers "who pray for the government are for the most part merchants, and those who do not pray are peasants."[123] One priestist merchant who advocated prayers for the tsar frankly admitted: "In the first place, we are not of the type of people who meddle in His Majesty's affairs or understand them. Our first concern is to stuff our pockets, even if the whole world goes to waste. We think about Mammon more than about the Christian faith. In the second place, our religion does not allow us to go against authority . . ."[124]

Another minor change in attitude toward the state among the capitalist merchants occurred with regard to the obligation to serve in public offices without pay. While traditional merchants generally avoided such service, the new group of wealthy merchants willingly bore the financial burden and derived a sense of status from their contribution. One such merchant of comfortable means was Nikolai A. Naidenov (1834–1905), the son of a former serf cotton printer, who began his public career by serving on the Merchant Board (1865–7). Naidenov rose steadily through various city offices to become a member of the prestigious Stock Exchange Committee in 1872 and its president from 1877 to 1905.[125]

An examination of the political ideas of Timofei V. Prokhorov provides a rare glimpse into the attitudes of the merchants in the 1850s. Prokhorov, a capitalist merchant whose utilitarian approach to education has already been discussed, delivered to a meeting of Moscow industrialists a moralizing speech that stressed religious reverence for the emperor and dedication to public service. "In our blessed fatherland, all are brothers, and our one common tsar-father unites us . . . [under] the heavenly guidance of God the Father." Because "our father's desire is the prosperity of his subject-children," industrialists were obligated to further the common good by increasing Russia's wealth. Merchants must also become useful citizens, for the accumulation of riches did not alone ensure an honorable life. "Honor from wealth" resulted not from personal "vanity and luxury," but from satisfying "the essential needs of our neighbors in the physical and spiritual respects of their lives." A merchant must have "richness of intellect" (*umstvennoe bogatstvo*) in order to be a credit to his estate. In particular, factory owners must care like dutiful fathers for their workers, "those fellowmen who by Providence are entrusted to our protection." Finally, merchants must obey "the laws which express the will of the tsar . . . as do other classes in the fatherland."[126]

It is remarkable that Prokhorov voiced strong religious and patriotic sentiments such as these in view of the fact that he and his brothers had been active in the merchants' struggles against the state's economic policies, already discussed. Although Prokhorov's thoughts on serfdom do not appear in available documents, his modern mechanized factory certainly suffered from the lack of a free labor force. Furthermore, he participated in the petition campaign of 1850 that sought continued tariff protection for Russian industry. In the 1840s and 1850s, he had also joined the merchants' vain appeals for large state subsidies to enable Russian industry to compete in Asian markets. In light of Prokhorov's opposition, timid though it was, to the economic policies of the tsarist government, it is all the more striking to observe the blind devotion to Emperor Nicholas that pervaded his speech. In this respect, the capitalist merchants perpetuated the dual attitude toward the government that had long been traditional in Russia: hatred and fear for the organs of state power and their officials, which they encountered at first hand, but mystical adoration for the abstract ideals of Russia and its autocrat.

The moralistic, patriotic, and religious currents that dominated Prokhorov's views provided the raw materials for the formulation of a merchant ideology in the mid-1850s. The enormity of the ideological evolution of the Moscow merchants can be appreciated only when the primitive conceptions pervading Prokhorov's speech are contrasted with the new consciousness that emerged out of the trauma of the Crimean War.

2

The formation of a merchant ideology,
1855–1860

By the mid-1850s, a number of Moscow merchants from the leading families had thrown off the most primitive aspects of their traditional culture and had become relatively educated and enlightened entrepreneurs. Yet they still had not developed a coherent ideology that could indicate solutions for the many political and economic problems facing Russian trade and industry. Such an ideology emerged between 1855 and 1860. The most prominent characteristic of the new ideology, which the merchants first articulated in public speeches and articles during and after the Crimean War, was its fundamental difference from the bourgeois ideology prevailing in Western Europe in the nineteenth century. Its distinctively Russian character derived both from the merchants' religious and patriarchal traditions and from their distrust of Western liberalism.

The Crimean War provided an emotional shock that impelled the merchants beyond a complacent faith in Russian autocracy to an aggressive, anti-Western nationalism. Simultaneously, the merchants' personal contacts with Slavophiles, which began during the tense days of the siege of Sevastopol, developed into a whole series of cooperative economic and publicist projects. This fortuitous partnership – designated here as an "alliance" between merchants and Slavophiles – had profound ideological consequences for the merchants. It turned them against Western "principles" – not only economic ones, but philosophical and political as well. The merchants' aversion to Western thought, previously only a vague attitude, became a major component of the new ideology that resulted from the merchant-Slavophile alliance.

The merchant-Slavophile alliance

Before the Crimean War, the merchants had gradually developed a sense of what they did not want from the West and from the Russian state. The "liberal" tariff reductions and the stifling regimentation of their businesses had provided issues around which their group identity could take shape. The final phase in the formation of the merchants' political ideology occurred when the British and French invasion of the Crimea in 1854 cast the West in the role of aggressor against their Russian homeland. The disastrous war made the merchants all the more hostile toward the West. It increased their disdain for Western "liberalism," and made the Slavophiles' xenophobic tirades seem all the more convincing.

At the outbreak of the war, the merchants showed little concern. Such apathy was to be expected from the traditional merchants like old P. M. Vishniakov, who neither knew nor cared where France was; but even within the new generation of capitalist merchants, "public interests were weakly developed, and political ones did not exist. The Crimean War thundered like a threatening storm, but it was almost unintelligible to us . . . All the political rumors and news had much less importance for the residents of Bolshaia Iakimanka [in Zamoskvoreche] than the death of some well-known person in the parish, the marriage of a local girl with a big dowry, or the birth of a first-born son in a family of our relatives."[1] When the Russian Black Sea fleet of sailing ships was destroyed by the British and French steam-powered gunboats, and the lack of a railroad from Moscow to the Crimea prevented Russian reinforcements from reaching the southern coast quickly, apprehension mounted. But only after the British and French laid siege to the Russian fortress at Sevastopol, late in 1854, did the merchants begin to realize that a national disaster might occur.

During the "Sevastopol winter" of 1854–5, the merchants had many long discussions in the taverns about the lack of Russia's military and political strength.[2] By the spring, merchants had started to give contributions to support the All-Russian Militia, as requested by Zakrevsky.[3] From the beginning of the war until the fall of Sevastopol in the autumn of 1855, the Moscow Merchant Society donated the enormous amount of 925,000 silver rubles to the war effort.[4] The war caused economic hard-ships as well. The Anglo-French blockade severely disrupted foreign trade, particularly at the ports of St. Petersburg and Odessa. Exports and imports fell in volume, and traders were forced to depend on land routes through Prussia. The decline of raw cotton imports from the American South compelled textile producers to increase the amount of cotton imported from Central Asia.[5] Their patriotism aroused, merchants gathered their families together to prepare bandages for the wounded soldiers.[6] Sergei P. Botkin, the son of a leading Moscow tea wholesaler and later the private physician of Alexander II, commanded the military hospital at Simferopol during 1855.[7]

The tension generated by the prolonged siege, news of which the literate capitalist merchants could follow from day to day in the newspapers, broke into a torrent of emotion when Emperor Nicholas I died in February 1855. According to Naidenov, the merchants interpreted the terrible blow to Russia as a sign of "the wrath of God." When the stunning news of the Allied victory at Sevastopol arrived on August 30, "everyone cried."[8] Anger toward the invaders reached new heights when the peace terms were made known in March 1856. Russia's stature was severely damaged: the treaty deprived the empire of part of Bessarabia, ended Russia's pretensions to act as protector of the Christians under Turkish rule, and abolished Russian fortifications and naval units on the Black Sea.

That the merchants fully appreciated the enormity of Russia's defeat in the Crimea is evident from the zeal with which they honored the defenders of the Sevastopol bastion. When eighty of the sailors and their officers returned to Moscow in February 1856, the Moscow merchant Vasili A. Kokorev led a huge crowd of merchants and *meshchane* to the city gates. The welcoming party carried large silver platters piled high with bread and salt. Kokorev, a stocky, bearded merchant wearing a peasant fur coat and cap, as if to personify the common Russian people, gave a short speech before falling to his knees at the sailors' feet: "Friends and brothers, we thank you for your labors and feats, for the blood you shed for us in the defense of your native land. Accept our heartfelt thanks and our deep bows."[9] Kokorev (1817–89), the principal organizer of this patriotic demonstration, was an Old-Believer merchant and liquor-tax concessionaire who had amassed a fortune of over three million rubles and, in spite of a meager education, had learned to speak in public and to write articles. During the ten-day celebration, which gained him nationwide fame, he spent 20,000 silver rubles on dinners, lodgings, and toasts for the Sevastopol heroes. Although S. T. Aksakov complained to his son Ivan that Kokorev's enthusiastic performance degenerated into a "disgusting comedy" because the officers were being moved from party to party "like animals," even he was touched by the ceremony at the gates of Moscow – "an extremely remarkable and instructive spectacle."[10] Kokorev's nationalist speech on the war's historical significance at the Merchant Assembly on February 28 impressed all those present by its patriotism.[11] Another wealthy liquor-tax concessionaire, Kokorev's friend I. F. Mamontov, gave a grand ball for the sailors.[12]

This outburst of patriotic fervor among the Moscow merchants in 1855–6 resembled somewhat their generous support of the beleaguered fatherland in the War of 1812, when 1.7 million rubles of merchant treasure went to the national defense effort.[13] But the merchants' patriotism then had been an elemental reaction to a foreign invasion of Moscow that destroyed by fire their trading offices, warehouses, and factories. Although the financial losses were many times greater in 1812 than in 1854–6, the war against Napoleon left no permanent ideological effects because the merchants had not yet learned to think in abstract political terms.

The shock of the Crimean War increased their sense of involvement in Russia's tragedy and brought their level of thinking up to a new, national plane. For almost two decades, they had feared the West as an economic threat because of the European domination of Asian markets and the "liberal" trend away from industrial protectionism. While they continued to borrow the Western technological improvements in trade and industry, they did so not out of admiration, but rather to protect themselves from the economic challenge. The Crimean War appeared to vindicate their earlier opposition to lower tariffs. By standing firmly in favor of their own industrial prosperity, they honestly began to consider themselves to be contributing to the defense of Russia's economic power in a hostile world. The merchants now identified the economic threat from the West with the frustration of Russia's Christianizing mission in the Near East. Personal economic interest and nationalist fervor reinforced each other entirely.

This patriotic conception grew directly out of the strong but poorly articulated love for "our dear fatherland" which had prevailed among both traditional and capitalist merchants before 1854. The new nationalist perspective transcended the older uncritical patriotic feeling by placing it in the context of the world political system, in which Russia was seen as a large but weak power threatened by the technologically superior armies and navies of the Western nations. This unprecedented nationalism, which took shape under the emotional shock of the war, became the dynamic center of the whole merchant ideology.

Other key concepts which blended with virulent nationalism to create the merchant ideology of the 1860s came to them from Slavophile intellectuals with whom they began to cooperate closely after the Crimean War. This "alliance" between Slavophiles and Moscow merchants constituted the single most important factor in the latter's ideological development during the nineteenth century.

What common purpose brought together two groups in Russian society so different in background and educational experience as university professors, journalists, playwrights, and philosophers on the one hand and merchants still bearing the marks of obscurantist tradition on the other? Their close working relationship in publishing journals, campaigning for higher tariffs, founding banks, and building a privately financed railroad lasted from the Crimean War until the late 1870s. Separate sets of causes impelled each group to seek the help of the other and to maintain the partnership.

The term *alliance* is appropriate because the Slavophile intellectuals, even when they became businessmen in order to promote Russian industry, remained foreign to the merchant culture, however attenuated in its modern or capitalist form; and even the capitalist merchants were unable to appreciate, much less adopt, the rich tradition of literature, history, and philosophy that lay at the center of the Slavophiles' whole existence. Yet if the two groups remained distinct, they were bound by shared concerns. The primary goal of both groups – state sponsorship of Russia's industrial growth – provided a sufficiently broad common ground for cooperative action. That the alliance continued in spite of personality clashes, differences in cultural backgrounds, and changing priorities through the 1860s and 1870s is testimony to the importance that both sides attached to their common endeavor. Furthermore, the alliance had unintended consequences as far as the merchants were concerned: where they sought nothing more than economic allies, they received some new ideas besides.

The Slavophile circle, which developed in the 1830s among students at Moscow University under the influence of German nationalist and romantic philosophy, was led by six thinkers.[14] By 1860, the Kireevskys, Khomiakov, and Konstantin Aksakov would be dead. Ivan S. Aksakov, who lived until 1886, gave personal continuity to the movement as it developed from speculative philosophy into aggressive Pan-Slavism. Slavophilism in the mid-1850s still incorporated several aspects of the original credo: Russia's distinct pattern of political development in contrast to the West's; the union of all Russians in the Orthodox Christian faith; a history allegedly free of internicine strife and class war; a mystical union of love between the gentle tsar and his obedient people; the deleterious effects of Peter's reforms, especially the growth of a westernized, tyrannical bureaucracy that allegedly cut the tsar off from the people; and the need for a free and loyal public opinion emerging from within Russian society to offset the bureaucracy's power.[15] The Slavophiles feared the influence of the West because of its allegedly "rational" and "Roman" religious and political principles. Western institutions – particularly parliamentary liberalism, which was founded on the principle of competition among opposing interests and parties – threatened to undermine what they regarded as Russia's unique cohesive spirit *(sobornost')*. The Slavophiles saw no logical contradiction between their veneration of Russian autocracy and their devotion to gradual political change through the growth of public opinion. They admired England for what they perceived as its nonviolent historical evolution; however, they failed to appreciate the crucial importance of institutional checks on the executive power (won, incidentally, by bloody revolution two centuries before),[16] which were central to the English form of government. This basic inconsistency of Slavophile thought – manifested in action by a refusal to press for constitutional reforms,– was one of the most important ideological legacies to the merchants in the 1855–1905 period.

The beards and long frock coats of the traditional merchants appeared to demonstrate the survival of a truly Russian culture into the modern age. Even the merchants of the new generation were closer to the peasant masses in their behavior and outlook than were the gentry. Furthermore, the merchants' growing economic power suggested that they might assume a greater importance in public affairs than they had in the past. Ivan Aksakov first perceived the merchants "as a link between the peasantry and the upper classes" in 1849–51.[17] Likewise, Fedor V. Chizhov, the Slavophile most strongly devoted to Russian industrial development, expected the merchants to play a central role in this effort.

Political economy . . . is the question of the day. Here is the true path to raising the lower strata of the people. Here, I believe, the merchants should come out as public figures. The merchants are representatives from the people. The merchants constitute the primary basis of our historical life, that is, the life of Great Russia proper, as exemplified by Novgorod and Pskov.[18]

In this connection, it is interesting to note the Slavophiles' attitudes on the benefits and dangers of industrial growth. Without abandoning their desire to protect the peasants from demoralization in the factories,[19] Aksakov and Chizhov publicly championed a new effort to increase Russian industrial power, regardless of the social consequences, so as to meet the challenge posed by Western Europe's domination of the world economy.

The Slavophiles' influence on the merchants appears to have begun even before the two groups started their conscious collaboration in 1857. The nationalism of the Slavophiles, in the dual sense of love for Russia and devotion to the common people, first inflamed the merchants' patriotism during the Crimean War. "A Slavophile," "a patriot to the marrow of his bones," and an actor with "colossal talent," the playwright Prov M. Sadovsky preached to the merchants about the war "until the tears came." The merchants in Pechkin's Coffee House "all gathered around Prov Mikhailovich and listened to his impassioned speeches."[20]

During the war, Slavophiles often paid friendly visits to the Botkin family, respected by both merchants and literary figures as "one of the most educated and cultured merchant houses in Moscow." Sadovsky and Ivan F. Gorbunov, a fellow playwright, went every Saturday to see Ivan P. Botkin, a young capitalist merchant. A "close and strong friendship" developed between Ivan and Petr Botkin and the literary Slavophiles, particularly A. N. Ostrovsky,[21] whose comedies depicted the foibles of the traditional Moscow merchants.

Friendly exchanges continued after the war, notably during Kokorev's ten-day festival for the defenders of Sevastopol in February 1856.[22] The historian and theorist of Official Nationality, Mikhail P. Pogodin, gave a dinner of Russian pancakes for Kokorev and the sailors. While Pogodin was not a Slavophile (he accepted the Petrine reforms and imperial bureaucratic rule), he shared with the Aksakovs and Khomiakov an intense devotion to Russian Orthodoxy and a hatred for Western liberalism. His "Political Letters" during the Crimean War condemned the repression of the Balkan Slavs and advocated the spread of Russian influence in Eastern and Southern Europe.[23] Several Slavophiles, including Konstantin Aksakov, Mikhail Odoevsky, and Aleksei Khomiakov, attended the dinner for the sailors at the Merchant Club.[24] At one of these banquets, Pogodin praised the merchants' financial sacrifices on behalf of the war effort and lauded their philanthropy: "Long live the success of the remarkable, benevolent Moscow merchants, in all their good deeds."[25]

Kokorev and Pogodin (the former's "constant shadow" during the celebration)[26] became close personal acquaintances at this time, apparently as a result of their cooperation on the patriotic display. In 1857, Kokorev and the merchants Ivan and Nikolai F. Mamontov often visited Pogodin, and also entertained him in their homes. During such social visits, these merchants and intellectuals spent whole evenings playing cards and discussing the urgent questions of Russia's future: economic problems, particularly the need for emancipation of the serfs and for bold new projects – "a railroad . . . ship building, consulates in Asia"; the baneful influence of the state bureaucracy; and the new tsar's "many wonderful aspects."[27] Kokorev and Ivan Aksakov celebrated New Year's Eve at the home of I. F. Mamontov.[28]

This fortuitous convergence of merchant and Slavophile activities between 1854 and 1857 engendered more than just new friendships. Unprecedented cooperative undertakings in the public arena soon began, which linked the two groups for more than a decade thereafter. First, the merchants provided funds for the Slavophile journals that appeared between 1857 and 1860. Second, Kokorev arranged banquets in late 1857 and early 1858 to applaud the government's decision to free the serfs; Slavophiles delivered dramatic speeches at these gatherings. Third, merchants and Slavophiles joined forces in opposing the reduction of the European import tariffs in 1857. Fourth, in order to reverse the trend toward freer trade and to encourage economic modernization, Slavophiles founded two industrial journals in 1858. Finally, the most enterprising Moscow merchants responded by helping the Slavophile intellectuals to build the first private railroad line in Russia, unaided by foreigners, as a demonstration of Russia's native economic and financial capabilities.

As soon as the censorship was lifted after the Crimean War, the Slavophiles immediately resumed their favorite activity: publishing journals. A police report of early 1859 clearly linked the Moscow merchants V. A. Kokorev, I. F. Mamontov, Osip Geer (a vodka producer), and K. T. Soldatenkov (a cotton manufacturer) with two new Slavophile journals edited by A. I. Koshelev: *Russkaia beseda* (*The Russian Colloquium*) and *Selskoe blagoustroistvo* (*Rural Welfare*). "The financial backer of the [Slavophile] society is Kokorev, who is supported by a multitude of merchants of the new generation, whom the Slavophiles are recruiting in every way possible."[29] How much money Kokorev and his friends in fact contributed to this publishing effort was not specified. In any case, the donations soon ceased, perhaps because the practical merchants were reluctant to support the purely literary and theoretical publication on which the Slavophiles throve. In early 1860, *Russkaia beseda* closed for lack of funds, and Ivan Aksakov's attempt to save it by raising a 20,000-ruble "Slavic Fund" among the merchants met with failure.[30]

Soon after the journals began, merchants and Slavophiles participated in the movement to demonstrate public approval of the state's announcement (made November 20, 1857) that serfdom was soon to be abolished in

the Russian Empire. To celebrate the historic decision, a banquet was
arranged for 180 persons by the reform-minded bureaucrat K. D. Kavelin
at the Merchant Club on December 28.[31] Seven speakers praised the
Emancipation declaration: M. N. Katkov, the publisher of *Russkii vestnik;*
A. Stankevich, the writer; Pogodin; Nikolai F. Pavlov, a member of
Stankevich's literary circle; Ivan K. Babst, professor of economics at Moscow University; Kavelin; and Kokorev, the merchant.[32]

Dinners held to applaud the Emancipation assumed special importance
for the merchants when Kokorev followed Kavelin's example. A second
banquet on January 16, 1858, at his own home attracted all "the most
distinguished Slavophiles in literature";[33] he also planned a third, for February 19 at the Bolshoi Theater. This last banquet is of great interest, in
spite of the fact that it was banned by the overcautious Zakrevsky, who
saw only sedition in the outpouring of loyal emotions. The guest registers
of the first two dinners have not been preserved, but the list of those
persons who planned to attend the third banquet demonstrates the growing political consciousness of the leading Moscow merchants. The 84
would-be guests included fully 27 merchants, among them the most important in Moscow; they outnumbered all other social groups among the
guests (15 bureaucrats, 10 professors and writers, 5 landlords, 5 staff officers, 3 generals, and 2 actors).[34]

Above all, the merchants received help from Slavophile intellectuals in
their struggle against reductions in tariffs by the Ministry of Finance. The
tariff reductions drawn up by the Ministry in 1857 had been kept secret
from the public. Industrialists, who had previously been allowed to
present their case for protectionism, were not summoned to give testimony before the Tariff Commission. In desperation, a group of textile
manufacturers[35] joined three Slavophile intellectuals in creating a new organization to articulate their economic demands: The Plenipotentiary
Representatives of Russian Manufacturers and Domestic Traders. The
group's long petition opposing freer trade was written by the economist
Pavel Kriukov, the writer and cotton spinner Dmitri P. Skuratov,[36] and a
Slavophile publicist on economic affairs, Aleksandr P. Shipov.[37] It
claimed that Russian industry needed protection because of specifically
Russian economic factors: the low level of applied science, the necessity
for large basic capital expenditures, the high interest rate on liquid capital,
long winters, great distances, poor transportation, heavy taxes, and the
lack of trained Russian technicians. In sum, the petition castigated lower
duties as a sterile, "theoretical" measure that derived solely from West-Eu-

ropean doctrines and endangered Russia's economic and social health.[38]

The Plenipotentiary Representatives also drew on Slavophile political ideas to make their point. First, tariff reductions and the "liberal" free-trade policy were simply another manifestation of the same sterile Western rationalism that had infected the Russian bureaucracy since the time of Peter the Great. Second, poverty among the peasants would result from lower tariffs, since the importation of cheaply produced manufactured goods from Western Europe would ruin Russian rural industry. Free trade might well cause revolution in Russia. "The loss of earnings could easily lead to consequences which are eagerly awaited by Western foreigners, as events in accordance with their democratic principles and their material and political interests, especially when, for other reasons, a dangerous spirit might arise in the people."[39] This argument, first used in 1857, was repeated often by the Moscow industrialists during the following decade. By claiming (or threatening) that autocracy in Russia could be spared revolution only by continuing to sponsor industry, the manufacturers benefited from the bureaucracy's fear of social unrest. Finally, the Plenipotentiary Representatives reiterated the usual Slavophile demand that the public have a voice in policy matters. Shipov insisted that the merchants be consulted in future tariff deliberations and that such discussions be held "in public" (*glasno*).[40]

These arguments had no noticeable effect on the Tariff Commission's work, and other attempts to prevent tariff reductions at this time also failed: brief letters in the St. Petersburg newspaper *Severnaia pchela* (*The Northern Bee*) in 1855 and 1856 by Iakov V. Prokhorov; a discreet gift of 5,000 rubles to the Tariff Commission president by Konstantin V. Prokhorov; and a series of petitions urging the establishment of a Society to Encourage Manufacturing and Trade.[41] The merchant-Slavophile campaign against free trade would gain victory only in later decades.

Theoretical journals, dinners to celebrate the forthcoming Emancipation, and unsuccessful attempts to preserve high tariffs were largely symbolic gestures that marked the first year of cooperation between merchants and Slavophiles. In 1858, the Slavophiles undertook a more serious venture on behalf of Russia's industrial development: the publication of *Vestnik promyshlennosti* (*The Herald of Industry*, 1858–61) and *Aktsioner* (*The Stockholder*, 1858–65, published as an appendix to Ivan Aksakov's *Den'* – *The Day* – in 1863–5). The merchants supported the journals by subscribing to numerous copies of each issue, which they promised to distribute among their friends and workers. While *Aktsioner*, a slim weekly paper, contained small articles, editorials, and commodity and stock market quotations, the monthly *Vestnik promyshlennosti* was a genuine "thick journal" of about five hundred pages. It presented such varied articles as descriptions of trade in the United States and Europe (from correspondents there), biographies of English inventors, explications of new industrial techniques, and surveys of recent developments in Russian manufacturing and commerce.

The organizers and editors of *Vestnik promyshlennosti* were intellectuals from the gentry who, out of nationalist motives, had forsaken their former literary and administrative careers for the unfamiliar world of business and industrial journalism. Each of the men had distinct approaches to Russia's economic problems. Fedor V. Chizhov (1811–77), the main editor, had come from the poor gentry of Kostroma province and had briefly taught mathematics before a tour of the Balkan lands aroused his concern for the Slavs in the Austrian Empire. The most practical of the Slavophiles, he sought to improve Russia's industrial strength through a myriad of projects: silkworm cultivation, industrial journalism, railroad construction, and bank management.[42] Chizhov hated above all the dominance of the foreign capitalist – "the exploiter" to whom "Russians and redskinned Indians are just one and the same."[43] He therefore sought to create an entire corps of native Russian industrialists and technicians to free Russia from the rapacity of the foreign expert. His concern with rapid improvements in industry led him to prod the Russian merchants out of *"blind protection"* and into the "stimulating and strengthening air of competition . . . "[44] Savva I. Mamontov credited him with inspiring a whole generation of young capitalist merchants to embark on bold schemes.[45] Under Chizhov's vigorous leadership, *Vestnik promyshlennosti* attracted the most enlightened Moscow merchants to discussions of current economic problems in the journal's editorial office. Here they learned to understand the Slavophiles' economic nationalism, slowly acquiring a sense of the political implications of Russia's industrial progress.[46]

Less of a Pan-Slavist than Chizhov and more of a proponent of the Western model of capitalist development for Russia was Ivan K. Babst (1823–81), who became the assistant editor of *Vestnik promyshlennosti* and *Aktsioner* in 1860. A professor of political economy at Moscow University from 1857 to 1874, Babst delivered a speech in 1857 that attracted national attention. It stressed the economic benefits of Emancipation, free competition, and a modern credit system.[47] At first, Babst ridiculed the romantic ideal of national economic self-sufficiency preached by certain Slavophile economists. "The point is not industrial independence from foreigners. These are Old-Believer [*staroobriadcheskie*] ideas which recall the landlord's notion that one's own homemade things are always cheaper and better."[48] Yet his growing appreciation for the concept of balanced growth propounded by the German economist Wilhelm Roscher led him to support Russian industrialization.[49] The Moscow textile producer Iakov Prokhorov expressed cautious approval for this most Western of the intellectuals aiding the merchants' cause. On April 12, 1857, he wrote to Babst:

I am scarcely acquainted with you, but in my soul love and respect you . . . I hope that you . . . will open wider, for us ignorant Russians [Babst appeared German because of his name], the way to moral and material enlightenment . . . Of course we see even in you the ideas of the new doctrine of free trade; but you articulate wisely, and we, who are not scholars, understand . . . Only prepare us for it wisely and perhaps after half a century we ourselves will desire it . . . For the sake of God defend us; your pen is stronger than all our cries.[50]

Babst, who in 1858 derided the merchants' fear of the very words "free trade," gradually accepted the economic nationalism of the merchants and Slavophiles. Although he did not adopt the Slavophile philosophy on non-economic matters,[51] Babst joined Chizhov as assistant editor of the two publications.

More attached to economic autarchy than Chizhov or Babst was the third organizer of *Vestnik promyshlennosti*, Aleksandr P. Shipov (1800–78), formerly a guards officer and a provincial official in the Ministry of State Domains. The first intellectual to speak out against the trend toward freer trade, he had written protectionist articles in 1852.[52] In 1857, his role in the Plenipotentiary Representatives so impressed the leading Moscow industrialists that E. F. Guchkov, V. Lepeshkin, and S. Alekseev recommended that he be seated on the MSMC. He became a member of that body in 1858,[53] served as its president in 1860–3,[54] and was elected president of the Nizhny Novgorod Fair Committee in 1864.[55] Shipov contributed 1,900 rubles to *Vestnik promyshlennosti* in 1857, and his brother Dmitri gave an even more substantial sum – 11,526 rubles – in 1858.[56]

Proceeding from a profound conviction that domestic raw materials should serve as the basis of industrial expansion, Shipov advocated the development of the Russian linen industry. By 1855, in Kostroma province, he had acquired his own modern flax-spinning mill equipped with 750 spindles.[57] His devotion to linen textiles rather than cotton (which depended on imported raw materials) at first earned him only ridicule; after he gave a speech on this subject to the Moscow Agricultural Society in 1854, this preference for linen became known as a "Slavophile" economic doctrine.[58] However, his close association with the Moscow cotton men taught him the economic benefits of part-time factory work by peasants, and in the late 1850s and 1860s he vigorously defended high tariffs for the Russian cotton industry.[59]

The journal's policy on industrial growth reflected the bold and unequivocal outlooks of its editors. To provide material well-being for the population and to increase the economic power of the empire, Russian industry needed several major reforms: free labor instead of serfdom ("this abominable lack of free hired labor . . . is everywhere a terrible hindrance");[60] replacement of bureaucratic regimentation with the principle of "laissez-faire, laissez-aller" in the domestic economy;[61] and moderate tariff protection from foreign competition until merchants mastered modern industrial techniques. Few merchants could write, but one anonymous "industrialist" who took advantage of Chizhov's new forum enumerated the obstacles he perceived to the untrammeled growth of industry: indirect taxes (perhaps a euphemism for bureaucratic bribe taking),[62] the lack of liquid capital and credit, poor roads, official hindrances at fairs, and the enserfment of workers.[63] This forthright article marked a significant change in the industrialists' public stance on the lack of a skilled and dependable labor force. Supported by the Slavophiles, they cast off their fear of making open statements on the question of serfdom.

Another scheme besides industrial journalism – the first attempt to construct a railroad in Russia with private capital and no state subsidies – involved Chizhov, Babst, and Shipov even more deeply in economic cooperation with the merchants. Just as Chizhov had begun a silk enterprise and A. P. Shipov had managed a flax-spinning mill, the Slavophile ideology led to the founding of a four-million-ruble railroad project in 1859: a line from Moscow to the Trinity Monastery at Sergiev posad (now Zagorsk), 43 miles to the northeast. "God save us," wrote Chizhov, "from foreigners and builders and enlighteners and administrators,"[64] referring to the Frenchmen who were running the state-financed Main Railroad Company into greater financial deficits each year.[65] The "Trinity Railroad," which reached the monastery in 1863 and later was extended to Iaroslavl and Vologda, became Chizhov's "beloved child," the all-consuming passion of his life after 1857.[66] Chizhov was willing to forsake art, literature, ethnology, and mathematics, his first intellectual interests, for the sake of economic nationalism. By 1863, he had "turned himself into a completely industrial man."[67]

Baron Andrei I. Delvig, a railroad construction engineer and inspector
of Russian railways in 1858, claimed credit in his memoirs for the idea of
the road to the Trinity Monastery. He asserted that during Shrovetide
(February 4–6) 1858, he proposed the undertaking to the Shipov brothers
(Sergei, Aleksandr, Dmitri, and Nikolai), who were already complaining
about the Main Company's financial "extravagances." The Shipovs were
soon joined by the liquor-tax concessionaires N. G. Riumin and I. F.
Mamontov and by Delvig himself.[68] The three latter men became the directors of the railroad in 1860. When the trains began running in 1863,
Delvig was replaced as the principal director by Chizhov, who had been
one of the main organizers of the project.[69] The prominence of Chizhov's
acquaintances from the Moscow merchants among the major stockholders
showed that Slavophile plans, funded by merchant capital, could create a
successful enterprise without any prior experience of either group in rail-
roading. Nationalism was enough. In 1858, Chizhov unveiled the idea in
Vestnik promyshlennosti: "We are glad about the new railroad, both in and
for itself, and because we see in it the movement of Russian capital and
Russian activity; only give free rein [*privol'e*] to industry, and she will soon
catch up to her European rivals."[70]

The significance of the Trinity Railroad lay not so much in the merchants' relatively passive role (owing to their dependence on the intellectuals for drafting financial plans and administering a complex organization) as in the extent to which both merchants and Slavophiles were
willing, after the Crimean War, to let nationalist ambitions overshadow
their earlier religious concerns. Religion still occupied a prominent place
in their ideology; the railroad went to Russian Orthodoxy's most hallowed
shrine, the Trinity Monastery, as well as toward the center of rural textile
industry, Iaroslavl province. But Chizhov felt no compunction about
"breaking the silence" at "our ancient holy place"; "real faith" required
loyal and devout Russians to "strive to free man from his subordination to
the unnecessary oppression of nature . . ."[71]

In spite of these unprecedented accomplishments, recurring tensions
marred the alliance and prevented the merchants and Slavophiles from
becoming a single cohesive group. The great divisive factor in the alliance
– the unbridgeable cultural gap – manifested itself in many ways.

Each side remained proud of its estate position within Russian society.
The gentry intellectuals, for their part, could not avoid feeling superior to
the merchants, of whom even the most modern and enlightened were far
from being genuine intellectuals (V. P. Botkin, the aesthete, excepted).

Chizhov and Babst, although they worked closely with merchants on mu-
tually beneficial projects like the founding and managing of railroads and
banks, treated them in a "bureaucratic and scholarly" manner, the merchant Naidenov recalled.[72] Their ultimate goal was the modernization of
Russia's backward economy, not the enrichment of the merchants. The
intellectuals sometimes openly belittled their merchant allies. "Chizhov
was proud of the fact that the gentry had given Russia the Decembrists,
and used to say to the merchants: 'You, moneygrubbers [*altynniki*], we put
our heads on the executioner's block, we had Decembrists, but you only
got rich.' "[73]

Conversely, the intellectuals' patronizing treatment stimulated the estate pride of the merchants. As early as 1858, young Savva Mamontov
expressed irritation upon reading Pogodin's toast in honor of the Russian
gentry at an Emancipation banquet. All the speeches were good, he wrote
in his diary, "except Pogodin's."[74] When Pogodin lectured Kokorev on the
need to improve his character, the earthy millionaire retaliated unkindly
by accusing the historian of "an ignorance" of the "Russian depraved nature, which is my nature."[75]

Separated from the intellectuals by this cultural rift, the merchants held
to their narrow conceptions of useful economic activity and resisted the
Slavophiles' prescriptions of enlightened self-interest. The capitalist merchants applied the latest technological innovations in their factories, but
often balked when the Slavophiles urged them to enter new economic
realms. Efim Guchkov, who led in the development of the Russian
woolens industry in the 1840s, refused to be distracted from the production of textiles. He replied to an offer to participate in the Trinity Railroad:
"I cannot and do not desire to meddle in the administration of a railroad
. . ."[76] Similarly, when Ivan Aksakov and a Bulgarian tobacco producer
tried to promote Russian activity in Balkan markets in the late 1850s, the
Moscow merchants ignored the idea; "each of them is involved in his own
affairs."[77] Contrary to Babst's idea that all merchant monopolies and privileges in the Russian economy should be abolished, K. V. Prokhorov stubbornly opposed a law of 1863 that allowed nonmerchants to engage in
most kinds of commerce upon the purchase of a simple business certificate.[78] The merchants' short-sightedness was particularly evident in the
tariff struggle of the mid-1860s, when unenlightened factory owners, who
had grown to regard protectionism as their "inalienable right,"[79] exaggerated their expenses in hopes of receiving higher tariffs than they really
needed. Chizhov, knowing that excessive tariff protection would only

hurt the Russian economy by encouraging technological stagnation and by raising prices, angrily insisted that the merchants furnish the Tariff Commission with accurate production costs.[80]

These cultural differences and the merchants' narrow conception of their economic interests combined to create serious misunderstandings on the crucial question of financial support for the two publications edited by Chizhov. After the Shipov brothers had supplied the basic funds in 1858, Chizhov felt it only fair that the merchants, as the direct beneficiaries of industrial progress, should pay for a number of subscriptions and distribute copies as widely as possible. The merchants readily subscribed to *Aktsioner*, the more practical weekly paper, and sustained it until 1865. It was, after all, a thin newspaper, and cheap. However, their appreciation for *Vestnik promyshlennosti*, the bulky and expensive monthly journal, quickly faded. Unfortunately, their thrift and practicality appeared to the Slavophiles as selfishness and ingratitude. When the industrialists fell behind in their subscription payments once too often, in 1861, Chizhov flew into a rage and vowed to stop it altogether. I. F. Mamontov, Chizhov's closest friend among the merchants, led a humble delegation of the most enlightened merchants (V. A. Kokorev, T. S. Morozov, and S. M. Tretiakov) to Chizhov's office with a cash offering of 20,000 rubles, enough to pay for the journal's publication through 1862. But Chizhov angrily threw the money down and shouted: "I will not do it; I refuse. You don't deserve our labors."[81]

After this unfortunate incident, the merchants continued to subscribe to *Aktsioner*; A. I. Khludov ordered ten copies for 1862 to be sent to his various offices and to several village public libraries.[82] Still, Chizhov had to remind Khludov and Ivan A. Liamin to "keep your word" in raising additional sums to support *Aktsioner* in 1862 after *Vestnik promyshlennosti* had been discontinued. [83] Chizhov, above all an economic nationalist who sought to improve Russia's economy in order to minimize the control of Europeans over it, evidently viewed the merchants as merely a means to this end. And although the merchants shared his ultimate goal, they did not always understand that moderate financial sacrifices were constantly necessary to achieve it. Thus, the Slavophiles' gentry pride and devotion to the abstract ideal of Russian economic power clashed with the merchants' cautious attitude toward innovation and their narrow concern with economic gain.

Because the merchants and Slavophiles each had their own reasons for engaging in the cooperative venture, they brought fundamentally different contributions to the alliance and expected different benefits from it. The Slavophiles sought from the merchants a new source of Russian public opinion that would be close to the people and relatively untainted by European ideas and manners. They also pressed the merchants to adopt modern industrial techniques so as to make the Russian economy independent of European experts and bankers. To encourage the merchants to become articulate public figures and rational businessmen, they were willing to put much personal energy into publishing and editing industrial journals for the merchants' benefit, help them draft pleas for high tariffs, and organize new industrial and financial enterprises. The Slavophiles expected from the merchants full monetary support for the journals and a willingness to abandon their most backward business practices.

The merchants, for their part, welcomed the aid and solicitude that apparently was offered at first by the Slavophiles unilaterally. Most of all, they appreciated the intellectuals' literary skill in drafting arguments for high tariffs. In exchange for this invaluable help, they were willing to contribute money to Slavophile publications and to subscribe to the industrial journals, although their proverbial stinginess kept them from providing the generous donations the Slavophiles expected. Inasmuch as they hoped to receive from the Slavophiles full sympathy for their economic problems, they were sometimes obstinate when pressed to adopt a more enlightened view of their needs. Despite periodic misunderstandings, their close working relationship with the Slavophiles between 1855 and 1875 caused them to imbibe many of the basic Slavophile ideological conceptions. These they would incorporate into their own merchant ideology.

The new merchant ideology

The traditional merchant political outlook prevailing before the Crimean War provided the raw material for the ideological synthesis that occurred between 1855 and 1860 as a result of the war's emotional impact and the alliance with the Slavophiles. Although the economic and political views that comprised the new ideology all had been present previously in rudimentary form, they received a logical framework from the Slavophiles that related each conception directly to the others. The resulting ideology not only represented a plausible interpretation of the merchants' economic needs, but also provided a guide to political action. Most importantly, besides having little resemblance to the bourgeois liberalism then current in Western Europe, it expressed a marked hostility toward liberal ideas and a strong devotion to tsarist autocracy.

Slavophile nationalism provided a rationale for the merchants' economic demands on three crucial problems: the balanced growth of the Russian economy, the economic policies of the Imperial bureaucracy, and the Western doctrine of free trade. Prior to their alliance with the Slavophiles, the merchants had sensed that the uneven growth of the empire's economy prevented Russians from taking full advantage of its enormous potential. In particular, some merchants saw the wisdom of using domestic raw materials in industry. As early as the 1840s, the benefits of using Transcaucasian madder instead of French dyestuffs had become apparent to I. F. Baranov, the Aleksandrovsk cotton textile printer and dyer. Not only was it cheaper to do so, but this substitution stimulated agriculture in the Transcaucasus and kept foreign dye merchants from draining Russia's gold reserves.[84] Second, a railroad network was needed that could reduce freight costs and provide year-round transportation. The Rybinsk grain merchant N. M. Zhuravlev, the Moscow industrialist Lepeshkin, and the Kharkov merchant K. N. Kuzin had proposed a rail line to the Crimea in 1840.[85] Moreover, V. A. Kokorev suggested that tracks, locomotives, and rolling stock for a modern Russian rail network be manufactured domestically with state subsidies, so as to develop Russian heavy industry and thus avoid paying for these expensive objects abroad.[86] In 1862, "several patriotic merchants" appealed (unsuccessfully) for Russian financing of a national railroad system.[87] Finally, the lack of a sound credit and banking system hindered the optimum course of commerce, as usurers and foreign bankers charged prohibitively high interest rates.[88]

Once allied with the Slavophiles, the merchants learned to perceive their economic needs within the nationalist philosophy of economic self-sufficiency propounded most eloquently by A. P. Shipov.[89] While the cotton factory owners understandably smiled at Shipov's and Kokorev's fascination with flax,[90] all of the leading Moscow merchants supported the creation of a sound railroad and credit network for Russia.[91]

On another issue, that of the treatment of the merchants' policy recommendations by the bureaucrats of the Ministry of Finance, the merchant-Slavophile alliance also had far-reaching ideological effects. The imperial bureaucracy had traditionally ruled arbitrarily, angering the merchants by regimenting industrial enterprises and lowering protective tariffs. The Slavophiles preached that Peter the Great had introduced an alien, Europeanized bureaucracy into Russian society. Now the merchants could see a threat to the Russian way of life in their economic enemies, the "liberal" officials of the Finance Ministry. V. A. Kokorev, for example, attacked "the evil influences of liberal despotism," claiming that the government in St. Petersburg brought into Russia alien ideas propounded by eminent economists whom he called "Them, Inc." (*firma "oni"*). They "radiated foreign book learning," but their projects, "cleverly draped in the mantle of liberalism," showed "not the slightest understanding of the needs and requirements of Russian life." Among the bureaucrats' worst "liberal innovations" and "Western doctrines inapplicable to our way of life" was the abolition of the liquor excise tax in 1863, which, he claimed, destroyed local distilling, stimulated drunkenness, and deprived agriculture in many areas of cattle feed (*barda*, or distillery refuse). By ruining agriculture, the misguided reformers were producing "at first the homeless man, and later the atheist and the desperate anarchist."[92] No less evil for Kokorev was the bureaucratic policy of borrowing capital from the West to build Russia's railroad network after the Crimean War. By requiring high interest payments on these loans, the Westerners drained off Russia's wealth, damaging the empire's trade balance and reducing the value of the ruble on the international market.[93]

Finally, the merchants' apprehension over Western free-trade theory received an ideological justification from the Slavophile concept that Russia differed fundamentally from the West. Free-trade ideas had directly inspired the precipitous tariff reductions of 1850 and 1857. The lowering of duties had threatened the very existence of the modern mechanized textile factories around Moscow. From 1857 onward, the textile men called in unison for higher tariffs on all imported products, whether raw materials, semimanufactures, or finished goods. They did so regardless of their personal position as importers or producers of yarn or cloth because the principle of protectionism appeared too important to be modified in special cases. (Moreover, a high duty on imported yarn provided the weavers with the grounds for seeking yet higher duties on imported cloth.) At the same time, the Slavophiles taught that Russian society in general was menaced by Western ideas; rationalism and liberalism gradually would erode the spirit of love and faith that had heretofore kept Russia free from the alleged blemishes of Western European history: class warfare and revolutionary violence. The interests of the merchants and the dogma of the Slavophiles coalesced in 1857 when the Plenipotentiary Representatives had called on the Finance Ministry to repudiate the principle of free trade as a manifestation of evil, Western rationalism.

How can the merchants' new ideology be classified in political terms? It is useful at this point to contrast it with the nineteenth-century liberalism of Western Europe. Liberalism is defined in this study by its salient political characteristics: the movement to put institutional checks on the power of the state; the securing of civil liberties for individuals; and the broadening of popular representation so as to include at least the educated and property-owning strata of society in some form of parliamentary body having the power to limit or control the state's executive actions.[94]

Comparing the behavior of the West-European bourgeoisie to this standard, we find that it was liberal in two respects. First, it opposed mercantilist regulations and advocated the free play of market forces with a minimum of state regimentation of commerce and industry; this was more the case in England than in France, where the bourgeoisie depended more on the state's power in the economy. Second, it endeavored to replace traditional patterns of representation with a governmental system that accorded the commercial and industrial interests a share of political power commensurate with their economic influence. By fighting for increased power, the West-European bourgeoisie struggled to weaken the centralized monarchy.[95]

The effort to ascertain whether or not there was indeed a liberal movement among the Moscow merchants is hindered by the peculiar usages of the term. Russians perceived Western liberalism in various ways, and for the most part incorrectly. In one usage, the capitalist merchants who were close to the Slavophiles received the label of "liberal" because of their public support for Emancipation. Early in 1858, Count Zakrevsky became enraged upon hearing rumors that V. A. Kokorev and two wealthy textile manufacturers, K. T. Soldatenkov and S. A. Alekseev, were causing unrest among the peasants near Volokolamsk by claiming to have already bought the serfs' freedom.[96] The tyrannical governor-general, who had put the Slavophile A. S. Khomiakov under police surveillance in 1856 for wearing a beard,[97] saw Kokorev as "a Westerner, democrat, and rebel [*vozmutitel'*]." Soldatenkov appeared to him as "a Westerner [and] friend of Kokorev, desiring disorders and rebellions."[98] Similarly, the young merchant Naidenov noted that Kokorev, the organizer of the Emancipation banquets, had friends who were thought to be "imbued with liberal tendencies, and therefore he was considered to be one himself."[99]

To further compound the problem of the meaning of the word, the reforming officials in the state bureaucracy who imposed lower import tariffs on European manufactured goods were castigated by the Moscow industrialists as "liberals." The Plenipotentiary Representatives in 1857 ominously warned that the reduction of tariffs, in accordance with Western "liberal" free-trade theory, might lead to the introduction of the pernicious "democratic principles" of Europe in Russia. Likewise, Kokorev himself accused educated people in and out of the state bureaucracy of "playing the liberal" (*liberal 'nichat'* – a term of opprobrium first used in the 1850s).[100]

These imprecise and misleading uses of the Western term in Russia served more to reveal the political perspective of the persons applying the label than to elucidate the specific nature of the merchants' or the bureaucrats' real political convictions. In both cases, the word had strong negative overtones. To the reactionary Zakrevsky and the politically unsophisticated Naidenov, Kokorev and the Slavophiles appeared to be liberal because they applauded the Emancipation. Conversely, for Kokorev and the Moscow industrialists, a bureaucrat devoted to free trade looked like a Russian-speaking Adam Smith. Yet neither group deserved the label. Emancipation was only a small step toward full civil liberties; and the reforming bureaucrats remained autocratic administrators who tolerated almost no consultation with public representatives. Indeed, this improper usage of the term *liberal* by Kokorev, the textile manufacturers, and the Slavophiles suggests that they so misunderstood the correct meaning of the word as to be unable to adhere to its principles.

In this connection, the issue of Emancipation provides a useful focal point, for it had both an economic and a moral dimension for the merchants. Superficially at least, the merchants, Slavophiles, and the economist Babst all appeared to be "liberal" on this issue because they favored Emancipation. Likewise, V. A. Kokorev, fresh from a tour of Western Europe, praised the economic advantages that would accrue to the whole of Russian society under a free labor system. He particularly admired the high level of efficiency in English agriculture, where "free, unobligated labor" stimulated domestic industry. He hoped that this symbiosis of the two sectors, impossible as long as serfdom held the peasants in dire poverty, would soon develop in Russia.[101]

The merchants' and Slavophiles' support for Emancipation cannot be understood solely in terms of economic interest or concern for Russia's economic progress, however. Of the seven speeches given at the banquet of December 28, 1857, in honor of the Emancipation announcement, only that of Babst, the economist, stressed the economic benefits of the reform.[102] Indeed, Kokorev's speech (undelivered at the dinner because of

its length, but printed in *Russkii vestnik*) urged merchants to contribute
their own capital toward the final redemption payments for peasant
lands,[103] and offered devout praises to the tsar for the gallant act of liberation. "The tsar sets his hopes on the people, and the people set their hopes
on the tsar. This is the mutual hope which is peculiar to Russia and which
sharply differentiates Russia from Europe . . . We have read the history of
the European peoples closely and have turned our very backwardness to
our own advantage."[104]

Mikhail P. Botkin wrote to his brother that these speeches, "which
breathed love for the great tsar," pleased him immensely, especially the
toast by N. F. Pavlov,[105] the most forthright about the human costs of
serfdom and the need for a "second transformation of Russia."[106] Perhaps
Kokorev and Botkin, a liquor-tax concessionaire and tea wholesaler, respectively, had a wider perspective on the significance of Emancipation
because they were not textile manufacturers, whose need for free labor
was so acute that it overshadowed other considerations. The moral basis
of their approval apparently owed much to the Slavophiles, who had long
advocated abolition, arguing that only free men could enter into the union
of Christian love between tsar and people, which they considered Russia's
unique destiny.

Whether from moral or economic motives, then, the leading Moscow
merchants appear to have supported Emancipation. However, the heated
debate within the gentry between 1857 and 1861 over the precise terms
under which the peasants were to be freed and endowed with land concerned the merchants not at all, since they owned no serfs. For this reason, there are few merchant statements relating to these financial details,
and even *Vestnik promyshlennosti* made no comments or proposals on the
matter.[107] Only Kokorev elaborated a plan for emancipation. He suggested that the peasants receive the land "they now work" as their "native
land which has been watered by their sweat and tears." They should pay
nominal rates for their plots, but should not be required to purchase their
personal freedom. The commune should be abolished (only here did Kokorev diverge from the Slavophile view), and all estates, including merchants, should be allowed to buy populated land.[108] The passport system
should be ended, so as to permit the free movement of the "common people."[109]

Although from humble Old-Believer merchant stock, Kokorev stood
out as a courageous spokesman for Emancipation after 1857, breaking
with the merchant tradition of silence, apathy, and inaction on public

questions. Yet he was not a liberal. He combined the traditional merchants' love for the tsar with the Slavophile notion of Russian uniqueness and the capitalist merchants' hope of receiving beneficial economic reforms from the state bureaucracy. A proponent of Slavophile faith in autocracy, he had close friends among conservative military and civil officials.[110]

Another merchant, almost as active as Kokorev in public affairs between 1855 and 1860, appeared to have advanced quite far toward a rudimentary liberalism. Kozma T. Soldatenkov (1818–1901), an Old-Believer cotton textile manufacturer, had studied history with the Westerner intellectual T. N. Granovsky in the 1840s.[111] Because Soldatenkov took part in the banquets welcoming Emancipation and in the alleged plan to free the serfs of Moscow province with Kokorev and Alekseev, he appeared to Count Zakrevsky as a revolutionary. He was also known for publishing, without profit, Russian and translated foreign books of the highest artistic, literary, and scientific quality with the editorial assistance of the municipal and zemstvo figure Nikolai M. Shchepkin (1820–86).[112] Some of these books were explicitly antiautocratic in tone: Ogarev's poetry (1856), Belinsky's *Works* (1859–62), Bryce's *American Republic*, and Chernyshevsky's translation of Weber's *Universal History* in fourteen volumes.[113]

But if Soldatenkov published liberal books and supported Ogarev's revolutionary newspaper for Old-Believer peasants,[114] he also worked closely with his merchant friends in the nationalist tariff struggles of the mid-sixties. Furthermore, he fully supported I. S. Aksakov and F. V. Chizhov in their Pan-Slavic schemes.[115] Unfortunately, because his archive (GBL-OR F 577) contains absolutely no written records indicating his political views, he remains a shadow figure among the merchants, emerging at a few crucial moments and then sinking back into obscurity. It seems that Soldatenkov "had only vague political convictions."[116] More precisely, he was a political omnivore. If he deserves the distinction of being the only merchant in Moscow with liberal tendencies, which he apparently acquired solely from his association with Granovsky, Shchepkin, and Ketcher, he also demonstrates precisely how weak that liberal current was among the Moscow merchants as they rose into positions of economic power and public leadership in the mid-nineteenth century.

Thus the Moscow merchants in the early reign of Alexander II advanced no demands on the three crucial issues of liberalism: individual rights, institutional limitations on autocratic power, and popular representation. The ideal of a *Zemskii sobor* (with merely consultative functions) came from radicals like Herzen and Ogarev, who sought peasant support; genuine constitutional plans were drawn up by only a few westernized intellectuals – notably P. V. Dolgorukov and M. P. Dragomanov – who had no ties whatsoever with the merchants.[117] The merchants themselves at no time between 1855 and 1905 sought to erect constitutional restraints on the power of the emperor. Indeed, as they grew closer to the state on economic and political issues, they seem to have held to the central inconsistency of Slavophile thought: that an enlightened public opinion should promote the peaceful political evolution of Russia, but that no constitutional checks on the state's executive power were necessary to this end.

A coherent merchant ideology – in the sense of an explanation of reality and a guide to action – did emerge in Moscow out of the trauma of the Crimean War. It was not "liberal," however. Russia's economic situation led the industrialists to adopt an anti-Western outlook based on an ideal of national economic self-sufficiency. Their political allies, the Slavophiles, lent romantic and anticonstitutional ideas of their own to the new outlook. By 1860, the capitalist merchants of Moscow had learned to wear the clothes and to enjoy the luxuries of the West-European *haute bourgeoisie*. But their political ideology was distinctively Russian in its nationalism and its devotion to the ideal of autocracy. It could not follow European lines, since to imitate Western liberalism would have required the destruction of Russia's industrial system and the ruin of its internal institutions. The contrast with the self-assured merchants and manufacturers of England and France, who had developed their liberal ideology over the course of three centuries of conflict with the church's moral strictures and the state's mercantile regulations, was indeed profound. And the gap between European and Russian merchant ideologies only widened as the nineteenth century wore on.

3

Economic challenges and accommodation with the state, 1855–1877

The Crimean War closed a period of Russian economic development characterized by gradual industrial growth under serfdom. During the years directly following the war, commercial, financial, light industrial, and transportation enterprises flourished with governmental aid. Joint-stock companies and share partnerships sprang up with unprecedented speed, and the first private banks in Russia were formed.

Inspired by their nationalism and by the continuing cooperation with the Slavophiles in banking ventures and railroad management, the Moscow merchants began to speak out more forcefully than ever before in defense of their economic interests. The government gradually began to heed their demands as it perceived that rapid economic development served the purpose of national power as well as the private economic interests of the merchants. Thus during these two decades an unprecedented spirit of mutual trust developed between highly placed government officials and the capitalist merchants of Moscow.

A determined campaign by merchants and Slavophiles against foreign control of Russia's railroad network finally won a favorable response from the Ministry of Finance. More dramatic was the merchants' success in the tariff struggles between 1864 and 1877; the trend toward free trade with Europe was reversed as the government heeded the protectionist arguments of Russian industrialists. Finally, the state in 1867 allowed the establishment of an independent organization, which held the first All-Russian Commercial-Industrial Congress in 1870. Thus by the mid-1870s the merchants had gained a favored position as consultants to the state on economic questions. This trend toward accommodation had a crucial political effect: to reinforce the nationalist, proautocratic strains in the merchants' ideology.

"To wrest Russian railroads from the hands of foreigners"

The personal contacts that took place between the most enterprising Moscow merchants and important officials after the Crimean War led directly to the satisfaction of the merchants' needs in the 1860s. The techniques that the merchants and Slavophiles used to influence state policy were first worked out in the dispute over the ownership and control of Russian railroads.

Because railroad building represented an especially fertile area for joint-stock activity after the Crimean War, both foreign and Russian entrepreneurs entered this new industry with enthusiasm. In 1855, there had been only 500 miles of track, 400 of it linking the two capitals; but by 1870 over 5,000 miles had been laid.[1] The railroad builders included few Moscow merchants. In general, the complex operations of planning a line, raising funds through the sale of stock, constructing the rail bed, and purchasing the cars and locomotives attracted seasoned bureaucrats and military officers like M. G. Cherniaev (cofounder of the Moscow-Rybinsk-Iaroslavl line in 1869),[2] Dmitri P. Shipov, and Ivan A. Vyshnegradsky (the future minister of finance).[3]

The new railroad companies brought mixed blessings to Russian economic life. In the first place, the self-confident officials who undertook these far-flung schemes often lacked the necessary managerial expertise, and mutual distrust frequently arose between corporate officers and stockholders. For example, the Rybinsk-Bologoe Railroad stockholders' general assembly, held in St. Petersburg in 1870, confronted the directors – an adjutant to Grand Duke Konstantin, a high official in the Ministry of Foreign Affairs, an actual privy councilor, and the rich St. Petersburg merchant Vargunin – with expressions of discontent over low dividend payments. As the directors began their report, there were shouts and cries, "Down with the board!" Speakers leaped onto tables; official papers were thrown on the floor; and the meeting adjourned in confusion.[4]

Poor management was not the only problem that plagued Russia's first railroad companies. The enmity of Russians toward foreign entrepreneurs became a major political issue of the 1860s. Slavophiles and merchants resented the extravagance of the Main Russian Railroad Company. Founded in 1857 with the participation of foreign banks, including the French Crédit Mobilier,[5] the company (*Glavnoe obshchestvo russkikh zhe-leznykh dorog* or *La Grande Société des chemins de fer russes*) immediately became the target of impassioned attacks, notably by Chizhov, Aksakov, and Kokorev, for its mismanagement, exorbitant profits, and corrupt dealings with high officials.[6] To the merchants and Slavophiles, whose economic nationalism had been intensified by the Crimean War, the Main company symbolized wicked foreign businessmen who took unfair advantage of Russia's lack of a modern financial system. It appeared to be robbing the riches of the helpless Russian giant through the imposition of heavy interest rates on foreign loans.

By any objective standard, the state-supported company indeed failed to construct railroad lines as quickly and as cheaply as it had promised. Its original contract of 1857 to build 4,000 versts (2,640 miles) of track over ten years had to be reduced to 1,616 versts in 1861. Only the lines from St. Petersburg to Warsaw and Nizhny Novgorod were to be constructed; the agreement to link Moscow with Feodosiia in the Crimea and Kursk with Libau was dropped. However, the company continued to receive outright grants from the Russian treasury of 1,250 rubles for every verst of completed road over the ensuing thirty years, and the state guaranteed stockholders a 5 percent annual return on their investment no matter what losses the company incurred. Thus encouraged to overspend, the company completed the lines to Warsaw and Nizhny Novgorod at the phenomenal cost of 125 million and 36 million rubles, respectively, or 104,000 and 88,000 rubles per verst.[7]

The Slavophiles became enraged at this enormous drain on Russia's gold reserves and the resultant pressure on the ruble in the European currency markets. What incensed them especially was the alleged arrogance of the French managers and technicians in the Main company; its headquarters were in Paris; 89 of the 117 board members were foreigners; and "only unskilled labor fell to the lot of the Russian man" as the cash for the salaries of managers and experts flowed abroad in torrents.[8]

To counter the Main company's disastrous railroad operations, the Slavophiles and the leading Moscow merchants cooperated in a number of economic ventures aimed specifically at showing that Russians could develop a rail network cheaply, efficiently, and without the tutelage of foreign bankers or engineers. The four-million-ruble railroad from Moscow to the Trinity Monastery had constituted the most impressive result of the merchant-Slavophile alliance. Its extension from the monastery to Iaroslavl between 1868 and 1870[9] reinforced the merchants' antipathy to foreign capitalists and produced a living demonstration of their pride, competence, and hope in Russia's native economic strength.[10]

At the commencement of construction beyond the Trinity Monastery in July 1868, a solemn celebration vividly illustrated the builders' nationalist and religious sentiments. After an Orthodox service was held in the Trinity Cathedral by Metropolitan Innokenti of Moscow, a procession of priests, merchants, Slavophiles, and assorted stockholders followed the monastery's abbot out to the new roadbed, which was blessed. The Honorary Citizen I. F. Mamontov gave a short speech:

> With the help of God we have undertaken the construction of this line, and happily completed it from its beginning to the Sergiev posad, with the intention of continuing it to Iaroslavl. Now the realization of this intention has been assured, thanks to the protection of His Imperial Highness, who has given to us his imperial allowance of 5 per cent [guaranteed return to stockholders] on twelve million. With this help alone, in the present difficult times, we are able to begin work and thereby provide earnings to those in the population who need them. Therefore allow me, gentlemen, to propose the first toast to the continued prosperity of our common protector, the tsar.

These words were greeted with cheers. Mamontov then toasted the late Metropolitan Filaret, his successor Innokenti, and the imperial ministers (especially M. Kh. Reutern, minister of finance). Innokenti blessed the crowd again, and those present expressed special gratitude to "F. V. Chizhov, I. F. Mamontov, N. G. Riumin, and V. A. Titov," the leading figures in the Moscow-Iaroslavl Railroad Company.[11] Thus devotion to the tsar, the blessings of the church, the employers' responsibility to the workingmen, and nationalist economic initiative were blended together in this private railroad endeavor.

Although the Slavophiles and capitalist merchants derived great satisfaction from their joint railroad project, they grew more and more alarmed as the Main company caused increasing havoc to the Russian economy. Then, in 1867, the Ministry of Finance announced that the railroad between St. Petersburg and Moscow – the state-managed "Nikolaev Railroad," named after its patron, Emperor Nicholas I – was to be sold. The Main company, with its large financial resources in foreign banks, seemed to be the most likely purchaser. Winans, "the crafty American" railroad engineer, also contended for the prize.[12] The idea that Russia's major rail line might fall under foreign control plunged Chizhov and his merchant allies into their most ambitious campaign to date: "to wrest Russian railroads from the hands of foreigners."[13] Motivated by both patriotism and the desire for financial gain, they began at once to organize a "Russian company" to acquire and manage the Nikolaev Railroad.

A simple document in Chizhov's archive marks the beginning of the campaign: a sheet of paper on which Chizhov wrote: "Those desiring to join a share partnership [*tovarishchestvo na paiakh*] to purchase the Nikolaev Railroad," the date (April 19, 1867), and his name. The other signers were among the most prominent merchants and Slavophiles involved in the alliance: A. Krestovnikov, D. Shipov, T. Morozov, I. Mamontov, A. Koshelev, I. Babst, I. Liamin, F. Rezanov, and Ivan Ananov.[14]

At first, this project appeared destined for success. The famous general M. G. Cherniaev wrote to Babst in July to seek a position on the board of directors, mentioning Chizhov, Aksakov, and "the Slavic cause, to which I thought to devote myself with full selflessness."[15] By March 1868, the company's sixty participants included the leading Moscow merchants, their Slavophile friends, and a number of sympathetic bureaucrats in St. Petersburg (see Appendix, Table I). Unlike the Main company, which proposed to operate the line while receiving constant state subsidies, the Russian company would lease the road for eighty years, providing 7.5 million rubles in clear revenue for the state each year, without state financial support or guarantees, and without recourse to a new burdensome loan from foreign bankers.[16] The company's elected representatives in talks with the St. Petersburg bureaucracy – Chizhov, Kokorev, Koshelev, the Mamontovs, Rukavishnikov, Gorbov, and Poletika[17] – won the approval of the majority in the Committee of Ministers; and a special council composed of ministers and other high officials voted 17 to 5 for the Russian company.[18]

The final vote on June 8, 1868, taken in the presence of the emperor himself, dismayed the Moscow merchants and Slavophiles; however, the Main company received the right to buy the Nikolaev Railroad. Kokorev claimed that the ministers who voted for the Main company had financial holdings in it; indeed, the value of its stock rose in European markets after the acquisition of the profitable line between the two Russian capitals.[19]

Yet Chizhov drew a different conclusion from the defeat: that Kokorev himself had contributed to the demise of the venture by failing to press vigorously enough on behalf of the Russian company among his highly placed bureaucratic contacts. "For this failure Chizhov blamed, more than anything else, the inactive participant Kokorev, and from that time always rejected his participation [in joint economic ventures]. Furthermore, F. V. [Chizhov] simply feared him for his endlessly grandiose fantasies, his purely American schemes, and feared being involuntarily drawn in and burned, without serious and fundamental consideration, as he had taught himself in his own affairs."[20] Chizhov's meticulous planning remained incomprehensible to the restless Kokorev, who had plunged into a multimillion-ruble debt in 1860 only to reemerge in the late 1860s as one of Russia's boldest oilmen, railroad magnates, and financiers. Kokorev's memoirs do not mention any rift with Chizhov over this matter, but his name does not appear among Chizhov's business partners in later projects such as the Moscow Merchant Mutual Credit Society.[21]

Although disappointed by their failure to acquire the Nikolaev Railroad, the merchants and Slavophiles finally received satisfaction three years later. In 1869, Chizhov and his merchant friends began petitioning for the purchase of the rail line from Moscow south to Kursk.[22] Chizhov's impeccable financial plan, which offered 57 million rubles for the road, mentioned "the many Moscow merchants" who had long desired to undertake railroad management in order to facilitate the movement of raw materials and finished goods between the Central Industrial Region and southern Russia.[23]

In May 1871, after nine months of final negotiations requiring repeated visits by Chizhov, Gorbov, Morozov, and A. N. Mamontov to St. Petersburg, their purchase of the Moscow-Kursk Railroad received approval – "almost a treaty with the government."[24] However, the participants in the plan found themselves without sufficient investment capital. As they prepared to begin operations, they found it necessary to sell bonds on European stock exchanges. In order to ensure adequate investor confidence to maintain a high price for the company's securities abroad, Chizhov made the Russian merchants who held stock in the company deposit their certificates in an ornate box in a vault of the State Bank. No stock was to be sold except as the company's debt was paid off gradually over eighteen years. Assured of the company's soundness, foreign investors promptly bought the bonds. Chizhov's ingenious scheme thus overcame Russia's lack of investment capital without resorting to an expensive foreign loan.[25]

Constantly urging his merchant acquaintances into more vigorous action on behalf of Russian economic development, Chizhov made the merchant-Slavophile alliance into a strong business partnership. Despite the cultural distance separating the merchants and Slavophiles, their joint effort to defend Russia from foreign predators continued. If they were not successful in every fight to assert domestic control over Russian railroads, they at least won a significant victory in the end. In the sixties and early seventies, the Moscow merchants' relations with the state also underwent gradual change. The joint stock companies and banks brought the merchants into personal contact with influential officials. Although these new enterprises received government aid ranging from subsidies to "irregular" State Bank loans, such relationships were occasional and tentative at first. The struggle over railroads reinforced the merchants' ties with the Slavophiles and taught them their first lessons of intrigue among high bureaucrats at court. It also served to strengthen the merchants' ideological commitment to nationalist principles as did no other question – except that of the tariff.

The struggle for tariff protection, 1864–1877

Because of the technical superiority that Western Europe enjoyed over Russia, the import tariff directly affected the Moscow merchants' economic survival. Although the new forms of economic enterprise and the railroads provided the first opportunities for Moscow merchants to become business partners with conservative state officials and to put their nationalism into practice, it was the tariff issue that brought them out into the public arena as a single unified force.

Following the defeats of 1850 and 1857, the merchants faced two new threats in the 1860s: a German proposal for a commercial treaty to reduce Russia's import tariff duties; and the plan of the Ministry of Finance to lower the European tariff still more. These events aroused the Moscow merchants and their Slavophile allies into a concerted public campaign for high tariffs on imported manufactured goods.

Much to the merchants' dismay, free-trade ideas continued to grow popular among educated Russians in the late 1850s and early 1860s. The journal *Russkii vestnik*, for example, expounded "Western science, beginning with free trade, in its whole content."[26] When, in 1864, the German Commercial Congress presented to the member states of the Zollverein a memorandum advocating a treaty to lower tariffs between Germany and Russia, the Moscow merchants grew apprehensive; and when, in July of that year, the Russian Ministry of Finance appeared to lend its approval to the idea by publishing a Russian translation of this document, the industrialists flew into a "frightful terror."[27] Official disclaimers that neither the Prussian nor the Russian government supported the proposal failed to calm them, even after a Slavophile in charge of the ministry's Department of Foreign Trade, Prince Dmitri A. Obolensky, sent a letter to this effect directly to Chizhov.[28]

Obolensky recommended that the Moscow industrialists "calmly en-

gage in a mature discussion of the questions raised by the commercial
estate in Germany and express their opinion on the needs and requirements of foreign trade." This invitation by a sympathetic bureaucrat encouraged the Moscow merchants to take "hitherto unprecedented action"
in order to attack the German proposal.[29] The MSEC called a meeting for
January 14, 1865, which attracted 195 persons. During a momentous session lasting six and one-half hours, the merchants created a new organization, the "Permanent Deputation of Merchant Congresses" *(Postoiannaia
deputatsiia kupecheskikh s"ezdov)* – an imitation of the German one.[30]

Its twenty deputies and twenty alternates included all the important
figures of the merchant-Slavophile alliance (see Appendix, Table I). In
general, younger and more dynamic merchants were elected as deputies
than the leaders of the MSEC and MSMC. For example, this was the
"first public activity" of the vice-president, Timofei S. Morozov,[31] who
remained an outspoken merchant figure until his death in 1889. Indeed,
older deputies who were "unable to work with written materials" (i.e.,
illiterate) needed the skills of the younger, better educated merchants.
The cultural development of the capitalist merchants was clearly manifested in the Permanent Deputation. Furthermore, the economic interest
that caused the merchants to attack the treaty proposal took the form of
nationalist antipathy toward Germans. Moscow merchants "who had foreign names, even like Kolli or Wogau, were elected only as alternates," as
were Zindel and Bostandzhoglo.[32]

The deputation promptly formed subcommittees for the compilation of
statistics showing the need for tariff protection. Chizhov immediately advised Babst to write "an answer to the German memorandum." He
stressed that one copy must be delivered "to the tsar. This is very important."[33] Babst's long and scholarly refutation of the German proposal
served as the introduction to the *Opinion of the Permanent Deputation of the
Moscow Merchant Congresses.*[34]

The *Opinion* admitted that free trade, like total disarmament, was a noble ideal,[35] but argued that the financial and industrial weakness of Russia
in the wake of the 1857 tariff and the Emancipation represented legitimate
reasons for high tariff levels. Russia's perennial impediments to an efficient industrial system also justified protectionism: the poor transportation and postal services;[36] the high cost of imported machinery;[37] the unfavorable balance of payments resulting from interest payments on foreign
loans;[38] and the high interest rate on commercial and industrial capital.[39] If
low duties like those of the disastrous "liberal tariff of 1819"[40] were ap-

plied to imported manufactured goods, the Russian Empire would remain a weak, purely agricultural country, exporting cheap raw materials and importing expensive finished products from abroad. On the other hand, maintenance of the protectionist system would prevent "the industrial conquest of Russia and the Eastern markets" by Germany.[41] In particular, the Russian merchant fleet, if expanded with government support, could prove useful as an auxiliary force in time of war.[42]

The merchants' emphasis on nationalist and military issues demonstrated that they knew precisely whom their book was intended to convince: members of the State Council and the emperor himself. These persons had the power to overrule the Ministry of Finance. Ivan A. Liamin, president of the deputation, sent copies of the *Opinion* both to the Finance Ministry and "to people with power in Petersburg."[43] In the end, the merchant-Slavophile publication succeeded; no more talk was heard about a commercial treaty with Germany until 1891.

A more serious battle between merchants and the Ministry of Finance erupted in 1867. At issue was not a treaty with Germany alone, but the modification of the entire tariff schedule that protected Russian industry from all European imports. Without warning, the ministry published a statistical survey that recommended sharp reductions in the 1857 levels;[44] and the MSEC was given only two months to submit its comments.[45] Once again, as in 1864, the Moscow merchants were plunged into a panic. Just as before, they undertook frenzied activity to defend the maintenance of protectionist tariff duties.

A delegation of merchants selected in October 1867 by the MSEC and the Council sections went to St. Petersburg to sit on the Tariff Commission, as they had done before 1857.[46] However, the bureaucrats and wholesale traders on the commission so angered the Moscow textile manufacturers by their opposition to protectionism that Morozov, Riabushinsky, Krestovnikov, and Zhurov resigned from the commission after displaying "extreme passion and anger."[47] They informed the MSEC on March 13, 1868, that a meeting on the order of 1864 and 1865 was necessary to discuss ways of fighting the free-trade trend. A special argument had to be presented to the State Council when it received the Tariff Commission's report.[48]

The Moscow mayor, Prince A. A. Shcherbatov, allowed the merchants to meet in the City Duma Building. There, fully 228 interested merchants assembled on April 2 to develop a two-fold plan. The MSEC would draft a statement to the minister of finance emphasizing the "danger threatening

Russian industry" under the proposed lower tariff rates; and then the most articulate merchants -- Morozov, Sanin, Naidenov, and Kokorev – would make personal appearances before the State Council.[49]

Between this April meeting and June 5, when the emperor approved the State Council's revised version of the tariff,[50] the merchants used all the skills they had developed for influencing state economic policy. First, they benefited from the journalistic endeavors of two Slavophiles. Chizhov filled the pages of Ivan Aksakov's newspaper *Moskvich* with protectionist arguments,[51] and A. P. Shipov published two books in defense of high tariffs for Russian industry.[52]

Second, they made formal presentations of statistical data to the State Council, whose members were more favorably disposed to protectionism than were the economists of the Finance Ministry. The merchants' traditional dread of uniformed officials and their respect for high rank were clearly evident at this time. The Old Believer, F. F.Rezanov, president of the Moscow Sections of the Manufacturing and Commercial Councils, shaved his beard in the middle so that his St. Stanislav medal would be visible and impress the Council members.[53] Even the capitalist merchant Naidenov, then 34 years old, was awed by the ornate chambers of the Winter Palace. As he gave his statement on wool textiles, he felt "a sensation which I had not experienced from the time of my school examinations; I was quaking in my shoes . . ."[54]

Third, they became more vigorous in their defense of protectionism for all of Russian industry, not just textiles, in order to forge an alliance with the proponents of Russian heavy industry in St. Petersburg.[55] Final victory on the tariff issue came only through the personal efforts of their intellectual allies. Babst, who was teaching economics to Grand Duke Vladimir Aleksandrovich, secretly kept the Crown Prince (the future Alexander III) informed of the protectionists' troubles on the Tariff Commission during the winter of 1867–8. He also arranged for a special audience between K. V. Chevkin of the State Council and the industrialists Morozov, Krestovnikov, and Baranov.[56] In April 1868, he coached the merchants on their presentations before the State Council and arranged two meetings between merchants and the Crown Prince at the Anichkov Palace.[57]

Consequently, the State Council formed a "special group" to review the tariff: Chevkin, the Crown Prince, Finance Minister Reutern, the former ministers Kniazhevich and Brok, and Nebolsin, head of the Tariff Commission. These officials, in response to the protectionists' lobbying, set the 1868 tariff duties at levels above those recommended by the Tariff Commission. Although the tariff of 1868 did not represent an abandonment of moderate protectionism (some important items received slightly lower duties than in 1857), the downward trend in tariffs was finally slowed.[58] Moreover, prices of imported goods were falling, so that even the lower duties on certain textile products represented high *ad valorem* rates: 60 to 63 percent of the price of ordinary calico, for example.[59]

Then, a decade later, the Finance Ministry turned back toward extreme protectionism. In an effort to solve its serious balance-of-payments problem, it implemented in January 1878 the suggestion of Chizhov and the Moscow manufacturers that all customs duties be levied in gold rather than credit rubles; all duties in the 1868 tariff were thereby increased by from 40 to 50 percent.[60]

The battle with the Germans in 1864–5 and the struggle over the tariff in 1867–8 represented a turning point in the merchants' campaign to gain a sympathetic hearing for their economic needs in St. Petersburg. The merchants learned how to bypass their antiprotectionist adversaries in the Ministry of Finance and its Tariff Commission and to take their pleas directly, through unofficial channels, to the highest levels of the imperial government. The tariff issue drew the Moscow merchants into public activity as no other question could. Only this mortal threat to their economic survival could cause them to forsake their traditional apathy on matters of state policy and their habitual preference for private dealings in small shops, warehouses, and taverns.

The merchants' long battle for protectionism, which began in 1850, had several ideological consequences. First, the merchants learned to equate the defense of their material interests with the development of a strong and self-reliant Russian Empire; the tariff struggles only intensified their self-righteous patriotism.

Second, the state continued to hold life-and-death power over the merchants' economic fate through its control over the tariff levels, and ceased to reduce Russian tariffs only because it at last accepted the validity of the merchant-Slavophile arguments. This was a passive sort of state sponsorship compared to later government measures, but it was absolutely crucial to the prosperity of the Moscow industrialists.

Third, it was during the tariff battles that the Slavophiles and other protectionists expanded their polemical attacks against the "liberal" economists close to the Ministry of Finance. V. A. Poletika, a foundry owner and mining engineer devoted to protectionism, criticized certain private dinners held in St. Petersburg in the 1860s. At these gatherings, the "liberal" economists Bezobrazov and Vernadsky discussed tariff reductions with state bureaucrats and with industrialists in the northern capital who would benefit from freer trade because they used imported materials in their factories.[61] Such "economic dinners," wrote the reactionary *Moskovskie vedomosti* (*The Moscow News*), represented nothing less than "a rehearsal for a parliament."[62] Similarly, K. A. Skalkovsky, like Poletika a protectionist mining engineer, called these dinners at the Donon restaurant "economic parliaments."[63] The anti-Western, antiliberal rhetoric of these protectionists (who were developing their own ties to highly placed bureaucrats opposed to free trade) strengthened the identification of tariff reduction with anti-Russian political principles.

The Russian Industrial Society

The cooperation between Moscow merchants and important government officials culminated, in 1867, in another gesture by the state to show confidence in the capabilities of the new generation of merchants. In that year, the state permitted the formation of a new Russian Industrial Society (RIS) in St. Petersburg, the first entity of its kind in the Russian Empire. The process of its creation, the composition of its membership, its economic demands, and its influence on the bureaucracy demonstrated the growing importance of the Moscow merchants in the economic debates of the 1860s. In sponsoring the First All-Russian Commercial-Industrial Congress in 1870, the society gave the merchants the public rostrum they had been seeking for decades.

Since the 1820s, Moscow merchants had occasionally petitioned for permission to establish their own organization. In 1823, they requested that the Ministry of Finance set up Manufacturing and Commercial Councils composed of distinguished industrialists and traders with powers to supervise local commerce and industry, submit statistics to the government, and – above all – defend themselves against the competition of trading peasants. When the Ministry of Finance instituted the councils in 1828 and 1829, however, it gave these bodies only consultative powers. Bureaucrats and scholars, as well as merchants, were appointed by the ministry, and the councils fell under the stultifying supervision of the ministry's Department of Manufacturing and Internal Trade.[64] The merchants and Slavophiles also failed to establish a semiautonomous Society to Encourage Manufacturing and Trade between 1856 and 1859.[65] Having won a major battle on the tariff question in 1864–5, and still actively pressing for the purchase of the Nikolaev Railroad, they refused to acquiesce before the usual bureaucratic tyranny. As they grew more and more confident of their increasing importance in the Russian economy, they realized the need for an independent organization to articulate their economic demands. When such an organization – the Russian Industrial Society *(Obshchestvo dlia sodeistviia russkoi promyshlennosti i torgovle)* – was formed on A. P. Shipov's initiative in St. Petersburg in 1867, the most dynamic Moscow merchants promptly joined it.

The society's founders – "several persons sympathetic to the nation's trading and industrial interests" – first met in St. Petersburg at the home of V. F. Gromov (1798–1869), a wealthy timber merchant, in February 1867.[66] The society was approved by the emperor in November of that year and had 138 members in the capital, 34 in Moscow (see Appendix, Table I), and 29 in Kazan by February 1868. The well-known protectionist sentiments of the society's leading personalities – A. P. Shipov, V. A. Poletika, and K. A. Skalkovsky – suggest that merchants and intellectuals in St. Petersburg as well as Moscow acquired a nationalist concern with the development of the Russian economy in the 1860s. By allowing the society to be founded, the Ministry of Finance also showed a distinct change in bureaucratic attitudes since the suppression of the Society to Encourage Manufacturing and Trade a decade before. Apparently, the new policy reflected the influence of the Slavophiles' incessant propaganda favoring economic nationalism. Despite the presence of a few antiprotectionist intellectuals among its officers,[67] the society rapidly became the empire's leading exponent of industrial protectionism and state-sponsored economic growth.

Although these policies favored the interests of Russian manufacturers, the society was not strictly an industrialists' organization. While Shipov, Poletika, and Skalkovsky themselves engaged in flax spinning and locomotive and warship production, respectively,[68] they were primarily educated men whose patriotism and concern for the future of Russia's economic development led them into the world of industry. Although the capitalist merchants formed the largest single group among the society's members in Moscow, the rolls of the St. Petersburg contingent were swelled by writers and bureaucrats devoted to economic nationalism. Articulate, educated publicists served in the society's elective offices and staffed its committees, while the merchants provided the funds (Gromov contributed 5,000 rubles in 1867),[69] made known their economic demands, and bene-

fited from its activities. RIS, like the Russian Technical Society founded in
1866, was thus what the Soviet historians call a "bourgeois intelligentsia"
organization. A group of educated spokesmen for so-called bourgeois policies – meaning capitalist development – predominated, while few genuine
capitalists (i.e., merchant traders and industrialists) acted as its leading
figures.[70]

This new organization clearly intended to circumvent the unresponsive
bureaucratic authorities. Various subcommittees recommended measures
to stimulate beet-sugar production; to promote the use of bills of exchange; to give merchants a voice in setting customs duties; to replace the
excise tax on liquor in order to decrease drunkenness; to supervise shipping at Nizhny Novgorod; and to improve the Russian merchant marine.[71] Other commissions of the society examined proposals of an even
bolder nature: that English *sukno* (thick wool cloth) samples sold in China
be analyzed to see "whether Russian *sukno* could be sold in China at the
same price"; that cotton cultivation be introduced on a large scale "*in our
Asian possessions*"; that trade routes to Central Asia be improved; and that
the economic effects of the Suez Canal (opened in November 1869) on
Russian trade with the Middle and Far East be explored.[72]

These proposals went far beyond the narrow economic concerns of the
Moscow manufacturers and traders, although, to be sure, they affected
them directly and in a positive manner. What was most striking in these
outspoken demands for action was the implicit identification of the vigorous expansion of Russian economic activity, both domestically and in
Asia, with the growth of the empire's political power and influence.
Perhaps this is why the tsarist government allowed the society to be established: the economic nationalism that emerged after the Crimean War developed not only among merchants and Slavophiles in Moscow, but also,
apparently, in certain chanceries and business offices in St. Petersburg.

A series of major economic proposals were presented at the Commercial-Industrial Congress held by RIS and the Russian Technical Society in
St. Petersburg in 1870. Despite its official name – "The First All-Russian
Congress of Factory Owners, Plant Owners, and Persons Interested in the
Nation's Industry" – few industrialists attended the congress. Just as they
played a passive role in RIS because of their lack of higher education and
their inexperience in public speaking, so they preferred to let the "guests"
– scholars, technicians, and government officials – dominate the proceedings. Yet the Moscow industrialists were by no means mute. Several important merchants, notably T. S. Morozov, N. A. Naidenov, and V. P.

Moshnin, ably defended in open debate a series of recommendations on economic policy: the tariff, representative organizations, and Central Asian cotton.

Each of the six sections of the congress discussed a topic approved in advance by the Ministry of Finance.[73] Industrialists and their critics were at odds from the outset, as the agenda showed. The merchants and their intellectual allies from Moscow and St. Petersburg sought such aids to industry as more banks for commercial credit, the creation of freely elected chambers of commerce, and high tariffs for imported industrial goods. They also requested that the passports regulating the movement of peasants into industrial centers be replaced with simple labor booklets. On the other hand, bureaucrats and scholars who disdained the merchants criticized the backwardness of Russians who used false weights, measures, and trademarks. They also raised the question of long hours and poor working conditions in Russian factories. The conflict between the free traders and the protectionists reached its climax in the discussion of the consequences of the 1868 tariff. Artur B. von Buschen (1831–76), a government statistician and official of the Geographical Society,[74] joined the economist Vernadsky in attacking the advocates of high tariffs, who included Chizhov, A. P. Shipov, Morozov, Skalkovsky, Moshnin, and Poletika. Yet these policy differences did not prevent the congress from issuing a series of forthright statements on the pressing needs of Russian commerce and manufacturing. Many basic concerns of the society received full expression in the final resolutions of the congress's sections.[75]

All the sections called for vigorous government aid to promote the expansion of Russian industry and trade: improved banking and mortgage facilities,[76] better railroad delivery service, and a government-subsidized merchant marine.[77] Expansion into foreign markets must be facilitated by several means: a commission, including elected merchant representatives, to study data on Russian exports; statistical expeditions to Western Europe and Asia; a Russian consular corps dedicated to the sale of Russian goods abroad; and low railroad rates for goods crossing the borders, especially in the south.[78] T. S. Morozov, the MSEC president, gave a thorough presentation of the problems that hindered the cultivation and transportation of Central Asian cotton: "If we can somehow improve our [Bukharan] cotton somewhat, then we will cease being under American tutelage, at least regarding cotton goods of average quality, in which we can then compete in quality and cheapness even in foreign markets, since the cotton must become cheaper with the improvement of means of communication and must become finer in quality with the improvement of cultivation."[79] Approving Morozov's call for Russian self-sufficiency in cotton production, the congress recommended the construction of a "safe, cheap, fast, and direct" transportation link with Central Asia to stimulate cotton deliveries to the Moscow region.[80]

The Commercial-Industrial Congress also expressed the merchants' determination, after the harrowing tariff struggle of 1867–8, to secure adequate representation in the semiofficial organizations of trade and industry. One resolution favored the "transformation" of the Manufacturing and Commercial Councils: members should be subject to removal, and the councils themselves should be made thoroughly elective bodies, like West-European chambers of commerce.[81] This request received prompt ministerial attention. At a meeting at Morozov's house in Moscow the following November, Chizhov helped a group of merchants (including Aksenov, Naidenov, A. K. Krestovnikov, Moshnin, and Sanin) to draft a formal proposal to this effect.[82] Less than two years later, in June 1872, the Councils were abolished and replaced by two new organizations, which were to last until 1917. A Council of Trade and Manufacturing (*Sovet torgovli i manufaktur* – CTM) now consisted of twenty-four members appointed by the finance minister: scholars, technicians, and merchants. A Moscow Section of the Council (MSCTM) elected its own president. In addition to the councils in the capitals, local Committees of Trade and Manufacturing (*Komitety torgovli i manufaktur*) were established. Elected by merchants in provincial cities, they could submit recommendations to the Ministry of Finance on their own initiative as well as upon the state's request. Although the semibureaucratic council and the committees were far from being self-governing chambers of commerce, they constituted a "great step forward."[83]

At this time, the Moscow Stock Exchange also received a new and less restrictive charter. On account of T. S. Morozov's "persistent petitioning" with Reutern, the emperor approved the change in March 1870, only four months after its submission. A Moscow Stock Exchange Society (MSES) of 100 members was henceforth elected by the guild merchants; the MSES in turn elected the Stock Exchange Committee, which received the right to discuss questions of economic policy and to submit unsolicited recommendations to the Ministry of Finance.[84]

To appreciate the far-reaching implications of the First Commercial-Industrial Congress and the significant changes for which the Moscow Merchant Society praised Reutern on the tenth anniversary of his appointment in 1872,[85] we need only recall the issues that most disturbed the merchants between 1840 and 1861. The abolition of serfdom alleviated the first major problem for the factory owners of the Central Industrial Region nine years before the congress took place. To be sure, the system of mutual responsibility for taxes and redemption payments kept peasants from leaving their villages at will. Before departing, they needed the permission of the commune's council, which remained liable for each person's payments. The council often allowed only unmarried sons to take work in factories, requiring them to return home each summer and on the completion of their factory employment. Still, this condition proved far less troublesome to the Moscow industrialists than serfdom in hindering the formation of a more stable and better trained labor force.[86] The second problem, that of declining tariff levels, was resolved by the concerted efforts of merchants and Slavophiles between 1857 and 1877. Third, the government's attitude toward sales in Central Asia changed significantly after Western Turkestan was conquered by Russian armed forces. Russian merchants poured their products into Bukhara and Tashkent,[87] and the state appeared sympathetic to their requests for better transportation links to the newly subdued territories. The final problem facing the Moscow merchants – government regimentation of commerce and industry – was also somewhat alleviated by the formation of RIS, by the Commercial-Industrial Congress of 1870, by the reorganization of the Moscow Stock Exchange that same year, and by the establishment of the CTM in 1872.

The antiprotectionist bureaucrat Buschen drew cheers at the 1870 congress when he declared: "I submit that the first and most important condition for the development of any industry is freedom! . . . Every regulation in industry is generally harmful; the less regulation, the better it is for business."[88] The Moscow industrialists certainly wished to be free from the bureaucratic restraints of the Finance Ministry and from petty interventions by local officials like Count Zakrevsky. On the other hand, because of Russia's economic backwardness relative to Western Europe, the merchants grew increasingly dependent on the state's measures for their continued prosperity – the protective tariff, financial support for corporations and banks, armed force for the conquest of Asian markets, and subsidies for shipping companies and railroads. It was indeed symbolic of the contrast between Russian and West-European patterns of economic and social development that Buschen, a government official, proclaimed the West-European bourgeois ideal of *laissez-faire*, while the industrialists

themselves, represented by Morozov, were calling for still closer cooperation between merchants and agencies of the state in efforts to increase the
economic might of the Russian Empire. Far more pleasing to the merchants' ears than Buschen's doctrinaire call for freedom of enterprise was
Reutern's promise to the MSEC in July 1872 to consult them in all future
policy deliberations: "the merchants could rest assured that as long as he
was Minister, not a single measure affecting industry 'would strike like a
bolt from the blue.' "[89]

The ideological consequences of the accommodation between the Moscow merchants and the state in the 1857–77 period can scarcely be over-
rated. The merchants' defense of their economic interests by nationalist
arguments, which proved successful in swaying the imperial bureaucracy,
strengthened their aversion to "liberal" free-trade theory and West-European parliamentary government. Indebted to autocracy for their economic
survival, and culturally remote from any sort of constitutional theory or
ideology, the Moscow merchants, once their needs had been met through
the solicitude of the Ministry of Finance, displayed little interest in questions of political reform.

4

The political impact of the reactionary
ideology, 1860–1890

Although the Moscow merchants derived immense benefit from the business acumen and literary skills of sympathetic bureaucrats and intellectuals, they paid little attention to questions of local self-government and
civil freedoms. Instead, they remained devoted to autocratic government
and economic nationalism, particularly since these political ideals represented the means by which Russia might parry the foreign economic
threat. The full extent of the merchants' indifference to political reform
emerges from an examination of their public activity during the era of the
"Great Reforms": their attitude toward several political issues of the
1860s; their role in the reformed Moscow Duma between 1870 and 1892;
their support of the Pan-Slav movement; their opposition to zemstvo liberalism; and their stands on various other political issues in the 1880s.

Political issues of the 1860s

The merchants' growing attachment to autocracy and nationalism manifested itself dramatically in a variety of events in the 1860s: the Polish
uprising of 1863; the visits of the American ambassador and of an American naval delegation to Moscow in that same year; and the demand for free
speech and freedom of religion addressed to the emperor by the Moscow
Duma in 1870.

The Polish uprising against Russian rule in 1863 prompted a great outpouring of loyalist sentiment in Russia. The journalist Katkov and the
Slavophiles, led by Aksakov, emerged as the most vocal advocates of
bloody repression. Those recent arrivals to public life, the Moscow merchants, also joined the display of patriotic devotion. The significance of
the merchants' emotional nationalism may be appreciated by comparing it
to their indifference to the Polish rebellion of 1830–1.

From the most educated merchant leaders to the simplest petty traders, feelings ran high against both the Polish nationalists of 1863 and the Russian radicals and liberals who urged leniency toward the rebels. For Vasili P. Botkin, the tea merchant and literary critic well known as an admirer of West-European culture, the Polish rebellion marked a political turning point. He confessed to his brother-in-law, the poet A. A. Fet:

The spiritual anxiety which the Polish troubles produced in me has . . . become chronic . . . I never suspected in myself such a national streak as has now become evident; everything else within me has died . . . Katkov's recent article on Poland is magnificent. Here is a real statesman's view of the matter. Our brainless progressists cannot understand it, draping themselves in their abstract and empty liberalism.[1]

Likewise, an uneducated Old-Believer bookseller hated the nihilists and despised the " 'literati,' as he christened the liberals, . . . to the marrow of his bones for their idle talk."[2] The lower orders of Moscow, including the merchants, hated the students and educated people in general; they mistakenly viewed the young radicals as "sons of landlords who were rioting against the tsar because he took their serfs from them."[3]

One clear indication of the merchants' nationalist fervor in this period was the change in political attitudes among the sizable minority (about 8 percent) who still belonged to the Old Belief.[4] Since the seventeenth century, these religious fundamentalists had viewed the tsarist state as an evil force and the tsar himself as the Antichrist. However, the new generation of capitalist merchants emerging in mid-century included several Old Believers who, although refusing to join *Edinoverie*,[5] broke with tradition on the issue of political support for the tsarist government. The journalist Katkov encouraged the leading Moscow Old-Believer merchants to show their approval of the Russian military action in Poland and circulated among them a petition of loyalty to the emperor for which I. K. Babst wrote the text. Such eminent Old-Believer merchants as T. S. Morozov and K. T. Soldatenkov signed it, as if to demonstrate unequivocally the final disappearance of the Schism's antitsarist sentiment among the wealthiest merchants.[6] When the revolutionist Kelsiev endeavored to incite Old Believers to revolt, he found only three kinds of merchants among the schismatics: capitalist merchants, who accepted the government's policy; many traditionalists, who bore religious persecution passively; and a small group of young traditional merchants concerned about freedom of religion and the convocation of a consultative *Zemskii sobor*, but no other political questions.[7]

Whereas the Polish uprising in 1863 thus provided an opportunity for the expression of nationalist feelings and of faith in autocracy, the attempted assassination of the emperor prompted the merchants to articulate their attitudes toward the monarch himself. The pistol shot aimed at Alexander II by the revolutionist Karakozov on April 4, 1866, provoked a flood of letters congratulating the emperor on his escape. Several such documents from the Moscow merchants are significant as indications that both Old-Believer merchant leaders and those in the Moscow Stock Exchange Committee totally disdained political radicalism. The address of the Priestist Rogozh Commune, bearing 103 signatures, promised "fervent prayers of thanks to the Most High for your escape; we implore Him to preserve you for the glory and well-being of our entire fatherland." Forty-nine members of the Priestless Preobrazhensk Commune assured Alexander, "Your life, tsar-liberator, is dear to us. May the Most High guard it as He preserved it now, to the well-being of all Russia." Nikitenko, the censor, greeted these unprecedented statements of loyalty with a joyful note in his diary: "A wonderful address from the Old Believers. Thank God!" Not to be outdone, the MSEC telegrammed: "Our tongues are unable to express to you, adored monarch, the sentiments which filled us upon the news of the terrible attempt on your precious life, by which all the good fortune and all the hopes of the Russian land are bound."[8]

Just as the events of 1863 and 1866 prompted the merchants to speak their mind publicly on political matters foreign and domestic, the manner in which they behaved is also of great significance. Two visits by American dignitaries in 1866 provided opportunities for the merchants to display their increasing self-confidence in public as they expressed their patriotic sentiments. Visiting Moscow in January of 1866, American Ambassador Clay and his secretary, Jeremiah Curtin, received a warm welcome from 150 merchants at a grand banquet in the Merchant Academy. Following a lengthy cheer for the emperor, Liamin toasted President Johnson; Gorbov cited the kindness shown to Russia's fleet during its recent visit to American ports; for the MSEC Chetverikov proposed a toast "for the protection and development of home manufactures in Russia and the United States" and to the growth of both countries' merchant fleets; and Ambassador Clay obligingly attacked European free-trade theory. Finally, Chizhov recalled de Tocqueville's prophecy about the rise of Russia and America, toasted Henry C. Carey (the leading American defender of high import tariffs),[9] and recited Konstantin Aksakov's poem to Moscow.[10]

More significant than the ideas expressed was the fact that this dinner was "the first in Russian history given by the merchants of Moscow in their private and collective capacity to representatives of a foreign nation." The only members of the gentry among the 150 guests were Mayor Shcherbatov, Katkov, and a provincial official, Curtin recalled. "The Moscow nobles wished to take part in getting up the banquet, but the merchants would not permit them to do so. . . . The merchants were just at that time beginning to get power. They were proud of their wealth and influence and wanted to make it felt as against the nobles."[11]

The merchants' patriotism was again demonstrated later that same year, during an American naval delegation's visit to Russia in August. On this occasion, Admiral Fox was treated to a banquet and made an honorary citizen by the Moscow Duma (in spite of his obvious ineligibility, Naidenov noted dryly).[12] The merchants' enthusiasm for the Americans stemmed largely from the fact that Washington and St. Petersburg had recently aided each other diplomatically in a time of crisis; the United States had supported the Russians' suppression of the Polish revolt, while the Russian government had, during the American Civil War, refrained from aiding the Confederate States despite the economic dislocations caused by the shortage of southern cotton. In his speech to Fox's group in St. Petersburg on August 3, Kokorev resorted once more to Slavophile rhetoric. "The citizens of America have understood the secret of Russian life and of Russian history; they have understood that the longevity and health of Alexander II constitutes for us a guarantee of strength, glory, and happiness."[13]

Loyal speeches were one thing; political action to attain the Slavophiles' most cherished goals were quite another, however. In the most dramatic event in municipal political life in this period,[14] the merchants displayed a total lack of initiative and resolve. In mid-November 1870, Ivan Aksakov drafted an address to the emperor praising Russia's unilateral abrogation earlier that month of the terms of the Peace of Paris. In 1856, the Western powers had forced Russia to dismantle its naval forces on the Black Sea, and now Alexander II took advantage of the Franco-Prussian War to annul this provision of the Paris Peace. In his congratulatory message to the emperor, Aksakov pledged the support of the whole Russian nation for the effort to "shake off the illegal bonds placed on [Russia] by her enemies," and praised "your great transformations" (that is, the reforms of the 1860s) as a "source of new strength" for the empire. Yet the need existed for several more reforms to further solidify the "unbreakable bond of tsar and people": "first of all, [wider] scope for opinion and the printed word, without which the spirit of the people will grow feeble and will lack sincerity and truth in its relations with authority; religious freedom, without which even the sermon itself is ineffectual; finally, freedom of conscience in faith, that most precious of treasures for the human soul."[15] This call for greater civil liberties received the endorsement of Mayor Cherkassky, former Mayor Shcherbatov, the Slavophile Iuri Samarin, and Pogodin. It was signed by all members of the Moscow City Duma present on November 17, 1870, and dispatched to the emperor.[16]

It is difficult to establish precisely the significance of the Duma's action, for it is not known how many merchants signed the address, nor how many of the sixty absent members were merchants.[17] Furthermore, the political motives of the signers were unclear because the document was both aggressively nationalist and timidly liberal; while it approved the emperor's bold move against the Western powers, it also advocated somewhat greater freedom for domestic public expression.

It is noteworthy, however, that at least four of the duma members who refused to sign were prominent merchants: S. P. Kartsev, N. A. Naidenov, M. E. Popov, and V. D. Konshin.[18] Kartsev explicitly urged the deletion of the passage on civil freedoms, arguing cogently that they did not pertain to the abrogation of the Peace of Paris. The most vigorous opposition came from Naidenov, who rejected Aksakov's claim that all estates stood ready to serve Russia, militarily if necessary, in order to avenge the humiliation of 1856. Merchants had long enjoyed exemption from military service, and Naidenov, although a modern capitalist merchant and staunch nationalist, here betrayed an old-fashioned concern over his estate's privileges.[19] Moreover, as Sukhotin noted, several merchants who signed the address "were in dread" about the angry reprisal that was expected from St. Petersburg. One "important merchant leader" exclaimed, "This is not an address, but the lead editorial of a suppressed newspaper."[20]

These fearful merchants understood the imperial bureaucracy all too well. The emperor refused to accept the statement; and both Governor-General Dolgorukov and Mayor Cherkassky received severe reprimands.[21] Disgusted, Cherkassky resigned as mayor soon afterward.[22]

Aksakov, who perceived a certain "civic spirit and political sense" among the merchant and *meshchane* duma members who signed his statement, had clearly overestimated their devotion to civil liberties. At a meet-

ing of forty duma members at Cherkassky's home on November 16 to
scrutinize "every word and every phrase" of Aksakov's text,[23] three merchants had been present (Naidenov, S. M. Tretiakov, and A. K. Krestovnikov), but they discussed only the question of military exemption.[24] Furthermore, when the statement was signed on November 17, the Duma
acted passively, approving the final version with little discussion of its
content.[25] Although the merchants voted in favor of the address, apparently in order to demonstrate their patriotism, they did not participate
actively in drafting it, and, except for the four who openly opposed it,
simply followed the gentry leadership of the Duma.

In the fifteen years following the Crimean War, the Moscow merchants
had emerged as public figures outside the narrow realm of economic policy. Yet as new arrivals to political life, they continued to rely on the
Slavophile intellectuals for guidance, just as they did in industrial journalism and railroad management. In the years to come, they would find their
own voice. Still, the most fascinating aspect of their cultural development
was the manner in which the ideology of the 1855–70 period colored all
their public activities in the late nineteenth century, long after the creators
of the merchant-Slavophile alliance had died.

Merchants in the City Duma under the reform of 1870

The city of Moscow enjoyed an unprecedented degree of self-government
under the law on municipal administration promulgated on June 6, 1870,
and finally implemented in Moscow on February 1, 1873.[26] By abolishing
the rigid system of representation of social estates in favor of the looser
principle of property qualification, this measure offered a new opportunity to the merchants. Would they assert the political power to which
their wealth now entitled them? Would they work to create a strong political base of liberalism analogous to that which the middle gentry fostered
in the Zemstvo during the same period? These were not idle questions, for
the tsarist government now promised Russian cities the right to manage
their public services "independently."[27] Specific responsibilities of the
Duma included management of the city's financial affairs; construction
and maintenance of streets, bridges, the lighting system, and other public-
works facilities; supervision of such essential services as the public health
system, markets and bazaars, the stock exchange, and municipal credit
institutions; and administration of city hospitals, philanthropies, and public schools "on the model of the zemstvo organizations," as well as munici-

pal theaters, libraries, and museums. Although the tsarist bureaucracy had no intention of creating a political competitor, the municipal dumas did in fact train public-spirited citizens in self-government and thereby prepared liberal Russians for the great struggle with autocracy in the early twentieth century.

The new voting system, based on taxable wealth, gave the merchants a preponderant voice in the selection of delegates to the Duma. Under the previous system of proportional representation, merchants and honorary citizens had cast less than two-fifths of the total votes for duma delegates. The law of 1870 restricted the suffrage to the tax-paying residents of Moscow, that is, those few (approximately 3 percent of the population) who owned real estate or who purchased annual commercial or manufacturing certificates. All those inhabitants of Moscow who rented their homes or who did not hold certificates – many gentry landlords, most professional men, and almost all artisans, workers, and peasants – were thus disenfranchised.[28]

Nor were the taxpayers' votes considered equal. Under the new procedure, the names of all taxpayers aged 25 and older were listed in descending order according to the amount of taxes paid in the two preceding years. Then the list was divided into three parts, each representing one-third of the revenues collected. The electorate was thus separated into a small group of rich industrialists and a few gentry in the first electoral assembly; a somewhat larger group of several hundred property owners, mostly merchants, in the second assembly; and thousands of small taxpayers, mainly *meshchane*, in the third. Because each electoral assembly chose one-third of the 180 delegates *(glasnye)* of the Duma,[29] the merchants listed in the first two sections of the tax rolls could conceivably have elected up to two-thirds of the duma members. The striking inequality of this system was evident in the election statistics. In 1880, the three assemblies contained 245, 1,558, and 20,405 voters, respectively; in 1884, 222, 1,360, and 18,310; and in 1888, 231, 1,474, and 21,966.[30]

From the list of all eligible voters aged 30 to 72, each of the three assemblies elected sixty delegates to the Duma. The first election was held late in 1872 and the first four-year term ran from 1873 through 1876. The composition of the Duma naturally reflected the unequal representation of social estates in the electoral assemblies.[31] In the first Duma, delegates from the gentry and officialdom numbered 86; merchants, 81; *meshchane*, 9; artisans, 3; and peasantry, 1.[32] In the second term (1877–80), 143 of the 180 delegates were merchants or honorary citizens, 26 were gentry, and

only 11 came from the lower estates.[33] The Duma, which was convened
regularly (at least twice a month in the 1880s), set general policy, and in
turn elected the members of the Executive Board *(uprava)* from the list of
eligible voters. The mayor, also elected by the Duma, acted as the president of the Duma, of the Executive Board, and of the electoral assemblies.[34]

Whether the commercial and industrial leaders of Moscow would use
their new-found political influence to best advantage depended on two
factors: the central government's toleration of vigorous self-government,
and the political aspirations of the merchants themselves. The provisions
of the law set firm limits on the independent action of the municipal government. The city's budget was kept small at first, and although it grew as
the city imposed new taxes, deficits mounted at an even faster rate.[35] More
serious was the constant threat of intervention by the tsarist bureaucracy.
The law itself listed dozens of cases in which official interference was
allowed. For example, the minister of internal affairs in St. Petersburg
could refuse to confirm the Duma's choice for mayor, and under Article
104 the chief of police could both initiate legislation in the Duma and
temporarily nullify decisions of the city government. Finally, the body to
which the city appealed decisions of the police – a seven-member provincial Board *(prisutstvie)* for City Affairs – was chaired by the Moscow governor-general, and four of its members, a majority, were administration
officials.[36]

The attitude of the provincial governor-general therefore emerged as a
crucial factor in the functioning of city government. Prince Vladimir A. Dolgorukov, an Adjutant General who assumed the office of
Moscow governor-general in August 1865 at the age of 56, occupied that
position for almost 26 years, until February 1891. A leading Moscow aristocrat later recalled that in the 1870s Dolgorukov "was unquestionably the
first person in Moscow . . . because of the nature of his obligations and his
role. In his hands were concentrated all the strings of that complex web
that constituted the life of the capital in its innumerable and various
aspects – administrative, in the broad sense of the term; public; commercial-industrial; and private."[37] Official displeasure at Dolgorukov's failure
to suppress the Duma's address of 1870 had almost caused his dismissal,
and he never again endangered his career by permitting such political displays. Indeed, the most telling fact in the history of the Moscow City
Duma between 1873 and 1892 is that five of the six mayors of this period
resigned from office, and only one of the five did so because of ill health.

The stories of the four politically motivated resignations reflect both the power of the tsarist bureaucracy and the unavoidable shortcomings of self-government by inexperienced merchants.

The comical resignation of the first of these mayors recalled Za-krevsky's petty tyranny in the reign of Nicholas I. Hereditary Honorary Citizen and Commercial Councilor Ivan A. Liamin became mayor in 1871 upon Cherkassky's departure, but he "seemed, in comparison to his prede-cessor, somehow pitiful" as he habitually shuffled his feet and followed the old merchant tradition of seeking approval from the provincial authori-ties.[38] After defeating former Mayor Shcherbatov in the election of 1872, he began his four-year term in 1873, but left office within only two months. Liamin, "a fine-looking person, clever, and home-made, as some-one said of him, [had] an absurd clash with the newly appointed [civi-lian] governor, Durnovo . . . This incident made a painful impression on Moscow, all the more so because [of] the cause – a calling card left [by Liamin] with the doorkeeper instead of a signature in the guest book . . ."[39]

Perhaps Liamin, a merchant ignorant of the manners of gentry society, committed more than one error of etiquette that day. According to a sec-ond version, he paid a courtesy call on Dolgorukov dressed, as was the mayor's privilege under the new law, in the uniform of the provincial bureaucracy. Dolgorukov, proud of his military position, told Liamin that he need not wear the uniform when presenting himself to the new civilian governor. When Liamin appeared in evening dress *(vo frak)* rather than in uniform, the insulted Durnovo "gave him such a tongue lashing that the bewildered millionaire, unused to such treatment, immediately resigned, and from then on never stuck his nose into the mayor's job . . . Liamin, [while] not a stupid man, . . . was without any education at all and had no significance as mayor. In public affairs he was famous only for his elo-quent delivery, by heart, of speeches that Aksakov wrote for him."[40]

The next two resignations revealed the inability of elected officials to meet the new challenges of public life. State Councilor Danilo D. Schu-macher, elected in 1874, enjoyed the merchants' respect as an energetic duma member, director of the Moscow-Riazan Railroad, and president of the board of the Commercial Loan Bank. Unfortunately, in October 1875 the bank failed, and it became known that shortly before the crash Schu-macher had withdrawn his own money and that of his nephews "in a moment of poor judgment." Although acquitted of criminal charges, he retired in disgrace early in 1876 from both his governmental and municipal posts.[41] Hereditary Honorary Citizen, first-guild merchant, and Commercial Councilor Sergei M. Tretiakov, "a gentle and good man who enjoyed universal favor" as an industrialist and patron of Russian art, served as mayor from 1876 to 1882. He failed, however, because of an alleged "lack of character," to prevent the board from abusing its power and ignoring the will of the Duma. Disagreement erupted over a minor issue: whether to manage the Sokolniki grove as a park or to fell the trees for lumber. The uneducated merchant P. V. Osipov denounced the board for proceeding to clear the grove without obtaining the Duma's consent. "After a stormy session, Tretiakov resigned and went abroad."[42]

State Councilor Boris N. Chicherin, a Tambov landowner and former professor of history at Moscow University, became mayor in 1882. Although successful in leading the Duma, he ran afoul of the tsarist officialdom by making two speeches (unrelated to municipal affairs) in May and June 1883, one defending the principle of university autonomy and the other calling for a national zemstvo organization. While Chicherin opposed constitutional rule for Russia and sought a "happy medium" between tradition and reform, his oratorical attack on what he called "the enemies of free institutions" led Emperor Alexander III to request his resignation.[43]

To what extent did the Moscow merchants use their control of the Duma to further the cause of independent local government? The available evidence suggests that, while their dedication to improvements in the city's management did increase markedly, few merchants distinguished themselves in the struggle against the bureaucracy. Instead, their traditional devotion to the more particular concerns of the merchant estate remained as strong as ever. In 1881, the merchants' close ally Ivan Aksakov offered a backhanded compliment to the recently deceased industrialist Aleksandr K. Krestovnikov, a duma member from 1863 to 1875: "there was in him none of the narrow estate spirit which unfortunately infects many of our outstanding merchants."[44]

Brief portraits of merchant duma members in the memoirs of Prince V. M. Golitsyn (1847–1931; mayor of Moscow 1897–1905) give useful indications of their peculiar behavior in the 1870s. The tobacco magnate and Merchant Society *starshina* Vasili M. Bostandzhoglo exhibited no special qualities except an exaggerated sense of his own importance; as was typical among rich capitalist merchants, his pretensions to polite manners were tinged with the coarseness of the traditional merchant *samodur*. "White-haired, with a clean-shaven and rather dark-complexioned face and black, penetrating eyes, he loved to emphasize his refined good breeding in dealing with others, even in the shortest conversations . . . Somewhat acrimonious and abrasive . . . he was feared; even merchants of his age were somewhat servile before him, while younger ones strove to imitate his elegant manners."[45]

Several merchants in the Duma exhibited a more serious attitude toward city government that did Bostandzhoglo, but they displayed in various ways a distressing lack of competence. Vasili I. Iakunchikov, who was "just as elegant" as Bostandzhoglo, "took an active part in city affairs." Having lived in England, he "always tried to mention examples of West-European cities as deserving of blind imitation by Moscow,"[46] but offered few practical ideas. Nikolai P. Lanin, a producer of mineral water and champagne, regularly made a ridiculous spectacle of himself by carrying to extremes a superficial devotion to European ways. He "considered it necessary, in spite of his poor education, to express an opinion on every report, and in all his speeches foreign words just poured out, whether they made sense or not . . ." Worse, Lanin's arrogance "caused more or less serious incidents with the presiding officer and with other members."[47]

In contrast, several merchants like Mikhail A. Gorbov "always spoke coolly, quietly, and moderately" in the debates. Yet Gorbov, like Lanin, had little influence.[48] The merchants responded less to rhetoric in open session than to personal persuasion by respected men of commerce. Thus, the most enigmatic figure among the Moscow merchants exerted great influence behind the scenes. K. T. Soldatenkov, "a wonderful conversationalist, . . . never entered into the public debates, but on the other hand worked a great deal in the commissions and talked even more in separate groups of duma members, when during recesses they would gather around the tea tables."[49]

Above all, the merchants seemed to prefer the favorite activity of rich men in search of status: philanthropy. Their own estate organization – the Merchant House, renamed in 1863 the Merchant Board *(uprava)* – had long managed a number of modest orphanages, poorhouses, and schools, according to the wills of rich Moscow traders and manufacturers.[50] In the 1870s, the merchant leaders of the Duma's philanthropy commission undertook similar projects on a larger scale, coupling municipal administration with private financing, as from the Bakhrushin brothers, M. I. Liamin,[51] and V. D. Aksenov. The latter, a "goodnatured and humane" septuagenarian, enjoyed great influence among his fellows, although to Golitsyn he appeared somehow "picturesque" because of his "delicate, almost child-like voice" and "his whole figure, skinny as a skeleton, with a deathly pale face and a long, white beard."[52]

The strongest merchant personality, for progress or reaction, in the Moscow government after 1870 appears to have been the prominent cotton textile manufacturer and banker Nikolai A. Naidenov, a duma delegate from 1863 until his death in 1905. He convinced L. L. Katuar and many other capable merchants of their civic duty to participate in public affairs.[53] Yet if Naidenov possessed the qualities of "a true Moscow patriot" and spoke well in the Duma on financial questions, he also demonstrated an extreme narrowness of vision that, together with his strongly antireformist views, served only to hinder the development of vigorous self-government. "Naidenov was a very intelligent and businesslike man, but [also] a cunning person who pursued his own personal goals; it was absolutely impossible to rely on him. For him, the interests of the merchant estate were incomparably higher than the city's, and his own personal importance stood highest of all."[54]

For all his faults, however, Naidenov appeared far more capable than his fellows. "The merchant majority was, in general, not of a high standard. There was very little education [among them] and perhaps even less [of an aptitude for] participation in public affairs. Very few knew how to work; most of them sat in silence and simply voted for their leaders."[55] Thus the Duma rarely witnessed discussions of issues of national importance such as those raised in the zemstvo assemblies of St. Petersburg, Tver, and Chernigov. Perhaps for that reason no general history of the Moscow Duma exists. In the absence of a detailed study, a discussion of four crucial incidents will suffice to illustrate important aspects of the Moscow merchants' political ideology in the 1870s and 1880s.

In mid-October 1876, during the Turkish offensive against the Serbs, the duma member and Pan-Slav activist D. F. Samarin assembled the delegates prior to a regular session and delivered an impassioned speech calling on the Russian government to intervene on behalf of the "brother Slavs." Ivan Aksakov, who was present at the meeting though not a duma member, promptly pulled from his pocket and read aloud an emotional appeal to the tsar urging intervention. The assembly then moved into the regular duma chamber and unanimously passed Aksakov's statement in the form of a resolution. As in 1870, the tsar refused to accept the address, but during a visit to Moscow just two weeks later he delivered an anti-Turkish speech to the Duma that foreshadowed Russia's declaration of war on April 12, 1877.[56] So strong was the merchants' patriotism that when war was declared the duma chamber resounded with "great ovations." The delegates voted overwhelmingly to include in the regular budget for 1877 one million rubles for the war effort, an enormous expenditure that drastically raised the city's debt.[57]

The merchants' sense of political priorities may be appreciated even more clearly by viewing these events of 1876–7 within the context of the city's chronic financial problems. While they readily approved the million rubles to vanquish the Turks, they proved less generous with revenues for the city's own needs. For example, in 1883, the tsarist government initiated a bill in the Moscow Duma to replace the existing tax on fuel with a new tax on the profits of commercial and industrial firms. Mayor Chicherin proposed a rate of 7 percent on net profits, but the Duma reduced the rate to 5. Then the government, taking the merchants' side, set the rate at only 3 percent, so that the city received even less revenue than before![58]

A third incident deserves extended discussion because it illustrated how the merchants intentionally exercised their voting power in the Duma to frustrate liberal reforms. In the summer of 1882, Chickerin appointed Baron Nikolai A. Korf (1834–83) as the new superintendent of the Moscow public schools. A well-known expert on education,[59] Korf received the endorsement of Iuri F. Samarin, the influential Slavophile publicist and proponent of public education. However, the appointment soon encountered difficulties. Most of the merchants were away at the Nizhny Novgorod Fair, and some resented Chicherin's failure to consult them. Moreover, the reactionary *Moskovskie vedomosti* attacked Korf for having publicly opposed the government's plan to establish church-controlled parish schools outside the jurisdiction of the Ministry of Education and local city dumas and zemstvos. Dmitri Samarin, Aleksandr Korsh, the dynamic merchant leader Nikolai A. Alekseev, "and the whole third group of delegates" in the Duma supported Korf; but "the old devout merchants" feared that Korf's preference for secular schools signified a principled opposition to Orthodoxy. Chicherin attempted to convince them by reading pro-Christian passages from Korf's published works, but to no avail. Traditional religiosity, the core of the merchant ideology, had obviously lost none of its force.

In the autumn of 1882, Korf himself aggravated the issue by publishing in *Golos* (*The Voice*), a liberal St. Petersburg newspaper, an article praising as a model for Russia the new French system of primary schools, which was completely secular. Now only those whom Chicherin termed "the radicals" (notably the zemstvo leaders S. A. Muromtsev and V. Iu. Skalon and the eccentric merchant Lanin) continued to defend the baron's appointment. When Korf rejected Chicherin's advice to withdraw from the post, the antiliberal merchants in the Duma began a full-scale campaign against him.[60] Konstantin P. Pobedonostsev, the most influential proponent of reaction in Russia, personally entered the fray at this point.[61] "Pobedonostsev wrote the most insistent letter to Bishop Amvrosi, Aksenov and Naidenov, prevailing upon them to influence all honorable people and to oppose Korf's candidacy by all means, as (in his words) a disgrace to Moscow. Amvrosi in fact assembled the merchants and read Pobedonostsev's letter to them."[62]

Naidenov, for his part, needed no such encouragement. On October 16, he thanked Pobedonostsev for his letter and expressed alarm at the support given Korf during the past week by Alekseev "and several young ones like him" (Alekseev was 30 at the time).

I know all this from one of our people, sent [to Alekseev's house] to observe. I thought it *premature* to come out *against* it then, in order not to intensify the activities of Korf's supporters; but *now all possible measures* have already been taken, and his own sin has implicated him as well; he damaged himself a great deal with his latest article in *Golos*. Two days ago D. F. Samarin openly renounced him . . . [Now] our merchants, except the youth, are *all* against Korf; the *meshchane* and artisans (the majority) also; the gentry, half and half; on his side there remains the red party [*sic!*], like Muromtsev, Skalon, Koshelev, etc.

This party is, I hope, not large . . . The big little boys [*vysochki-mal'chishki*] have now taken over the leadership of this party. They are no good. Once encouraged from above for their liberal views, they do not know their own worth.[63]

The Duma carried out Pobedonostsev's wishes at its next meeting; even the younger merchants had apparently realized the hopelessness of the baron's cause. "A great multitude of delegates and the public gathered; there was great excitement. Aksenov told me that the whole crowd had come to vote against Korf," Chicherin recalled. When the mayor announced that the baron had at last withdrawn his candidacy, "the tense mood of the assembly was promptly dispelled." Only Muromtsev and other "radicals" objected to the outcome, in a "caustic little article that was never answered."[64]

In a fourth episode – the Duma's protest after Chicherin's forced resignation in August 1883 – some hesitant moves by merchant leaders toward the defense of self-government were evident, but the matter ended in a typical display of fright and passivity before the tsarist bureaucracy. At first, many delegates, including Naidenov, expressed their sympathy for the ex-mayor.[65] Among the merchants still in Moscow and not away in Nizhny Novgorod or at a dacha for the summer was V. D. Aksenov, the oldest duma delegate. After meeting with sixteen other merchants, including Naidenov, at Rukavishnikov's house, he drafted a speech in Chicherin's honor, which he read to the Duma on September 12. The merchant delegate S. V. Lepeshkin then proposed that Chicherin be made an honorary citizen of the city, and the motion passed.

Soon, however, "the city leaders panicked," Chicherin recalled ruefully. In the eyes of the bureaucracy, their mild statement "was like a protest against the will of the tsar."[66] Although Dolgorukov was then abroad, his assistant moved quickly to settle the matter. The seven-member Board for City Affairs reviewed Chicherin's honorary citizenship, and "as usual, by a vote of four to three," it overruled the Duma's action (on the grounds that the question had been introduced and passed on the same day, instead of in two separate sessions, as the rules required). On his return, Dolgorukov was surprised to find that neither Aksenov nor Lepeshkin cowed before him when he threatened them with exile from Moscow. Both stood firm in expressing admiration for Chicherin's performance as mayor, though not for his speeches that had angered the tsar.[67]

At the same time, the merchants sought to reverse their hasty action unofficially, as they dreaded the dilemma – either capitulation or insubordination – that awaited them in the Duma's reconsideration of the verdict of the Provincial Board. Aksenov, former Mayor Tretiakov, and even Ivan Aksakov suggested to Chicherin that he politely refuse the title of honorary citizen. When the desired letter arrived from Chicherin, Tretiakov cried, "This is wonderful!" and Aksenov agreed, despite the letter's angry mention of "the weakness of Russian [educated] society . . ." As Chicherin wrote later, "I earned the right to speak of the indifference, the inertia, and the servility of Russian [educated] society. If I was not supported, it was not I who was guilty."

Chicherin put primary blame on the Duma's gentry leaders, since they had failed to show the requisite qualities of independence in this affair despite their superior education. As for the others, he offered a less harsh judgment. "It was difficult to expect civic courage from the merchants and *meshchane*. They had long been accustomed to bow before authority. Their private interests were completely dependent both on the Ministry [of Internal Affairs] and on the governor-general, especially in view of the wide-ranging powers that the latter enjoyed."[68] The merchant P. V. Osipov had once justified their behavior with characteristic bluntness: "If we decided to put up opposition, we would be twisted into a ram's horn."[69] All the same, Chicherin expressed bitterness at the servility displayed by Naidenov, "who had just recently boasted to me that he did not belong to the party of Dolgorukov."[70]

It was Naidenov who arranged, in a secret meeting with Aksenov, to put forward a candidate for mayor who could be trusted to cooperate fully with the authorities. They chose S. A. Tarasov, an aged delegate and former bureaucrat who had gained a fortune by marrying a rich merchant woman. Chicherin recalled that "many delegates, to whom this was not at all becoming, went along with the deal." Alone among the merchants, N. A. Alekseev became "indignant," but his bid for election failed by several votes, so that Tarasov, "the lackey of the governor-general," became the new mayor of Moscow.[71] Chicherin once remarked pessimistically that during its first decade the reorganized Moscow Duma represented "the absent gentry, the indifferent merchants, and the impertinent democracy."[72]

The municipal government flourished, however, in the late 1880s and early 1890s. Tarasov resigned because of ill health shortly after taking office,[73] and the vice-mayor, M. F. Ushakov, was succeeded in November 1885 by Tarasov's recent challenger, Nikolai A. Alekseev (1852–93). The scion of a rich manufacturing family that had produced a Moscow mayor in 1840, Alekseev served as mayor from 1885 to 1893, and was generally regarded as the most dynamic leader that the city had ever seen. The imposing new duma building (constructed 1890–2, now the Lenin Museum) and the Upper Trading Rows (1886–93, now the GUM department store) expressed in their neo-Slavic ornaments the Muscovites' growing civic pride. Yet Alekseev's contributions to the cause of self-government are difficult to measure because of the complexity of his character and the contradictions that marked his unusual public career.

Some duma leaders viewed Alekseev as a dangerous man. Naidenov, in his letter to Pobedonostsev in October 1882, had spoken of Alekseev as the mastermind of the pro-Korf faction, "more vigorously and more insolently active than the others," a man who already harbored ambitions of becoming mayor. Alekseev's report before the State Council favoring schools for industrial workers showed no fear of the contagion of radical propaganda in the factories, and now he "thinks everything should be constructed in a new way – everything old is no good. Woe to us from these reformists!"[74] Naidenov's antipathy dated back at least to the trial of the directors of the bankrupt Commercial Loan Bank in October 1876, in which Alekseev, out of "the extreme cruelty of his character," allegedly testified falsely against two innocent relatives.[75] Yet if "Naidenov hated him, and the old merchants in general did not like him," the duma delegates, impressed by Alekseev's great energy and enthusiasm, elected him mayor by 123 yea votes to only 23 nays.[76] Of course, Alekseev had supported Korf in 1882, but not so adamantly as had the liberals Skalon and Muromtsev. Indeed, the antipathy between Naidenov and Alekseev was apparently based on nothing more substantial than personal animosity and the all-too-common distrust of the young (or rather, middle-aged) generation by the old.[77]

The dramatic improvements that took place during Alekseev's term had been foreshadowed in the previous decade. S. M. Tretiakov (1876–82) had added to the staff of the Executive Board capable young engineers, architects, and doctors.[78] Likewise, during Chicherin's brief tenure (1882–3) the city had begun issuing long-term municipal bonds to maintain public services (including "horse-drawn streetcars, gas and electric lighting, expanded water mains"), and had planned to extend the sewer system.[79] Still, Alekseev's energetic leadership resulted in unprecedented improvements. Not only was the sewer system completed, but a new water main and municipal slaughterhouses were constructed.[80] Mayor Alekseev was perhaps best known for his program of building many public hospitals, including an insane asylum, the first in Moscow and one of the finest in the world at that time. (It was indeed ironic that he would be murdered in the Duma building by a lunatic's pistol shot.)[81]

Of the many anecdotes told about Alekseev, one illustrates best his flamboyant personality and his unbounded dedication to the city's improvement. Because the new psychiatric hospital cost 1.5 million rubles, the city treasury required donations from the public. As usual, rich merchants were invited to contribute. When one wealthy trader offered 10,000 rubles, Alekseev addressed him loudly at a party in the presence of many important merchants, saying that 10,000 was shamefully little. But if 50,000 were pledged, Alekseev announced, he would bow down before the donor in public. The merchant replied that it would be worth such a financial sacrifice to humble the mayor of Moscow. Alekseev immediately dropped to his knees and said, "I won't stand up until you write out a check for 40,000 rubles." The embarrassed merchant had no choice but to comply. Alekseev stood up, pocketed the check, and dusted off his trousers, saying, "There, you see how it turned out; you know, I had almost decided to kneel down for only 25,000!" The flustered donor left the party amid general laughter.[82]

Chicherin, who knew Alekseev well, admired him for defending the city government against the arbitrary interventions of provincial officials; "this son of our Russian merchant estate did not cringe before the authorities, but knew how to remain independent . . . Like a brilliant meteor, he flashed over Moscow, which will never forget him."[83] Unfortunately, Chicherin specified no facts in this regard, except that Alekseev encouraged him to return to the Duma as a delegate in 1888.[84] The best-known case of Alekseev's resistance to outside interference – several unsuccessful attempts in 1887–90 to prevent the provincial Zemstvo from taxing real estate within the city limits – scarcely reflected a commitment to vigorous self-government.[85] Moreover, contemporary observers emphasized the dark side of the mayor's public career. Alekseev's tendency to pursue his goals with extreme vigor made him, paradoxically, an enemy of democracy in Moscow. Far from being a "red," as Naidenov held, Alekseev implemented his apolitical program of public-works construction by personal fiat, and rudely discouraged the Duma from offering any criticism or advice; "in everything he undertook he was a despot."[86] Even Chicherin admitted, "This was no longer self-government, but despotism in the public arena."[87] A delegate once quipped that Moscow knew three kinds of mayors: those who asked what the Duma wanted, those who told the Duma what it needed, and Alekseev, who shouted, "I want this and that is how it will be!"[88]

Alekseev's loyalty to autocracy was never doubted by the bureaucracy. Having worked diligently preparing for the coronation of Alexander III in 1881–3, he became in 1885 the merchant representative on the Special Board *(osoboe prisutstvie)* of the Governing Senate considering the crimes of revolutionary terrorists, and he was reappointed to this post annually. For his many services, he was awarded several tsarist medals. His eulogy for the reactionary journalist Katkov ended with an emotional tribute: "We grieve over the death of Katkov, and we regret that Russia has lost this highly gifted statesman of the press. Katkov was dear to us as a Russian thinker and patriot."[89]

In conclusion, the available documents give scarcely any signs of genuinely liberal political activity within the Moscow city government under the law of 1870. The few voices of reform in the Duma were those of zemstvo leaders from the gentry, like Muromtsev and Skalon. Alekseev hardly deserved the description of a liberal merchant spokesman leading a bloc of "people from the educated bourgeoisie" in a "class struggle" against their "mortal enemy," an alleged "gentry party" of reactionary landlords.[90] The real political split in the Duma, when it occurred at all, formed between the mass of merchants who followed their leaders (first Naidenov and Aksenov, later Alekseev) and a small band of dedicated reformists, notably the gentry liberals who vainly supported Baron Korf to the bitter end in 1882. It remained to be seen whether the merchants would further the cause of liberalism under the Municipal Statute of 1892, whose restrictive electoral system gave them still greater power to control the institution of self-government in Moscow, the Duma.

Militant Pan-Slavism

The Moscow merchants' unwillingness to challenge the tsarist autocracy in the name of municipal self-government should not be interpreted as evidence that they lacked political sophistication. In the 1870s and 1880s, at the very time that the duma leaders Chicherin, Koshelev, Skalon, and Muromtsev encountered what appeared to them to be the merchants' apathy, these same merchants were openly and enthusiastically engaging in a highly political campaign in favor of Pan-Slavism and the Russian military assault on Turkish territories in southern Europe and Transcaucasia.

Aggressive nationalism had been implicit in the merchant ideology during the early years of Alexander II's reign; but the outward manifestations of that nationalism had then been tentative and feeble. During the Crimean War, the merchants had begun to recite Slavophile diatribes against the West and had given symbolic cash donations to the war effort. Yet even Kokorev's grandiose ceremony honoring the returned defenders of Sevastopol in 1856 had been only an exercise in vicarious patriotism. For two decades the Moscow merchants, no longer political neophytes, played their supporting role in the Pan-Slav movement with a new sense of self-assurance. Active participation in the Pan-Slavic cause, notably in the form of generous financial support, so strengthened the merchants' commitment to Russian nationalism that this element of their political outlook persisted with undiminished power for decades thereafter. The significance of the merchants' Pan-Slavic adventure lay in its ominous ideological consequences, particularly the stifling of liberal sentiments among merchants who were active in the zemstvos and other political forums in the later nineteenth century.

The Moscow Slavic Benevolent Committee, the central organization of Russian Pan-Slavism in the two decades following its creation in 1858, included many intellectual allies of the merchants among its founders: the

Slavophiles (including A. P. and D. P. Shipov), Pogodin, and Katkov, to name a few.[91] The merchants themselves were slow to join at first, owing to their traditional distrust of political schemes that might entail financial sacrifices without tangible rewards.[92] By the early 1870s, thirty Moscow industrialists, essentially the same men who had gained control of the Duma at about that time, made up about 10 percent of the committee's membership.[93] Nikitin surmised that these rich merchants joined because of their close relations with the committee's gentry and professional leaders on other matters, not because of a commitment to Slavic liberation or of an urge to conquer Balkan markets.[94] Yet in the decade from 1856 to 1865 the merchants had acquired a conscious ideological outlook based firmly on nationalism. Their shyness, inexperience, and perhaps financial caution, not any philosophical opposition to the Pan-Slavic ideal, delayed their involvement in the cause.

Merchants figured prominently among the duma members at the Pan-Slavic "Ethnographic Exhibition of Representatives of the Slavic Peoples" in Moscow in 1867. In Naidenov's words, the Duma gave "the drawing together of the Slavs" a certain "political character" by organizing a ceremony and outdoor party at the Sokolniki park on the outskirts of Moscow.[95] In addition, the visiting Slavic scholars and nationalist leaders were provided with lodging in merchant homes. Besides the Slavophile, Iuri F. Samarin, and the Official Nationalist, M. P. Pogodin, the hospitality committee included the merchants V. A. Kokorev, F. F. Rezanov, T. S. Morozov, A. N. Volkov, A. K. Krestovnikov, V. M. Bostandzhoglo, and S. M. Tretiakov. The latter organized the housing and transportation facilities and collected from his fellow merchants the necessary 4,000 rubles for the visitors' carriages during the exhibition.[96] The most influential merchants also donated money in 1867 to a campaign sponsored by the mayor of Moscow "to aid Christians suffering on Candia island" (Crete). Amid the names of various princes and Slavophiles, several merchants – Rezanov, Chetverikov, Liamin, and Konshin – appeared prominently as donors of between 25 and 100 rubles; Soldatenkov gave 200, while Bostandzhoglo and K. A. Popov each contributed 300 rubles.[97]

The strength of the merchants' Pan-Slavic sentiments may be seen in their active support for the Russian drive against Turkish and Austrian rule in the Balkans in the 1860s and 1870s. In 1866, Kokorev discussed with Field Marshal Prince A. I. Bariatinsky the need for a preemptive Russian assault on the Hapsburg territories. The ideal solution would be the partition of the Austrian Empire, "this hotbed of intrigue and traitorous activities that hamper the formation of independent life in the Slavic lands."[98] Between 1870 and 1875, the merchants played an increasingly important role in financing the Slavic Committee's philanthropic and organizational projects: a school for Balkan Slav women in Moscow,[99] restoration of a church in Prague,[100] and gifts of uniforms and money to the Montenegrins.[101]

Following anti-Turkish uprisings in Herzegovina and Bosnia in the summer of 1875, the Slavic Committee intensified its campaign in favor of Russian intervention. It found a vociferous spokesman in General Mikhail G. Cherniaev, a military hero whose close ties with important Moscow cotton textile producers dated back to 1865, when Ivan and Mikhail A. Khludov had accompanied his troops in the conquest of Tashkent.[102] Mikhail Khludov and Kokorev had stood by Cherniaev during the years of his political frustration (1869–74), when the cautious policy makers in St. Petersburg denied him an influential military post and ignored his pleas for a Russian diplomatic and military offensive in the Balkans.[103] The merchants also provided Cherniaev with financial aid for his reactionary and chauvinist newspaper, *Russkii mir (The Russian World)*, which did more than any other periodical to whip up Pan-Slavic emotions in Russia. Acting on a request transmitted by Chizhov, they provided the necessary funds in 1874 in exchange for the printing of economic news in the paper.[104]

As diplomatic tensions continued to mount, Cherniaev left for the Balkans in April 1876 to take personal command of the Serbian offensive against the Turks.[105] The Slavic Committee financed the outfitting and transportation of hundreds of Russian volunteers who followed him to Serbia. When Serbia officially declared war on Turkey at the end of June, the Pan-Slav fever became endemic in Russia. By the summer of 1876, Slavic Committees throughout the country were collecting thousands of rubles from all social groups to support the Serbs.[106] The excitement was especially intense in Moscow, where the merchants now committed huge sums to the undeclared war against the Turks. Aksakov chose as the Slavic Committee's new command post the spacious office in the Moscow Merchant Mutual Credit Society, of which he was a director.[107] One of the largest contributions to the committee came from the Moscow Old-Believer merchants, led by K. T. Soldatenkov and T. S. Morozov: an entire 100-cot field hospital, with a full staff of Russian medical personnel.[108] So many military volunteers flocked to the Moscow committee that in August one of its members, the merchant Aleksandr A. Porokhovshchikov

(1809–94), set up a special branch office in his "Slavic Bazaar" restaurant. Here, in the heart of the commercial district, committee workers carried out the enormous tasks of bookkeeping, coordination, and storage of materials in support of the Serbs.[109]

After a Turkish counterattack in the autumn of 1876 wiped out Cherniaev's early gains, the Pan-Slavists intensified their campaign for official Russian intervention in the Balkans. On September 21, in Livadia, Porokhovshchikov presented to the tsar a persuasive case for war with Turkey, and afterward sent to Aksakov, Katkov, and Dolgorukov a triumphant telegram: "Complete confidence. The situation is secure. Unlimited goodwill."[110] Despite the misgivings of the Ministry of Foreign Affairs, Russia finally declared war on April 12, 1877.[111]

Like the Serbian campaign, the short-lived uprising in Bulgaria (April 1876) also received enthusiastic support from the merchants. In July, with the consent of the crown prince, the reactionary General R. A. Fadeev[112] personally came to Moscow "to obtain money from the purses" of the merchants for the Bulgarian independence movement. This call for funds received the official endorsement of Governor-General Dolgorukov, Mayor Tretiakov, the MSEC, and the Merchant Society. Fadeev emphasized to Aksakov that Tsar Alexander himself approved, as long as aid to the Bulgarians remained unofficial and did not implicate the Russian government directly. "The Tsar knows that the contributions are for the purpose of arming the Bulgarians; he has been given the names of the founders [*sic*] of the patriotic movement: Tretiakov, Morozov, Naidenov." This appeal to the merchants' loyalty and self-esteem paid handsome dividends. By the end of August, Fadeev's target of 150,000 rubles had been surpassed, and by November the merchants' donations had provided the Bulgarians with twelve Krupp cannons and 2,500 rifles.[113]

However, Fadeev's handling of the Bulgarian campaign soon gave Aksakov and the merchants second thoughts. Fadeev irritated them by attempting to keep their friend, Cherniaev, from taking a leading role in the Bulgarian revolt. Furthermore, it appeared that the Slavic Committee's funds would be severely depleted, as the cost of the new military operation might reach a million rubles. They were quite relieved, therefore, when the Russian government allowed the establishment of a new commission to help the Bulgarians. Headed by Aksakov and including General N. G. Stoletov as military quartermaster, S. M. Tretiakov, T. S. Morozov, and N. A. Naidenov, this commission, acting with the tsar's full approval and supported by governmental funds, outfitted the Bulgarian militia with uniforms in late 1876 and early 1877.[114]

Soon after Russia declared war in April, the Slavic committees received full official status, and the merchants had the enormous satisfaction of serving the great nationalist cause in such activities as raising funds for the army and organizing facilities for the wounded. Frustrated during the Crimean War by the news of defeat and by the lack of opportunities to aid the war effort, the Moscow merchants now gloried in their well-publicized role as financial and administrative coordinators of auxiliary organizations in the Balkan war. The Moscow Duma's contribution of one million rubles to the war effort and the establishment by the Merchant Society and the MSEC of an additional one-million-ruble fund to aid families of Russian war casualties symbolized this chauvinist enthusiasm.[115]

Mayor S. M. Tretiakov's speech to the Duma on March 2, 1878, breathed this spirit of militant Pan-Slavism. He mourned the death of Prince V. A. Cherkassky, the prominent Slavophile, Pan-Slav leader, and former mayor, "who left Moscow ten months ago in the prime of health and strength in order to serve the sacred cause of the liberation of our brothers . . ." The fact that Cherkassky had suddenly fallen ill and died in the war zone just as Russian troops were approaching the Turkish capital made his death an especially tragic one for Russian patriots.[116]

The Russo-Turkish War, even more than the Crimean War two decades before, left a lasting impression on the ideology of the Moscow commercial-industrial leaders. As their chauvinist enthusiasm mounted in the midst of military campaigns and visits by the tsar, the merchants developed closer contacts than ever before with four spokesmen of national stature who stood on the extreme right of the political spectrum.

By the late 1870s, Ivan S. Aksakov had become the foremost proponent of Pan-Slavism and Russian expansionism. His angry denunciation of Russia's acceptance of the peace terms imposed by the major European powers at the Congress of Berlin (July 1878) earned him exile in Vladimir province for several months. During his ordeal, he received strong expressions of sympathy from Moscow merchant leaders, who continued to donate funds to the Pan-Slavic cause as late as 1885.[117]

Moreover, the merchants provided financial backing for Aksakov's last venture in journalism, the Moscow weekly newspaper *Rus'* (*Ancient Russia*, 1880–6; biweekly in 1883 and 1884). As in the 1860s, Aksakov set the editorial policy, while the merchants expressed their views on current

questions of finance, taxation, and industrial policy.[118] While Aksakov
retained until his death a residual Slavophile hatred for bureaucratic tyranny, especially censorship of the press,[119] it was clear to all, including the
merchants, that the implications of his critique were hardly liberal. He
castigated the tsarist bureaucracy for its lack of aggressiveness in foreign
affairs, for its approval of "the great sin" of the Bulgarian constitution of
1878, and for its failure to implement fully the reactionary policy of Russi-
fication: the cultural suppression of Jewish, German, Polish, and other
minority populations within the empire.[120] Although it is unlikely that the
Moscow merchants understood Aksakov's purely theoretical arguments
against the government in the 1880s any more than they had twenty years
before, this last episode in the merchant-Slavophile alliance tied them
closer than ever to the antiliberal camp.

General Cherniaev, the merchants' favorite military hero, in 1876
"sought to become military dictator of Serbia" and to destroy the parliamentary institutions of that country.[121] After the failure of the Serbian
revolt, M. A. Khludov accompanied Cherniaev to Prague, where the pop-
ulace gave him a triumphal welcome in January 1877. On his return to
Moscow, two hundred people, "mostly merchants," cheered his parade.[122]

Another man on horseback adored by the merchants was General
M. D. Skobelev (1843–82). After distinguishing himself in the Bulgarian
campaign of 1877, he gained eternal fame in the massacre at Geok-Tepe
(1881) of 8,000 Turkmen natives resisting the Russian conquest of Central
Asia.[123] In 1881–2, Skobelev, a fanatical enemy of Germany, joined
T. S. Morozov, N. N. Konshin, and other Moscow merchants in a plan
for a Russian trading company to undertake an offensive against European
commercial firms operating in the Balkans. The project was abandoned
only because, as Morozov explained to RIS, it would constitute "a declaration of war against the entire industry of Western Europe" at a time when
the Russian economy was not yet strong enough to win such a contest.[124]

Finally, the Moscow merchants established close relations with the
most illustrious reactionary in late nineteenth-century Russia: Konstantin
P. Pobedonostsev. As the war drew to a close, the merchants sought new
means to strengthen Russia's economic and military power. Early in 1878,
"a group of Russian patriots, largely Moscow merchants and officials at
first," collected funds for the establishment of a Volunteer Fleet.[125]
Cargo vessels were to be donated to the navy and outfitted with armaments, so that they could augment the regular naval forces in a future
war.[126] A number of Moscow notables, including Prince Dolgorukov, the

Samarin brothers, Ivan Aksakov, Bishop Amvrosi, Professor Babst, the merchant leader T. S. Morozov, and the St. Petersburg banker I. E. Ginzburg, convinced Pobedonostsev to become the executive director of this novel patriotic scheme. The enormous sum of six million rubles, raised between May 1878 and December 1879, provided an initial increment of six ships. In the several years following Pobedonostsev's first meeting with the Moscow merchant leaders in April 1879, he found himself learning the rudiments of the shipping business for their sake (much as Chizhov had been obliged to master the techniques of railroad management twenty years before!). Although Pobedonostsev despaired when his newfound friends soon lost interest in maritime commerce, the fleet remained in operation for decades.[127] We need only recall the scorn with which tsarist bureaucrats had treated the manufacturers in the 1855–70 period to appreciate the significance of their relationship with Pobedonostsev, who in 1882 described them to Alexander III as "the most Russian, the most conservative, and the most devoted to the tsar in the name of Russian and national interests."[128]

In conclusion, the merchants' activism on behalf of patriotic and reactionary causes earned them considerable prestige. By supporting Pan-Slavism, the most extreme form of Russian xenophobia in the 1870s and 1880s, the Moscow commercial and industrial leaders learned a lesson in aggressive nationalism that was to remain strong through the fatal adventure of World War I.

The struggle against zemstvo liberalism

Less apparent, but far more significant for the political evolution of Russian society than Pan-Slavic agitation, was the Moscow merchant's hostility to the only native source of liberalism in Russian, the movement to strengthen the new institution of rural self-government – the Zemstvo. Created by the state in 1864 simply as an elective body entrusted with the maintenance of roads, schools, hospitals, agronomical stations, and similar rural services,[129] the Zemstvo soon became a forum for enlightened landowners who hoped to replace tsarist autocracy with a constitutional regime. The role of the merchants in this political drama is difficult to reconstruct because of the paucity of documentary materials, but it appears to have been fully consistent with their ideology of the 1860–90 period. Merchant participation in zemstvo work remained at a low level; their lack of concern was founded on a clear perception of their economic interests;

and when they did participate, notably in industrial areas, they emerged as outspoken opponents of zemstvo liberalism.

Hostility toward the Zemstvo may be seen, then, as the reverse side of their active support of reactionary causes. The merchants' early antipathy to zemstvo liberalism generally took the form of inaction rather than outright acts of opposition, at least in the 1860s and 1870s; yet the very fact of nonparticipation assumed central importance. In the half-century prior to 1917, the fate of zemstvo liberalism because the fate of political freedom in Russia. The merchants may have made their most profound political impact by refusing to donate to the Zemstvo as much energy and money as they provided to numerous antiliberal and xenophobic purposes in these years.

From the very outset, the complicated zemstvo electoral system in effect from 1864 to 1890 limited the merchants' role in the new institution. To be sure, merchants were not excluded from the district *(uezd)* assembly, the local zemstvo body that elected from its midst the district Executive Board *(uprava)* and the delegates to the provincial assembly. Individuals of any social category who owned real estate worth at least 15,000 rubles or industrial or commercial enterprises with a yearly business volume of at least 6,000 rubles were entitled to vote in the first electoral college *(kurial'nyi s"ezd)*, together with large and small gentry landowners and the clergy. The second college, comprised solely of merchants and *meshchane* in district towns, included owners of 6,000-ruble industrial and commercial establishments and of urban real estate worth at least 500 to 3,000 rubles, depending on the size of the town. Only the third college, established for peasant communities, excluded merchants.[130]

Instead of allowing each electoral college to elect one-third of the delegates to the district assembly, however, the law erected a complex system of proportional representation based on the actual amount of land owned by the members of the colleges. Thus the number of delegates elected by the wealthy gentry in the first college made up, on the average, almost half of the total (47.8 percent), while peasant communities elected less than two-fifths (39.7 percent), and urban delegates (merchants and *meshchane;* the latter owned relatively little land) occupied only 12.5 percent of the seats.[131] Despite the merchants' dominance in the second college, they were far outnumbered by gentry landlord electors and delegates in the first and most influential college, where they made up only 5.1 percent of the delegates. In this college, 78.1 percent of the delegates came from the gentry, 5.6 percent from peasant landowners, and 11.2 percent from the clergy in twenty-four provinces for which detailed information is available.[132] The highest percentages of merchant and *meshchane* delegates in district assemblies in 1865–6 were to be found in the industrial area around Moscow, but even there the gentry predominated.[133] A similar pattern prevailed in the administrative boards, which were elected by the district assemblies.[134]

More significantly, even smaller numbers of merchants served in the provincial zemstvo assemblies, whose members were elected by the district assemblies in each province. An English journalist who studied several zemstvos at firsthand observed that "the District Assemblies choose their most active members to represent them in the Provincial Assemblies, and consequently the choice generally falls on landed proprietors."[135] Average percentage figures for provincial assemblies and boards in the period from 1864 to 1890 were as follows: gentry and bureaucrats, 81.5 percent in assemblies and 89.5 percent in boards; merchants and *meshchane*, 11 and 9 percent; and peasants, 6.9 percent and 1.5 percent.[136] It must be pointed out that although merchants comprised about 10 percent of the membership of the Pan-Slav Committee and the provincial zemstvo assemblies, these figures had entirely different political implications. In the Pan-Slav movement, the merchants played an active financial role, whereas in the zemstvos they appeared far less willing than gentry landowners to promote projects of rural improvement.

The primary reason appeared to be economic. In the first two years (1864–6), the gentry majority in many areas imposed extremely high taxes on the merchants' commercial and industrial enterprises. Complaints by traders and manufacturers led Finance Minister Reutern to recommend strict limits on zemstvo taxation, embodied in a law of November 21, 1866.[137] Still, the initial financial attack on the merchants left a bitter legacy of distrust, reflected in Naidenov's caustic remarks on the zemstvos:

As practice everywhere showed, they scarcely achieved the goal for which they were introduced: to attract the population into independent activity for the improvement of the local economy and the satisfaction of local needs. From their very origin, large new expenses appeared, and new taxes were levied. The zemstvos' efforts in industrial localities were primarily directed toward increasing the taxes on factories and plants, frequently to extreme levels . . .

The zemstvos, he claimed, were "always hostile" to industrialists, and this poor relationship "did not improve with time, but significantly worsened."[138]

Indeed, both the zemstvo leaders and the manufacturers protested the law of November 1866. The St. Petersburg Zemstvo felt so strongly about this issue that in 1867 it requested permission to participate in the drafting of governmental legislation, a brazen challenge to autocracy that led the tsarist administration to close down this body and banish several of its leaders from the capital.[139] During the same year, Naidenov himself drafted the MSEC's complaint to the Ministry of Finance against the zemstvo tax policy. In a ruling that satisfied neither side, the government in July 1867 approved taxes on the value and profitableness (*tsennost' i dokhodnost'*) of machines and implements, as well as of factory buildings. However, the percentage restrictions established in 1866 remained in effect, as did the ban on taxing gross capital turnover (*oboroty*) and net profits of the enterprise.[140] As a result, industry and trade were henceforth taxed at a rate that was "abnormally low in comparison to the taxation of land and other real estate." Deprived of a fair and rational tax system, zemstvos in some areas imposed their levies arbitrarily and, in fact, constantly sought to "evade the law."[141] Thus in Naidenov's words, an eternal "struggle between zemstvos and industry" took shape, so that complaints "have not ceased to this day" (1905).[142]

Wallace explained the merchants' apathy by focusing on this very problem. For a number of years after 1867, local taxes constituted a far smaller percentage of the total national tax burden in Russia than in other European countries,[143] so that factory owners' complaints, Wallace felt, merely displayed their selfishness. The most important consequence of the government's restrictions was that, until the 1880s, "the mercantile class, sure of being always taxed at a ridiculously low minimum . . . lost all interest in the proceedings."[144] After 1867 the merchants, in effect, rationalized their apathy to the zemstvo leadership in these terms: "There is nothing here for us to do; you will not take less than what has been authorized, and you dare not demand more."[145]

A second reason for the merchants' failure to participate during the 1860s and 1870s may be found in the relative liberalism of the dedicated gentry leadership of the zemstvos. At the same time that the merchant ideology was evolving in a clearly authoritarian and xenophobic direction, Russian liberals embraced the Zemstvo as an institution of self-government that would one day place constitutional restraints on the autocratic ruler.[146] Naidenov's acid commentary on the "liberal views" (*liberal'nost'*) of the most visionary zemstvo leaders and their efforts to achieve "the subsequent transformation of the state structure,"[147] eloquently testified to the great ideological rift between the Moscow merchants and the zemstvo constitutionalists on this crucial issue.

The actions of those merchants who served on zemstvo boards in the 1870s reflected this attitude. In Vladimir, the industrially developed province northeast of Moscow, the assemblies on both the district and provincial levels "consisted exclusively of factory owners, merchants, landlords, bureaucrats, peasant elders, and rich peasant industrialists."[148] Up to a third of total revenues was spent on salaries for board members; public health services remained poorly developed, especially in the factory villages; the tax burden weighed more heavily on the poor than on the rich; and the manufacturers seemed to show enthusiasm only in routing railroads past their properties (they sought the northern branch of the projected Trans-Siberian) and in receiving medals from the bureaucrats for having established schools in their factories.[149]

In the course of two decades, the social composition of district zemstvo assemblies underwent a distinct change which reflected the merchants' increased economic strength, particularly in the Central Industrial Region. As they purchased more and more landed property, merchants obtained a preponderant voice in the first electoral college. The number of gentry delegates from this college, their traditional bastion of power, fell below 50 percent by the mid-1880s throughout the Moscow region, notably in six districts in Vladimir province, two in Kaluga, six in Kostroma, six in Moscow, four in Nizhny Novgorod, and two in Iaroslavl.[150] Accordingly, merchant and *meshchane* strength in the district assemblies of the central provinces rose significantly: in Vladimir, to 29.1 percent; Kostroma, 25.4 percent; Moscow, 23.9 percent; Kaluga, 22.5 percent; Pskov, 20.8 percent; Iaroslavl, 17 percent; Tver, 15.8 percent; and Nizhny Novgorod, 14.5 percent.[151]

In the 1880s, merchants actively challenged the gentry leadership, especially in industrially developed regions. Two trends seem clear. First, the nongentry oppositionists sought control of the zemstvos in order to neutralize the threat to their economic interests, particularly the arbitrary tax assessments on "machines and equipment in industrial enterprises";[152] second, they proposed no bold new reforms. V. Iu. Skalon, the liberal editor of the journal *Zemstvo*, complained in December 1880 that the merchants, rich peasants, retired bureaucrats, and wealthy tavern owners who had recently gained control in some areas were leading the zemstvos "into a condition of lifelessness and stagnation."[153]

One case of such aggressiveness by merchants occurred in the election of 1880 in the Moscow district. There the owners of brick factories *(kirpichniki)* "made their first onslaught" against the liberal gentry and voted out of the assembly several progressive zemstvo men. As a result of a second electoral struggle in 1883 that was "even more bitter," the brick-makers "held the Zemstvo in their hands" until the Zemstvo Statute of 1890 altered the electoral system in favor of the economically weakened gentry.[154] These "factory owners who strove to slow the tempo of zemstvo activities in the name of economy and reduced taxes" ended "forever" the zemstvo career of Skalon, the Moscow district board president since 1874 and author of three books on rural self-government.[155]

Also in 1880, evidently in retaliation against zemstvo reports of filth and disease in his father's huge textile complex in Iartsevo,[156] M. A. Khludov "seized control" of the Zemstvo in the Dukhovshchinsk district of Smolensk province. In flagrant violation of the law, Khludov employed false voter lists and used his sales agents to offer bribes and promises of zemstvo offices to gentry voters, while appealing to the peasants with "curious slogans" attacking "pans [Polish landlords] and priests" (the latter paid no taxes). Although these illegal electoral maneuvers provoked a judicial inquiry, Khludov's political offensive proved successful. He scored a stunning victory over the liberal landlords who had previously controlled this district zemstvo.[157]

Whether from estate jealousy or from devotion to progressive zemstvo ideals, the liberal gentry condemned the new merchant and peasant delegates from the first electoral college as "dirty-faced" *(chumazyi)* or "fatbelly" *(maslopuzyi)* upstarts who lacked any commitment to reform.[158] Only Lanin, the indefatigable merchant publicist enamoured of West-European theories, claimed that the growing influence of the merchants and rich peasants represented the rise of a progressive force, which he called "our third estate." Commenting in 1884 on the zemstvo elections of the previous year, he wrote, "The commercial class," together with the kulaks, "has declared a serious war on the gentry-landlord element." Far from imposing a policy of political stagnation, as gentry liberals contended, "the Russian bourgeoisie [*sic*] is striving to take control of public and political affairs and to assume leadership of local self-government." In a rare declaration of merchant self-confidence, Lanin asserted that, "taken as a whole, the bourgeoisie is a more progressive class than the gentry."[159] However, in the absence of evidence to support the notion of merchant liberalism in the Zemstvo or elsewhere in this period, Lanin's grandiose generalization must be viewed as simply an empty boast.

Perhaps the election of Sergei I. Chetverikov and Nikolai A. Alekseev to the Moscow provincial assembly after serving as "ardent zemstvo members" on the district level may be considered a concrete example of the merchants' alleged devotion to zemstvo liberalism in the 1880s. In the course of introducing a double-entry bookkeeping system to put the provincial board's finances in order, these two merchants bewildered the old landlords with their modern terminology: transfer, balance, debit, and credit.[160] (Here was a revealing example of cultural progress among the merchants, which reversed the traditional contrast between the educated gentryman and the ignorant merchant!) Yet this devotion to the Zemstvo led to nothing more reformist than technical improvements in the method of record-keeping; in the Zemstvo, as in the Moscow city government, Alekseev remained aloof from the constitutional movement. The prevailing merchant attitudes toward the Zemstvo – ranging from political apathy to outright hostility – appeared all the more clear in contrast to the desperate struggle for vigorous self-government waged by the zemstvo liberals, whose leaders came almost exclusively from the middle gentry and the professions, and not from the merchant estate.

The merchant ideology of the 1880s

In addition to the Moscow merchants' actions in the City Duma, the Pan-Slav movement, and the zemstvos, their stands on other important issues of the 1880s provided indications of their political opinions. Their attitudes toward the revolutionary movement and the government's policy of religious persecution defined their position on the political spectrum of that period; and V. A. Kokorev's last polemical articles expressed several ideas of the utmost political significance.

In the late 1870s and early 1880s, the antipathy of merchants toward the revolutionary movement drove them to commit acts of violence so extreme that the tsarist regime itself moved to restrain them. In two particular incidents, the merchants deserved to be classified as "ultrareactionary" on the basis of their actions against the radicals. On April 3, 1878, petty merchants and butchers *(miasniki)* in the central commercial area of Moscow known as "Hunters' Row" viciously attacked a group of students from Moscow University who were marching to demonstrate their solidarity with some student prisoners from Kiev who had been arrested for revolutionary activities.[161] Only after N. S. Skvortsov, a liberal journalist, made it clear to Prince Dolgorukov that the failure of the authorities to punish such "beastly violence" would serve as an invitation to similar acts by the city's many thousands of factory workers did the governor-general prudently decide to arrest and punish the rioters.[162]

If the butchers' riot demonstrated the intensity of reactionary feeling among the lower stratum of the Moscow merchant population, a mood of desperate hatred for the enemies of tsarism also emerged at the very pinnacle of this social estate in the aftermath of the assassination of Alexander II in March 1881.[163] Dissatisfied with the measures taken by the government to combat the revolutionary movement, several hundred nobles and bureaucrats in St. Petersburg created a secret counterrevolutionary force – the "Holy Host" *(sviashchennaia druzhina)* – and appealed to proautocratic industrialists for financial support. Seventy-four of the 709 members of this illegal reactionary organization were merchants and honorary citizens, primarily from Moscow, St. Petersburg, and Nizhny Novgorod. They included the most illustrious figures in the Moscow industrial world.[164] Among the 96 members of the Moscow section were 23 merchants: "the mayor (S. M. Tretiakov), duma members, delegates of the Moscow Merchant Society, members of the [Moscow Section of the] Council of Trade and Manufacturing (Sanin, Diachkov, Prove), big Moscow merchants and philanthropists (Shelaputin, Lepeshkin, Losev), and even their *intelligenty* (Maklakov and Liamin); and to them can be added large-scale trader-industrialists and stock exchange merchants . . ."[165] Moreover, the Moscow Holy Host leader, assistant *okrug* court procurator Anatoli I. Chaikovsky (whose brother, the composer Petr, also joined the organization), worked closely in public affairs with N. A. Alekseev and Mayor Tretiakov. A frequent dinner guest in eminent merchants' homes, he married Tretiakov's niece, the daughter of the venerable textile magnate V. D. Konshin, in the spring of 1882.[166]

The Holy Host, created in October 1881, had become moribund by the beginning of 1883. However, its fanatical campaign to employ secret agents against the radical underground and to establish counterfeit leftist periodicals that would confuse and discredit the real revolutionaries symbolized the growth of a reactionary political psychology further to the right than that of the government itself: a domestic counterpart of the virulent Pan-Slavism of the previous decade.[167]

Such reformist sentiments as existed among the Moscow industrial and commercial leaders appeared in connection with the issue of civil rights, particularly those of persecuted religious minorities: Old Believers and Jews.[168] T. S. Morozov, V. A. Kokorev, and K. T. Soldatenkov remained true to the old faith all their lives and resented governmental measures to suppress it. Yet to speak of the "North Russian democratic tradition" as something that, after surviving tsarist persecution since the seventeenth century, emerged intact at the beginning of the twentieth in the form of an Old-Believer "liberal bourgeoisie"[169] is to ignore the crucial antiliberal phase of the entire Moscow industrial leadership, Orthodox and Old-Believer alike, from the 1850s through the 1890s. (It also exaggerates the liberalism of Old-Believer merchant leaders like the Riabushinsky brothers in the 1907–17 period; see Chapters 7 and 8.) The most that can be made of this idea is that the merchants' religious faith strengthened their alliance with such publicists as Ivan Aksakov, who consistently defended "the freedom of conscience" for the Old Believers in *Den'*, *Moskva*, the 1870 duma address, and *Rus'*. By the same token, Pobedonostsev's active opposition to religious toleration[170] apparently strained his relations with Old-Believer merchants. While T. S. Morozov and other schismatics supported the Volunteer Fleet, Pobedonostsev's closest acquaintance among the Moscow merchants was the devoutly Orthodox N. A. Naidenov.

The merchants' solicitude for religious minorities extended on at least two occasions to the Jews, who in the 1880s began to suffer from blatantly lawless attacks, condoned by the police, in the southern areas of the empire. T. S. Morozov protested to the Minister of Internal Affairs in May 1881 that because of the pogroms Jewish shopkeepers could not pay their suppliers, so that "for the most part it is [the industry of] Moscow that will have to pay for the disorders in the south of Russia." He urged that the police protect Jewish merchants' "property and security";[171] economic activity was impossible in the midst of rioting and destruction, no matter what religion the affected merchant professed. Likewise, in the 1890s Mayor Alekseev, with the support of Finance Minister Witte, successfully challenged a decree by the Ministry of War, which, by restricting the commercial activities of Jews in Bukhara, threatened to disrupt deliveries of raw cotton from Central Asia to the Moscow area.[172]

It seems clear, however, that the Moscow merchants' defense of Jewish traders owed less to a principled belief in religious toleration than to a narrow concern for economic gain. In the 1880s these same industrial and commercial leaders successfully petitioned the government to expel certain Jewish merchants from Moscow, on the grounds that the latter were competing unfairly by not purchasing the requisite certificates and by charging greatly reduced prices.[173]

In light of these opinions on the revolutionary movement and religious toleration, the ideas expressed by V. A. Kokorev in 1887 take on special significance. Kokorev cannot be dismissed simply as an eccentric Old-Believer millionaire who, shortly before his death in 1889, filled the pages of *Russkii arkhiv (The Russian Archive)* with a Slavophile diatribe masked as a memoir. True, his series of recollections (entitled "Economic Failures") prescribed dubious economic notions wrapped in self-righteous, patriotic rhetoric,[174] but he was generally regarded as the most articulate Moscow merchant of his generation. His many provocative statements, therefore, provide crucial evidence to illuminate the shadowy world of the capitalist merchants' ideology.

At the heart of Kokorev's outlook remained the Slavophile concept of a contradiction between true Russian civilization and the evil influence of Western European ideas. Quoting "the great patriot . . . the most worthy Ivan Aksakov," Kokorev exclaimed at the outset, "It is time to go home!" – to Moscow; "time to stop searching for economic principles outside the nation's borders and cluttering the native soil with violent transplantations; time, long since, to return home and come to know *our own strength in our own people.*"[175] Angrily he blamed foreigners for Russia's large debts, the inability of the poor peasants to sell flax, and the decline of the gentry: "happy America, fleecing us for cotton for fifty years and extracting billions from us; happy Germany, increasing its political importance at the expense of our declining political strength; happy Europe, sucking from us all the old coin of the time of Peter, Catherine, and Alexander I and all the Siberian gold, and seizing many Russian lands as deposits by means of mortgage writs."[176]

Kokorev still found refuge in the main tenets of the merchant ideology that had formed three decades before: traditional religiosity, fervent patriotism, and hatred of foreign ideas, particularly liberal constitutionalism. "Not flowery orations on political economy, not cunning parliamentary speeches or various kinds of constitutions will give us the wisdom for Russia's well-being and exaltation, but the Word of God living in plain, simple hearts. *This is the one thing; this* will put us on the path of truth and justice."[177] Yet in the final analysis, salvation lay less in Christian love than in the power of the autocratic state, wielded by hardhearted statesmen. "This article posed the question: 'what do we need?' and has answered in one line: 'We need just a dose of Bismarck.' "[178] A clearer expression of the merchants' crude hatred for liberal reform could hardly be imagined.

The merchants' use of Slavophile and Pan-Slavic ideas appeared to one perceptive foreign observer as the most distinctive feature of their political behavior in the late nineteenth century. The eminent German scholar Gerhart von Schulze-Gävernitz, who spent several years studying the Russian economy, particularly the cotton textile industry of the Central Region, saw in the reactionary policies of the Russian state proof that the Moscow manufacturers wielded great influence. The secret of their success, he believed, lay in their use of the Slavophile "nationalist economic theory, which as far as possible rebels against Europe and its liberal ideals."[179] Aided after 1870 by various reactionary spokesmen who advocated protectionism, including Katkov and Pobedonostsev, the industrialists had succeeded in neutralizing the challenges of German economic power and European liberalism.[180]

At the same time, however, Schulze-Gävernitz predicted that industrial development would eventually undermine this reactionary tendency in Russian political life; liberalism would inevitably follow capitalist expansion. With great optimism, he wrote that already industrial protectionism was creating a new class, the capitalists, whose "representatives now make up the nucleus of the first party, in the West-European sense, on Russian soil . . ."[181] Through a "striking irony of fate," the crude bosses of the factories were more "European" than the civilized but impoverished gentry landlords, since the penetration of capitalism into Russian society forced ever greater numbers of peasants to abandon subsistence farming and to take up production of agricultural and handicraft goods for the market. Other European political institutions, notably constitutional liberalism, would develop in turn; the Slavophile and Pan-Slav visions would eventually perish.[182]

Thus Schulze-Gävernitz correctly perceived not only the close ties between the Moscow industrialists and reactionary ideologues but also the logical contradiction in the merchant-Slavophile economic program of bolstering the traditional Russian society by industrial development. However, Petr Struve noted in his incisive introduction to the Russian edition of this book (1899) that Schulze-Gävernitz "strained his point" in identifying Slavophilism and Pan-Slavism "as the pure ideological expression of the interests of the large-scale industrial bourgeoisie." Ivan Aksakov had consistently held cultural progress to be a far higher good than the satisfaction of the narrow economic demands of manufacturers; and Katkov, "the ideologist of red tape and conventionalism," had always defended the interests of the tsarist state and the gentry more actively than those of the industrialists. It was not so much the manufacturers' demands for tariff protection as the antiliberal stance of the far more influential gentry that had actually determined the government's reactionary policies in the 1880s.[183]

Struve, far better than Schulze-Gävernitz, realized that because the merchants lacked direct access to political power within the autocratic system, they exerted their greatest influence on the government when they argued that aid to industry would increase the power of the state to the detriment of Europe and of the Russian liberal and radical movements. Thus the German economist had underestimated the tendency of the Russian industrialists "to play a deeply reactionary role. . . . Personally, I have always thought that in Russia what is progressive is not so much an emerging and rapidly growing bourgeoisie as the general conditions of economic and cultural life in which it develops."[184] (Indeed, to appreciate the impact of the merchants' political activities, we need only compute their total financial contributions to municipal and religious philanthropies, reactionary newspapers, the Slavic Committee, the war effort of 1877–8, and the Holy Host, for example, and imagine that the zemstvo constitutional movement, the liberal press, and the revolutionary socialist groups had received these millions of rubles in the 1870s and 1880s.)

The primary example of a regressive capitalist institution in the 1890s was, for Struve, the Russian factory. By degrading the workers with low pay, unsanitary and dangerous working conditions, and arbitrary punishments, it stifled the development of modern culture among the masses. The relationship between the Moscow industrialists and the workers whom they employed thus became an important factor in the manufacturers' ideology in the late nineteenth century, when the "labor question" assumed great significance as a political issue.

5

●━o━●━o━●━o━●━●━o━●━o━●━o━●━●━o━●━o━●━o━●━o━●━o━●━o━●━o━●━o━●━o━●━o━●━o━●━o━●━o━●━●━o━●━o━●━o

Industrial growth and the challenge of the
labor movement, 1880–1900

Protected from European competition by steadily rising tariffs, Russian
industry developed at such a rapid pace in the last two decades of the
nineteenth century that the Moscow manufacturers' relationship with
other social groups underwent a profound transformation. In the aftermath of the Commercial-Industrial Congress of 1882, the government
continued to accommodate the manufacturers' economic demands by fur-
thering the development of Russian industry. At the same time, however,
the expansion of factories in the Moscow region caused serious labor disorders. These disputes led the Ministry of Internal Affairs, with the reluctant approval of the Finance Ministry, to implement a series of strict factory laws. Moreover, in 1896, at the last Commercial-Industrial Congress,
the Moscow manufacturers once more encountered strong antiprotectionist arguments from spokesmen partial to agricultural interests: landlords, economists, and certain government bureaucrats.

As the euphoria of the 1880s gave way to a grim defense of industrial
capitalism in the face of opposition from the disgruntled workers on the
one hand and the antiprotectionist gentry on the other, the manufacturers
gradually acquired a consciousness of the profound economic difference
that separated them from other social groups. The manufacturers did not
yet perceive the tsarist state as an adversary, despite the animosity caused
by the factory inspection system and other, more traditional, bureaucratic
hindrances on industry and trade. Indeed, the growing conflict with the
gentry and the workers only strengthened the industrialists' already close
political ties with the tsarist state and with conservative statesmen and
intellectuals: Vyshnegradsky, Witte, Pobedonostsev, Katkov, and Mendeleev. Thus while the merchant ideology grew stronger and became
more clearly defined, it still did not deserve to be called at this point a
bourgeois class consciousness.

The golden decades of Russian industry

The Commercial-Industrial Congress, held by RIS in Moscow in June 1882 during the Industrial Exhibition, discussed current economic issues of interest to the Society's members and government departments. It differed in several important respects from the St. Petersburg Congress of just twelve years before. Not only did the agenda include a broader range of questions than in 1870; manufacturers, although evidently outnumbered again by bureaucrats and economists, spoke with far greater assurance on major policy issues and met less opposition from proponents of free trade. In addition, the final resolutions, which filled a fifty-three-page pamphlet, outlined a comprehensive plan for Russian industrial growth that made the statements of 1870 seem timid in comparison.[1] The lengthy agenda, approved in advance by the Ministry of Finance, consisted of thirty-six discussion questions arranged under such headings as industrial production in factories and plants; trade; finances and credit; transportation; postal and telegraph communications; and statistics and vocational training. Although it is impossible to classify the 257 participants by occupation, since only their names were given, both the reduced size of the congress (171 fewer persons than in 1870) and the increased self-confidence of the Moscow manufacturers following their tariff victories of 1868 and 1877 gave them a more prominent role than before. Mayor S. M. Tretiakov served as one of two vice-presidents; T. S. Morozov chaired the sections on trade and communications; and ten other leading Moscow merchants appeared on the official list.[2] (See Appendix, Table I.) Furthermore, in contrast to the Moscow Duma and the Zemstvo, where the merchants mostly sat in silence, the Commercial-Industrial Congress served as an open forum for spirited discussion by the merchants themselves. The stenographic report of the speeches brought into clear view the distinct personalities and policy stances of the industrial leaders.

A major organizational proposal dominated section one, which dealt with the needs of large-scale industry. The president, the eminent chemist D. I. Mendeleev (1834–1907), advocated the creation of a new Ministry of Industry and Trade, which would take from the Ministry of Finance the huge task of promoting industrial development.[3] T. S. Morozov strongly supported this idea of a "real defender" of the merchants' interests, and offered a logical corollary: "Then industry would deal directly with its own minister, and subsequently a Chamber of Commerce could be established under its auspices."[4] Mendeleev and Morozov thus presented a barely veiled critique of the Ministry of Finance for having paid less attention to the protection of Russian industry than to the fiscal and balance-of-payments functions of the import tariff. Furthermore, Morozov's call for a national Chamber of Commerce indicated the industrialists' displeasure with the new Council of Trade and Manufacturing (CTM), created in 1872. During the previous ten years, the council had remained "semibureaucratic" and unrepresentative because its twenty-four members (merchants, technicians, and government officials) were appointed by the minister, not elected locally; they served indefinite terms, with little rotation; meetings took place only once or twice a year; and there was no coordination with stock exchange committees.[5]

One who spoke eloquently on this issue of chambers of commerce was a Krestovnikov (apparently this was Valentin K. Krestovnikov's nephew Grigori A., who was born in 1855 and had married T. S. Morozov's daughter Iuliia in 1878). He endorsed the idea of a new organization, but warned against allowing chambers of commerce to be elected locally. His disparaging remarks about freely elected representative institutions, aimed obviously at the zemstvos and municipal dumas, evidently reflected both a distrust of European political principles and a belief that the manufacturers' economic interests could be served without any democratic reforms. "Elective institutions are in general new in Russia and they can scarcely be considered well established; therefore I submit that the benefit to the interests of industry and trade from such institutions is doubtful . . . What is especially and urgently needed now is a separate Ministry of Industry and Trade, which could then encourage those local institutions that would correspond to our conditions."[6] Of course, neither Krestovnikov, Morozov, nor Mendeleev viewed the recent activities of the Finance Ministry and the lack of a Chamber of Commerce as major obstacles to continued economic growth. Rather, they appeared optimistic that the generally successful policies of the past decade could be enhanced by the government's adoption of their specific proposals for improved coordination. They spoke not as victims of bureaucratic neglect or oppression, but as junior partners eager for closer consultation, less direct supervision, and a more responsible role.

Section three of the congress, which dealt specifically with foreign and domestic commerce, provided an even more useful forum for the Moscow industrialists. President Morozov, by his calmness and deference to all speakers (in contrast to his tantrum in the Tariff Commission in 1868), demonstrated his confidence in the outcome of the debate on tariffs, export strategies, and domestic railroad rates. The two advocates of reduced import duties, V. P. Diushen and Professor V. A. Goltsev, met fierce opposition from the locquacious Krestovnikovs. In response to Diushen's warning that a prohibitive tariff would encourage monopoly pricing and technological stagnation, V. K. Krestovnikov countered audaciously, "I am convinced that there is no such thing as a tariff duty that is too high." No monopolies could grow up because higher prices would attract domestic competitors, who would soon force prices down to a reasonable level. Without high tariffs, however, domestic raw materials – cotton, silk, and wool – would remain largely unused because of the importation of foreign (*chuzhoe*, literally "alien") goods from America, Egypt, and Austria. "Consequently, we must have not only a protective duty, but also one that is firm and constant in one direction, until we come out on the smooth road. Then we will have our own cotton and our own wool."[7]

Just as his venerable uncle pounced on Diushen, so G. A. Krestovnikov scathingly dismissed as "a total anachronism" Professor Goltsev's claim that a high tariff could not stimulate industry because Russian entrepreneurs lacked "knowledge and energy."[8] "Capital needs not energy or patriotism; it needs profit [*vygoda*]. Show it the ways of profit, blaze the trail to it, and capital will gallantly [*bogatyrski*] rip out from the bowels of the earth all Russia's incalculable riches for use by what the professor called the wretched popular consumption." To ensure adequate tariff levels, the government must consult the manufacturers, and discussions must be conducted "publicly and openly [*glasno*] . . ." Following remarks in a similar vein by his uncle and father-in-law (Morozov had called the present tariff system "extremely irrational"), the younger Krestovnikov criticized the Finance Ministry for maintaining relatively free trade in raw materials. When asked what kind of tariff was needed, "we reply: a completely different one than is now in effect. The present one is no good at all."[9] With considerably less hyperbole, one of the Krestovnikovs (no first name given) had made this same point in section one: "Russia has undergone many [governmental] measures that were not always wise, many passions, bad and good, and many desires, often coming from above, that have wiped out whole branches of industry. Our capitalists are not assured of support or even of the immutability of the conditions [necessary] for the existence of production. One stroke of a pen in Petersburg can destroy production." Under a completely protective system, the Russian consumer would pay "only a worthless penny" more, so that "not [only] individual persons would benefit, but all of Russia."[10]

Discussions of export strategy, the second major issue before section three of the congress, revealed the Moscow merchants' new sophistication in seeking the aid of the Russian state to win or maintain control of foreign markets in the face of increased competition from high-quality European goods. As long as the domestic market remained incapable of absorbing the entire output of Russian factories (as it had since the 1840s, owing to the poverty of the peasant masses), the Moscow manufacturers would look beyond the borders of the empire for their economic salvation. At the 1882 congress, they placed primary emphasis on selling Russian goods in Asia, with the exception of some probing into Bulgaria in order to weaken Austria's economic and political influence in that agricultural country.[11]

On the issue of railroad rates, A. S. Cherokov, secretary of the third section, strongly appealed for governmental subsidies. He cited transport cost scales that clearly favored the European owners of Russian railroads (85 kopecks per pud Warsaw–Moscow, compared to 66 kopecks Berlin–Moscow, double the distance; 1.10 rubles Warsaw–Petersburg, compared to 58–60 kopecks Berlin–Petersburg) and discriminated against Russian exporters (1.5 or 1.8 rubles Moscow–Berlin and Petersburg–Berlin). Cherokov, using rhetoric worthy of his late mentor F. V. Chizhov, denounced "the evil that oppresses our export trade; and it will be impossible to eradicate this evil until our Russian railroads pass into Russian hands, since at present the foreigners who control them can only be expected to promote their exports to us, and not our exports to them."[12]

In contrast to the humble statements of 1870, the final resolutions of 1882 reflected the unambiguous desire of the Moscow merchants for a comprehensive policy of state support for economic development, coupled with a reduction of bureaucratic tutelage over the merchants' consultative organizations. The first section of the congress called for a relaxation of the Finance Ministry's control over the CTM. Members of local representative bodies should be chosen "on a strictly elective basis," not appointed by the ministry. Furthermore, every important industrial and commercial region should have its own elected institution; "a central organization" (the provocative term, *chamber of commerce*, was not used) "should be formed with the function of the Manufacturing Council, consisting of elected delegates from local institutions"; regional industrial congresses should be held periodically; and "a Ministry of Trade and Industry should be formed." Finally, in support of section three's demand for "a completely protective" tariff, to be established through a "general *rational* re-

view" with the participation of industrialists and traders, section one recommended tariff increases not only on finished products but also on raw
materials and semimanufactured goods such as coal, oil, and pig iron (the
latter to receive a duty of 25 kopecks per pud for fifteen years!); on finer
grades of linen and wool cloth; and on peasant-produced coarse linen bags,
threatened by a flood of cheap jute bags.[13]

The recommendations of the third section, on measures to meet European competition abroad, urged that merchants be elected to serve in customs offices in St. Petersburg and Taganrog, and that customs officers
stamp out smuggling. The expansion of exports required the development
of a merchant marine and coastal shipping; the immediate construction of
railroads to Asia; reduced railroad rates to stimulate exports (section one
had specifically advocated low rates for machinery, salt, coal, and chemi-
cals); and a museum in Moscow to display samples of foreign goods. Special measures to expand trade with Bulgaria, Turkey, and China were
proposed: commercial expeditions, Russian schools in Constantinople and
Kiakhta, a Russian bank office in China, and the abolition of the transit
trade of European goods across Transcaucasia to Persia. In the realm of
diplomacy, Russian consuls in America, Europe, and Asia should be required to provide current information on foreign market conditions, and
Russian merchants should be consulted prior to the negotiation of commercial treaties with foreign powers.[14] Finally, in a gesture of concern for
agriculture, the third section recommended the establishment of a govern-
ment-financed system of grain elevators to facilitate exports to Europe,
where in recent years competition from the United States had grown increasingly severe.[15]

The resolutions of the other five sections had less direct political significance, but they too testified to the Moscow merchants' great influence at
the congress. The fourth section (finance and credit) called for more state
aid for private joint-stock banks and mutual credit societies and, by advocating "the productive use of bank loans by borrowers," implicitly criticized the spendthrift gentry. Domestic railroad regulation was proposed
in the fifth section, including controls over rates imposed by competing
lines and a ban on discounts to large shippers, as well as a special fourth-
class passenger rate for migrant factory workers. No precise route for the
Siberian railroad was proposed, but the suggestion of thirteen merchant
firms for a rail link between the Ob and Volga river basins was approved.[16] The sixth section called for more efficient postal and telegraph
systems, and the seventh urged a more practical orientation in technical

schools. All the sections' resolutions were approved by the General Assembly.[17]

Although a Ministry of Trade and Industry was not created until 1905, in several instances the Ministry of Finance duly responded to the manufacturers' requests of 1882, and in some cases of official resistance the merchants, through relentless pressure, achieved eventual success despite the absence of institutional changes. As in the past, the merchants enjoyed no real power to determine official policy, but their recommendations appeared reasonable to the ministry in light of the instructive example of Bismarck's industrialization drive in Prussia.[18] The various techniques that the merchants had learned in the previous quarter-century enabled them to exert direct influence on policy makers: the submission of carefully worded petitions and personal statements to the Finance Ministry, special commissions, and the tsar himself; lobbying at court through influential ministers and advisors; and favorable articles in the press. Especially significant was the tsarist government's acquiescence of five central questions of the 1880s and 1890s: consultation with commercial-industrial representatives; tariff protection; the cessation of the foreign transit trade through Transcaucasia; development of "domestic" (i.e., Central Asian) sources of raw cotton; and improvement of the Russian railroad system.

Leading factory owners continued to serve as "experts" on temporary governmental commissions and to testify before them. Moreover, three permanent bodies provided increased leverage on the official decision-making process, because they spoke with collective authority. To be sure, the manufacturers would have preferred to debate economic questions in a national Chamber of Commerce; but since their requests in 1870 and 1882 for the creation of such an organization would remain unfulfilled until 1917, they learned to utilize three existing bodies, which together served approximately the same purpose.

Although the RIS Congress of 1882 had criticized the ineffectiveness of the CTM, the merchants of the Central Industrial Region used its Moscow Section (MSCTM) to considerable advantage. Throughout the late nineteenth century, particularly in the debates on the tariff and labor questions, members of the MSCTM regularly presented their collective arguments to the Finance Ministry through petitions and personal visits.

RIS, the first private industrial organization in Russia and the sponsor of the two Commercial-Industrial Congresses, continued to serve the manufacturers well. Its Moscow Section (MSRIS), created in 1884, elected T. S. Morozov as its first president and included on its Executive

Council some of the most eminent names in the Moscow business world: N. N. Konshin, P. P. Maliutin, M. A. Gorbov, A. L. Losev, V. D. Aksenov, and A. I. Abrikosov.[19] MSRIS constituted an effective forum in the next two decades because the society's leadership in St. Petersburg periodically endorsed the Muscovites' aggressive policy of economic nationalism.[20] On the other hand, RIS never became "their" organization. Among the society's twenty-six officers elected in 1892, none came from Moscow.[21] Furthermore, the economic interests of the Moscow Section often conflicted with those of the St. Petersburg, Warsaw, and Lodz manufacturers, as will be mentioned later.

Prevented from forming a Chamber of Commerce and obliged to use the local sections of CTM and RIS, the Moscow manufacturers might have been expected to create their own regional organization. In fact, numerous precedents existed. The mine owners and metallurgists of southern Russia, who had held their first congress in 1874, met annually from 1877 onward, generally at Kharkov, to discuss current questions of coal and iron production. The Baku oil producers began holding congresses in 1884, and the iron manufacturers established a permanent coordinating body in 1887.[22] The "Petersburg Society of Manufacturers" (or PSM, created in 1893 and officially confirmed in 1897) became the first regional organization of representatives from various industries.[23] Four years before, such leading textile magnates as N. A. Naidenov, S. I. Prokhorov, I. A. Baranov, and M. L. Losev had indeed established a "Moscow Industrial Society" (see Appendix, Tables I and II); but despite the similarity between its name and that of PSM,[24] it confined its activities to the dissemination of chemical and mechanical improvements in textile production. The Moscow merchants, it seems clear, saw no need to create a new representative body. Instead, they continued to strengthen the organization that had stood at the center of their life since 1839: the Moscow Stock Exchange Committee.

Since 1870, the MSEC functioned not only as the executive arm of the stock exchange but also as an organization entitled by the Ministry of Finance to express the views of its members on questions of economic policy. In the last four decades of Imperial Russia, it acted with unchallenged authority as the most influential body of commercial and industrial leaders in the Central Region. Buryshkin and Lure stressed the primacy of the stock exchange committees over the CTM and its local committees; and both asserted that the Moscow committee, the largest in the empire, remained for many years the most influential.[25] The MSEC derived its importance from two factors: it represented the interests of industry as well as of commerce; and it drew its membership from all the provinces of the Central Industrial Region, not Moscow alone. Constantly engaged in "systematic collaboration" with the Finance Ministry in setting economic policy for the whole empire, it acted as the "militant" defender "of industry, especially the textile sector."[26] In addition to its permanent subcommittees on cotton supply and spinning and weaving, as well as a commission on banking, it also established temporary commissions on such vital questions as taxation, labor unrest, and chambers of commerce and industry.[27] Reutern's successor, Samuil A. Greig (1878–80), initiated a new practice: not long after taking office, the minister of finance (and, after 1905, of trade and industry) would visit the MSEC to pay his respects.[28] Although the committee, of course, had no veto power over such bureaucratic appointments, these courtesy calls demonstrated St. Petersburg's solicitude for the economic opinions of Moscow. Such a ritual visit was known humorously as a "bride-show" (*smotriny*), as it recalled the traditional merchants' habit of parading eligible daughters before the families of prospective in-laws.[29]

The lack of any real electoral contests between 1876 and 1905 demonstrated that N. A. Naidenov, the MSEC's ten-term president, enjoyed the unqualified respect and admiration of the thousand richest traders and manufacturers of the Central Region.[30] A "slight, lively, and fiery [*ognennyi*]" person whose "importance and authority" were "very great" among merchants,[31] Naidenov displayed a rare determination to fight the St. Petersburg bureaucracy whenever it resisted the MSEC's recommendations. His political and economic views, as expressed in his memoirs and policy statements, must therefore be considered broadly representative of the opinions of the Moscow merchants as a whole, at least before the crisis of 1905 provoked disagreements over the pace of reform.

No less significant, although for different reasons, was the composition of the MSEC and the Delegate Assembly. Even a cursory examination of the membership lists reveals a remarkable pattern: the several leading Moscow merchant families that had risen to prominence in the textile industry during the 1840s continued to predominate well into the last decades of the imperial period. The complex ties of intermarriage among these eminent merchant families (see Genealogies), as well as the stable composition of the committee and the assembly, gave the Muscovite spokesmen great authority in their discussions with the government.[32]

Thus the lack of a Ministry of Trade and Industry and of a Chamber of

Commerce did not prevent the Moscow merchants from communicating their views directly to the government. In the absence of democratic political institutions, the manufacturers developed what Berlin (quoting Plekhanov) called "political gills," which allowed them to breathe in the stifling atmosphere of tsarist Russia, where a West-European bourgeoisie would have "suffocated" for lack of freedom. "Here the fate of the Russian bourgeoisie took a distinctive turn . . . [It] was able to find ways and means, without creating the corresponding European political forms, to exert a strong, constant pressure on governmental policy on whatever side and at whatever point it deemed necessary. Under these conditions, the bourgeoisie developed some extraordinarily instructive devices for exerting influence on the governmental authorities."[33]

Several specific questions of economic policy were resolved to the merchants' satisfaction in the late nineteenth century. Particularly successful was the perennial campaign for increased tariff protection. The instruments of pressure, notably petitions from representative bodies and incessant demands for protectionism in the periodicals of Aksakov and Katkov, proved sufficient because the tsarist government had become receptive to the patriotic slogan of a "national economic policy" based on high tariffs. The German economist Schulze-Gävernitz correctly perceived the importance of this "alliance" (*Bündnis*) between "businessmen and ideologues, industrialists and nationalists." He was mistaken only in claiming that "free-trade ideas began to be labeled 'antinational' " in the 1880s,[34] a quarter-century after the merchant-Slavophile alliance first formulated this xenophobic slogan.

The steady tariff increases of Bunge, Vyshnegradsky, and Witte caused what Arcadius Kahan aptly termed "a conflict between [the state's] short-run fiscal interests and the objectives of industrialization," since the higher duties on imported raw and semimanufactured goods such as iron, coal, cotton, and wool called forth further increases in tariff rates for cotton yarn, woolen cloth, and metal products. This "chain reaction" had the unfortunate effect of raising prices paid not only by the already poor Russian consumer but also by Russian manufacturers, and therefore created the "paradox" of "higher prices for the types of imports which were to foster industrialization." Instead of attributing these blanket tariff increases to either "ignorance" or "bureaucratic routine" on the part of the policy makers, Kahan explained them in terms of "the overriding priorities of fiscal needs." Two other policy goals also legitimized this extreme protectionism. Although Kahan mentioned in passing that tariffs on capital goods imports were intended, together with treasury orders, to cause "the expansion or improvement of domestic output,"[35] it must be stressed that this goal seems equal in importance to the purely fiscal purpose of the tariff. Moreover, by limiting imports and stimulating domestic industry, the tariff would reduce the outflow of specie and prevent the further erosion of the ruble's value abroad.

Proof of the success or failure of these policies depended on the precise measurement of both the cost of increased duties to consumers of imported and domestic goods, and the speed at which infant industries developed in Russia, a formidable statistical problem. So complicated were the equations involved that both the advocates of increased tariff duties and the critics found plentiful data to support their opposing arguments. Numerous economists, notably those of the Free Economic Society, accused the Moscow manufacturers of demanding higher tariff duties than were absolutely necessary to forestall competition from foreign producers. For his part, Schulze-Gävernitz opined that probably nowhere in the world were both tariff levels and corporate profits so high as in Russia.[36] More was involved than pure greed, however. Nikolai A. Naidenov of the MSEC, "one of the most fervent and extreme representatives of the protectionist tendency among the Moscow merchants, . . . from the 1880s onward participated in all government decisions with demands for the highest duties." In other words, the merchants spoke as patriotic defenders of Russian industry in general, whether or not they benefited personally from higher tariffs on iron, coal, or machines. (From 1857 onward, manufacturers of the Moscow region who used imported materials in their factories advocated a high tariff on such goods, as long as the import duties protecting their own finished products were raised correspondingly.)[37] A convincing indication of the sincerity of their ultranationalist feeling appeared in a private letter from the railroad magnate S. I. Mamontov to his wife during a discussion of the coal and pig-iron tariff in February 1884: "Toward the end of the sessions, the passions of the hostile sides were running very high (on the one side Germans, foreigners, and parasites in general; on the other, Russian producers) . . . The general impression is gratifying; in Russia there are forces that are capable of serving her well, and it is necessary only to summon them to work."[38]

These conflicting arguments had, of course, been heard before, in the 1850s and 1860s. The major difference between the earlier debates and those of the later period seems to be that formerly the Moscow merchants' clamoring for high tariffs had been restrained somewhat by the erudite

admonitions of Chizhov and Babst, who realized that excessive protectionism would encourage not industrial growth but stagnation. In later decades, however, no such moderating influence existed in Moscow, so that
the impartial observer feels far less sympathetic to the merchants' claim
that increased protection necessarily served the national interest.

Indeed, in the momentous tariff debates of 1890–1, which led to the
establishment of the highest duties yet seen in Russia, Naidenov, Savva
T. Morozov, G. A. Krestovnikov, and other spokesmen for the MSEC
and MSCTM demanded something new and rather bizarre: the tariff
should protect not only all existing industries but also nonexistent ones,
which would need prohibitively high tariff duties in order to be created by
Russians.[39] Because such arguments, couched in patriotic rhetoric, satisfied both the manufacturers' sense of nationalism and their desire for increased profits, it is perhaps impossible to separate their motives. In any
case, their successes in the tariff debates following the Commercial-Industrial Congress of 1882 encouraged them to speak as industrialists and patriots in the largest sense for many years to come.

Besides reorganized representative bodies and higher tariffs, the Moscow merchants in 1882 had urged the abolition of duty-free European
trade from the Black Sea to Persia via Transcaucasia. At stake, argued
Katkov's influential *Russkii vestnik*, was not only the Russian export trade
in Persia but also the government's ability to prevent massive shipments of
contraband goods into adjacent regions of the Russian Empire: Transcaucasia, the Caucasus, and Central Asia. Following the opening of the
transit trade in 1878 and the completion in 1883 of the railroad linking
Batumi on the Black Sea to Baku on the Caspian, increasingly large
amounts of European manufactured products, primarily English textiles,
flowed illegally into Russia along the Caspian shores, where the customs
inspection was particularly lax. The nationalist argument also included
the ritual expression of solicitude for the Russian workers, since such rhetoric had softened the hearts of Finance Ministry officials in the past. Abolition of the transit trade would protect "Russian production"; on the other
hand, if no action were taken, "how many factories would have to close
down and how large a mass of working people who are fed by these factories would be left without work . . . [?]" (The veiled threat of disorder
among unemployed workers also lurked in this ominous question.) Manufacturers and traders in Nizhny Novgorod, Ivanovo-Voznesensk, Shuia,
Kineshma, Tashkent, and Lodz, joined by the Vladimir provincial
Zemstvo, supported the MSEC's unanimous decision in December 1882

to send a special deputation to the tsar himself.[40] Naidenov's strongest ally at the imperial court, K. P. Pobedonostsev, duly urged Alexander III to accept the deputation's petition, as this issue was causing "alarm" among the merchants.[41]

The petition of December 1882, an extensive article of early 1884 in *Russkii vestnik* written at the behest of T. S. Morozov,[42] and further pressure from I. A. Zinoviev of the Asiatic Department of the Foreign Ministry (and perhaps also from Pobedonostsev) finally produced the desired result. Alexander III, having become "politically motivated" to challenge the English commercial threat, abolished the transit trade in 1884, and for several decades thereafter, the Russians enjoyed commercial supremacy in the Transcaucasion region and a somewhat strengthened position in adjacent northern Persia as well. "The conquest of the north Persian market was seen from St. Petersburg as a part of the larger task of establishing Russian hegemony in the Middle East."[43] Economic nationalism had triumphed once again.

Another hope of the Moscow merchants in 1882, that production of Central Asian cotton could be expanded and improved, also became a reality in the succeeding decades. Following the introduction of American varieties of cotton (1884), the extension of the Transcaspian railroad to Samarkand (1888) and Tashkent (1899), and the completion of the Orenburg-Tashkent rail link (1906), cotton deliveries from Central Asia increased dramatically, from 873,000 puds in 1888 to 4,960,000 in 1900 and 13,697,000 in 1913. By 1899, Central Asian plantations supplied 50 percent of the raw cotton processed in Moscow province and 47 percent of that used in Vladimir province.[44]

This drive for self-sufficiency succeeded largely because of several changes in the government's policy on railroads, the final major issue raised by the merchants in 1882. The Ministry of Communications began in 1880 to reduce the degree of foreign control over Russian railroad companies by building lines itself and by purchasing privately owned lines, especially those in financial difficulty. By 1894, the state owned approximately one-third of the total rail mileage in the empire, and by 1912, 78 percent.[45] Furthermore, after numerous discussions with Moscow merchants, the government established in 1889 a comprehensive system of railroad rates that set the price per verst of long-distance freight shipments below the price for short hauls.[46] This innovation ended the pro-German bias in Russian rail rates, about which Cherokov and Morozov had complained bitterly at the Commercial-Industrial Congress.

The merchants apparently viewed the state's control of railroads as no threat to their economic well-being. Given the great financial risks and their lack of specialized training in the fields of heavy industry and railroad construction, most Moscow merchants prudently left these fields to the government or made their fortune quickly before selling out to the state. The sudden demise of S. I. Mamontov's railroad and steel empire in 1899[47] dramatically illustrated the difficulties that faced even the boldest Russian entrepreneurs in the railroad industry.

The guiding role of the tsarist state in the economy apparently had a subtle but powerful political and psychological effect on the Moscow manufacturers' outlook. Although less directly dependent on the government for their prosperity than, for example, the rail and arms producers who sold their output to the state itself, the textile manufacturers of the Central Region clearly perceived their economic weakness in the world economy and realized that without the kind of aid already described, they most likely would have perished.[48] Thus despite the annoying bureaucratic fetters that they encountered at every turn, the Moscow merchants regarded the tsarist state as their indispensible economic patron. In a sense, the resolution of the various economic problems raised in 1882 dampened their resistance to bureaucratic interference in their business affairs, for it was clearly impossible to invite the government to stimulate commerce and industry without surrendering wide realms of economic freedom. Although they occasionally indicated their desire for a *laissez-faire* policy, until approximately 1900 they reluctantly paid the price of red tape, knowing that the alternative, governmental inaction, would have left them defenseless against the economic threat from the West.

Labor unrest and factory legislation

Although the Moscow merchants received satisfaction from the government on most economic issues, they failed completely during the term of Nikolai Kh. Bunge (minister of finance, January 1882 to December 1886) to block the passage of legislation regulating the working conditions in their own factories. However false its official pretension to protect equally the interests of all social groups (especially since it openly favored the gentry against the peasantry in the Emancipation Statute and numerous subsequent measures), the tsarist government in this instance strove to defend the rights of the poor. In the late nineteenth century, the Ministries of Finance and Internal Affairs intervened directly to ameliorate the wretched conditions that led factory workers to strike and commit acts of violence. Although intended to reconcile the opposing parties, such interference encountered fierce opposition from factory owners in the Central Region. Blinded by illusions of their own benevolence, the merchants unwittingly helped create a legacy of working-class resentment that smoldered for decades before bursting into revolutionary flames in 1905.

Simple condemnation of the merchants' greed and cruelty would, however, leave obscure the reasons for their tragic myopia. Their behavior had strong roots in the family-centered, patriarchal culture of the traditional merchants. In one typical "Old-Testament factory," the eminent gold-braid producer Semen A. Alekseev (1746–1823) made the transition from peasant artisan to factory owner very slowly, hiring relatives and friends from his native village to work in his growing shop in Moscow. Like a medieval European master craftsman, Alekseev lived and worked alongside his three dozen employees, and spoke to all of them as intimates, using their middle names. His son, Vladimir (1795–1862), whose experience on the Nikolaev railroad did nothing to overcome his distrust of modern machinery, continued the old traditions. At morning tea, he would gently admonish any employee who had not returned to the house by 10:00 the night before. The factory "lost its patriarchal character" only after Vladimir's grandson, Nikolai A. (1852–93, the mayor) installed machines.[49]

Patriarchal attitudes remained so strong among the workers themselves that exponents of Official Nationality, Slavophilism, and free trade agreed (despite their philosophical differences on other issues) that the Russian laborer might well never lose his ties with agriculture. As long as the Russian worker belonged to a rural commune, to which he regularly returned to till the land, he would remain immune from class hatred and faithful to autocracy and Orthodoxy – unlike the European proletariat, which lived entirely from wage labor in the factory and, in the course of its struggle with the bourgeoisie, developed a socialist political consciousness. Although this official view owed much to wishful thinking, as late as the 1890s strong evidence of the workers' traditional submissiveness to partriarchal authority could still be found. One socialist observed with dismay:

The outlook of the workers, molded by the centuries and carried from the landlords' villages, was as follows: the proprietor, the landlord, the industrialist, were all father-benefactors who provided work for thousands and tens of thousands of workers, and gave them food and drink. Consequently, if there were no manufacturers and proprietors, the workers would die of starvation. Such patriarchal notions prevailed among the laboring masses almost until 1905.[50]

As spontaneous labor protests began to threaten Russia's political and social stability, the perceptions of intellectuals, state officials, manufacturers, and workers changed rather more slowly than did the objective economic conditions that were dividing employers and laborers into antagonistic classes.

Unbiased descriptions of working conditions in the Central Region between 1861 and 1900 leave the impression that only economic necessity and a long tradition of submission drove peasants into the factories and prevented constant rebellions. Work in the textile industry demanded a strange and unpleasant surrender to the tyranny of the machine in crowded, noisy, and unsafe factories, where workdays lasting twelve to eighteen hours were common. Moreover, because of the large pool of unskilled labor, the boss (*khoziain*) kept wages to a minimum and fired with impunity any worker who dared to complain. Wages were usually at their lowest level in the winter season (October to Easter), when the lack of agricultural work forced peasants into the factory. When labor was in short supply (from Easter to October) or in periods of slack market demand, the boss often abolished the night shift in order to reduce his labor costs. The only limitation on his arbitrary power to change wage rates was the risk of "unpleasantness" from angry workers, who demanded at least a subsistence wage from the factory work on which their livelihood depended.[51] Even such an enlightened merchant as P. M. Tretiakov, who built barracks, reading rooms, schools, and hospitals at his huge Kostroma Linen Factory, could not care personally for all his workers; the flax spinners and weavers, together with their families, numbered several thousand men, women, and children. To his daughter Vera, the machines roared "like huge, fantastic dragons," and the children working in the carding rooms appeared pathetic, their mouths bound with rags as protection against the choking dust.[52]

Especially burdensome to the workers were various financial devices that favored the boss. Fines imposed for substandard workmanship, absence from work, and other shortcomings routinely amounted to "several thousand rubles a year and served as an important income for the boss," the more so because fine levels and the reasons for their imposition were never specified in writing. Likewise, paydays were held infrequently, sometimes only at Easter and Christmas, so as to prevent workers from leaving the factory at mid-season. Payment in coupons from state bonds that had to be held to maturity (*dosrochnye kupony*) performed the same function. Finally, a manufacturer would often require workers to buy food, clothing, and other necessities at his factory store, so that their net wages amounted to only a few rubles at year's end. Indeed, owing to exorbitant prices and credit charges, these stores often brought in more profits than did the factory itself![53]

While incidents of strikes and other protests dated from the inception of large-scale factory production in the Moscow region, Soviet historiography has strained the evidence in an attempt to demonstrate the growth of a self-conscious "labor movement" in the mid-nineteenth century. Rather, sporadic strikes before 1880 represented simply a series of angry outbursts against acts of chicanery by the boss. One typical strike, at T. S. Morozov's Nikolsk factory in 1863, ended without punishments or a court suit; after the police had restored order, the boss simply refunded some fines and paid out the wages of those workers who wished to leave.[54] The inconclusive resolution of this strike suggested that the tsarist authorities cared more about the restoration of order in the factory villages than about the permanent diminution of the boss's near-absolute control over the workers. In any case, three official commissions that attempted, between 1859 and 1880, to draw up mandatory legislation on factory conditions failed to draft rules acceptable to the tsarist government, and so the power of the industrialists remained unchecked.

The first commission, under Adolf F. Stackelberg (1808–65), labored from 1859 to 1862 on a bill to end the employment of children; to limit adolescents to a daily maximum of ten hours and ban night work for them; to establish a system of factory inspectors; and to institute special courts to arbitrate labor disputes.[55] The St. Petersburg textile manufacturers in fact favored the abolition of child labor because of the competitive advantage that their capital-intensive factories would thereby gain over the labor-intensive ones of the Central Region. Against them the Moscow cotton-spinning magnate A. I. Khludov argued with characteristic bluntness that the cessation of night work for children would force manufacturers to abandon night work entirely because of the prohibitive costs of an all-adult shift. Posing as a benefactor of the young, he declared that "children who are denied wages in the factory will not bring any pay home to their parents; they will pass the time in idleness, which is harmful for [those of] their age, and will ruin their health in the stuffy air of their huts, instead of living in the bright and healthy accommodations of the factory." Khludov, Morozov, Solodovnikov, Tretiakov, and Prokhorov offered Stack-elberg an ingenious plan for the factory inspection system: it should be administered by the CTM through its local branches (e.g., the Moscow Section), that is, more or less by the manufacturers themselves! After a second round of hearings in 1863 and 1864, the commission's bill was rejected by the State Council.[56]

The second commission to discuss labor regulations met under the direction of Adjutant-General P. N. Ignatiev in 1870–1. Its bill, in addition to prohibiting the employment of children, would have regulated adolescent labor; set minimum wage levels; and required the construction of barracks, hospitals, and schools. This bill's most ardent opponent before the State Council was N. A. Naidenov. Repeating the warning that any diminution of child and adolescent labor would increase production costs, he shrewdly borrowed a debating point from the tariff controversy: "this will affect the price of the goods themselves, to the benefit of foreign competition." These "arguments of a patriotic nature" proved effective. Both the State Council and the Ministry of Internal Affairs rejected Ignatiev's bill in 1872.[57]

Likewise, the recommendations of the commission chaired by former Interior Minister Petr A. Valuev (1814–90) between January and March 1875 failed to satisfy the State Council in 1876 and 1880. Naidenov's concern for the child's essential wage-earning role in the family was echoed by several commission members who owned factories: I. A. Vargunin and A. E. Struve of St. Petersburg and V. A. Kokorev and S. M. Tretiakov of Moscow.[58]

It is perhaps impossible to compute the precise effect of the manufacturers' opposition on the government's decisions not to regulate factory conditions. It seems clear, however, that bureaucrats, not merchants, exercised predominant influence within the consultative bodies such as the MSCTM, which recommended against labor legislation, and that in any case the MSCTM could hardly have dictated policy to the State Council, the supreme legislative body of the Russian Empire.[59] While largely skeptical of the transparently self-serving pleas of the factory owners, the State Council agreed that the labor situation did not yet require extensive regulation by the government. When serious labor troubles did erupt in the 1880s, the state moved decisively and with impunity against the merchants' most cherished prerogatives and remained indifferent to their cries of anguish.[60]

The merchants apparently had no one but themselves to blame for the eventual change in governmental policy, for few made any effort to improve working conditions. One factory disturbance proved especially embarrassing because it indicted A. I. Khludov, the eminent merchant leader and solicitous guardian of children's right to work. Khludov had built a five-story cotton-spinning mill in Iartsevo (Smolensk province) in 1874–5. Valued by the district Zemstvo at a million rubles, it earned a clear profit of 45 percent annually.[61] From neighboring provinces the huge complex drew thousands of peasants, who called it *Khludovshchina* – "the Khludov thing." Zemstvo inspectors in 1879 found that men, women, and children labored in two shifts, six hours on the job and six off, day after day; disease reached epidemic proportions in the filthy and crowded barracks, where open ditches served as latrines; temperatures were kept uncomfortably high, between 77 and 86 degrees Fahrenheit, because the cotton fiber required it; and although there was a tavern in the town, Khludov had built no kindergarten, school, library, or church for his workers.[62]

A violent confrontation erupted in September 1880, when Khludov reduced wages by ten kopecks, as was customary at the beginning of the winter season. At first, Khludov's son Mikhail calmed the angry workers with an offer of free drinks at the tavern, but when the police arrived he refused to reconsider the wage reduction. The crowd, now a thousand strong, began shouting; some factory windows were shattered by thrown rocks; and several machines were damaged. In the end, five hundred soldiers were needed to restore order, and hundreds of striking workers suffered eviction to their native villages.[63]

When A. I. Khludov died in March 1882, N. N. Subbotin, a frequent contributor to *Russkii vestnik*, pointed with satisfaction to the old merchant's many accomplishments: his government titles (manufacturing councilor and St. Vladimir medal, third degree); his friendship with General Cherniaev; "his fervent and sincere devotion to Orthodoxy"; and even "God's benediction on his business affairs." But Subbotin's claim that Khludov "always wanted to be and was in fact not only a boss but also a benefactor and father" to his workers rang false in the aftermath of the strike of 1880 and of a terrible fire at the Iartsevo factory in early 1882.[64] If the most honored merchant leaders maintained inhuman conditions which could at any moment kill dozens of helpless workers or make thousands go on strike, might not the danger of mass violence be even more acute in the factories of less conscientious manufacturers? It was this question (and the terrifying answer that now loomed before the government) that led the tsarist bureaucracy to enact a series of labor laws in the wake of the Iart-sevo strike and numerous less serious disorders.[65]

Bunge, soon after assuming the title of minister of finance in January 1882 (he had been the ministry's interim head for seven months), placed before the State Council a bill to ban child labor and to establish a ten-hour daytime limit for adolescents. During the State Council's debate, T. S. Morozov and other eminent manufacturers summoned as "experts" attacked the bill; S. I. Chetverikov argued that a prohibition of night work for adolescents would destroy the cohesion of the workers' families by separating their members for extended periods.[66] This time, however, the State Council and the tsar disregarded the Muscovites' objections. Factory owners must thenceforth employ no children under twelve years of age; must limit to eight hours the workday of adolescents aged twelve to fifteen; must remove adolescents from the night shift and from Sunday and holiday work; and must, at their own expense, provide primary education to the workers' children. A corps of factory inspectors would enforce the new law of June 1, 1882, upon its implementation in April 1884.[67]

This law did not, however, deal with the crucial issue of wages and fines. Only after the largest and most serious strike yet seen in Russia – the great "Morozov strike" of 1885 – did the ministry take such action. Like the Khludovs, the proprietor of the Nikolsk cotton textile complex had received ample warning of his workers' resentment during strikes in 1863 and 1876,[68] but T. S. Morozov nevertheless persisted in his patriarchal ways. Even the laudatory history of the Russian cotton industry published by the Moscow manufacturers themselves characterized Morozov as "a complete *samodur* . . ."

On the days when the boss came to the factory everything trembled, as before a storm. The only supervisors who were considered valuable were hardhearted and callous executors of the boss's will. Having received [only] a psalm reader's education, Morozov was unable to understand that he could have quickly achieved the results he desired by the improvement of the factory's machinery and the proper selection of techniques. His faith in the stick and belief in the fist left a black mark on the history of the Nikolsk factory.[69]

Morozov apparently believed that only by disciplining his workers "mercilessly" could he protect his reputation as one of the few producers of high-quality cotton goods in Russia. In remorse, he spent hours in his private chapel praying tearfully to his Old-Believer God for forgiveness of the sin of imposing heavy fines.[70] Despite Morozov's secret torments, however, the documentary record of this massive strike[71] indicated that the workers' spontaneous outrage against economic injustice should have come as no surprise. Real wages in the textile factories of Vladimir province had fallen between 1857 and 1883 by as much as 43 percent for spinners, 47 percent for machine weavers, and 52 percent for hand weavers.[72] For his part, Morozov had not only lowered wages but had increased his fines by over 150 percent between 1881 and 1884, so that the average worker lost a quarter of his wages in fines, while some forfeited up to half their entire pay. Apparently, only one worker, P. A. Moiseenko, had come in contact with socialist theory, but his resolve "to wage a struggle against the insatiable vampire who has sucked all our blood" spread quickly. When the administration demanded a full day of work on January 7, a traditional holiday, several thousand spinners and weavers walked off their jobs.[73]

The workers' demands seemed reasonable: an increase in wages to the levels of 1880–2; a maximum on fines (5 percent of the basic wage) and a one-ruble ceiling on fines for missed work; observation of the existing law regulating firing and quitting (fifteen days' notice by either side); established rates of pay for specific tasks; a refund of all fines collected since Easter 1884; free food during the strike; and the right of workers to elect a spokesman (*starosta*) and to compel the firing of any factory official or foreman whom they considered unbearably cruel. Morozov, unwilling to relinquish his position as autocrat of the factory, saw only one way to end the disturbance: the prompt application of armed force. His urgent telegram to Minister of Internal Affairs D. A. Tolstoi requesting "more rapid measures to end the disorders" vividly reflected his sense of near-panic and his total dependence on the government's repressive apparatus.[74] By refusing to feed the strikers or to grant most of their other demands,[75] Morozov carried on a test of strength during the ensuing week. The workers, for their part, had limited their aggression to minor outbursts of violence: window breaking, pilfering of goods from the company store, and threats against certain foremen. Morozov gained the upper hand when two detachments of Cossack troops arrived. He then dismissed six hundred striking workers, increased wages very slightly, and kept the Cossacks at the factory until April.[76]

Although work resumed on January 14, Morozov had lost an inestimable amount of prestige in Russian society. An administrative trial in February 1886 imposed very light sentences on seventeen strike leaders, and a jury the following May acquitted all thirty-three accused workers.[77] On the streets of Vladimir during the second trial, the crowd cheered the defendants and showered Morozov with boos, whistles, and cries: "Rob-ber, sorcerer, bloodsucker, you drink our blood!" The final acquittal, ac-cording to a gendarme colonel, "caused panic among the factory owners and perplexed them, but it produced jubilation among the factory workers." Organs of enlightened public opinion such as the liberal *Vestnik Evropy* greeted the verdict with joy.[78]

The ministers of finance and internal affairs, who, of course, cared more for the maintenance of public order than for the manufacturers' right to exact maximum profits, reacted quickly to prevent a recurrence of labor violence. In a memorandum to Bunge dated February 4, 1885, less than a month after the massive disturbance, Count Tolstoi recommended the establishment of strict regulations "which, by limiting the factory owners' arbitrariness to a certain degree, would help in the future to eliminate the deplorable cases that have occurred in Moscow and Vladimir prov-inces."[79] Yet another commission, headed this time by Viacheslav K. Plehve (1846–1904), began deliberations; but unlike those of Stackelberg, Ignatiev, and Valuev, it produced two strong measures in spite of the Moscow manufacturers' objections.

The first law, dated June 3, 1885, prohibited the employment of women on the night shift and raised to eighteen years the minimum age of night workers. Begun for a three-year trial period the following October, it remained in force until 1917. As in the past, the St. Petersburg manu-facturers supported the measure, while those of the Central Region (I. I. Baranov, N. A. Naidenov, A. L. Losev, P. A. Maliutin, and N. N. Kon-shin) vociferously opposed it. Even Pobedonostsev's personal appeal on behalf of Naidenov ("one of the best representatives of the Moscow mer-chants") to delay implementation of the law until 1887 was disregarded by Bunge, who now showed little sympathy with warnings from Moscow that labor laws would cause industrial crises and unemployment.[80] This measure, in fact, did not seriously disrupt factory production in the Cen-tral Region. By defining "night" as the period from 10:00 P.M. to 4:00 A.M., it left two full nine-hour "day" shifts during which women and adolescents could tend the machines! Furthermore, many manufacturers introduced the piece-rate system, which raised productivity to compen-sate for the shorter hours. Finally, in view of the current economic reces-sion, several Moscow merchants, including T. S. Morozov, S. I. Chet-verikov, and N. A. Alekseev, welcomed the cessation of night work as a solution to the overproduction problem.[81]

A far more comprehensive law drafted by the Plehve Commission received the tsar's confirmation exactly one year later on June 3, 1886. It virtually outlawed the old patriarchal order by imposing strict standards and by strengthening the enforcement powers of the factory inspectors.[82] So far-reaching were these changes that even the enlightened manufacturers (Chetverikov and Alekseev) briefly supported Naidenov's unsuccessful "freedom of labor" campaign.[83]

Fighting to defend their economic power against what they viewed as "a spirit of hostility or antipathy toward the upper capitalist class and . . . of biased patronage toward the hired, lower working class,"[84] the Moscow merchants sought aid from their allies in journalism. As usual, they still found publishing too difficult a task to undertake themselves; T. S. Morozov sold his unsuccessful paper, *Golos Moskvy (The Voice of Moscow)*, shortly after its creation in January 1885.[85] Of particular benefit to them was Ivan Aksakov's weekly newspaper *Rus'*, to which they donated funds, and whose economic section was managed by Sergei F. Sharapov, secretary of the MSRIS. (In January 1885, *Rus'* had denied that Morozov's policies constituted "the single reason" for the great strike.)[86] Moreover, within a year after Aksakov's death in January 1886, several manufacturers, including T. S. and D. I. Morozov, N. N. Konshin, and A. F. Morokin, provided Sharapov with funds to support his own daily paper, *Russkoe delo (The Russian Cause)*. Sharapov obediently printed a stream of articles attacking Bunge's laws and the factory inspectors. Disagreements over Sharapov's appropriation of funds from the newspaper's office caused the merchants to end their financial support in 1888, however, and the paper closed at the end of 1890.[87]

Although hampered by recurrent troubles with "their" editors in the late 1880s, the Moscow merchants received welcome assistance from a number of other reactionary periodicals that were aiming increasingly hysterical attacks against Bunge. One Moscow paper, *Sovremennye izvestiia (Contemporary News)*, "saw in the laws of 1882, 1885 and 1886 something approaching socialism. Increased agitation began against the new laws. Minister Bunge, who was responsible for having passed these laws, was accused of not understanding the conditions of Russian life, of having a doctrinaire attitude, and of being carried away by pernicious West-European theories."[88] Likewise, Katkov's influential *Moskovskie vedomosti*, which in 1881 had opposed Bunge's appointment, repeatedly called for his dismissal in order to defeat "the party that stands in opposition to the current regime."[89] Similar demands came from two archreactionary St. Petersburg papers: *Grazhdanin (The Citizen)* of Prince V. P. Meshchersky and *Novoe vremia (New Times)* of A. S. Suvorin. Although opposition to factory legislation figured less prominently in their diatribes than criticism of currency policies, high taxes, and the tariff on imported iron, the press campaign achieved a complete success from the Muscovites' point of view. Katkov's preferred candidate, Ivan A. Vyshnegradsky (1831–95), replaced Bunge on January 1, 1887.[90]

Berlin's claim that the tsar appointed Vyshnegradsky "in order to establish good relations with the dissatisfied bourgeoisie" certainly exaggerated the Moscow manufacturers' influence on the state's economic policy. There is no doubt, however, that they "sighed with relief"[91] as Bunge left office, and immediately urged the new finance minister to weaken the factory inspection system. The MSRIS, at the suggestion of A. I. Morozov and I. P. Kopanev, submitted to him a petition of grievances drafted by a commission of leading manufacturers (A. L. Losev, P. P. Maliutin, I. E. Guchkov, and J. P. Goujon) chaired by N. K. Krestovnikov. The "extensive Slavophile arguments about the 'patriarchal nature' of relations between capitalists and workers" made this petition of March 4, 1887, an extremely significant statement. To view these arguments cynically (as did Laverychev: "In all probability many capitalists did not much believe in them")[92] is to overlook the indelible imprint of Slavophile concepts on the merchant ideology.

From the very beginning of the application of the new factory law, disagreements and arguments arose between factory owners and inspectors. As these grew more and more aggravated, they inevitably affected the mutual relations of bosses and workers . . . Polemical articles in newspapers and official complaints about the factory inspectors resulted from their unreasonable demands, which were completely inconsistent with the law and did not at all benefit the workers who were supposedly being defended, but only inconvenienced both the factory owners and the workers and interfered with production. These conflicts made it appear that some sort of struggle was going on between the inspectors, as defenders of the workers, and the bosses of the factories, as their exploiters in the most extreme sense of the word.

The inspectors' view of the mutual relations between factory owners and workers is based on the completely false idea of a conflict of interest between the two sides . . . The Moscow Section, on the contrary, considers the collaboration of bosses and workers in the factory to be an alliance [*soiuz*] based on a similarity of interests and a difference of abilities that supplement one another.[93]

Rarely had the patriarchal idea been expressed so clearly.

For his part, Vyshnegradsky needed little urging. A former "denizen of industrial and stock exchange institutions who had made a fortune in shady deals,"[94] he willingly revised Bunge's factory laws. Under a new law of April 24, 1890, inspectors could allow adolescent labor on Sundays and holidays, and provincial factory boards or governors could permit night work for women and for adolescents aged fifteen to seventeen. With the approval of both the Ministries of Finance and Internal Affairs, children aged ten to twelve could be put to work temporarily in certain factories. A number of inspectors who had defended the workers' interests were dismissed, and many others resigned in protest rather than act as "factory police chiefs" whose primary task would now be "the protection of workers not from exploitation and lawlessness but from sedition . . ."[95]

To a considerable extent, the counterreforms of Vyshnegradsky simply legitimized the manufacturers' noncompliance with Bunge's laws. One of the most dedicated factory inspectors in the Central Region, Professor Ivan I. Ianzhul, reported widespread violations of the laws and extremely few cases of punishment. A series of threatening letters prompted him to carry a pistol for self-defense. For his part, the inspector S. Gvozdev encountered only one manufacturer who treated his workers with respect. Petty factory owners seemed to him "typical village kulaks," whereas large-scale industrialists acted like "tsars of their realm" who regarded their workers as "servants and slaves . . ."[96] Even N. P. Lanin, whose *Russkii kur'er* had called for "the most comprehensive" labor legislation and had praised the omnibus regulations of 1886, himself continued to employ children in defiance of the law. Tried in court like any obdurate patriarch, Lanin was forced to pay a 100-ruble fine that was upheld on appeal all the way to the Senate.[97]

Despite the persistence of traditional methods of exploitation in the Central Region, the German scholar Schulze-Gävernitz nevertheless found reason for optimism. He perceived in the 1890s a gradual improvement in labor conditions, which he explained in terms of a four-stage process of "Europeanization" in Russian industry, that is, the application of technologically advanced machinery. The first stage, that of occasional work by unskilled peasants in factories without even barracks or dining halls, already belonged to the past. All factories in the Central Region had reached at least the second phase, in which manufacturers, viewing the worker as essentially a peasant on extended leave from the village, paid extremely low wages, especially when bad harvests drove masses of peasants, with their families, to the factory in search of subsistence. Unbearable conditions of work (six hours on the job and six off, in an endless cycle) forced the exhausted peasants to return to their villages periodically to regain their health. "For a permanent work force such a workday would be physically unthinkable," but "the teaching of the Slavophiles" about the Russian workers' permanent ties to the commune conveniently justified "the personal interests" of such factory owners, who were among "the most ardent followers" of the Slavophile doctrine. Of course, the high rate of labor turnover made this system economically irrational. On account of the unskilled workers' low productivity, labor costs per unit of output in the Moscow region remained above those in England, despite the four-to-one ratio between the hourly wages paid to individual English and Russian textile workers.[98]

The owners of the largest and most highly mechanized factories of the Moscow region, in the "third stage" of industrial evolution, provided hospitals, schools, and private rooms in the barracks for workers' families. Consequently, they profited greatly from the workers' increased productivity, even when they shortened the workday to nine hours.[99] The "fourth stage," in which an educated, highly skilled working class broke completely free of the village, existed as yet only in Poland, the St. Petersburg area, and in several leading factories of the Moscow region. Here a thousand spindles required the care of only ten to twelve workers, compared to the Russian average of 16.6 and the English average of 3.[100]

In light of this stage theory, it is not surprising that in 1894 the modern capitalists of the Lodz (Poland) Section of RIS petitioned Finance Minister Sergei Iu. Witte (1849–1915; minister, 1892–1903) for a total ban on night work and certain limits on the length of the workday. Likewise, it is clear why the MSRIS strove to delay the abolition of night work for four years and to retain a maximum workday length of twelve hours (eleven for mechanical spinning and weaving). In discussions of Witte's bill on the length of the workday, the MSCTM recommended a system of two shifts, each ten hours long, that would leave the machines idle for only four hours (at "night," to be defined as the period from 12:00 midnight to 4:00 A.M.!). Furthermore, such eminent Muscovites as S. T. Morozov, N. A. Naidenov, and G. A. Krestovnikov argued that even the twelve-hour shift should not be banned entirely.[101]

Witte's law of June 2, 1897, generally satisfied the manufacturers of the Central Region. It set eleven and one-half hours as the maximum average length of the workday (ten hours on Saturdays and before holidays); permitted work by adolescents for up to ten hours on shifts that went into the night (10:00 P.M. to 4:00 A.M.); and allowed single shifts for adults to last up to twelve hours. In addition, the law imposed no penalties for noncompliance; and shortly afterward, the Ministry of Finance in effect circumvented its own rules by allowing unlimited overtime work.[102]

The Moscow manufacturers' vigorous resistance to strict labor legislation seems in retrospect to have been a tragic mistake. The merchants appeared unaware of the fact that they were running a dangerous race against time. Schulze-Gävernitz had explicitly predicted an increase in violent strikes as Russian factories made the transition to modernity; "only the worker who is pretty well fed finds within himself the strength and inclination for resistance. In Western Europe, strikes are the weapon of the best-paid workers, while the lower strata of the working class endure their fate much more humbly and for the most part in silence."[103] The wisest course, then, might well have been to pass as quickly as possible through Schulze-Gävernitz's turbulent "third phase" into the final one, in which the educated, highly skilled, and well-paid workers would defend their economic interests by peaceful strikes, not blind outbursts of violence. Instead, bloody clashes only became more common as the textile industry expanded at an ever quicker pace. Although a decrease occurred in the number of small, medium, and large factories (those employing from 16 to 49, from 50 to 99, and from 100 to 499 workers, respectively), the numbers of very large factories (with 500 or more) increased from 12 to 19, and the total number of workers in the city of Moscow rose from 38,128 to 46,922 between 1890 and 1900. In the latter year, the three largest textile complexes – those of the Prokhorovs, A. Hübner (Giubner), and E. Zindel (Tsindel) – together employed 8,944 workers, or 19 percent of the total (the Prokhorovs' Trimount alone had 5,263), and the next largest eight factories, each with more than a thousand workers, accounted for another 40 percent of the textile labor force.[104]

Furthermore, just as Schulze-Gävernitz had foretold, the workers gradually outgrew the traditional patriarchal attitude extolled by the reactionary press. The contrast between the manufacturers' view of themselves and their workers' opinion of them may be illustrated by juxtaposing the merchants' speeches in honor of Sergei I. Prokhorov (on his death in 1899 at the age of 40) with the testimony of the workers at his Trimount factory. Various officials of MIS praised Prokhorov for his service as president of the organization since 1893, as an expert on chemical processes used in textile manufacturing, and as a proponent of commercial and technical education. In the spirit of "constancy, energy, and most of all love" toward those less fortunate than himself, Prokhorov had worked diligently to improve the lot of the masses in the Presnia district, where the

Trimount factory was located, "one of the poorest in Moscow." Indeed, on Prokhorov's initiative, the society had established a special commission to protect the workers' health. In his own factory, he had maintained a hospital, offered technical education, and presented a series of wholesome entertainments for the workers.[105]

Yet this same boss appeared to his workers as a cruel taskmaster, one who cheated them by falsely computing output under the piece-rate system and who allowed despotic foremen to molest workers' wives. Dangerous equipment and poor ventilation injured the workers' health, and a system of mandatory overtime labor easily circumvented the law of 1897. Especially harsh were his methods of discipline. "As soon as Sergei Ivanovich came to the factory, fines began to rain down right and left. The boss would spend the whole day rushing from one workshop to the next, imposing fines on everybody. Prokhorov even went to the lavatories and drove the workers out." Finally, in order to minimize the threat of workers' reprisals, Prokhorov periodically "purged" his labor force by refusing to rehire troublemakers after the Easter break and, with the help of police agents, maintained a blacklist of workers fired for bad conduct and for complaining to factory inspectors.[106]

Even when allowance is made for the exaggerations of his friends and for the hyperboles of a Stalinist historian, a tragic discrepancy remains between the images of Prokhorov as enlightened philanthropist and as heartless exploiter. Unable to admit the passing of the old patriarchal order amid the rising anger of the workers, the merchants were poorly prepared to face the revolutionary movement. Decades later, one merchant recalled sadly:

At that time, in the 1880s and 1890s, a fundamental change occurred in relations between bosses and workers. The patriarchal period, with its good and evil, its simple-heartedness and sin, its protection and help, and its cheating and injury, came to an end . . . Before then an old factory owner, fully confident of his righteousness, would say: "I have many faults, but can give myself credit for one thing: I set up a factory and developed the business, and now I feed ten thousand of the people." And for this the old workers also gave credit to the boss, with whom they had played knucklebones in childhood. But years passed, and in his old age the same boss would hear young workers cry out during a strike: "We are ten thousand, and all of us are just feeding you, you pot-belly!"[107]

Neither the merchants nor the workers had yet achieved the consciousness of irreconcilable class antagonisms that was to separate them in the 1905–17 period, but a wave of strikes between 1880 and 1900 showed the direction of the inexorable process. The number of violent protests increased markedly in these years, particularly at the factories of the most illustrious Moscow merchants: Prokhorov, Khludov, Baranov, and Konshin. At the huge Vikula Morozov cotton textile complex next to the Nikolsk factory in Orekhovo-Zuevo, "great excesses" occurred in 1897: workers broke into the director's house, drank three hundred bottles of "strong Scotch whisky," and then set fire to the house, threatened the cotton warehouses with arson, and smashed twelve thousand windows. During the strikes that swept the Prokhorov, Hübner, Morozov (in Tver), and Konshin factories in 1898–9, the two Morozov factories in Orekhovo-Zuevo began to house a permanent mounted guard of twenty-five Astrakhan Cossacks, at a cost of over 4,000 rubles. This practice spread quickly after the Ivanovo-Voznesensk manufacturers received the tsar's approval for the hiring of such guards.[108] Thus even as the traditional bonds of trust between workers and employers gradually dissolved, the latter responded not only by resisting the state's factory legislation but also by repressing labor unrest by force, in total disregard of the outmoded principles of patriarchal love to which they remained publicly committed. Even Buryshkin admitted that the Moscow manufacturers, by resisting the emergence of a vigorous and mature labor movement, "showed neither an understanding of contemporary circumstances nor foresight of the future."[109] In effect, they only prolonged the dangerous transition period described by Schulze-Gävernitz. The more they refused to improve conditions in their factories, the more they obliged the tsarist government to intervene, whether with legislation to protect the labor force or with armed troops to suppress it.

As the problem of labor unrest became more and more acute toward the end of the century, relations between the manufacturers and the Ministry of Finance also deteriorated. While Witte appeared far less sympathetic than Bunge toward the workers, his ruling in 1897 that bosses must not discuss any demands until strikers returned to their jobs further limited the industrialists' ability to make whatever concessions they considered necessary. Moreover, unlike the secret agents employed by manufacturers since 1880, who had remained "entirely dependent on the factory that paid for their services, . . . the police forces introduced [in 1897] were maintained by the state treasury and were independent of the factory owners; very likely, this was rather irritating to them."[110] Yet so powerful was their ideological heritage from the 1860s and so precarious was their economic situation that they persisted in seeing the autocratic government as an all-powerful patron whose policies could be influenced by nationalist rhetoric.

The tariff war with Germany and the
Commercial-Industrial Congress of 1896

In the early 1890s, even as the labor question eluded a satisfactory solution, the Moscow industrialists faced two unpleasant challenges to the import tariff, the foundation of their economic prosperity. The unusually high tariff of 1891 appeared too good to last, for the tide of public opinion shifted quickly against it.[111] Even more disruptive was the Finance Ministry's use of the tariff schedule as a diplomatic weapon in a two-year commercial dispute with the German Empire.

Between late 1891 and March 1894, when the tsar finally approved a comprehensive commercial treaty with Berlin, the Moscow industrialists suffered from abrupt vaccilations in tariff levels. The dispute began when Germany reduced import duties on most foreign grain up to 30 percent, but refused to allow Russia to benefit from the change on the grounds that the two countries had failed to conclude a most-favored-nation treaty earlier in 1891. Angered by the resulting decline in Russian agricultural exports to Germany, Witte counterattacked. On June 1, 1893, he raised the tariff rates of 1891 by an additional 15 to 30 percent for all countries without most-favored-nation status, and thereby hindered the flow of German exports to Russia. When Berlin retaliated with a further 50 percent increase on imports from Russia, Witte promptly responded in kind. Since the "tariff war" now threatened to put an end to all commerce between the two countries, negotiations for a new treaty began in Berlin in mid-September.[112]

Throughout 1893, Naidenov and other manufacturers in the Central Region, as well as the mineowners of the Ukraine, endorsed Witte's countermeasures. In a "bellicose" address, S. T. Morozov, president of the Nizhny Novgorod Fair Committee, declared that "it did not befit the richly endowed Russian land and the greatly talented Russian people to be tributaries to an alien treasury and an alien people. . . . Russia, owing to its huge natural wealth, the exceptional keen-wittedness of its population, and the rare fortitude of its workers, can and must be one of the leading industrial countries of Europe."[113]

Perhaps the most fascinating statement of anti-German feeling came from one of the old Krestovnikov brothers in an interview with the reactionary newspaper *Novoe vremia* in 1893. Although his chemical business depended on the exportation of glycerine to Germany, Krestovnikov declared himself ready to suffer temporary economic losses in order that Russia might emerge with both honor and high tariffs intact.

Now you probably read that we no sooner announced our raised tariffs than several factories immediately closed, in Poznan, if I am not mistaken. . . . It means that they existed exclusively at our expense, like alien, poisonous little mushrooms and tumors [*kak chuzheiadnye gribki i polipy*]. . . . There is also a benefit from the simple realization that they can't do without us, while we can do without them. . . . Here I can't help recalling Peter the Great, him and his club. He would give a beating to this [Russian] who buys Poznan suitcases. . . . No, absolutely, no matter what, we must stand firm, make sacrifices, but come out, finally, on our own road. . . . We will get along somehow without their suitcase makers and handbag makers, but see how well they will manage without our grain producers – we shall see about that. . . . It's kind of hard to get along without grain. It's even possible to die from hunger.[114]

As in the labor disputes, the Ministry of Finance avoided the rather crude and short-sighted policy advocated by the Moscow merchants. The final treaty (March 1894) reduced certain Russian duties, notably on chemical products, pharmaceutical goods, specialized metal implements, and high-quality wool textiles, while Germany made corresponding concessions to Russian agricultural exports. Furthermore, because the duties remained unchanges for ten years, and the treaty was renewed in 1904 with increased rates, Russian industry enjoyed two decades of tariff stability with Germany, its most important trading partner. As Witte told the State Council, the costs to Russia "will be expressed only in a certain reduction of our factory owners' profits, which will scarcely cause them great difficulties."[115] The dire warnings of Naidenov and Morozov, to say nothing of Krestovnikov's blusterings, thus failed to sway Witte. Russian industry continued to flourish in the 1890s before suffering a depression in 1900–3. The Morozovs' Nikolsk factory, for example, earned pure profits of 2.8 million rubles (56 percent of basic capital) in 1893–4 and 3.1 million (62 percent) in 1894–5.[116] The pride of the Moscow industrialists apparently suffered more grievously than did their prosperity; and the reactionary press's encouragement of xenophobic hatred served as a balm. The primary impact of the tariff remained, therefore, more ideological than economic. The virulent anti-German nationalism of the commercial treaty struggle (1864–5) and the aggressive Pan-Slavic crusade (1875–8), instead of dying out in the late nineteenth century, received an additional stimulus in 1891–4.

Russian manufacturers obtained another opportunity to express their economic demands two years later. The last Commercial-Industrial Congress in Imperial Russia occurred in the summer of 1896, in conjunction with the great "All-Russian Exhibition of Industry and Art" near the fairgrounds at Nizhny Novgorod. Like the Congresses of 1870 and 1882, that of 1896 seemed an ideal forum at which the merchants could articulate their economic views. Under Witte's solicitous policies of state-sponsored railroad expansion, transition to the gold standard (1897), and massive loans from Europe, industry flourished in the 1890s at an unprecedented rate, and the exhibition featured the finest products of Russian factories. The most impressive building at the exhibition, the Pavilion of the Russian North, had been designed by the artists Korovin and Vrubel "in the old-Russian style" under the personal supervision of the art patron and railroad magnate S. I. Mamontov.[117] The theme of merchant power appeared most conspicuously in the Nizhny Novgorod newspaper *Volgar'* *(The Man of the Volga)*, shortly before the congress opened. Reiterating in an uncanny way N. A. Polevoi's call for merchant self-esteem over six decades before, the editors boasted that for the first time in history, the tsar himself would soon visit the fair and address the merchants there.

Having made great progress and having received from the hand of Alexander II (of blessed memory) wide access to education, the merchants now count in their ranks a mass of people with a European education, while the children of merchant families render equal service to the state together with other privileged estates. . . . At the same time, because it stands in close contact with the common people and comprises its strongest element, the merchant estate, more than all other estates, has preserved within itself the distinctive Russian spirit, and national feelings have nowhere appeared with such force, confidence, and breadth as in this estate.

There was, it seemed, no limit to the editors' self-confidence. The merchant estate, they claimed, "can do anything [*Ono vse mozhet*]. And if in the time of Minin [1612], the townspeople were the source of the financial means to hire warriors for the liberation of a Russia held captive by enemies, then the Russian merchants of today are capable of overcoming far greater ordeals and of defending the honor and glory of their native land."

Polevoi's call for equal status now gave way, in fact, to pretensions of absolute superiority. First, the editors impugned the gentry's loyalty to autocracy by an oblique reference to the fact that liberal and radical movements had been led by scions of gentry families, not the sons and daughters of merchants. "Here, indeed, is that Russian estate which has not betrayed the legacy of its forefathers, but which is accustomed fervently

and selflessly to love Russia, with all that is good and bad within her."
Second, they emphasized that during the tsar's visit only merchants
would serve in the ceremonial honor guard. Rich merchant families now
appeared superior in dignity to the boyar dynasties of Russian history.
"For the first time, merchant children from the old-line [*rodovitoe*, literally
"well-born" – as if merchants had noble pedigrees!] merchants of Moscow
and Nizhny Novgorod are preparing to form an honorary bodyguard for
the tsar, as the gentry children in ages past served their tsar." Finally, the
growing economic power of the merchants in the age of industry spelled
the doom of the agricultural estates: the gentry and the peasantry. "At a
time when many estates, because of changing social conditions, are unable
now to manifest their strength and position in the development of the
nation's productivity as they did in ages past, the merchant estate has
become sufficiently strong in society to be the very foundation on which
the state can rightly depend, as education among the merchants develops
still further."[118]

Just before the congress opened, however, a shortage of credit obliged
the merchants to obtain from Witte an extension of the normal nine-
month time limit on bills of exchange issued at the fair. Cynics saw in this
episode an admission of economic weakness by the social group that
claimed to be able to "do anything"![119]

Even at the congress itself, the industrialists found themselves on the
defensive. In addition to representatives from stock exchange committees,
the CTM and its local branches, RIS sections, and other industrial and
commercial groups, the Ministry of Finance also invited numerous government officials, economists, technicians, zemstvo officers, and representatives of consumers' organizations. In all, 1,100 persons received permission to attend, and perhaps 700 actually did so. Out of apathy,
ignorance, or confidence in their permanent consultative bodies, merchant
leaders neglected to appear in full force; at the congress, nonmerchants
outnumbered them by a ratio of approximately four to three.[120] In all, the
five sections (devoted, respectively, to industry in general, the effects of
the 1891 tariff, commerce, consumers' societies and handicrafts, and technical education) met in forty-nine sessions, in which 171 official reports
were given and numerous policy resolutions passed after extended debate.
In the joint sessions of sections one and three, the manufacturers of the
Central Region recommended several kinds of governmental action: a sim-
plified railroad rate structure (the MSEC having established its own committee on freight rates in 1893); a less cumbersome system of import du-

ties; improved telegraph, transportation, and harbor facilities in northern Persia; and less interference by the Moscow governor-general with the establishment and expansion of industrial enterprises. In general, the manufacturers' speeches reflected concern over minor bureaucratic obstacles to business activity, now that Vyshnegradsky and Witte had provided extensive state aid, as the Congress of 1882 had advocated. The manufacturers had every reason to be satisfied; free trade had been abolished recently even in the Russian Far East, to the benefit of Russian manufacturers and traders.[121] Yet their triumph remained incomplete. The symbolic issue of the tariff arose once again in section two, and the partisans of protectionism – G. A. Krestovnikov, his brother-in-law S. T. Morozov, the Kharkov mine owner N. S. Avdakov, and Professor D. I. Mendeleev – waged a losing battle against proponents of lower import duties.[122]

The significance of the congress lay primarily in the free-traders' victory on two of the most important issues under debate: the import duties on agricultural machinery and implements; and those on the metals used in their manufacture. Landowners, zemstvo officials, and bureaucrats in the Ministry of Agriculture greatly resented the high duties on imported farm machines and tools.[123] They argued that such duties unfairly burdened Russian agriculture by raising production costs at a time when the country was struggling to produce increased amounts of low-cost grain for domestic use and for export. In vain, the protectionists retorted that encouragement of the Russian farm machinery industry would benefit the country in the long run by reducing the outflow of specie spent on imported equipment and by eliminating transportation costs on American and European machinery. The opponents of the tariff answered that Russian manufacturers, assured of high profits behind the tariff wall, failed to produce enough machines and tools to meet the huge demand. At the end of the long and acrimonious debates between Mendeleev (for the tariff) and Professors Khodsky and Zhitkov (against it), the second section voted 51 to 44 to repeal the import duty. The General Assembly upheld this position even more emphatically, 140 to 63.[124]

The principle of Russian industrialization under the Witte system had been publicly repudiated. Such was the anger of the protectionists that the Fair Committee arranged a special banquet in Witte's honor, at which President S. T. Morozov condemned free trade and lauded the development of Russia's industrial power under Witte's forceful leadership. "We firmly believe that, no matter what circumstances may arise, we shall always have in the person of S. Iu. Witte the same champion of Russian industry that we have known him to be up to now."[125]

Witte's reassuring answer carried enormous implications, both economic and political. The idea of free trade had merit, he said, but Russia would not lower its import tariffs unless all other countries did the same. Since Germany, "pardon the expression, skins us alive for our products, it is impossible to think about reducing our duties" in the foreseeable future. Indeed, Witte laid to rest the industrialists' fears about the significance of the congress's resolutions. The essence of Russian autocracy would remain unchanged; the government would disregard any advice on "public questions" that it did not already accept as valid. Witte left no doubt as to this last point: "What kind of government would it be if it came to a congress for instructions on the means . . . necessary to achieve its goal? . . . In this regard the conclusions of the congress were for me not entirely worthless, but of extremely little value. . . . Whether a thousand people or ten say something makes no difference to me, since ten people can speak wisely and a thousand foolishly. The ideas of the former will be adopted, those of the latter, not."[126]

The merchants drew a clear lesson from Witte's speech. The minister, still a friend of industry, would reject antiprotectionist resolutions, even those approved by a majority vote. This last consideration carried special weight. Those who benefited directly from high tariffs, the employers and perhaps also the workers, comprised only a tiny fraction of the Russian population. Even if the franchise were restricted to wealthy and educated persons, the majority of voters would surely have favored at least a partial dismantling of the tariff wall, since opposition to protectionism was particularly strong among landlord, zemstvo, technical, and professional circles. The vote at the Commercial-Industrial Congress of 1896 showed that the interests of democracy and of industry stood diametrically opposed.[127]

Yet while it is true that the tariff system and the state's other programs for industrial development served "to hook the representatives of capital by the cogs of the wheels in the bureaucratic machine,"[128] an exclusively economic explanation cannot account fully for the manufacturers' loyalty to the government. Such an analysis cannot explain, for example, the fact that bureaucratic controls over the economy, which caused perennial conflicts between the ministry and the merchants,[129] did not engender a spirit of political opposition among the latter. Working within the Marxist framework, the Menshevik Ermansky was puzzled by the "curious" way in which the industrialists' stubborn resistance to tax increases[130] and to labor legislation "coexisted perfectly with their readiness to accept the old-fashioned forms of state organization and methods of bureaucratic tutelage."[131] Despite the paucity of documentary information on the crucial question of the relationship between the state's economic policy and the manufacturers' political loyalty, it seems clear that the influence of psychological and cultural factors, at least as much as economic ones, must be admitted.

Of special interest in this regard is Buryshkin's remarkably perceptive sketch of the attitudes of the MSEC leaders at the end of the nineteenth century. He admitted that they preferred to concentrate on the narrow concerns of trade and industry, and not to raise political issues. No one "even thought of discussing questions which related to politics in one way or another. True, there was no direct surveillance over the activities of the stock exchange organizations, but anyone who bore the entire burden of work never entered into any conspiracy, and never would have." Whatever resentment existed against the autocratic system, as distinct from the Finance Ministry and its bureaucrats, was kept hidden; "both in industry and in trade there was a certain element of Fronde [opposition] – but they did not want to take risks and feared for the safety of the organization. Also, to tell the truth, few were ready to deal with questions of the most general kind." Naidenov and his fellow merchants therefore engaged in "discussions of chambers of commerce, tariff policy, regulation of the sugar industry, and the revision of taxes on businesses; but no one raised questions about what was necessary for the development of the country and the growth of the Russian national economy. Also, these questions were not raised partly because the answer was known in advance: it was necessary to change the general conditions of Russian life, both political and social."[132]

One is struck by the frankness of this account. Were the Moscow merchants before 1905 yearning secretly for a constitutional regime in which their businesses could flourish freely, released from the annoying constraints of the Ministries of Finance and Internal Affairs? Buryshkin tended toward a positive answer. "The thought arises, of course, that general questions were not raised because the membership [of the Stock Exchange Society] was 'right-wing' and too 'loyal.' This is not at all true. Of course Naidenov was no leftist, but there was never a trace in him of the Black Hundreds [protofascist mobs]." Instead, the merchants dared not risk criticizing their all-powerful patron, the tsarist state; their silence stemmed as much from the state's awesome power as from their own timidity. "Conditions of life at that time created their own kind of vicious circle: the political situation did not allow the raising of questions whose discussion would have facilitated the development of groups and of a class consciousness; and the lack of such a consciousness allowed an acceptance of the conditions of life prevailing at that time."[133]

This brief but penetrating explanation cannot be dismissed lightly, for Buryshkin, like his father, served in the Merchant Society and the MSEC and personally knew the eminent leaders of his estate. Yet two major qualifications must be made. First, his claim that the merchant leaders, including Naidenov, conscientiously avoided political activity before 1905 is contradicted by the evidence contained in the present study. Of Naidenov's successful appeals to Pobedonostsev and Katkov; of the merchants' active support for Pan-Slavism, the Holy Host, and Ivan Aksakov's numerous periodicals; and of their blatant hostility toward zemstvo liberalism, Buryshkin said nothing. Moreover, Buryshkin appeared to be attributing to Naidenov his own political outlook, which was rather enlightened for a Moscow merchant of the early twentieth century. To borrow his phrasing: Naidenov, of course, was no protofascist, but there was never a trace of liberalism in him. He stood far to the right on the political spectrum, not midway between the Black Hundreds and the radicals, as the quoted characterization implied.

On the merchant political spectrum of 1906–17, the leaders of the 1880–1900 period such as Naidenov and the elder Krestovnikovs would scarcely have found a place, so reactionary were their views. Indeed, far from advocating *laissez-faire* policies even in the domestic economy, N. Krestovnikov of the MSRIS called for "special laws relating to commercial brokers and agents" in 1888.[134] Even more striking is the fact that the merchants' hired pen of the 1880s, S. F. Sharapov, became a founding member of a reactionary gentry party in 1905.[135] Buryshkin's concept of a "vicious circle" therefore seems to owe too much to hindsight. It may be considered accurate only to the extent that it described the frustration of the few moderately reformist leaders like S. I. Chetverikov, who in the decades before 1905 was moving toward a mature class consciousness opposed to both autocracy and radical revolution. Naidenov, for his part, had no such misgivings about the government's monopoly on political power. He and his supporters, who remained dominant in Moscow merchant circles throughout 1905, refused to draw liberal political conclusions from the intermittent disagreements on economic policy that marred their partnership with the tsarist state.

In order for political frustration to emerge, the merchants had to realize their own importance as a class in social and political terms. Insufficient for this purpose were the antigentry blusterings of *Volgar'*, which echoed the narrow estate consciousness of the time of Nicholas I, still strong in the provinces and among the less educated merchants of Moscow. It was in the fields of culture and local self-government, not economics, that the elements of a truly bourgeois consciousness would first become manifest.

6

●━■●■●━■●━■●━■●━■●━●━━●━━●━■●━■●━■●━■●━━●━━●━●━■●━■●━■●━■●━━●━━●━●━■●━━●━━●━■●━■●━■●━●

Toward a bourgeois consciousness: culture and politics, 1880–1904

The merchants' improved education in the late nineteenth century produced an unprecedented diversity of cultural styles. While the traditional
merchant way of life persisted among poorly educated and less affluent
traders and manufacturers, many capitalist merchants became famous as
patrons of culture. The political consequences of their cultural activities
were not immediately apparent, however. The merchants had not yet attained a genuine class consciousness in the sense of rejection of the estate
structure of society and an awareness of social antagonisms based on economic function. Certain duma leaders like S. V. Lepeshkin and A. I.
Guchkov abandoned the rigid conservatism of Naidenov's generation, but
their ideological evolution hardly signified a major step toward liberalism
by the merchants as a group. Rather, conflicts between industry and the
state might have been resolved, as before, by mutual compromise had the
Revolution of 1905 not emboldened the manufacturers to press their demands for a larger role in public affairs.

Demographic change and cultural development

It has often been argued that the political and cultural feebleness of the
"Russian bourgeoisie" derived from its numerical weakness; as a tiny urban group engulfed in an ocean of peasants and landlords, it had no chance
to dominate the course of public affairs. This interpretation has a certain
historical foundation. The merchant estate, at best regimented and at
worst crippled by a system of expropriations and bureaucratic controls
that was unknown in Western Europe, remained outnumbered by the
rural masses well into the twentieth century. Yet to explain the docility of
the Moscow merchants in the late nineteenth century by recalling the
tsarist oppression of the sixteenth is to overlook both their growing numerical strength and their distinctive ideological coloration following the

145

Crimean War. Even if the industrialists' demographic position remained far weaker than that of the liberal bourgeoisie in Europe,[1] their political aversion to liberalism cannot be explained simply by pure numbers and without reference to the cultural and economic factors peculiar to Russia at this time.

Statistical records and analyses, while far from thorough, permit a tentative resolution of this question. The Russian merchant estate in 1881 included from 800,000 to one million persons, or approximately 1 percent of the population of 92 million, of which 50,000 to 60,000 were the richest and most influential: the "big bourgeoisie" of the Marxist terminology.[2] In Moscow itself, the guild merchants and their families numbered 22,916 persons in 1882. To them must be added most of the city's 9,223 honorary citizens (allowing the remainder as artists, actors, and other professionals), for a rough total of 32,000 persons, or 4.3 percent of the city's population of 753,469.[3] In 1897, merchants comprised 1.3 percent and honorary citizens 1.1 percent of the empire's urban population of 16.8 million. Together these two groups constituted about 0.5 percent of the total (126 million). By then, the number of merchants and their families in Moscow had shrunk to 19,491, but this decline was offset by a substantial increase in the number of honorary citizens (21,603). In 1902, merchants (18,500) and honorary citizens (40,700) together comprised 5 percent of the city's population.[4]

The population statistics themselves masked another important dimension of the Moscow merchants' demographic weakness: the considerable rate of turnover and the resultant low degree of continuity. Detailed quantitative analyses of this factor have yet to be undertaken, and so its effects cannot be measured precisely, but Laverychev correctly noted that "merchants' sons became bureaucrats, jurists, doctors, surveyors, engineers, foremen, private tutors, and even singers and painters . . ." Already in 1873, more than half (333) of the 623 first-guild merchants had entered the merchant estate after 1861.[5] On the other hand, because honorary citizens remained secure in their social status regardless of economic misfortune, they provided a strong element of continuity at the very pinnacle of commercial-industrial life in Moscow.

Soviet historians have produced very few empirical studies of the economic activities of the various social estates, but one recent analysis of the Moscow Merchant Board's records from 1865 to 1898 showed that merchants and honorary citizens maintained their traditionally predominant position in Moscow province, where nearly 20 percent of all first-guild

merchant certificates in European Russia were issued. This group purchased more first-guild certificates in both 1870 (76.0 percent) and 1898
(58.9 percent), as well as more second-guild certificates (74.2 and 45.7
percent for the same two years), than any other social category. The apparent decline was largely offset by the large increase (from 3 to 25.7
percent in this period) in the number of first-guild certificates owned by
small firms, which were almost exclusively under merchant control.[6]
Moreover, this rudimentary analysis ignored the merchants' role in the
new, large corporations – joint-stock companies and share partnerships[7] –
and thereby understated their economic power still more. Storozhev,
writing in 1912, clearly exaggerated when he compared the "transition of
the estates into social classes" to a great "earthquake in society"; but he correctly saw that the merchants' considerable influence over "the principal
vital nerve of the country – capital" gave them an increasingly important
role in Russian society, despite their small numbers. In this respect, the
nineteenth century was unique in Russian history, for among the wealthiest Moscow merchant dynasties, whose multiple intermarriages further
consolidated their social position, family businesses were commonly
handed down over many generations.[8]

Merchant leaders, weak in demographic terms yet secure in their economic prosperity, were able to devote their energies to new undertakings
that implicitly challenged the old estate structure of Russian society. The
hallmark of this dynamic merchant culture was a striving to displace the
gentry as the leading force in public life. As the playwright Vladimir I.
Nemirovich-Danchenko recalled, the merchants' challenge stemmed from
a residual feeling of cultural inferiority despite their superior wealth. "The
gentry envied the merchants, and the merchants flaunted their striving for
civilization and culture." The two groups therefore "regarded each other
with external amiability and concealed hatred; on the side of the first was
illustrious birth, on the side of the second, capital. Each with skilled diplomacy tried to flaunt its superior virtue before the other." The appointment of the tsar's uncle and brother-in-law, Sergei Aleksandrovich, as
governor-general of Moscow in 1891 greatly pleased the gentry, which felt
"that the grand duke would show it preference over the mercantile class."
The millionaire Savva T. Morozov retaliated shrewdly when the governor-general requested an invitation to his lavish new mansion. Morozov
was nowhere to be found when his honored guest arrived at the appointed
hour. "This was a very subtle snub, which was equivalent to saying, 'You
have a desire to see my house, but you're not coming to see me. The house

is at your service, then. Have a good look 'round. But don't imagine that I'll be here to meet you with genuflections.' "[9] Because the merchant, in the words of Vladimir P. Riabushinsky (1873–1955), "felt himself to be 'the first man' " of Moscow, superior to the gentry, "there was little contact between these two worlds. Families were very rarely acquainted, and mixed marriages were exceptional. The Moscow lords [*bary*] looked with scorn on the 'little merchants' [*kupchishek*], and the Moscow merchants, owing to an abundance of 'their own,' did not pay attention to the gentry." The old dream of gaining gentry status as a reward for outstanding public service gradually lost its luster; "it was better to be first among the merchants than to be last among the gentry."[10]

A haughty article of the late nineteenth century in the conservative *Novoe vremia* expressed the gentry's reciprocal condescension.

The merchant is in fashion. People expect the "real word" from him. And everywhere he promptly obliges. He produces speeches, drafts measures, publishes books, manufactures high-quality policies, organizes public meetings, etc. . . . The merchant is an organic part of Moscow – its mouth, its nose, its teeth now beginning to emerge . . . Glance into a worthy institution, and without fail you will meet the merchant there, very often in uniform, with the "Eglish crease" [deliberately misspelled], with a French speech, but a merchant all the same, with all his "Ordynka-Iakimanka" [merchant-quarter] characteristics, which no trends nor civilization can air away.[11]

This implication that the merchants' traditional crudeness followed him about like stale air overemphasized the negative aspects of their old ways. It was only because the merchant leaders of this period felt secure in their traditions that they would eventually muster the courage to challenge the autocratic state. For better or worse, the bourgeois consciousness of the 1905–17 period grew directly out of the estate pride of the nineteenth-century merchants. Riabushinsky's memoirs make clear, for example, that the great merchant families who sat smugly in their homes "like West-European medieval feudal lords in their castles"[12] kept alive at least two beneficial traditions: the strong religious spirit and devotion to the family business.

Of his father, Ivan V. (1817–90), Petr Shchukin wrote, "We often went to church with father; he was very religious." Every Old-Believer merchant family "without fail" had a private chapel in the house "with ancient icons and liturgical books."[13] As in the past, religiosity continued to be expressed publicly by "generous annual donations" to churches and parish schools, but now, competition over building the most beautiful churches

Figure 1. Top left: The museum of art collector Petr I. Shchukin, which was constructed between 1892 and 1898 in the neo-Slavic style. Top right: The chapel in the poorhouse established by Pavel M. Tretiakov. Middle: The Trimount cotton textile factory of the Prokhorov family in the mid-1890s. Bottom: The Moscow City Duma Building, constructed between 1890 and 1892 in the neo-Slavic style.

gave way to "competition among eminent families . . . over *who does more for the people.*" To his brothers, Pavel P. Riabushinsky (1871–1924) often paraphrased the aristocratic French motto "noblesse oblige" by saying "richesse oblige" (*bogatstvo obiazyvaet*); "the underlying spirit of it, although often unconscious of course, was the firm Christian faith of fathers and grandfathers."[14] In addition to maintaining the guild records, the Moscow Merchant Society Board organized special religious funds for the construction of Orthodox churches in Batumi, Kars, Prague, and even Buenos Aires; granted pensions to merchants' widows; and instituted a quaint form of "guardianship" (*opeka*), usually exercised by close relatives, over merchants whose physical infirmities or lapses into drunkenness and debauchery jeopardized their families' great fortunes. The society's annual revenue of over one million rubles went primarily to maintain the many philanthropic institutions that rich merchants had established in their wills.[15] The biblical injunction about the difficulty of a wealthy man's entering heaven weighed heavily on the consciences of the religiously oriented merchants, and the way to salvation – to serve the common people (*narod*) through philanthropy – continued to be preached by leaders of the estate even as the old patriarchal order was crumbling.

Useful old habits persisted in this period in the realm of business as well. Literary works must, in general, be treated very carefully by the historian, but Riabushinsky recommended as an "ideal" the stories and novels of Ivan Shmelev about the world of petty merchants under Nicholas II, in which simple devotion to the patriarchal father, the family business, the church, and the tsar constituted the dominant theme.[16] Nikolai Chukmaldin (d. 1901), who moved his tea and wool wholesaling business from Siberia to Moscow in 1872, naively expressed this religious approach to commerce. "Only he who provides a service to society prospers and grows rich in trade. The most valuable commodity is trust, and faith is given only to irreproachable honesty and to unselfishness in trade . . . Everything that is gained unjustly, through cheating, self-interest, and evil bears death within itself. Only the good is vital and strong."[17] The Moscow textile manufacturer Lev Rabenek left the same impression of devotion to traditional virtues in the final prerevolutionary decade.[18] Thus, Buryshkin argued, a leading Moscow merchant, unlike the calculating American or European businessman, saw in his enterprise "the fulfillment of a task, his own type of mission entrusted to him by God or by fate." Those who were merely wealthy enjoyed less honor than cultural and public leaders like P. M. Tretiakov, N. A. Naidenov, and G. A.

Krestovnikov. Likewise, the most respected firms were those whose clerks served loyally for decades and left only to start their own businesses, not because of poor treatment by the boss.[19]

Even the Riabushinskys, who diversified from textiles into banking and international trade in the early twentieth century, held to many ways of the past, when there were no " 'employers' and 'employees,' but an elder [*starshina*] and his clan [*rod*]." Where the boss had total power, he was "bold, enterprising and flexible, and did not have to look back." Next best was a family firm, in which "brothers polished one another, conflicts were absent, and there was support and replacement for rest." The European joint-stock company functioned less satisfactorily in Russia, allegedly because the management "*wasted time on explanations, self-justifications, apologies, and self-glorification.*" Still worse were municipal and state enterprises, because of their monopoly position. The traditional "unwritten merchant hierarchy" reflected these values. Most status accrued to manufacturers, somewhat less to traders, and least of all to the banker the "interest-monger" (*protsentshchik*) – whom industrialists avoided by financing expansion out of current earnings or by establishing their own banks, as did Naidenov and the Riabushinsky family. Moscow banks followed the English model, holding savings accounts, discounting bills of exchange, and giving "careful loans with securities as collateral," in contrast to the St. Petersburg banks, whose establishment of new industrial enterprises (*griunderstvo*) in the manner of the French *banques d'affaires* and the large German banks risked disaster. "The Moscow industrialist sat in his warehouse or factory like an appanage prince in his princedom, snorted at Petersburg, and did without it."[20]

Likewise, personal dealings based on mutual trust remained typical well into the twentieth century. In times of financial emergency, merchants helped their closest friends first. Another unwritten rule required that every bundle of cash be counted whenever it changed hands. Once an outsider, "not knowing our customs," took payment from an important merchant without counting the bills. "For goodness sake, I trust you, " he explained. "Of course! How dare you not trust me!" bellowed the Muscovite. "But I could make a mistake. Count it!"[21]

The weight of tradition, if beneficial in the realms of religion and business, also had negative consequences, however, especially among the thousands of petty merchants who lacked higher education. Documentary evidence from this period, cited above, reveals little that is new in the coarse habits of this lower stratum compared to fifty years before, but precisely because of this fact, the later sources bring into clear focus the persistence of the traditional merchant culture into the twentieth century. The failure of the self-conscious bourgeois leadership to draw the uneducated merchants away from their age-old political outlook in the final decade of Nicholas II's reign can be explained only by the tenacity of this traditional culture, which was inculcated into the last generation of Moscow merchants by the familiar indoctrinations of stern patriarchs.

To illustrate the perennial strength of the old habits, it suffices to mention just one aspect of traditional merchant life, the short-sighted urge for maximum profits. Riabushinsky recalled learning a harsh proverb in childhood, "Moscow does not believe in tears,"[22] that is, failure in the economic struggle won no sympathy. The competitive spirit kept alive the virtuoso skills of cheating for which the uneducated Moscow merchants were justifiably famous. When the university-educated S. I. Chetverikov advertised the thirty-year-old debts of his late father, his honesty appeared unique, to say the least. Far more common were false declarations of bankruptcy by unscrupulous petty merchants, who, though nominally religious, often disregarded the Eighth Commandment. Unfortunately for the cheated creditors, Russian law gave little protection against such abuses. Of course, the wealth thus obtained conferred no social status, but for merchants of middle and lower rank the money itself served as adequate compensation.[23] In 1886, one Old-Believer merchant complained to his diary: "Everywhere filth, loathsome, venal filth . . . And all are hiding behind a screen of piety; they bear on their criminal brow the mark of the ardent Christian."[24] Riabushinsky appealed for Christian charity toward the shortcomings of his unenlightened fellows: "misers, mischievous people with no crosses on their necks, plunderers who swallowed their prey live, unbridled gray horses, blockheads, good-for-nothings, fraudulent bankrupts, skinflints, windbags, cunning rogues, and other people of every loathsome and idle rank and habit."[25]

Even among some of the newly educated leaders of the Moscow merchant estate, great wealth untempered by true Christian humility or by a sense of public duty often led to wild extravagance. Mikhail A. Morozov (1871–1903), who left his family's textile complex out of boredom, reportedly wrote novels and historical studies and gave lectures at Moscow University, but he found his true vocation as a famous bon vivant. In 1901, his personal expenses amounted to 196,675 rubles, or 1,035 times the average wage of his textile workers that year! According to legend, he lost more than a million rubles in one night while gambling at cards.[26] With princely disdain, V. M. Golitsyn condemned the "epic feasts" of the nouveaux riches; "people talked of smashing hundreds or thousands of rubles' worth of dishes, of washing the floor with champagne, and of throwing unopened bottles out into the street."[27] In this way, the merchants kept alive the Russian peasant tradition of the blindly destructive drinking bout (*zapoi*), but in a high style commensurate with their new bloated fortunes, as denoted by the special Russian words for the rich reveler (*kutila*) and his carousing (*kutezh*).

The most enlightened merchants strove to eradicate such baneful effects of tradition by providing their children with a good education. By the end of the century, it was no longer unusual to encounter Moscow merchants with university degrees.[28] In addition to the Practical Academy (since the 1860s supported by a portion of the profits of the Moscow Mutual Credit Society) and the Duma's network of public schools, two projects demonstrated the leading merchants' commitment to enlightenment. In 1897, the banker Aleksei S. Vishniakov organized a Society for the Propagation of Commercial Education (*Obshchestvo rasprostraneniia kommercheskogo obrazovaniia*) to train foremen and clerks already employed and to prepare young students for careers in business. Over a hundred leading manufacturers contributed 60,000 rubles during the initial subscription of funds. Vishniakov's society also created a Moscow Commercial Institute to provide education beyond the secondary level.[29] These measures encountered considerable resistance from traditional merchants, however. Inasmuch as they had learned their business techniques by direct observation and practice, they disdained "theoretical disciplines" and valued only "basic knowledge of bookkeeping or even simply the ability to compute on the abacus." In fact, graduates of elementary schools often found jobs more easily than did holders of diplomas from the merchants' own institutes![30] The tension between tradition and modernity continued to cause tragic consequences. The family of a Kursk fish merchant who moved to Moscow in 1890 suffered from the all-too-common pattern of decline and fall. The well-meaning but ignorant patriarch, Iasha Polunin, slipped into financial ruin while pathetically mouthing old proverbs.[31]

Several cultural leaders of the Moscow merchant world, having acquired enough education and wealth to be capable of establishing new institutions, undertook in the late nineteenth century a myriad of projects in virtually all realms of public life. In this respect, they did not yet constitute a self-conscious bourgeoisie, since their cultural activity bore the stamp of the old merchant psychology of religiosity, peasant orientation, and a striving for gentry rank. Yet many of their contributions in diverse fields – historical preservation, the theater, and art collecting – remain famous to this day.

In order to demonstrate their ancestors' contributions to Russian history and thereby counter the unflattering stereotype of the greedy "little merchant" (*kupchishka*) and "dry-goods peddler" (*arshinnik*),[32] the Moscow merchant leaders spared no expense in resurrecting the past. In 1883, N. A. Naidenov began the monumental task of publishing the Merchant Society's archival records.[33] Several other merchants – notably A. I. Khludov, Petr I. Shchukin, Aleksei P. Bakhrushin, and Pavel A. Buryshkin – rescued from oblivion great numbers of Russian antiques, rare books, and historical documents that now constitute the core collections of Soviet museums in Moscow.[34] Wealthy young merchants now found it especially fashionable to display their good taste by congregating with their friends and relatives at the theater. The most famous of these young aesthetes, Mayor Alekseev's cousin Konstantin Sergeevich (1863–1938), took the stage name Stanislavsky. With the playwright Vladimir Nemirovich-Danchenko, he founded in 1897 the Moscow Art Theater, which became under his direction a world-renowned institution of modern drama. The irrepressible Savva T. Morozov provided crucial financial support to the fledgling company in its early difficult years (1900–4).[35]

Most impressive of all were the great art collections of the Moscow merchants, which, in the words of the eminent critic Stasov, demonstrated their "benevolence and proud patriotism . . . " From the late 1850s onward, the merchants K. T. Soldatenkov, S. A. Mazurin, G. I. Khludov, and V. A. Kokorev had encouraged the work of young Russian painters. The leading merchant patron, Pavel M. Tretiakov (1832–98), had vowed as early as 1857 to collect Russian paintings exclusively. With his brother Sergei (1834–92), he built a private collection of 1,276 works that far exceeded the number of Spanish paintings in the Prado (500) or of English ones in the National Gallery, London (335).[36] Repin, Surikov, Kramskoi, and the other creators of the great masterpieces of Russian realism, who called themselves "the Itinerants" (*peredvizhniki*) because of the annual exhibitions which they circulated throughout the country from 1870 to 1923, were supported financially not only by the Tretiakovs but also by Soldatenkov and Chizhov's protégé in railroad management, Savva I. Mamontov. The illustrious "Mamontov circle" also included composers, musicians, and singers, who performed the great works of Mussorgsky and Rimsky-Korsakov in the ebullient impresario's private opera, founded in 1885. With Sergei P. Diaghilev, Mamontov later published the lavishly illustrated journal, *The World of Art* (1898–1904), which encouraged the development of the new postrealist styles of the Silver Age.[37]

Because rich merchants' daughters had traditionally received better training in the arts than their practically oriented brothers, it is not surprising that the most cultured merchant salon of the period was maintained by a woman: Margarita K. Morozova (1872–1958, née Mamontova). A patron of music who sustained the eccentric genius A. N. Scriabin during several difficult years,[38] she was best known for her intellectual salon, where the Soloviev Religious-Philosophical Society (founded in 1907) gathered to hear such major thinkers as the Trubetskois, Berdiaev, and Bulgakov. While the liberal historian and politician Pavel N. Miliukov spoke at her house on several occasions in 1905, he was indeed a rare phenomenon in merchants' living rooms at this or any other time. Moreover, the influence of the merchant ideology of the previous decades may be discerned in the philosophical journal edited by M. K. Morozova, which "represented the Slavophile and Russian Orthodox trends in Russian philosophy."[39]

So powerful was this cultural tradition that when educated young merchants entered the world of government service they tended to maintain a conservative outlook. D. I. Abrikosov (1876–1951) despised the radical youth he met at the university.

I must confess that . . . political indifference corresponded much more to my inner feelings than self-sacrifice for some vague promise. I was accustomed to the idea that Russia was a monarchy. It was the monarchy that had created contemporary Russia and ruled, as far as I could see, without any display of inhuman cruelty . . . To destroy all that and to start some political adventure seemed absurd to me.

The scion of a Moscow family famous for manufacturing jams and candies, he overcame the stigma of his merchant origins ("I was greatly embarrassed that my name was associated with sweets and caramels") by becoming even more snobbish than his fellow clerks at the Ministry of Foreign Affairs. Throughout his diplomatic career, he demonstrated an unshakable loyalty to the tsarist regime.[40]

Likewise, Petr S. Botkin, son of the eminent professor of medicine from the famous tea importing family, cultivated an air of discriminating culture, and in his memoirs dropped the names of famous writers he had met in childhood: Fet, Turgenev, and Mendeleev. He took special pride in an incident that occurred when he was serving as a junior diplomat in Washington, D. C. George Kennan, author of the famous indictment of the Siberian exile system (1891), was giving public lectures critical of the tsarist autocracy. Young Botkin printed a patriotic rebuttal in *The Century Magazine* (February 1893): "Autocracy is as natural and satisfying to Russia as is the republican form of government to the United States; . . . [the people] submit cheerfully to be ruled by it and . . . they prosper under it." He also intended to go on a speaking tour himself, but was restrained from further public displays of patriotism by the Ambassador, Prince Kantakuzen, who regarded such blatant propaganda as unbecoming a gentleman.[41]

In view of the growing prominence of rich Moscow merchants in the arts and government service, one is struck by the fact that they had little impact on the most political aspect of public life, the periodical press. To be sure, from 1890 until his death in 1896, the textile magnate D. I. Morozov had maintained a reactionary monthly, *Russkoe obozrenie (The Russian Survey)*,[42] but this brief foray by a merchant into the world of political journalism remained a unique episode. In 1899, S. T. Morozov and S. I. Mamontov prepared to publish a proindustrial newspaper to be entitled *Narod (The People)*. We can only infer from the title and from these merchants' own dedication to economic nationalism that the self-righteous and patriotic rhetoric of their fathers' old Slavophile mentors would again have resounded in the pages of *Narod*. Like so many other publishing ventures proposed by Russian merchants, however, this project somehow never reached fruition.[43] Laverychev concluded his fascinating tour through the dim byways of merchant journalism with the curious statement that "the big bourgeoisie actively strove to utilize the periodical press for its own purposes,"[44] but even as these words conjured up the familiar West-European image of a culturally dominant bourgeoisie, his own account convincingly demonstrated the perennial pattern of the merchants' feebleness in journalism.

While the "big bourgeoisie" failed to create a powerful organ to defend its material interests and express its political views, several publishers among the merchants did earn substantial incomes from popular dailies. The editor of *Russkoe slovo (The Russian Word*, 1894–1918), the book publisher I. D. Sytin, strove simply to produce "a nonparty, nonclass, well-informed newspaper with a large circulation and great influence."[45] Still less attention was paid to questions of political reform by the so-called "boulevard press," utterly devoid of serious ideological content, which appealed to the middle and lower strata of the urban population, especially the merchants. Such was N. I. Pastukhov's "merchant newspaper," *Moskovskii listok* (*The Moscow Sheet*, 1881–1918), whose spicy anecdotes entertained petty merchants and clerks of the kind described in Shmelev's stories.[46] (These were precisely the two papers read by the pathetically fatalistic patriarch of Polunin's memoir, who cared nothing for constitutional ideas on the very eve of the Revolution of 1905.[47])

A sense of what was and was not typical of Moscow merchant culture, particularly in journalism, is too often lost in historical discussions of the link between Varvara A. Morozova (née Khludova, b. 1848) and the leading liberal newspaper in Moscow, *Russkie vedomosti* (*The Russian News*), published from 1882 onward by her second husband, Vasili M. Sobolevsky (1846–1913). Here is the only opportunity to paint the "Russian bourgeoisie" in liberal colors, and Soviet historians generally make the most of it.[48] If her father (A. I. Khludov), her first husband (Abram A. Morozov, 1839–82), and her sons by this marriage (Mikhail and Ivan) had, like her, poured their millions into liberal journalism instead of religious manuscripts, the family cotton textile mill, luxurious parties, and French Impressionist paintings, respectively, then a bourgeoisie worthy of the name might have emerged in Moscow prior to 1905. Instead, this rich but modest lady, who seems to have "arranged her whole life in the manner of the noble, restrained tone of this newspaper," played the role of the enlightened manufacturer almost alone. Among her unique philanthropic projects were women's and workers' education, student scholarships, and the first public library in Moscow, named after Turgenev.[49] Moreover, her houseguests included Tolstoi, Chekhov, and various "liberal-minded Muscovites . . ." The main female character in P. D. Boborykin's colorful novel of merchant life, *Kitai-gorod* (*The Commercial District*, 1882), was based on V. A. Morozova, but Buryshkin opined dryly that "the original was far more remarkable than the copy."[50] Indeed, Morozova's commitment to *Russkie vedomosti* made her, in Buryshkin's words, "somewhat exceptional among other public figures from the Moscow merchant estate." The decisive gap between the merchants and her newspaper was political. During the darkest days of reaction under the last two tsars, *Russkie vedomosti* defended the ideals of the liberals who eventually formed the Constitutional Democratic (Kadet) Party. While after 1905 "the Kadet influence on it was strong," the Kadets had, in contrast, "no such influence" in commercial-industrial circles.[51] Only a handful of merchants ever published articles in the newspaper,[52] whose cosmopolitan, humanitarian, and liberal creed – "the awakening of the public's consciousness of law and independent activity, directed toward democratic, political, and socioeconomic reforms"[53] – remained foreign to the nineteenth-century merchant ideology.

All in all, therefore, the Moscow merchant culture of the late nineteenth century, although far more variegated and dynamic than before, nevertheless maintained its old hallmarks: a low educational level among the mass of smaller merchants, and ostentatious displays of wealth among the rich. Cultivation of the fine arts and genuine benevolence founded on the concept of "richesse oblige" and the more traditional precepts of Christian charity somewhat mitigated the dominant impression of ignorance and frivolity. An individual like V. A. Morozova might show some striving toward a class-conscious bourgeois outlook based on a realization of the power of capital in the new industrial society then being formed in Russia, but others climbed the status ladder into the gentry or expressed pride in their accomplishments as merchants, from a purely estate point of view. Against this cultural background, the behavior of merchant leaders in the political arena before 1905, particularly their indifference or hostility toward liberalism, is to be seen not as an aberration but as one aspect of their public activity that was fully consistent with the whole.

The merchants in municipal politics, 1893–1904

The Imperial decree of June 11, 1892, which restructured municipal dumas in Russia, strengthened the influence of the merchants in local self-government. Whereas in 1870 all male taxpayers aged 25 or more were allowed to vote in city elections, the law of 1892 reduced this small electorate to miniscule proportions through a high property qualification. No one could vote unless he owned real estate that generated annual taxes of at least 500 rubles (if a house, 5,000 rubles), or purchased a commercial or industrial certificate that cost 500 rubles a year. (Jews were excluded totally; but electoral rights were granted to the various philanthropic, scholarly, governmental, and educational institutions that owned sufficient real estate.) Whereas in 1889, 23,000 persons, or 2.7 percent of the population of Moscow, had enjoyed the franchise, in the election of 1892 for the ensuing four-year term (1893–6), only 6,260 qualified, or 0.5 percent of the population. Four years later, this figure fell to 0.3 percent![54] Those privileged to vote and to serve showed little interest in doing so. In the campaign of 1892, only 14 percent of those eligible bothered to cast their votes. Four years later, 17 percent turned out, but still the number of candidates "almost equalled the number of voters: thus they came to the election not so much to elect as to be elected!" Moreover, of the 160 seats in the Duma (reduced by the law from 180), up to one-fourth remained unfilled because of the lack of candidates.[55]

Such apathy was understandable in light of the repressive features of the new system. The law severely restricted the Duma's legislative power, both by subordinating the municipal institutions to the bureaucracy and by limiting their financial resources. The governor-general enjoyed veto power over all measures passed by the Duma, subject to the decision of the Provincial Board (*prisutstvie*) on zemstvo and municipal affairs. Also, the Executive Board, duma commissions, and even hired staff now became subject, like the mayor, to confirmation by the administration before taking office. As de facto civil servants (one liberal dubbed them "elected bureaucrats"), executive board members wore official uniforms and became subject to administrative discipline.[56] The city's real estate taxes could not exceed 10 percent of the annual net profitability, or 1 percent of the value of a piece of property, and commerce and industry were taxed "at the most insignificant level." Furthermore, although the city government drew up its own budget, the administration had the power to alter it. The annual budget did rise appreciably, from 1.7 million rubles in 1863 to 4.7 in 1887, 15 in 1901, and 22.3 in 1905, thanks to the expansion of municipal enterprises – slaughterhouses, laundries, the municipal savings bank – after the turn of the century. The overall picture remained somber, however. "The needs of the population . . . grew and accumulated, but the most urgent measures had always to be postponed for lack of funds."[57]

The political consequences of the law were unclear. According to the liberal Shreider, the counterreform "met the desires and aspirations of the upper economic strata of the urban population" and thus strengthened the existing "ties of solidarity" between rich merchants and the regime.[58] At the same time, however, constant interference by the Ministry of Internal Affairs inevitably provoked resentment. Maintenance of the ministry's police force and mounted patrols, night watches, and other services pressed the Duma to "financial exhaustion." The tsarist bureaucracy also appropriated municipal funds for its own use and raided "the pockets of the ruling minority itself" by requiring homeowners to maintain yardkeepers and lighted house numbers at their own expense. Particularly frustrating were administrative delays affecting "hundreds of decisions . . . on the most urgent and vital questions"; often "approval was given after the decision itself had lost all significance."[59] The result was a "chronic war" between the Duma and the administration. Instead of cowing the municipal leaders, the law of 1892 "created with one hand and destroyed with the other."[60]

As in the past, spokesmen for municipal independence came more from the professional intelligentsia and the gentry than from the commercial-industrial leadership. Still, the merchants who served in the Duma gained firsthand experience in elaborating a rationale of antiautocratic political action. Requests by the Duma for municipal fire brigades were, of course, far from demands for constitutional liberties and universal suffrage, but they foreshadowed one of the major political demands of 1905: an end to irresponsible and arbitrary intervention by the bureaucracy in local affairs.

The two mayors who presided over the Duma from 1893 to 1905 strove to avoid open confrontations with the overwhelming power of the bureaucracy. An obsequious merchant, Konstantin V. Rukavishnikov (1848–1916), succeeded the murdered Alekseev and then served a full four-year term (1893–6). Prior to his election, Rukavishnikov "never entered into the debates and rarely participated in commissions because of an innate shyness," but to demonstrate his devotion to the city, he made large donations (50,000 rubles on one occasion) to the Duma's treasury. Elected mayor "almost against his will," he served as a competent administrator; "no better choice could have been made."[61] His family had become famous for its philanthropic undertakings, particularly a home for young criminals supervised by his pious elder brother, Nikolai (1845–75).[62] Already a privy councilor, Konstantin became an actual state councilor while mayor, and so clearly enjoyed the confidence of the governor-general. He improved the financial condition of the city, strengthened the institutions created by Alekseev, added a pawnshop to the list of municipal enterprises, established a pension fund for city employees, and introduced a trusteeship council to coordinate various philanthropies.[63]

Prince Vasili M. Golitsyn agreed to serve as mayor when Rukavishnikov declined reelection in 1896 on the grounds of fatigue and the press of business. Essentially an "unpretentious, tender, and well-mannered" aristocrat, Golitsyn had been dismissed from his position as civil governor of Moscow after refusing to comply with petty regulations of the Ministry of Internal Affairs. The leading Moscow merchants, who called him "our prince," elected him mayor as if to demonstrate their "self-reliance in judgment and choice: Moscow had its own opinion and Petersburg cannot lay down the law for it." At the same time, Golitsyn, like the gentry mayors Shcherbatov and Cherkassky in the 1860s, posed no threat to the tsarist bureaucracy. Although personally sympathetic to "progressive and liberal ideas," he presided over the Duma so calmly and quietly that some members recalled nostalgically Alekseev's "stormy, fiery, and exuberant activity" and Rukavishnikov's "businesslike and tightly formal administration." His defenders explained that the mayor purposely avoided dominating the Duma, so as to encourage members to participate more actively than in the past.[64]

The social composition of the Duma from 1893 to 1905 reflected the stifling effect of the 1892 law. Yet the merchants by no means exercised the political monopoly that the law seemed to grant them. Because merchants gained neither financial benefit nor personal prestige from sitting in the Duma, few of those who were eligible bothered to run. In this quiet decade, members were primarily "those who wanted to serve their city, just as the zemstvo men wanted to serve their village."[65] In 1893–6, for example, merchants and honorary citizens numbered 86 of the 139 members; gentry, 40; *meshchane*, 10; and peasants, 3.[66]

In any case, there never appeared any tendency within the Moscow merchant estate . . . to seize complete control of the Duma . . . On the contrary, . . .there was a definite desire to bring into the Duma representatives from the intelligentsia who did not own enough property to qualify. This was possible because the electors included various scientific and philanthropic societies that owned real estate. Under the law, they could give power of attorney to anyone they pleased, not just to someone from their staff. By this means, several persons were elected who played an outstanding role in the Duma.[67]

Accordingly, in 1897–1900 the merchants kept preponderant influence but not absolute control, having increased their numerical strength only slightly, to 67.5 percent from 61.9 four years before. Of the 120 members (40 seats remained vacant), there were 81 merchants, 22 professionals (lawyers, professors, doctors, architects), 10 nobles or civil or military officials, 6 *meshchane*, and one priest. Despite their comfortable majority, the merchants did not participate as actively as did other members. Thirty-five merchants (or 43 percent of all merchant members) served on no commissions whatsoever, compared to 36 percent of the professional men, 33 percent of the *meshchane*, and 30 percent of the nobles and rankholders. Twenty-one merchants undertook administrative work on the audit, tax, and financial commissions, for which their business experience gave them special expertise, but their relative showing here (26 percent) remained lower than that of the nobles (30 percent) and *meshchane* (33 percent). Most merchants preferred to give silent support, like old Aleksandr A. Bakhrushin, whose family had donated more than two million rubles for the construction of a hospital and a school and had built a children's home and a rooming house for the poor. He "has never talked in the Duma, but together with his brothers has done as much for the city as dozens of duma members who do talk"![68]

These tranquil years witnessed the appearance of a small group of younger merchants who urged the Duma to act more decisively. As yet lacking a program of political liberalism, these members "were, however, the forerunners" of the Constitutional Democratic and Octobrist leadership. This mildly oppositional faction earned the mercantile name "Guchkov brothers, Shchepkin, Mamontov, and Co.," for it acted as the "driving force" in the field of economics: the budget, construction of electric streetcar lines, and supervision on the city's various enterprises.[69] K. V. Rukavishnikov's father-in-law, Ivan N. Mamontov, for many years the president of the Finance Commission, had published in 1893 the first explicit criticism by a merchant of the Moscow Duma's lack of "independent activity and initiative" under strong-willed mayors like Chicherin and Alekseev. He proposed the creation of an "editorial commission" to coordinate the tasks of the Duma and the Board, as in the Tver Zemstvo (a hotbed of liberalism, of which he was then a member). Chicherin, however, despised this "stutterer and idle talker," whose many grandiose schemes "lacked the slightest political sense." Still, Mamontov had enjoyed the support of the *meshchane* when he ran for mayor in the 1880s.[70]

Other members of this group also qualified as experienced duma men. N. N. Shchepkin, Rukavishnikov's talented vice-mayor, refused to serve under Golitsyn and lent his efforts to the opposition.[71] Aleksandr I. Guchkov (1862–1936), the scion of a prominent textile family, served on the ten-man Executive Board. After taking a degree in classics at Moscow University in 1885, he had studied for three years in Berlin, where he had learned to appreciate "the German *Rechtsstaat* and . . . the successful operation of its semiconstitutional order. The model of a strong, efficient, and independent monarchy free of party determination but with nominal links to a popular legislature was one which Guchkov held before him as the Russian ideal . . ."[72] His brother, Nikolai (b. 1860), the holder of a law degree, pursued an active career in banking and insurance, but also represented the city in the provincial Zemstvo and served on the duma commissions on horselines, military affairs, and philanthropy.[73] Aleksei S.

Vishniakov, a close associate of Mayor Rukavishnikov, joined the anti-Golitsyn group in 1897 after the older merchants tried to prevent the creation of his Commercial Institute.[74] Finally, the board member Semen V. Lepeshkin, grandson of the Moscow Mayor Semen Loginovich, distinguished himself as a statistician, builder of municipal dormitories for students, and editor of the Duma's *Izvestiia* (*News*). Educated at Dresden University, he displayed obvious displeasure at the counterreform of 1892 and, out of frustration, eventually contributed funds to extreme parties of the left.[75]

These young merchants and intellectuals took a certain pleasure in "the persecution of some rather elderly and lazy Board members, settling scores with N. A. Naidenov's group, which consistently supported Prince Golitsyn"; but theirs was a formidable task.

Naidenov had a severe disposition and a severe hand. A very clever man who had a high opinion of himself and did not grovel before the powerful of this world, he liked to show his power and influence. Small and wizened, with lynx-like, shifty little eyes and a head that always swung from side to side, he . . . would not allow objections. The Moscow merchants dependent on him executed his orders unquestioningly . . . in commercial affairs and also in the City Duma, in the Stock Exchange Committee, and in the Merchant Society. Naidenov's dictatorship oppressed many in the 1890s.[76]

The intense conservatism of Naidenov's dominant faction colored the few political statements that the Merchant Society and the Duma made in this period. In sharp contrast to the zemstvo leaders' call for constitutional reforms on Nicholas II's accession to the throne in 1894, the merchants' message of condolence to the new tsar on the death of his father radiated the traditional spirit of firm loyalty. "The Moscow Merchant Society, meeting in extraordinary session, resolved most humbly . . . to present to the HOLY FEET of the EMPEROR the feelings, inherited by the merchants from their ancestors, of reverential love and unlimited devotion, by which Russia is strong and happy . . ."[77] Two years later, outgoing Mayor Rukavishnikov declared that it was "entirely possible to work independently for the good of the city" under the law of 1892.[78]

On the eve of the Revolution of 1905, therefore, the Duma publicly expressed no dissatisfaction with the tsarist system. Yet while the bond of trust and affection that allegedly united the Russian tsar and his people seemed unbroken, the merchants' perennial feeling of fear and antagonism toward the bureaucracy persisted. Two actions by the government at the turn of the century weakened the merchants' faith in the autocratic system and drove the younger leaders into open opposition: police-sponsored labor unions and the repression of the moderate zemstvo reformers.

An overzealous official of the Moscow secret police (Okhrana), Sergei V. Zubatov, sought to solve the labor problem by creating illegal unions under the veiled control of the Ministry of Internal Affairs. By this means, he hoped to gain influence over the disgruntled workers and steer them toward the purely economic struggle for higher wages and shorter hours, and away from the political movement for a democratic and constitutional republic, led by liberals and Marxists. Early in 1901, Zubatov established mutual aid societies in Kharkov and Moscow, and the Moscow Textile Weavers' Union. On February 19, 1902, the forty-first anniversary of the emancipation of the serfs, Zubatov organized a huge crowd of 50,000 workers, who demonstrated their loyalty to tsarism by laying a wreath before a monument to Alexander II.[79]

Two days later, however, strikes led by Zubatov's agents erupted in Moscow, in Mussi's silk factory and at Goujon's metallurgical plant. The workers demanded higher wages and the return of monies illegally deducted in past years. Goujon complained to the Moscow police chief, D. F. Trepov, but the latter began to harass Goujon for his violation of the sanitary code. Trepov thus blamed the manufacturers, not his agents, for the strikes. The textile manufacturers Prokhorov and Beliaev met similar abuse: unless Prokhorov made concessions, he would be exiled from Moscow. The factory owners, realizing that such punishment would mean financial disaster, reacted immediately. A deputation from the MSEC to Witte denounced Zubatov and Trepov as creators of a movement that had gone out of control. Just prior to the strike, on February 17, one workers' assembly had discussed the current state budget of the Russian Empire.

The unification of workers belonging to various factories and different strata of the working class is extremely dangerous, particularly [when they are] in such a mood as to undertake an analysis of questions of state policy. If the purpose of granting them a certain organization is to attract them away from participation in antigovernmental activities, it is no less dangerous to permit them to engage in anticapitalist activities, which unquestionably have the same political significance.[80]

Witte agreed, and relayed the warning to the Minister of Internal Affairs, D. S. Sipiagin. Already alarmed at the huge demonstration, the latter forbade further commentary in Russian newspapers about the working class. The strikes were repressed; and priests and the repentant revolutionary Lev Tikhomirov now lectured to workers on the "harmony of interests between labor and capital." So docile became the police unions that some industrialists agreed to support them financially.[81]

Most of the Moscow manufacturers did not forgive Zubatov, however, even after he gave an impassioned defense of his program before a group of factory owners at Testov's restaurant on July 26, 1902. He could hardly have won their support by his claim that the workers, the intelligentsia, and the priests all viewed capitalists as "swindlers" whose only defender was General Trepov. Even Zubatov's superiors soon lost faith in him. He was transferred by the new Minister of Internal Affairs, Viacheslav K. Plehve, and in August 1903 he was exiled to Vladimir province.[82]

Zubatov's demise did not end governmental interference in the factories. In June 1903, the state required manufacturers to compensate victims of industrial accidents except in cases of "gross negligence" by workers, and also allowed workers to elect an elder (*starshina*) to represent them in dealings with the boss. Although Iakunchikov welcomed this latter plan as a way of forestalling labor unrest, most manufacturers opposed it in the drafting stage and refused to implement it after it became law.[83]

Both the government and the manufacturers faced unique dilemmas. The bureaucracy, fearing that unregulated exploitation would lead to mass revolts, passed increasingly strict factory laws. At the same time, the State Council emphasized on May 9, 1903, that "appropriate protection" must be given to the industrialists, "all the more so since they unquestionably constitute the class that is directly interested in the maintenance of public order."[84] The Zubatov fiasco demonstrated, however, the difficulties of protecting either the workers or the bosses without injuring the other side. It was all too easy to anger both parties without resolving the labor question. Neither side, for example, believed that the factory inspectors acted fairly.

For their part, the industrialists had no choice but to rely on the armed force of the state in quelling huge strikes. On the other hand, with few exceptions they continued to resist the government's labor laws as unwarranted intrusions into their private domain. Before 1900 they had grudgingly accepted factory legislation for the sake of tangible economic benefits from the state: tariff protection, low taxes, and the repression of strikes. Now the Zubatov movement and the new edicts on factory inspection, the length of the workday, elected elders, and accident compensation undermined their devotion to the autocratic regime. The rule of law began to appear attractive to them as "a powerful protection against arbitrary acts by the government."[85] Moreover, the severe recession of 1900–3 called into question Witte's emphasis on state-sponsored heavy industry and pointed to the need for a vigorous mass market within Russia, hitherto limited by the crushing tax burden on the peasantry and the communal agricultural system.[86] Never enamoured of the St. Petersburg bureaucracy, the Moscow industrialists now began to doubt the worth of the tsarist system as a whole. In Weberian terms, the rationalism implicit in modern capitalism – the need for impartial and predictable rules – more and more conflicted with the arbitrariness of the autocratic system. Yet to reject the proautocratic ideology of the past forty-five years would require great effort. Those few who dared to break with the past received encouragement from the strongest native Russian source of liberal constitutionalism: the Zemstvo.

The ideological influence of the zemstvo men on the Moscow merchant leaders grew despite several serious obstacles. First, the law of June 12, 1890, had thoroughly reorganized the zemstvos so as to increase the power of rich landlords at the expense of the less wealthy. Also, merchant landowners now voted in urban electoral assemblies regardless of how much rural land they possessed. Denied equal rights in the Zemstvo "even in the most industrially developed districts," merchants showed little desire to participate.[87] Second, the "sharp and fierce" battle over taxes between the Moscow provincial Zemstvo and the Duma, begun in Alekseev's term, did not abate under Rukavishnikov. After winning the right to impose property taxes within the city, the Zemstvo levied them with enthusiasm, so that "the City Duma as a whole was not favorably disposed" toward it. The district zemstvo president, N. F. Richter, outraged the Duma by selling the land for the city's new sewage plant for 3.3 million rubles, seven times its actual value.[88]

Yet for decades, a small band of Moscow liberals had sat both in the Zemstvo and in the Duma, and since 1872 the Duma had elected one of its members to the provincial Zemstvo Assembly. By the 1890s, these tenuous contacts had grown into "close and organic" ties. Duma members in the provincial assembly now included A. I. Shamshin (on the zemstvo tax board), S. N. Mamontov (formerly a district assembly and board member), and the dynamic N. I. Guchkov. Some of them, like old A. A. Shilov, "always fervently defended the city's interests," presumably by advocating lower taxes, but others, like S. V. Lepeshkin, served selflessly on many zemstvo commissions and helped gather essential statistics.[89]

The drift toward a critical view of autocracy apparently began as early as 1891–2, when a severe famine and cholera epidemic ravaged the Russian countryside. Participants in the humanitarian cause included Mayor Alekseev, appointed to the Moscow Committee for Famine Relief, and Varvara A. Morozova, whose Literacy Committee fed masses of starving peasant children. Viewed in the context of the merchants' traditional commitment to philanthropy, the campaign signified no new departure. It seems that few, if any, merchants who donated money to the cause drew any political conclusions from it. Alekseev's committee acted under the patronage of the Grand Duchess Elizaveta Fedorovna, in whose honor a new Benevolent Society was formed in Moscow in 1892. Yet the structural flaws of the tsarist regime had been demonstrated to all, and by visiting the villages at this time "many members of the upper classes first discovered the wretched conditions under which peasants lived (or died) in Russia."[90]

The common devotion of both zemstvo men and merchants to the improvement of living conditions among the peasantry led to cooperation in other projects. In 1899, for example, a League dedicated to the commercial production of folk crafts established a Cooperative and Handicraft Goods Trading Company. Its fifteen-member council included the industrialist Sergei T. Morozov, his late cousin's wife V. A. Morozova, the former municipal official M. P. Shchepkin, and the zemstvo leaders V. Iu. Skalon, Professor M. V. Dukhovskoi, D. N. Shipov (president of the Moscow Provincial Board, 1894–1904), and D. A. Khomiakov (son of the Slavophile).[91]

Ironically, the manufacturers were drawn toward political liberalism by the zemstvos' rural philanthropy at a time when peasant handicrafts faced eventual extinction by the advent of industrial mass production. Yet even the merchants who believed in monarchy respected the zemstvo opposition's brave defense of local initiative against the arbitrary dictatorship of the bureaucracy. An informal "Colloquium" (*Beseda*) of prominent zemstvo men – the twin Princes Dolgorukov, D. I. Shakhovskoi, Prince M. V. Golitsyn (evidently a son of the Moscow mayor), D. N. Shipov, and others – met several times a year in Moscow from November 1899 to early 1905. Among the nine "steady attendants" were two merchants: N. I. Guchkov and a brick manufacturer from an old merchant family, Mikhail V. Chelnokov (b. 1863). A future mayor of Moscow (March 1914 to March 1917) and Kadet party leader, Chelnokov had worked with Shipov since 1893 in zemstvo mental health and educational projects and had presided over the district zemstvo board (1891–4).[92] Thus a third era in merchant-zemstvo relations had begun. Open hostility had given way to infrequent cooperation (like that of Alekseev and Chetverikov) in the 1880s, to be followed now by occasional participation in political opposition to the regime.

At first, these *Beseda* discussions explored avenues of reform that the tsar himself might espouse, but the need for constitutional changes became clear as the government attempted to cripple the Zemstvo's activities.[93] Even the anticonstitutionalist members of *Beseda* like Shipov, who were called "Slavophiles" because of their adherence to the autocratic principle, soon grew disgusted with the obtuse interventions of the bureaucracy. In April 1904, when Plehve refused to confirm Shipov's reelection as president of the Moscow Zemstvo Board, both the Zemstvo and the Duma issued strong protests. "It was impossible to remain indifferent . . . Only [Vice-Mayor] Ivan A. Lebedev and a handful of old members remained grimly silent or made unfavorable remarks on the ever more frequent expressions of dissatisfaction sent to the [provincial] government and Petersburg."[94] S. I. Chetverikov, calling himself "an old and convinced zemstvo man," publicly recommended the abolition of the high property qualification for zemstvo board members in favor of an educational criterion, and criticized the "introduction of the bureaucratic principle in the affairs of the Zemstvo."[95] Duma members began reading *Osvobozhdenie* (*Liberation*), the illegal newspaper of the constitutionalist Union of Liberation that Struve published abroad, and often asked each other in low voices "if there was anything new from 'Stuttgart.' " Although the majority in the Duma did not yet seek political change, two small extremes had formed by 1905: Naidenov's diehard reactionaries, who showed "unconcealed irritation and hatred" toward reform, and the liberals, whose influence grew stronger with each repressive act from St. Petersburg.[96]

This tentative drift toward opposition took place against the background of highly patriotic statements by Duma and merchant leaders during the war with Japan. On January 28, 1904, after the Japanese attacked Port Arthur, Mayor Golitsyn called upon the Duma to set an example of self-sacrifice. As in 1877, it enthusiastically appropriated one million rubles for the war effort and began collecting private donations to aid the sick and wounded. The duma member A. E. Armand was sent to the Far East with a large medical detachment.[97] Likewise, the Merchant Society on January 28 unanimously pledged to aid the wounded soldiers and sailors and the families of the dead by contributing the 800,000 rubles still remaining from the Turkish war and by creating a new fund of one million rubles, to be raised by the society and the MSEC, under the patronage of former Empress Mariia Fedorovna. The society and the MSEC also presented an icon and a banner to the Russian commander in Manchuria.[98]

However, the steady deterioration of the Russian armed forces undermined the patience of the most patriotic merchant leaders. A. I. Guchkov, a brave and even reckless student of military affairs, had visited Anatolia during the Armenian massacres (1894), commanded a guards unit in Siberia (1898), fought against the British in the Boer War (1899), witnessed the Boxer Rebellion in China (1900), and observed the Macedonian uprising (1903). His experience as the assistant chairman of the Russian Red Cross and as manager of a field hospital in Mukden, where he was captured by the Japanese in February 1905, strengthened "his Russian nationalist fervor" and convinced him that the army and navy had been betrayed by an incompetent bureaucracy in St. Petersburg. As president of the Third State Duma in 1910–11, he was to launch a "barrage on the monarchy for its neglect of the military establishment."[99] The Guchkov brothers became disillusioned with the tsarist regime more rapidly than did their fellow merchants. By the end of 1904, however, even the conservative leaders felt the severe economic dislocations of war: credit restrictions, transportation problems, delays in importing machinery, disruptions of exports to Central Asian markets, and the reduced purchasing power of the urban population.[100]

By November 1904, a firm program of political reform had been enunciated by the Zemstvo Constitutionalists (led by *Beseda* members, including Chelnokov) and the Union of Liberation, the political precursor of the Kadet party. The Moscow manufacturers' attraction toward liberalism now became clear. The members of the Union's "Group A" in Moscow, "the most active and important branch in the country," included not only renowned zemstvo liberals but also the industrialists N. I. Guchkov and S. T. Morozov.[101] Their presence had special significance because the program of the Union, drawn up in January 1904, verged on radicalism: "the liquidation of autocracy"; "universal, equal, secret, and direct vote"; "defending the interests of the working class"; and "the right to self-determination of the various nationalities."[102] Morozov, in particular, had undergone a dramatic ideological change since the Commercial-Industrial Congress of 1896. Having lost faith in tsarism, he gave "24,000 rubles a year" (beginning apparently in 1901) to Lenin's newspaper *Iskra (The Spark)*. In October 1904, he loaned money to a Union of Liberation member through his friend Maksim Gorky to finance two daily newspapers designed to spread constitutionalist ideas among the workers, *Nasha zhizn' (Our Life)* in St. Petersburg and *Bor'ba (The Struggle)* in Moscow. The first issue of *Nasha zhizn'* appeared on the opening day of the national Zemstvo Congress, held in St. Petersburg from November 7 to 9, 1904.[103]

Under the presidency of D. N. Shipov, this congress passed eleven resolutions calling for political freedoms (of conscience, speech, the press, assembly, and association), inviolability of persons, civil equality (including equal legal rights for peasants), reform of zemstvos and municipal dumas, political amnesty, abolition of the states of emergency, and – most important of all – the convocation of a national, popularly elected representative body. A majority of the delegates (seventy-one to twenty-seven) favored a legislative assembly with the right to limit the autocrat's power, as proposed by the Union of Liberation and the Zemstvo Constitutionalists. Shipov and his "Slavophiles" stopped short of such a major constitutional change, preferring a purely consultative body, like the *Zemskii sobor* of the sixteenth and seventeenth centuries. In the interest of harmony, both the majority and minority versions were submitted to the tsar, but the Union of Liberation actively promoted its view by organizing in major cities during November and December a series of banquets at which constitutional speeches were made and resolutions passed.[104]

As in the preceding April, the Moscow Duma approved a special resolution in support of the zemstvo leadership. Led by the liberals S. A. Muromtsev and N. N. Shchepkin, seventy-four members met privately to prepare a cautiously worded statement, which the Duma adopted unanimously on November 30. It appealed to the self-interest of the taxpayers by listing such bureaucratic outrages as the unfair tax structure, the administration's refusal to share revenues with the city, and the imposition of governmental expenses on the city treasury. It also avoided the provocative phrase "Constituent Assembly" and the delicate issue of the State Duma's power (legislative or consultative).[105] Just as in 1870, the most conservative members of the Duma refused to participate; "before the vote, three members took to their heels: the priest, [A. or N.] Naidenov, and [Professor V. I.] Guerrier."[106] Most of the merchants approved the resolution, however. "An especially strong impression was made by the fact that the Duma, the stronghold of the biggest merchants, passed a resolution calling for the immediate convocation of popular representatives . . . An Old-Testament merchant in a long frock-coat and high bottle-shaped boots . . . pointed out to me the statue of Catherine II which adorned the Duma chamber and said with a sigh, 'What is she thinking now, little mother?' "[107]

This incident revealed the emergence of a new political consciousness. For the first time, merchant leaders in Moscow occupied positions all along the political spectrum, from radical (S. T. Morozov) to moderately liberal (M. V. Chelnokov, S. V. Lepeshkin, and N. I. Guchkov) to staunchly proautocratic (N. A. and A. A. Naidenov). In the duma elections for the 1905–8 term, held in late 1904, the liberal-democratic and promonarchist tendencies, which would soon form the Kadet and Octobrist parties, were already contending for influence. Buryshkin asserted that these "progressive" and "moderate" slates of candidates in no way expressed class interests. "On those comparatively rare occasions when a struggle in the Duma went along political lines, one group of merchants opposed the other on the same grounds as did the representatives of the intelligentsia."[108]

In certain areas this pattern prevailed. In Ward 5 (Iauza, Basmann, and Rogozh), a private meeting of fifty people endorsed a return to the less restrictive Municipal Statute of 1870; a broadening of the public school curriculum; the formation of an independent agency within the board to reduce "red tape and formalism"; open discussion (*glasnost'*) in the Duma; and the election of twenty two progressive candidates, including six lawyers and judges, two doctors, two engineers, and several merchants (P. D. Botkin, M. N. Bostandzhoglo, and the leading vote-winner, N. I. Guchkov).[109] On the other hand, in Ward 1 (Gorodsk, Tversk, Miasnitsk, and Sretensk), a "struggle" occurred between "the merchant and intelligentsia" parties. The latter's slate of progressive candidates scored an impressive victory. Only three merchant delegates not listed on it won reelection (F. E. Guchkov, P. S. Rastorguev, and S. I. Liamin – the latter left off by mistake). Of the new members, three were endorsed by the intelligentsia party, and only two – the well-educated S. T. Morozov and K. A. Iasiuninsky – were not.[110] After the election, the growing political tension between the Duma and the government impelled the newly elected members to declare their solidarity with the liberals. The first act of these members was the signing of the November statement. Although some new members, like Buryshkin's father, feared reprisals from the government, this demonstration of unity forestalled any retaliation.[111]

In all the momentous political events of the 1900–4 period, the Moscow merchant leaders who sought reforms generally followed the political lead of Shipov's conservative wing of the zemstvo opposition. By late 1904 they, like Shipov himself, were exasperated by the intransigent bureaucrats who refused to trust loyal Russian citizens with local self-government and who proved incapable of averting famine, economic recession, and military defeat. Their own interests were affected, to be sure; the merchants were still smarting from the Zubatov experiment and the labor laws. Yet once again, progressive ideas had come to the merchants from outsiders: Shipov and, to a lesser extent, the Union of Liberation. The strength of the merchants' new commitment to fundamental political reform would be tested in the great drama of revolution.

7

The failure of the bourgeois revolution, 1905

The Russian Revolution of 1905, in retrospect, appears to have been the crucial event during which autocracy might have been abolished by the briefly unified liberal-radical movement of zemstvo men, professionals, workers, and peasants and replaced by a constitutional regime strong enough to defend itself against both the revolutionary left and the reactionary right.[1] The war with Japan had destroyed the government's legitimacy and had temporarily drawn the armed forces away from the centers of peasant and worker discontent, but the country was spared the economic chaos and wholesale slaughter of the army that, during the Great War, finally doomed both the tsarist regime and the liberal Provisional Government.

Peasant unrest, workers' strikes, constitutional demands from zemstvo leaders and professors, and calls by national minorities for autonomy had all been heard before. Yet the most remarkable political phenomenon of the Revolution of 1905 was the public expression of liberal ideas by Russian manufacturers and traders. The change in allegiance from tsarism to constitutionalism by several of the richest and most articulate businessmen in the empire brought the prospect of the tsar's downfall into clear view. By the beginning of 1905, even some of the most reactionary of the commercial and industrial leaders of Moscow saw their erstwhile patron and mentor, the Russian state, as an obstacle to further economic prosperity. The activities of the Finance Ministry had always entailed both aid and bureaucratic obstruction, but the latter now seemed to outweigh the former. The opportunity to obtain a voice in political affairs at the expense of the tsar and his officials would not be missed by the Moscow manufacturers in 1905.

Although this liberalism constituted a break with tradition, the coordinated efforts of the Moscow commercial-industrial leadership to subdue the tumultuous strikes staged by thousands of angry workers in 1905 signified a no less epochal turn. The dual struggle against the recalcitrant state on the one hand and the unruly laborers on the other brought to the Moscow merchants a new consciousness of their common interests and their isolated position in a postrevolutionary Russian society. Conscious of their identity as a minority separated by fundamental economic and political differences from the state and the workers as well as from the peasantry and the gentry, the leading Moscow merchants by the end of 1905 had become a bourgeoisie in fact.[2] Not only Marxist and academic liberals, but now businessmen themselves began to speak of the "Russian bourgeoisie"; after 1905 the word *class*, appropriate to a rapidly industrializing society, slowly began to displace the centuries-old word *estate* in their public pronouncements.

And yet if it is possible to speak of the maturation of a genuine bourgeois consciousness in Moscow during the Revolution of 1905, the merchant ideology of the past by no means faded away. Indeed, the events of the revolutionary year appear comprehensible only in the light of that ideology. This was so because a sizable portion of the Moscow commercial-industrial leadership, especially the older merchants who controlled the MSEC, continued to adhere to many of its tenets. Together with the newly emergent liberal bourgeoisie, therefore, there formed in Moscow a conservative bourgeoisie as well, one whose will would prevail at the end of the year.

The emergence of bourgeois liberalism in Moscow, January to May

The first five months of the revolutionary year witnessed unprecedented political activity by Moscow merchants. For the first time, they reacted to labor unrest by calling for political reform rather than instant repression. While the partisans of constitutional liberalism were far outnumbered by those who sought merely to modify the Russian autocratic system by including wealthy manufacturers and gentry in deliberations on national policy, both the liberals and the conservatives in the Moscow merchant leadership insisted on structural reforms in this moment of bureaucratic weakness.

The indiscriminate shooting by the police of peacefully protesting workers in St. Petersburg on "Bloody Sunday" (January 9, 1905) provoked an angry reaction in Moscow. The Duma's protest, an unprecedented challenge to the autocratic principle, constituted a major political event because of the new tactic urged by a group of "liberally inclined" manufacturers. At the request of V. S. Bakhrushin, K. A. Iasiuninsky, I. A. Morozov, and P. P. Riabushinsky, the Duma petitioned the government to forestall further labor violence at this crucial moment by legalizing peaceful strikes and granting to all Russian citizens the right of assembly and association. It also recommended that "civil authorities" prevent troops from injuring "peaceful residents" during street disorders. While at this point only a minority of the MSEC favored the legalization of strikes and labor unions, a large number of manufacturers meeting on January 13 agreed on a new tactic to bring about political reform. They resolved not to appease their workers by making any concessions in wages and hours. This stand cleverly united self-interest and political acumen. The cost of labor would not be raised, and at the same time the government would be made responsible for soothing the angry mood of the workers by political reforms. On January 24, the minister of finance, V. N. Kokovtsov, met with the Moscow manufacturers but failed to convince them of the need for wage increases.[3]

The liberally inclined minority among the rich Moscow industrialists, known as the "young group,"[4] proclaimed their new political views in a remarkable memorandum of January 27. The backwardness of Russian industry reflected the lack of a firm legal system, including "freedom of the individual and of initiative," freedom of scientific inquiry, and adequate public education. By means of "endless and needless formalities" the "ruling circles" had blocked the expansion of public schools, libraries, and reading rooms for the poor and ignorant – the merchants' own philanthropic enterprises.[5]

This call for civil rights on the West-European and American model was promptly followed, and to some extent contradicted, by the invocation of a strongly non-Western, Slavophile idea that would be inexplicable except in light of the merchant ideology of the past five decades. Russian industry suffered, for example, because "the common people [*narod*] are cut off from the Supreme Bearer of true authority" and cannot "express their needs" to the throne because of the "tutelage of the bureaucracy . . ." In a passage worthy of F. V. Chizhov, the industrialists complained: "Russia's position in the world market is shaken by economic backwardness, the direct result of the weak legal system, and her role as an industrial country is also thereby pushed into the background."

The memorandum expressed special concern for the problems of the lower strata of Russian society. The peasant masses, steeped in ignorance, tied to inefficient farming techniques, and unable to purchase the products of Russian industry, remained hopelessly poor, the victims of periodic economic crises. (The part played by high import tariffs in reducing the peasants' purchasing power was not mentioned.) Because of the close links between the Russian workers and the village, industrial prosperity would directly aid the peasants.[6]

The "ruling administration" erred, furthermore, in blaming peasant and worker unrest on the agitation of evil individuals. "No, the general disorganization of state life; the lack of political rights; the lack of open intercession before the throne on behalf of the interests of the people, in the form of freely elected representatives; and the lack of other prerogatives that constitute the inalienable appurtenance of a free individual in a free state – here must be sought the main reasons of periodic workers' disturbances." To be sure, certain changes were needed in "the economic position of the working estate," but only under a free legal system could the workers and their employers jointly seek improvements. By all means, the regime must avoid enflaming class tensions by "shooting peaceful, unarmed residents" (a clear criticism of "Bloody Sunday") and by encouraging labor protests. The Zubatov experiment, discussed at length in six paragraphs, had been particularly harmful in "demoralizing the working masses . . ."[7]

The solution lay, therefore, in a system of equality of all citizens before the law, in which social strife "could take the form of a peaceful, legal type of struggle, as is observed in Western Europe and America, where industry has not only not suffered as a result, but on the contrary has achieved such prosperity as is yet far from being witnessed in Russia."[8] Posing as "the class that is the most cultured [*intelligentnyi*] and devoted to the throne," the young Moscow industrialists offered a far-reaching political program intended to promote industrial growth, ensure social justice, and avert a violent revolution. It was necessary to adopt "elementary conditions of a state governed by law" (*pravovoe gosudarstvo*, a direct translation of the German *Rechtsstaat*): "equality of each and every person under firm laws," and "complete inviolability of person and residence . . ." Both workers and industrialists needed "the complete right to hold meetings and assemblies" in their free time, and to organize "unions and all kinds of other societies for self-help and the defense of their interests . . ." Each worker must be free "to refuse work, individually or in common," and at the same time to accept work "under conditions that he finds admissible," as long as they are not prohibited by law. Contrary to the demands of the socialists, workers who preferred not to strike must be allowed to stay at their jobs, protected from "the violence of striking workers." The factory owners must retain full control over wages and piecework rates and the assignment of employees, subject only to norms established by law. Labor disputes must be resolved "peacefully and legally" by the two sides, acting as legal equals. Indeed, sweeping reforms were needed for purely economic reasons: "freedom of speech and press," essential to industrial growth and the improvement of working conditions; "the participation of representatives from all classes of the population, including workers and industrialists," in the establishment of "legislative norms," especially the state budget; and "universal and compulsory education," the lack of which had contributed directly to Russia's defeat in the war with Japan.[9]

The memorandum ended with some rhetorical flourishes aimed against the gentry and bureaucracy. In 1861, the tsar-emancipator had wisely granted the Russian people their physical freedom, "in spite of the wishes of the upper strata of society at that time." Now the hour had struck for "the emancipation of the spirit from the tutelage of the bureaucracy," and the threat was scarcely veiled. In the "wise words" of Alexander II, it would be in the interest of both the country and the throne "to give freedom from above . . ."[10]

Although the memorandum was printed anonymously, its authors clearly included some of the best-educated Moscow manufacturers, and it reportedly received loud applause from "more than two hundred" industrialists. Thus it may be considered largely representative of the mood of many manufacturers of Moscow and the Moscow region.[11] Several conclusions can be drawn from this document. First, the authors transcended the immediate problem of labor unrest and gave a comprehensive critique of "bureaucratic tutelage." Hardly a good word was said for the Witte system of industrial growth, which, despite its undeniable achievements, had constrained free enterprise by a myriad of regulations and which in spirit did not differ essentially from the hated *Zubatovshchina*. Second, the call for equality before the law and for a "peaceful struggle" over working conditions illustrated the industrialists' new confidence in their economic power. Precisely by endorsing the right to strike, the employers abandoned their age-old opposition to labor unions, declared their independence from the state in matters of internal factory management, and countered Kokovtsov's policy of unilateral economic concessions.[12]

Finally, however, the overall impression left by the memorandum was one of ideological confusion. The Slavophile references to an alleged Russian heritage of free speech and direct access to the loving tsar appeared most striking. Thirty-five years after the Moscow Duma had submitted Ivan Aksakov's address to Alexander II, the Moscow manufacturers had at last learned the rudiments of Slavophile liberalism. Indeed, in failing to specify the actual powers of a future national assembly, they reiterated the Duma's formula of November 30, 1904, and the "Slavophile" position of Shipov's zemstvo minority.[13] At the same time, the favorable allusions to West-European and American legal and economic practices (particularly the legalization of unions and peaceful strikes) demonstrated the manufacturers' new appreciation of modern capitalist and liberal principles, although the provocative word *constitution* was avoided. The demand for "a firm legal order" (*prochnyi pravovoi poriadok*) directly contravened the Slavophile idea of a benevolent tsar whose whim had the force of law, and invoked the essential feature of the *Rechtsstaat:* the government itself must obey the law.[14]

The ideological ambivalence implicit in this memorandum typified the Moscow manufacturers' political activities in the first half of 1905. Only in July would factional splits become firm. For example, the MSEC, which openly repudiated both the Duma's statement of January 13 (favoring the right to strike) and the manufacturers' memorandum of January 27,[15] sent a curious petition to the tsar on February 3. In addition to N. A. Naidenov, of whose reactionary views there could be no doubt, the seventy-six signatories included P. P. Riabushinsky, A. S. Vishniakov, and even the rebellious S. T. Morozov. A vaguely reformist suggestion that the tsar summon popular representatives on the basis of "their type of occupation" for "work in the field of state activity" (an innovation that would, of course, have given the MSEC an important consultative voice in legislation) was followed by a strongly proautocratic conclusion that echoed the spirit of the 1880s: "Casting at the feet of your imperial highness its sentiments of unlimited devotion, the commercial-industrial estate . . . expresses its unshakable conviction that only under the supreme leadership of the autocratic authority is it possible to preserve the power and security of Russia and her further prosperity." Nicholas found it "especially comforting" that the merchants remained "true to the age-old principles of our state system."[16]

This striving of the conservative Moscow manufacturers to limit the scope of any political change became especially apparent after February 18, when the emperor released three important statements. A ukase instructed the Council of Ministers to review all suggestions sent to the tsar from Russian citizens and organizations for improving the public services and well-being of the population. The emperor's rescript to A. G. Bulygin, the minister of internal affairs, ordered him to explore ways of including popularly elected representatives in a new "National Council" (*narodnyi sovet*) or "Popular Assembly" (*narodnoe sobranie*), which would play a new consultative and advisory role within the autocratic system. As if to deny that any real concessions were contemplated, however, the tsar's third document, a manifesto, called on "all true Russians," "everyone in his place and estate," to aid the government in fighting its enemies and upholding the principle of "true autocracy."[17] The extraordinarily patriotic reply of the Moscow Merchant Society praised the manifesto and ignored the promises of modest reform. "The Moscow merchants, devoted from time immemorial to the throne and the fatherland and true to the legacy of their native land," offered their "aid to the TSAR in conquering foreign and domestic enemies . . ." Indeed, the society subtly criticized the emperor's own weakness: "[we] firmly believe that the Lord will fulfill the wishes of his Anointed one and will send Him the strength and fortitude to lead our native land out of the difficulties that it is now experiencing."[18]

In accordance with its statement of two weeks before, the MSEC welcomed the rescript of February 18, but recommended severe restrictions on representation of less educated social groups. Because of "their general level of development and culture," it would be "far from appropriate to the tasks that will face the National Council" to include peasant and worker representatives.[19] Stressing the need for "the broad development of [Russia's] productive forces," the committee impatiently requested for itself "an active and direct part in the work of the future State Duma on economic problems."[20] For its part, the Moscow City Duma approved the rescript's promise of reform, but pointedly expressed the hope that the elected representatives would "participate in the exercise of legislative power," in order to create "firm law and order" (*prochnyi pravoporiadok*) in the country.[21] So strong was the mood of change within the Duma that by May most members, including the merchants, supported the constitutional movement. The old reactionaries – A. A. Naidenov, Kaznacheev, Professor Guerrier, and Vice-Mayor Lebedev – had formed an "opposition" of sorts, but it remained unorganized and "kept to the sidelines . . . They grumbled, looked askance, and objected in private conferences. But they did not come out into open battle." The conservatives' timidity apparently stemmed from several factors: the tsar himself had encouraged the expression of opinions; their group had become small by early 1905; and they were annoyed by the government's military defeats and by its indecisive political tactics.[22]

Another reason, however, appears to have outweighed all these: the unresolved differences with the tsarist bureaucracy over the labor problem. At both meetings of the short-lived Kokovtsov Commission (March 16 and May 16–18) the government's recommendation – immediate economic concessions to the workers in order to avoid major political reforms – angered both the "young group" and the conservatives, led by G. A. Krestovnikov.[23] There appeared to be two reasons for the industrialists' attitude of self-assurance in opposing Kokovtsov's policy: their successful organization of collective action to resist the strikers' economic demands, and their more ambitious (but less fruitful) attempt to create a national political party. As early as mid-February, the MSEC had created a special Commission on the Labor Question, chaired by S. I. Chetverikov, which met six times between February 14 and March 8. Its first action was to specify what kinds of labor violence must be punished: any presentation of demands by a crowd of workers; any threatened or actual violence against workers who refused to strike; and any destruction of factory property, including incidental damage resulting from a sudden stoppage of work. Then a detailed "convention" was drawn up for general adoption by the factory owners of the Moscow region. The main points left no doubt as to their determination to refuse economic concessions: no reduction in the length of the workday without a new law; no payments to workers for time spent on strike; no participation by workers in any managerial decisions, such as setting wage rates and firing workers; and no establishment of a minimum wage, abolition of fines, or regulation of overtime work. Ending on a liberal note, the convention endorsed the right of workers to create their own organization, just as the manufacturers had done, but its form was left undefined.[24]

While the employers' organization marked a break with tradition, an even greater innovation in the crisis of 1905 was the Russian manufacturers' attempt to create a national political party of their own. The debates brought into clear relief the political outlook of several leading figures of Russian industry, particularly the hesitancy of the majority to adopt a thoroughly liberal program. Just after the Moscow Labor Commission had been created, but six days before the Kokovtsov Commission was convened, a group of representatives from all the major industrial centers in the Russian Empire except Lodz assembled at the Moscow Stock Exchange. Savva T. Morozov presided. This meeting discussed not only the labor question but also the possibility of endorsing a clear political credo. V. I. Kovalevsky of the Ural mineowners argued in favor of the zemstvo-liberal program, stressing that without "basic reforms" the solution of "particular questions like the labor problem" would be impossible. Others, like Nobel (St. Petersburg) and Zhukovsky (Dombrovo, Poland) preferred to have a national bureau of manufacturers instead of a political party. The immediate task was to draft a comprehensive labor law to quell the workers' violence. I. I. Iasiukovich, a South Russian mineowner, exclaimed, "In the South there is panic, pillage, and arson. People are fleeing. Under such conditions it is impossible to talk of reforms; we must be given means of existence." A twelve-man commission was elected to draft the charter of a new industrialists' bureau, but the tactical disagreements between Kovalevsky and the southern, Polish, and most Muscovite manufacturers over the pace of political reform, coupled with the evident distrust of the MSEC toward a new and potentially more influential industrial organization, foredoomed this bureau to failure.[25]

At the same time, the March conference provided a forum for industrialists to comment on the nature of the new representative body that Bulygin was in the process of forming. Speaking for the Moscow conservatives, G. A. Krestovnikov outlined a plan that further refined the MSEC's statement of mid-February. The National Council should enjoy only consultative powers and should stay in session only for short periods. Rural representatives should be elected by the existing zemstvos (provinces where they did not exist would thus be denied a voice) and urban representatives by stock exchange committees and municipal dumas. Because of their "immaturity," no workers or peasants would be allowed to vote.[26] Krestovnikov's fear that Bulygin might draft an electoral law so democratic as to swamp the tiny "commercial-industrial estate" in a sea of rural representatives was shared by many leading Russian industrialists. In a special petition delivered to Bulygin on March 19 by the elected delegates of the March conference (S. T. Morozov of Moscow, E. Nobel of St. Petersburg, and N. Avdakov of the southern mineowners), they pleaded for adequate representation of all "the most important groups of the population" in the conference that would draft the final electoral law. Manufacturers should participate "in proportion to the great significance [of industry] in the life of Russia," particularly for the government's financial system, and toward this end the existing consultative organizations now permitted by law to issue opinions should be allowed to select spokesmen to advise Bulygin.[27]

Bulygin's failure to honor what Laverychev called his "half-promise" to summon representatives from existing commercial-industrial institutions caused the signatories of this petition great anxiety in the ensuing five months, before the plan for the creation of a State Duma and the reorganization of the State Council as an upper chamber (including twelve industrial representatives) was finally unveiled on August 6.[28] Even before mid-year, however, the misgivings of certain Moscow industrial leaders became clear. What was perhaps most interesting about the political views of two such men, S. I. Chetverikov and S. T. Morozov, was their willingness to lend their names to the blatantly undemocratic statements made by official organizations in February and March, while voicing at precisely the same time individual opinions of quite a different political complexion.

Chetverikov's letter in March to the editor of *Russkie vedomosti* constituted perhaps the only public statement of principle by an individual manufacturer in 1905. In it, we see not the carefully phrased formulas of a committee, but the personal views of a veteran zemstvo and stock exchange leader, or rather the generous side of one signatory of the statement of March 19. This letter showed both a willingness to accept the principle of worker and peasant representation in the future Duma or Council, and the persistence of the old "tsar and people" myth, which had given the semiliberal statement of January 27 its unique flavor.

Although narrower than the electoral plan of the Union of Liberation, Chetverikov's program went far beyond the rigid and negative stand of the MSEC. All social groups must be allowed to elect representatives to the State Duma, in limited numbers, "to ensure that that body could work efficiently." Furthermore, "strong links between voters and the elected representatives" must be maintained, so that the Duma would reflect the real concerns of the population. To this end, "consultative and electoral committees" should meet periodically in provincial capitals, in apparent imitation of the local caucuses of the Moscow Duma members and voters in late 1904. Each would be composed of 150 members from existing provincial and district institutions, including marshals of the gentry, zemstvo board presidents, city mayors, and selected zemstvo and duma members, together with elected representatives of the clergy, universities and schools, stock exchange committees, labor unions, and the peasantry (one delegate from each canton). Every three years, these bodies would elect their representatives according to a proportional system, so that the Popular Assembly would reflect the social composition of the local committees. In addition, bills before the assembly would be discussed locally at annual committee meetings. This system appeared complicated, "but at the same time the goal is so exalted that the people, who are thirsting for a renewal of life and find it absolutely impossible to reconcile themselves any longer to their present condition, must not fear the selfless labor which is needed to complete the great work of the liberation of the 'spirit' of the Russian people."

Chetverikov saved his strongest demand for the end of the letter. The new National Council must not be "a consultative organ, an appendage to the bureaucratic structure." Rather, its full participation must be "acknowledged as an indispensible condition of the implementation of [each] governmental bill and new law." However, he still was not ready to endorse the concept of a truly legislative Duma empowered to overrule the tsar, and carefully denied any wish to infringe "on the prerogatives of the supreme authority . . ."[29]

Chetverikov's moderate position, too cautious for the zemstvo constitutionalists, yet too daring for the stock exchange leaders, consigned him and the small group of like-minded Moscow industrialists to isolation and impotence. The one merchant who did go beyond the position elaborated by Chetverikov came to a tragic end in 1905. Savva T. Morozov had begun in 1901 to donate 2,000 rubles a month to Lenin's revolutionary periodical *Iskra* (*The Spark*) through an electrical engineer at his factory, Leonid Krasin. According to Maksim Gorky, who encouraged him in his radicalism, Morozov in 1903 spoke of Russia's need to overtake Europe through a "fatal leap" (*salto mortale*) into violent revolution. While he denied being a Slavophile or a Populist, he endorsed Nietzsche's idea that Europe was spiritually impoverished; Russia could "revivify Europe" only by destroying autocracy and releasing the energy of the masses. He also apparently felt guilty about the working conditions in his factories, especially since the old merchant tradition of philanthropy and benevolence had obviously proved inadequate to maintain a personal, humane relationship between employers and workers in the giant textile complexes. When at home in his lavish mansion, Morozov preferred to live modestly in the small rooms upstairs and was so "stingy" with himself that he often wore tattered boots in public. He once told Gorky, "I hate money! I love the people!" Like a repentant nobleman in a Russian novel, Morozov sought expiation, first in marrying a woman who had once tended spinning machines in his Nikolsk factory and later by carrying suitcases of socialist literature to his workers. In the summer of 1902, he heeded Chekhov's personal appeal to introduce the eight-hour day in his distillery and vinegar plant in the Urals.[30]

Morozov's many acts of benevolence to revolutionary activists in 1905 cost him the support of his business associates and even of his family. As punishment for sharing the profits of the Nikolsk factory with striking workers there, he was ousted from the board of directors in April by the factory's manager and major stockholder, his mother. When the Moscow police threatened to publicize his ties with the revolutionary underground, Morozov fled abroad, to Nice. There, plagued by the fear that he was losing his sanity, he ended his life with a pistol shot through the heart on May 13/26, 1905. His suicide scandalized the merchants because he had named as the beneficiary of his 100,000-ruble insurance policy not a relative but M. F. Andreeva (1872–1953), the Art Theater actress and mistress of Gorky. Upon winning the court battle with the Morozov family, she donated sixty thousand rubles to the Bolsheviks.[31]

Morozov's death did not signify an end to the activities of the so-called young group of Moscow businessmen. Within days of his suicide, the public received the most devastating news of the entire war: after sailing for seven months to the Far East, the Russian Baltic fleet had been destroyed by the Japanese navy in the Strait of Tsushima (May 14/27). Zemstvos, dumas, and newspapers all over Russia demanded the prompt negotiation of a peace and insisted that popular representatives be elected without delay to debate the terms of the settlement.[32] The plodding work of the Bulygin commission now appeared totally inappropriate in the eyes of the most dynamic political leader among the Moscow merchants. A. I. Guchkov had returned to Moscow from Manchuria in the spring of 1905. In the City Duma, ably assisted by his brother Nikolai (whose political views appear to have corresponded to his at every juncture), he pressed for political reforms of the kind advocated by Chetverikov and Riabushinsky at this time, that is, representation of all social groups in a State Duma with less than full legislative power. After attending the third Zemstvo Congress (Moscow, May 24–6), he met with Nicholas II and Empress Alexandra for two and a half hours on May 26. Guchkov urged the tsar to grant "a fundamental change in domestic policy" that would improve the army's morale, for "the *leitmotiv* of *his* opposition to the Romanov dynasty was always to be its failure to manage military affairs properly." The tsar promised to receive a delegation of zemstvo and city leaders on June 6, and Guchkov gathered the distinct impression that the tsar would heed his advice to convoke a *Zemskii sobor*. The next day, however, Guchkov was astounded to learn from former Mayor K. V. Rukavishnikov that Nicholas had decided instead "to conclude peace and to grant no reforms of any kind"![33] Ineptitude and unresponsiveness of this sort only strengthened the resolve of the liberally inclined manufacturers to seek an end to the tsarist system. However, if in the period from May to mid-October the idea of a limited constitutional monarchy grew more attractive to these men, it did not draw the Stock Exchange Committee away from its staunch defense of autocracy and of the interests of industry, narrowly conceived. The Russian government would ultimately profit from this political division within the Moscow bourgeoisie.

Stalemate between liberalism and reaction, May to mid-October

By midsummer, the constitutionalist position of the Moscow merchant minority had brought it into direct conflict with the conservative majority. The battle raged at several national meetings, including a conference of industrialists in early July and the Zemstvo-City Congresses in July, September, and October. Especially bitter were the debates in the Moscow Duma and the MSEC, as the strike wave grew in intensity and finally, in mid-October, engulfed the entire Russian economy.

In early July (4–6), the MSEC held a national conference of fifty-two representatives from twenty-three commercial-industrial organizations to draw up a clear economic and political program, including a demand for an important role for business leaders in the State Duma. The prospects for success were not bright, however. In the preceding month, Bulygin had discussed an electoral plan that would have given manufacturers "almost no hope of entering the State Duma," and had shown no interest in the industrialists' proposal to elect their own special delegates to the Duma "directly" from existing commercial-industrial organizations.[34] Moreover, although Naidenov's offical agenda specified that political discussions must deal only with the nature of a consultative Duma, several St. Petersburg manufacturers (Glezmer, Nobel, and Norpe), as well as the MSEC minority, favored broader changes.[35] In defiance of the agenda, the presiding officer, the Ural mineowner V. I. Kovalevsky, promptly raised the question of a legislative Duma. Incensed, Naidenov denounced the meeting to the governor-general, demanded that it be closed by the police, and set out for St. Petersburg to report the dreadful news to Kokovtsov in person. On the second day, however, Kovalevsky's motion won the support of everyone present, except the remaining representatives of the MSEC (G. A. Krestovnikov, N. I. Prokhorov, I. A. Baranov, and A. L. Losev). Abstaining or absent were those of five small organizations that also opposed it (from Elets, Kazan, Kostroma, and Ivanovo-Voznesensk, plus the Moscow Meat Exchange). Spokesmen for the other seventeen organizations approved the resolution before the police arrived and dispersed the meeting.

That evening, the representatives of the twenty-three organizations reassembled at the spacious home of P. P. Riabushinsky. The MSEC was now represented by a number of men excluded from the meetings of July 4 and 5 because of their penchant for reforms, among them Riabushinsky's brothers Nikolai and Dmitri, N. D. Morozov, and A. S. Vishniakov. After long discussions on July 5 and 6, the group endorsed a liberal political program: a two-chamber legislature; an upper house to be elected by existing institutions; for the lower house, equal but indirect suffrage in two stages (only three organizations favored direct elections) and universal male suffrage (women to be excluded because of peasant resistance to female equality). Also approved were "equality of all before the law; freedom of speech, conscience, press, assembly, and association; and inviolability of person and domicile . . ." A bureau of twenty-four men, headed by M. F. Norpe of the St. Petersburg iron producers and including P. P. Riabushinsky, A. I. Konovalov, J. P. Goujon, S. I. Chetverikov, A. S. Vishniakov, and N. N. Shchepkin of Moscow, was elected to organize an "All-Russian Congress of Industry and Trade," to be held within a month. This congress would draft a charter for the new organization, set up central and local offices, establish newspapers to "disseminate a correct view toward industry and trade," and prepare for the first time an explicit "economic program of Russian industry." Finally, the meeting took an enlightened stand on the labor question. In addition to the freedom of workers to form unions, bargain over wages, and participate in nonviolent meetings and strikes, it supported government regulation of female and child labor, and of health and safety conditions in factories; a national system of workers' insurance; and mediation of labor disputes by boards composed of both employers' and workers' representatives.[36]

The July meeting did little to strengthen the Russian liberal movement, however. First, Kovalevsky demanded political reforms only in order to rescue industry from "a desperate and utterly precarious position"; he rejected Bulygin's plan of a consultative Duma with restricted suffrage only because it could not "calm the existing disorders" among the disenfranchised peasants and workers.[37] Second, although the resolutions coincided with those of the Zemstvo Congress of May, the first national Zemstvo-City Congress (then meeting in Moscow, July 6–9) refused to receive a delegation from the manufacturers' bureau. The gentry and professional men feared that an open alliance with the industrialists might discredit liberalism in the eyes of the peasants and workers.[38] For its part, the bureau rejected as excessively liberal important aspects of the Zemstvo-City Congresses' political and social programs: direct elections to the State Duma; the expropriation of private lands and the establishment of independent farms (*khutory*) on state properties; the eight-hour workday and other economic norms; and freer international trade.[39] Finally, the bureau members found themselves isolated not only from the political center but also from their fellow industrialists on the right. Representatives of the three organizations that withdrew from the Moscow meeting on July 6 (the Moscow and Elets Stock Exchange Societies and the Ivanovo-Voznesensk Committee of Trade and Manufacturing) affirmed angrily that "a basic difference in views and convictions about fundamental questions of the future political system of Russia" now separated the minority from the majority. Naidenov and his followers in the MSEC, who had again endorsed the principle of "autocratic power" in a letter to Kokovtsov in mid-June, prevailed upon the bureaucracy to prevent the National Industrial Congress from meeting.[40]

The tension reached its height in late July. Exasperated by Naidenov's unwavering support of autocracy, "up to thirty" MSES members met at Ivan A. Morozov's apartment sometime between July 20 and 26 to chart a new strategy "in case the future State Duma were to be only consultative, and not legislative, in character." S. I. Chetverikov suggested an unprecedented plan of action: to apply economic pressures against the state. All commercial and industrial leaders should refuse to participate in the Duma; "all possible opposition" should be mounted against the new loans issued by the beleaguered government; manufacturers should refuse to pay the recently increased tax on industry; and, perhaps most ominously, "all factories and plants should be closed in order to create a mass labor movement." These ideas proved too strong for some young liberals, however. P. P. Riabushinsky and A. S. Vishniakov considered the refusal of the state loan as a weapon of last resort; it could be employed successfully only with the support of a "broad union" of Russian industrialists at a national congress. The proposal to close all factories also aroused heated objection. Even Chetverikov's idea of boycotting a consultative Duma was rejected, the majority arguing that a conservative stranglehold on the Duma could be averted only by the election of liberals committed to its legislative function. It was finally agreed to arrange a national commercial-industrial congress; to put Chetverikov's plan of action on the agenda; and to urge all industrialists "to organize a mass labor movement in protest against the government's arbitrariness."[41]

These men then published in *Russkie vedomosti* a letter that they circulated to all stock exchange committees in an attempt to muster support for a legislative Duma. Yet even in this constitutionalist statement, "the highwater mark of business 'radicalism' in 1905,"[42] the authors' reliance on the Slavophile rhetoric of the past betrayed their political weakness and immaturity. "We love our native land no less sincerely than do our opponents; we are no less ready than they are to stand in defense of our tsar. But we, like the majority of the Russian people, now affirm that autocracy in Rus' should not be identified with *the right of the tsar's servitors, in their actions, to disregard the opinions and desires of the people* . . . No renaissance, moral or material, is conceivable without the conviction that the experience and wisdom of the people will in fact stand guard over the interests of the native land." The fifteen delegates of the MSES who signed the letter were seconded by twenty-four other merchants three days later[43] (see Appendix, Table II).

The tsar, his advisors, and most Russian manufacturers were not impressed. As long as the Naidenov-Krestovnikov faction continued to control the MSEC, "the most important representative institution in the country would remain hostile to the idea of unity around a liberal political program."[44] Indeed, Bulygin's announcement on August 6 of a consultative Duma to be elected by unequal and indirect suffrage like the zemstvos caused rejoicing among industrial leaders all over Russia.[45] Like the city dumas of St. Petersburg and Kiev, the stock exchanges in Moscow, Nizhny Novgorod, Rybinsk, Saratov, Astrakhan, and elsewhere greeted the new Duma with expressions of loyalty and devotion. The South Russian mineowners, in *Gorno-zavodskii listok (Mining Leaflet)*, criticized only the fact that the commercial-industrial representatives received "third-rate" status in comparison to those of the gentry. Completely ineffectual were the condemnations voiced by ten city dumas (among them Moscow's), the Samara Stock Exchange Committee's demand for a legislative Duma, and a petition by the MSEC minority urging that "the working estate" (*rabochee soslovie*) be allowed to vote.[46] During the Nizhny Novgorod Fair in late August, P. P. Riabushinsky and other members of the MSEC minority met on a Volga steamer and decided not only to campaign against Naidenov's candidates in the Duma elections but also to elect a new MSEC president in 1906. Plans for a mass newspaper with a progressive orientation, to be called *Narodnyi trud* (*The People's Labor*), were also discussed by the industrialists' bureau, elected in July.[47] All these projects failed, however, owing to the numerical weakness of the reform-minded industrialists. In particular, the national meeting of constitutionalist manufacturers, which Chetverikov had advocated as a means of blocking the Bulygin Duma, simply never materialized.

In September and early October, the political conservatism of the Moscow merchants hindered the efforts of Russian liberals to solve two new issues of crucial importance: the nationality question and the problem of increased labor violence. At the Zemstvo-City Congress of September 12 – 15 in Moscow, attended by 126 zemstvo men and 68 municipal leaders, A. I. Guchkov caused "a great deal of confusion" in the already "extremely difficult situation." Like the "young group" in the MSES, Guchkov found himself politically isolated from both the tsarist bureaucrats and the liberals, but unlike them he felt less exasperated with the tsar than four months before and now directed his anger against the forces of change. Not only did Guchkov lead a sizable minority (37 votes) of mainly urban representatives in opposing the liberals' familiar call for universal suffrage; by demanding a roll-call vote on the question of autonomy for Poland and other minority nationalities he precipitated a "clear schism" (*iavnyi raskol*) in the constitutionalist movement. Mayors Nemirovsky (Saratov) and Memorsky (Nizhny Novgorod) supported Guchkov's uncompromising rhetoric, which echoed the implacable hatred of Katkov, the Slavophiles, and the chauvinist merchants against the rebellious Poles in 1863. "If we disagree on this single question, we are political enemies; if we agree, we are allies." *Gorno-zavodskii listok*, in a scathing attack on the zemstvo-city liberals, declared common action impossible.[48]

The angry mood of the workers in Moscow also drove the manufacturers back into increased dependence on the state's repressive power. On September 21, the MSEC implored the governor-general to retain in Moscow the Cossack detachments that "democratic circles" wished to have removed. The committee saw these mounted soldiers not as a vicious oppressive force, but as the only available protection for banks, factories, and other private property.[49] The situation reached a critical state in mid-October. The Black Hundreds roamed the streets attacking Jews, liberals, and students, while 1,500 radical students and workers held demonstrations at the university and technical school, built barricades, and gathered guns. Although the Duma stayed in session day and night, it could reach no solution because of a serious tactical split between Muromtsev's liberal group and the advocates of order, now led by A. I. Guchkov. Alone among the merchants, M. V. Chelnokov argued that demands for an end to the strike would fan the flames of popular anger. Guchkov's impassioned oratory proved more persuasive: "The population is only punishing itself by political strikes . . . We are committing not only a political error but also a grave crime."[50] By the dim light of the kerosene lamps (electricity had been shut off by striking municipal workers), a futile debate raged over resolutions to condemn the Black Hundreds and establish a militia to restore order. When angry radicals streamed into the main hall on October 15 demanding total power, Mayor Golitsyn and Vice-Mayor Lebedev announced in despair their intention to resign.[51]

Confusion reigned in the MSEC as well. On October 14, Naidenov's majority passed a resolution calling on Governor-General Durnovo to introduce martial law without granting any reforms at all. S. I. Chetverikov objected in vain that "it would be we ourselves who would seem to be guilty for the massacres that might occur . . ." He then led seventeen stock exchange members to Durnovo with an emotional petition for restraint on the part of the tsar.[52] The violence of the " 'social-revolutionary party' must be counteracted with violence, and military measures should be applied with all severity," especially to restore public services. At the same time, however, "both the personality and the property of citizens must be defended," and pacification must be based on the granting of legislative power to the Duma, abolition of the property qualification for voting, and extension of the franchise to "the entire class of the factory population."[53]

Durnovo's nonchalant response dumbfounded the manufacturers. "How impatient you are! Especially you, the merchants, who live for your tsar, as in the bosom of Christ [*kak u Khrista za pazukhoi*], what kind of freedom are you petitioning for? The tsar knows without us what he must do for the well-being of his people."[54] In desperation, Chetverikov's Labor Commission sought on October 17 to reopen the municipal gas and electricity plants by using strikebreakers from the provinces. The restoration of these services would create a "schism" among the workers and impel the majority to return to their jobs. As G. A. Krestovnikov noted with disgust, the liberal Union of Unions planned to continue the general strike until the convocation of a Constituent Assembly, "but it would be necessary to wait about six months for that." Chetverikov believed that the "light and water will be more calming than an atttack and offensive," but the mood of some verged on hysteria. V. P. Riabushinsky, for one, hotly defended the policemen who had recently opened fire on a crowd of peaceful strikers.[55]

In the hope of forcing political concessions from the government, several Russian manufacturers encouraged the October general strike by closing their factories and paying their workers for time spent in the streets and at Soviet meetings.[56] This practice was quite rare in Moscow, however. We can only speculate about the political reforms that Witte and the tsar would have granted had the forty-seven signers of the February memorandum simultaneously discharged their 125,000 workers in mid-October. As it was, Chetverikov's plan for a mass lockout had been tabled even by the liberally inclined minority in late July; and now the Labor Commission strove not to intensify the general strike but to put an end to it as quickly as possible. Factories and banks in Moscow closed only when workers went on strike, or when mobs of outsiders arrived threatening violence unless work was halted.[57] Large numbers of workers were paid during the strike, but only because, as Chetverikov noted on October 17, the law required the payment of up to a week's wages whenever a factory shut down on account of unavoidable circumstances.[58] Far from supporting the general strike, the Moscow industrialists of both conservative and reformist convictions did their utmost to end it, even before the October Manifesto appeared.

The Imperial Manifesto and demands for order,
October to November

Witte's Manifesto, signed under duress by Nicholas II on October 17/30, 1905, succeeded in its political purpose: to destroy the united opposition of liberals and radicals by promising a new order based on full civil freedoms (of speech, press, religion, assembly, association, and personal inviolability), universal suffrage, and a Duma with the power to approve or reject legislation and to supervise the bureaucracy. Although the word "constitution" was avoided, the tsar's program satisfied in almost all respects the substantive demands made by the Zemstvo and City Congresses during the previous twelve months. The radicals, who demanded even greater changes (an end to the monarchy, the eight-hour day, and the seizure of state and landlord properties by the peasants), were now isolated, prey to the brutally effective repression of the armed forces in ensuing months.

Already eager for the establishment of order before October 17, the

Moscow manufacturers, liberal and conservative, threw all their political influence to the cause of the new principle of constitutional monarchy. Although their various parties reflected the ideological diversity characteristic of the previous ten months, Witte's program created a common ground on which the most liberal industrialists joined all but the most reactionary. In the crucial period from mid-October to mid-December, both the liberal and conservative Moscow manufacturers helped to destroy the momentum of the revolution by supporting the tsar's shaken power and by stubbornly resisting labor radicalism.

When the news of the Manifesto arrived by telephone at the darkened Duma building, the municipal leaders cheered and embraced each other; "the old men had tears in their eyes." A triumphal banquet at the Merchant Club, attended by "everyone," was marked by "drunkenness from both joy and wine."[59]

The next day, however, a heated debate in the Duma revealed the damaging effect of the Manifesto on the opposition movement. After a religious service in honor of the great event, S. A. Muromtsev read his draft of a telegram to the tsar: a memorial should be erected "to those who gave their lives for the cause of Russian liberation"; full amnesty should be granted to all political and religious prisoners, together with the cessation of the states of emergency; and a special fund should be established to aid the families of workers deprived of wages during the strike. Although this motion carried by a wide margin (62 to 24) and was supported by several influential merchants (A. E. Armand, M. V. Chelnokov, S. I. Liamin, A. V. Buryshkin, P. D. Botkin, A. A. Bakhrushin, and S. N. Mamontov), its effect proved short-lived. A. I. Guchkov promptly introduced for the Duma's approval a telegram to the tsar which implied that no further political reforms were desired.

The Moscow City Duma, having heard with a feeling of profound satisfaction the Manifesto of October 17, 1905, which grants to the entire population of Russia, regardless of religion or nationality, the rights of civil and political freedom, a firm system of law and order on unshakable foundations, and active participation in the construction and administration of the state, regards this great document as the guarantee of the greatest free development and complete renewal of the entire life of the nation, and conveys sentiments of gratitude to its monarch, in the name of the henceforth free population of the city of Moscow.

Guchkov's version passed by a vote of 66 to 18. The fragile consensus created by the Duma liberals – Astrov, Shchepkin, and Muromtsev – ended in a "definite schism" when the liberals' proposal for a militia to control the Black-Hundred mobs was soundly defeated by Guchkov's new conservative majority.[60]

The "progressive group" had shrunk to such a small minority that when Mayor Golitsyn resigned in mid-November the liberals made no attempt to put forward a candidate. Most members agreed that one of the Guchkov brothers should replace Golitsyn. As Aleksandr preferred to act as the spokesman for Moscow in the State Duma, Nikolai easily won election, by a vote of 101 to 21, and remained mayor until January 1913. The new mood was stern and vindictive. All municipal employees who had gone on strike in October were summarily fired. When Astrov asked his close friend Konstantin I. Guchkov to support an appeal to the throne to spare the lives of mutineers awaiting execution in Sevastopol, the latter exclaimed: "What are you saying! How can that be considered! They must all be hanged. No! Now all those little jokes will be stopped. There will be no more sentimentality!" Indeed, when the question came to a vote on November 29, Mayor Nikolai Guchkov defeated the motion for clemency by breaking a 37–37 tie, whereupon the Duma passed another resolution, by Aleksandr Guchkov, strongly denouncing the mutiny in Sevastopol.[61]

General satisfaction with the promise of constitutional reform also characterized the joyful celebration at the stock exchange on October 18. After a solemn church service, S. I. Chetverikov leaped on a bench and cried, "Citizens! Allow me to initiate the use of the [newly] granted freedom of speech . . ." "Glory to the tsar" for placing "the welfare of the people" higher than his own prerogatives; "glory to the great citizen Witte" for his role in promulgating the Manifesto; and "glory to the people, who desired to love their tsar not out of fear, but according to their conscience!"[62] The MSES's telegram of October 19 proclaimed the unity of feeling. "Most gracious tsar! At the dawn of a new life for Russia, the assembled delegates of the Moscow Stock Exchange, filled with a sense of joy and gratitude, unanimously affirm that the commercial-industrial estate of Moscow is just as devoted to you, O tsar, as in the past, and is just as ready to serve the interests of the free native land on the [basis of the] new principles that you have granted."[63]

One wonders whether Naidenov and the other reactionary merchants resented the government's promise to implement a constitutional regime. If so, they expressed their disappointment only indirectly. In a statement of loyalty sent in mid-November, the MSES subtly criticized the new freedoms, which allowed the radical parties to enflame the masses. Alarmed by the revolt at the Kronstadt naval base, unrest in Poland, and new strikes, it advised Witte "to take heart and carry through to the end" in preparing the new State Duma, despite the "cries and demands of the extreme parties [and] all those tiny groups that cause turmoil and stop the life of the country . . . " The "great multitude" of Russians believed in Witte and "the system of freedom that the tsar has granted to them."[64]

The manufacturers' happiness owed much to the creation of a new Ministry of Trade and Industry on October 26. Witte's bill, signed promptly by Nicholas without any discussion by the Council of Ministers or the State Council, removed from the Ministry of Finance the supervision of commerce and industry and of various consultative bodies, and took from the Ministry of Internal Affairs control over merchant and handicraft matters. The new ministry's jurisdiction included trade, industry, factory inspection, mining, railroads, and maritime commerce.[65] It was as if the merchants' loyalty to the government had finally been rewarded at a crucial moment, over forty years after they had first petitioned for a Ministry of Trade and Industry to replace the Ministry of Finance as their patron.

On the national scale as well as in Moscow, a serious political rift occurred immediately. The liberal zemstvo and professional leadership (organized in mid-October as the Constitutional-Democratic, or Kadet, Party) encountered the firm opposition of the more conservative gentry and business groups. Although the last Zemstvo-City Congress, held November 6–13 in Moscow, passed Kadet proposals for Polish autonomy (St. Petersburg would control only military, diplomatic, and budgetary affairs) and for the power of the State Duma to write a new constitution, a determined minority among the delegates refused to endorse further reforms such as a Constituent Assembly. A. I. and N. I. Guchkov, Count P. A. Heiden, D. N. Shipov, and M. A. Stakhovich openly denounced these two resolutions. Perhaps the most impassioned speech at the congress was given by A. I. Guchkov against Polish autonomy. Defending the government's imposition of martial law in Poland, he intoned, "Only the unity of Russia constitutes its power"; it was a matter of "instinct, feeling, and faith." P. B. Struve argued in vain: "It is autonomy which will give Poland order. Why, then, do you, a man of order, a Guchkov of Moscow and Russia, disarm the Guchkovs of Poland?" Guchkov's fervor did not submit to such logic, however. On November 12 he prophesied darkly that excessively liberal policies would bring disaster. "The people, who are tired of this chaos and are completely ravaged, will welcome every Cossack whip . . . With our own hands we are piling brushwood on the bonfire that will consume us all."[66]

Within days of the October Manifesto's promulgation, the Moscow manufacturers undertook serious political activity outside the Duma, the MSES, and the Zemstvo-City Congress. Safe at last from reprisals from the governor-general, they began to speak frankly about all manner of current issues, and between October and December they formulated several distinct political programs. If the tragedy of the Russian bourgeoisie between 1905 and 1917 lay in its political immaturity in dealing with the tsarist government and in the fatal division between a strong conservative tendency and a weak liberal one, the pattern of eventual disaster was clear at the very beginning of the new era.

Like the industrialists of St. Petersburg,[67] those in the Central Region elaborated such precise concepts of an ideal political order that several parties, not one, emerged. The Moderate-Progressive Party *(umerenno-progressivnaia partiia)* presented the most liberal program. Led by P. P. Riabushinsky, A. I. Konovalov, the wine trader V. I. Gornung, and other members of the MSEC "young group," this party stood squarely with the Kadets in supporting liberal reforms: four-way suffrage in local and national elections, ministerial responsibility to the State Duma, legislative power for the Duma, and the expropriation of state, crown, church, and private land (with state indemnification) for the peasants' use. Rejecting key tenets of the merchant ideology of the past half-century, the Moderate Progressives endorsed equality before the law regardless of sex, religion, or nationality; freedom of speech, assembly, press, association, unions, and petitions; inviolability of the person and the domicile; prosecution of officials who flouted these principles; abolition of special courts and land captains; an independent judiciary elected without property qualification; and decentralized universal public education.[68] Even the economic platform offered enlightened reforms based on modern capitalist principles: abolition of peasants' redemption payments; a direct progressive income tax; somewhat lower tariffs and reduced excise taxes on mass-consumption goods such as tea and sugar; freedom of nonviolent union activity and strikes; an independent factory inspectorate and mediation service; strict laws on female, child, night, and overtime work; health and accident insurance, to be paid for by the manufacturers; and state-funded old-age and disability insurance.[69]

All the more significant, therefore, were the issues that set these liberal Moscow businessmen apart from the Kadets: nationalism and labor legislation. The Russian state must remain "united, whole, and indivisible"; autonomy for minority peoples was inadmissible; and Russian must remain the official governmental language. Likewise, the eight-hour day, advocated by the Kadets, must be rejected "in view of the world competition and the excessive number of holidays in Russia . . . " The party welcomed a national limit on the length of the workday, provided the total hours worked in Russia would equal those in the most advanced European country in a given year,[70] but this unprecedented gesture of compromise failed to bridge the chasm between it and the Kadets. (The strongly anti-protectionist stance of the liberals also undermined any possible political accommodation. P. B. Struve, who as a Marxist had formerly advocated high tariffs to encourage industry, by 1905 supported freer trade as a means of reducing consumer prices.) As P. N. Miliukov had declared at the founding congress of the Kadet Party: "Our party will never stand in defense of [landlords' and industrialists'] interests!"[71] Thus traditional merchant nationalism, the manufacturers' irreducible economic needs, and the Kadets' striving to remain "above class" prevented the formation of a strong left-center coalition of Kadets and liberally inclined Moscow manufacturers in the fall of 1905.

The Moderate Progressives appeared far too liberal, however, for the majority of Moscow manufacturers. Led by G. A. Krestovnikov, the conservatives created their own organization, the Commercial-Industrial Party *(Torgovo-promyshlennaia partiia)*. While it pledged to support the October Manifesto and the "creative activity of the State Duma" in implementing broad reforms (universal primary education, local self-government, equal suffrage in the Zemstvo, equality before the law, free exit of peasants from the commune, and a graduated income tax), its primary concern was political stability. This party not only stood firmly for the unity of Russia, but called for the "regulation" (rather than the full implementation!) of the civil liberties promised in the October Manifesto. Its program explicitly denounced radical demands for a federal state structure, a Constituent Assembly, and massive transfers of land to the peasants.[72]

The party's detailed economic program reflected a clear class bias. The need for labor legislation on the European model was admitted: peaceful union activity, including strikes, and state-funded worker insurance against accidents, illness, disability, and old age. On the other hand, bosses and workers must be left free to negotiate the terms of employment; in effect, the labor laws enacted between 1882 and 1903 should be rescinded. In particular, the eight-hour day, which existed nowhere in the world, could not be accepted, for it would cause Russian industry to be ruined by European competition.[73] As for the tariff, no change could be contemplated in the foreseeable future. Raising import duties would merely prompt German retaliation against Russian wheat exports and would reduce the purchasing power of both peasants and workers, while lowering them would cause unemployment and would benefit only European manufacturers. The ultimate solution to Russia's backwardness lay in a program of industrial expansion that would eventually reduce consumer prices and would also guarantee the Russian army adequate supplies of cannons, weapons, powder, shoes, and heavy cloth. Kokorev's polemics resounded loudly in 1905: "No, it is essential that we produce everything at home . . ."[74]

Far more vociferous in its calls for political order than the Moderate Progressives, Krestovnikov's party declared open war on the radicals: "all vital questions of the state and nation must be decided in the State Duma [free from] turmoil, rebellions, murders, and strikes . . ." Above all, the party demanded "strong governmental power, without which calm is unthinkable . . ." The political significance of these statements lay in the fact that the Commercial-Industrial Party, "the most conservative of the business political groupings" in Russia at this time, clearly represented the views of most leading Moscow manufacturers (see Appendix, Table II).[75]

By far the most successful party to the right of the Kadets was the Union *(Soiuz)* of October 17, commonly called the Octobrist Party, although its founders, devoted to the "tsar-and-people" myth, tried to avoid the appearance of partisanship. While it was never considered to be a strictly merchant party,[76] both its leadership and its political program were congenial to the majority of the Moscow manufacturers. They sincerely admired and respected D. N. Shipov, the grand old man of the zemstvo movement, whose opposition to a legislative Duma had set him apart from the liberal Union of Liberation. Like Ivan Aksakov and Fedor Chizhov a half-century before, Shipov always upheld the ideal of a benevolent tsar while tirelessly attacking the oppressive imperial bureaucracy. Despite the great contrast between Shipov's "dreaminess" and the industrialists' "sturdy realism, . . . great common sense, and genuine businesslike efficiency,"[77] Shipov's political outlook strongly appealed to them after October 1905.

The other Octobrist leader, A. I. Guchkov of the eminent Moscow merchant family, spoke boldly for the conservatives in the City Duma in the fall of 1905, and, while not a member of the MSES, for the majority of manufacturers. Although he once declared, "I never shared the views of the old Slavophiles" with regard to Russia's cultural uniqueness, he reiterated many of the traditional Slavophile ideals, as when he urged Nicholas II in May 1905 to call a *Zemskii sobor*. Representing Octobrism as "an act of faith in the Sovereign," he urged the monarchy to reform itself, but also remained a true "Moscow bourgeois," "a rabid Great Russian nationalist and a dyed-in-the-wool monarchist. In Guchkov his class had a formidable protagonist prepared to go to any lengths to ensure the glory of Russia and the stability of her monarchy." Guchkov particularly admired Prime Minister P. A. Stolypin (1906–11) for his "civic fortitude" (*grazhdanskoe muzhestvo*) – the ability to uphold state power through decisive action, including the bloody repression of unruly workers and peasants.[78]

Accordingly, the Octobrist political agenda emphasized stability and national unity (allowing limited autonomy only for Finland). Denouncing "both stagnation and revolutionary shocks," the party called for "peaceful reforms" under the direction of the tsar, who "in unity with the people . . . receives new power and a new, exalted task: to be the supreme leader of a free people." Peasants must be granted full civil rights, efficient farmsteads should replace the commune, and state and crown properties should be given to landless peasants, but private lands must be expropriated for the peasants' use only in extreme cases of "state need." Various forms of labor legislation were advocated, including the legalization of unions, but in the "economic struggle" violence must be outlawed, and strikes must be banned in enterprises serving public health or the national security. The Octobrists' endorsement of municipal and zemstvo reforms, universal primary education, and a progressive income tax closely paralleled those of Krestovnikov's and Riabushinsky's parties.[79] In fact, in late November the tiny business parties formed with the Octobrists a United Committee, which addressed a common appeal to the voters. The signers included not only Shipov and the Guchkov brothers but also G. A. Krestovnikov, S. I. Chetverikov, and P. P. Riabushinsky. The latter admonished the peasants in folksy language not to seize the landlords' property.[80]

While there can be no doubt of the rightward evolution of the Moscow business leaders after October, even Guchkov and Krestovnikov welcomed the civil liberties contained in the Manifesto. From 1905 onward the educated Moscow manufacturers remained politically distinct from the Black Hundreds and other proponents of the old system of social estates, unlimited autocratic power, and anti-Semitism.[81] Moreover, the Octobrists, in their talks with Prime Minister Witte within weeks of the Manifesto's publication, refused to accept any ministerial posts if the notorious reactionary P. N. Durnovo were appointed minister of internal affairs.[82] Confident of their economic power and intent upon defending their clearly conceived interests, they refused to be treated as pawns of the prime minister.

At the same time, the government's promise of modest reforms dampened the oppositional feelings within the Moscow industrial leadership in the last three months of 1905. The ominous specter of labor violence had the same effect. Radical socialists urged factory workers to fight for the eight-hour day, the abolition of the monarchy, and the convening of a Constituent Assembly elected by four-way suffrage. The unruly workers' councils or soviets, which sprang up in major Russian cities, made preparations for a general strike and an armed uprising. By November, the Moscow Soviet of Workers' Deputies contained 204 representatives from 134 factories employing 100,000 workers.[83] Out of the grim class struggle of 1905, the Moscow manufacturers developed several strategies to deal with labor unrest. The first reflex was to appeal directly to the government for the reimposition of law and order. On November 11, for example, the MSEC called on the Moscow governor-general to send armed units to quell a strike in the Lefortovo area of the city.[84] By December 2, the Ministry of Finance had issued new antistrike regulations that imposed a prison term of up to sixteen months for participating in a violent strike and even longer sentences for plotting one.[85] Although the manufacturers had earlier demanded the legalization of all peaceful strikes, both economic and political, the ministry's prohibition of all political strikes "perhaps met the desires of the industrialists" in early December.[86]

The MSEC's Labor Commission, chaired by Chetverikov, specifically condemned strikes by public employees. On this issue, P. P. Riabushinsky and his followers "were of one mind with Naidenov's hard line majority." On November 23, a special commission of the MSEC, headed by Goujon, branded the strike by postal and telegraph workers "a criminal undertaking" that "must be sternly prosecuted by law."[87]

Moreover, the Moscow manufacturers created new organizations to coordinate their antistrike campaign. The MSEC's Labor Commission became a manufacturers' union, also headed by Chetverikov. By November 16, its retaliatory lockout embraced twenty-six enterprises employing 58,634 workers. In the ensuing months various employers' unions in Russia, including the "Central Society of Manufacturers (composed of factory owners in that region),[88] would coordinate lockouts, refuse wage increases and reductions of the length of the workday, and maintain a common strike fund.[89] Chetverikov boldly announced that the new organizations,

by creating a certain support for [the manufacturers] in their struggle with the labor movement, would establish a certain discipline in implementing various measures. I use the word "struggle" and believe that there is nothing to fear in doing so. The old foundations are crumbling, and many prerogatives of capital are turning out to be extremely unstable; a struggle, in the sense of a test of each other's forces, is absolutely inevitable . . . As long as they do not meet the necessary resistance, the workers will find it hard to understand the possible limits to their demands.

Mediation committees composed of employers' and workers' representatives could "settle disputes" and "avert strikes," but it was "absolutely essential that both sides equally acknowledge the strength of the opposition."[90]

Chetverikov's blunt statement demonstrated the manufacturers' refusal to accept what they regarded as ruinous changes: substantial wage increases and the introduction of the eight-hour day. After they had welcomed the October Manifesto, the Moscow industrialists could not return to their old role as supplicants of tsarist political and economic tutelage. However, the violence with which the workers pressed their demands would soon place a firm limit on the factory owners' political estrangement from the government.

The popular uprising and the conservative resurgence, December

The strikes and mass violence in Moscow during December 1905 provoked not only governmental reprisals but also a crucial political shift among the business leaders. The Moscow Duma and the various commercial-industrial organizations now called on the tsarist government to end the popular disturbances by indiscriminate massacres. Furthermore, in order to wage the difficult struggle with the workers, the manufacturers strengthened the employers' unions and joined a new organization to coordinate national economic policy – the Association of Industry and Trade (AIT).

Serious labor disturbances broke out in many factories in the Moscow region in early December, and the Moscow Soviet began a general strike at noon on December 7. Perhaps the worst violence occurred in the Presnia quarter (christened "Red Presnensk" by the Bolsheviks in honor of the bloody fighting in 1905), where the huge Trimount factory employed several thousands of workers. By December 10, Presnia was cluttered with barricades from which armed workers exchanged rifle fire with Cossack detachments the next day. Fresh troops arrived shortly from St. Petersburg to lay siege to the area, and by December 16, when the workers' uprising had been quelled elsewhere in the city, the stage was set for the final assault. During the afternoon of December 17, a full-scale artillery barrage set the Schmidt furniture factory ablaze and caused the chemical tanks of the Mamontov paint and varnish plant to burn brightly for several days and nights thereafter. Water from the sprinkler system in the Trimount factory prevented fire, but damaged the machinery. Although about two hundred armed workers offered resistance, their rifles proved ineffective against the artillery bombardment that demolished the workers' dwellings. People who ran into the street to escape the flames were shot by the soldiers. After a white flag appeared over the Trimount factory kitchen, army troops moved in and summarily executed members of the workers' militia. A British eyewitness commented, "It was about as leisurely and safe a piece of slaughter as was ever seen."[91]

The government's repression also included unprovoked floggings and executions of both male and female students and the shooting of doctors tending the injured. The heavy hand of arbitrary authority was felt even by Chetverikov, who had averted an armed uprising of the workers at his woolens factory in Gorodishche by threatening to resign as director unless all the guns recently distributed were turned in to the office. Yet after a young radical spirited the weapons off to Moscow, Governor-General Dubasov summoned Chetverikov and accused him, "in a sharp and even nasty manner," of complicity in the popular uprising. On his way back to the factory, Chetverikov was accosted by three Cossacks, one of whom cut his cheek with a whip. "I look upon him as the blind tool of the arbitrariness which now reigns in Rus', an arbitrariness that is unthinkable in any cultured country."[92]

Although the government's brutality represented an explicit repudiation of the spirit of the October Manifesto, the Moscow business leaders rallied to the aid of the state even as the gunfire and artillery bombardment echoed over the city. In the Moscow Duma, "the old friendship" between Shchepkin and the Guchkov brothers had ended. "Politics drove them apart, into different camps." While the Duma mildly criticized the government on December 13 for having delayed implementation of the October Manifesto, Mayor Guchkov refused to mediate the terms of surrender between the Presnia workers and the governor-general. Instead of organizing a militia to halt the Black Hundreds' violence, the Duma simply appealed to the population "in the name of Christian love, mercy, and love of country to cease the struggle and bloodshed." When a Kadet proposed that the Duma condemn the army and police for murdering innocent civilians, Mayor Guchkov claimed that this "would only pour oil on the fire. It would appear to the workers as a new call to violence." The Duma then appropriated 5,000 rubles to aid policemen and army personnel injured in the fighting; approved the mayor's firing of twenty-three striking city employees; and defeated Professor Levitsky's proposal for universal suffrage in the coming elections to the State Duma.[93] As if to seal the alliance with the government, several important industrialists attended a banquet given by Admiral Dubasov on New Year's Day, 1906. There Mayor Guchkov pronounced a toast that contrasted sharply with his liberal speeches of the previous summer: "I can say to you in the name of all of us that you must not doubt our support; each of us is prepared to devote to it all our abilities and our strength."[94]

Even more vociferously than the Duma, the Moscow manufacturers' organizations encouraged armed repression in December 1905. G. A. Krestovnikov, who succeeded the recently deceased N. A. Naidenov as MSEC president,[95] donated to the governor-general 165,000 rubles collected from local businessmen to aid the forces of order. Likewise, instead of condemning the arrival in Moscow of troops from the Far East, the Merchant Society appropriated "up to 10,000 rubles" to arrange a celebration to greet them.[96] As the Commercial-Industrial Party warned in late 1905: "The country is in a panic; the life of the country is at a standstill; the country is perishing from turmoil. It is necessary immediately to unite persons of law and order . . . to form a mighty party to assist the governmental authorities in the cause of pacifying the country and implementing the newly enunciated principles."[97]

At the same time, the labor violence of late 1905 finally convinced the Moscow manufacturers of the impossibility of taming the mob by appeals to the old patriarchal values. Although N. I. Prokhorov blamed outsiders for the revolt at his Trimount factory, it was clear that his family's famous system of schools, libraries, chapels, and religious literature had simply failed to maintain the workers' loyalty. In order to defeat the militant labor movement, the new employers' unions organized lockouts, blacklists, reprisals against strikers, recruitment of strikebreakers, and a strike fund (in the Central Industrial Region, ten rubles per year for every worker employed became the assessment), and most employers lengthened the workday back to ten or eleven hours.[98] The manufacturers thus at last admitted the failure of the old factory system. Just as their enthusiasm over the October Manifesto signalled their desire to end the pattern of governmental tutelage, so their grim declaration of a "struggle" with the workers marked their transcendence of the patriarchal mentality.

The trauma of December intensified the Moscow business leaders' conservatism during the electoral campaign to the State Duma. In early 1906, the Commercial-Industrial Party, together with the St. Petersburg Party of Legal Order, Progressive Economic Party, and All-Russian Commercial-Industrial Union, joined the Octobrists in a single "electoral bloc." Although the Moderate Progressives did not enter this coalition or join the Octobrist Party as a unit (as did the Commercial-Industrial Party), P. P. and V. P. Riabushinsky and S. I. Chetverikov were among the twenty-two Octobrist Central Committee members from St. Petersburg and Moscow who met on January 8, 1906.[99] At this meeting, the committee approved the tsar's retention of the title of "autocrat" as long as the government recognized the new "fundamental laws" (a very precarious stance) and demanded vigorous measures, including martial law "for a period," to repress "revolutionary violence and armed insurrection." Indeed, when the Octobrists won only thirteen of 448 seats in the State Duma, the Moderate Progressives two, and the Commercial-Industrial Party one (G. A. Krestovnikov entered the State Council as one of twelve representatives of business organizations), these minor parties and their counterparts in St. Petersburg "merged" into the Union of October 17.[100]

The success of the Kadets and Trudoviks (Toilers), who had won 153 and 107 Duma seats, respectively, demonstrated the need for a new industrial organization to resist their vigorous social-reform programs. At the same time, however, the Moscow manufacturers consciously avoided party politics as a potential source of acrimony and division. The formation of the Association of Industry and Trade (AIT) in 1906 represented an effort to transcend party differences for the sake of coordinating a national economic policy. Although the MSEC displayed a certain distrust and envy toward the Petersburg, Donbas, and Polish coal and steel men who organized and led AIT, several eminent Moscow industrialists – J. P. Goujon, A. L. Knoop, G. A. Krestovnikov, A. I. Konovalov, P. P. Riabushinsky, and S. N. Tretiakov – were elected to its Council and Executive Committee.[101]

AIT's Moscow Bureau issued a programmatic statement that commented in detail on the full range of problems facing Russian society in the aftermath of revolution. It is, indeed, a testament to the Moscow merchants' political evolution that their clear positions resembled those of the Kadets on civil equality, personal freedoms, and the power of the State Duma (subject to the tsar's veto) to pass legislation, impose taxes, and control the ministers. On specific matters of legal, educational, nationality, and labor policy, the Moscow Bureau closely followed the Moderate Progressives. To a certain extent, its program of economic and financial reforms echoed the perennial demands of the past five decades: a tariff policy that would ensure "the best protection and development of national labor"; improved communication and transport; and technical education for the masses. Yet a new aggressiveness pervaded its attacks on bureaucratic controls over business. Chambers of commerce should be created with the power to hold periodic congresses and to issue mandatory regulations on trade; state agencies dealing with industry must be reorganized in the interest of efficiency; the "concessionary" system of creating new companies (which required the confirmation of the ministry and the tsar) must give way to incorporation by simple registration of the charter without prior official permission. Finally, the manufacturers' endorsement of a progressive income tax, which would of course place a disproportionate burden on themselves, not only demonstrated their good faith but also indicated that they now considered purely economic distinctions to be of primary social importance.[102] Among the best-educated manufacturers of Moscow, though not the petty traders and factory owners of the provincial centers,[103] the old estate consciousness was dead at last.

It is, unfortunately, impossible to say precisely when the conservative leaders like Krestovnikov became so disgusted with the state's interference and mismanagement that they jettisoned certain reactionary ideas of the past half-century and, like the younger and more liberal industrialists, embraced some ideas advanced by the zemstvo reformers of the 1890s. It seems likely, for example, that they had long resented the provisions of the 1836 law on incorporation, yet except for isolated cases – Chizhov's *Vestnik promyshlennosti* and the one complaint at the Commercial-Industrial Congress of 1896 – they had previously remained silent about it. In any case, by the end of 1905 they had recognized that fundamental economic differences separated them not only from the workers' movement but also from the bureaucratic state. Until 1917, chambers of commerce were illegal, the 1836 law remained in effect, and the state continued to dominate the economy, so that AIT and the government were divided by a number of serious economic issues in the coming years.[104] Thus the Moscow manufacturers had become a bourgeoisie, a genuine "class" (the Marxian *Klasse für sich*): "separate individuals" conscious of their economic interests, who "have to carry on a common battle against another class."[105]

At the same time, however, the timidity of these proposals must be emphasized. United around a common political program, conservatives like Krestovnikov and Knoop and the reformists like Riabushinsky and Konovalov placed their faith in the tsar's promises for reform and turned their energies and financial resources to an implacable struggle against the lower classes, the radical left, and minority nationalities. Naidenov, who had been enraged to hear industrialists proclaim constitutional slogans in the Moscow Stock Exchange in June and July, seems to have won a posthumous victory. Whether or not the tsar would have granted a genuine constitution in the face of insistent demands by the manufacturers is not an entirely hypothetical question. Between mid-October 1905 and April 1906 (the "Fundamental Laws" were issued on April 26), precisely when the tsarist regime's fate was decided by the support of the educated strata of society and the loyalty of the army troops,[106] the Moscow bourgeoisie threw its considerable organizational resources against the forces of change. The industrialists' role in the salvation of the tsar appears to have been far greater than their small numbers might at first suggest. Thus, owing in large measure to the political conservatism of the Russian manufacturers, the revolutionary wave had spent itself by early 1906 without achieving the destruction of the autocratic system. Before the cataclysm of World War I and the Revolution of 1917 there would be no second chance.

8

The fateful legacy of reactionary nationalism

The social and ideological evolution of the Moscow merchants has been analyzed in the present study with reference to three distinct stages. First, a social type labeled here as *traditional merchants* predominated in commerce and manufacturing from the sixteenth to the early nineteenth century. In accordance with the Muscovite cultural heritage of patriarchal family life and rudimentary education based on the Bible, these men, typified by P. M. Vishniakov and A. P. Shestov, relied on personal dealings in taverns and shops, to the virtual exclusion of rational economic innovation, and remained faithful to the autocratic principle in politics. Second, by the 1840s leadership in economic affairs and municipal government passed to a new group of somewhat better trained and more enterprising *capitalist merchants*, devoted to advanced technology and modern corporate forms of enterprise, which a number of them observed at firsthand in Western Europe. It was this group, led by the MSEC presidents A. I. Khludov, T. S. Morozov, and N. A. Naidenov, which after the Crimean War participated in the *merchant-Slavophile alliance*. With the aid of sympathetic Slavophile intellectuals – I. S. Aksakov, F. V. Chizhov, and the Shipov brothers – as well as M. P. Pogodin and I. K. Babst, these merchant leaders elaborated a comprehensive program of high tariffs and other government aid to economic development in the name of Russian nationalism.

Third, a new generation of merchant leaders, many with university educations, emerged from the trauma of the Revolution of 1905 as a mature, class-conscious *bourgeoisie*. Renouncing their habitual reliance on the autocratic state, they sought both to curb bureaucratic tyranny and, through new "employers' unions," to quell labor violence without relying entirely on the armed might of the state. The majority of the Moscow bourgeoisie, led by A. I. Guchkov and G. A. Krestovnikov, viewed the October Manifesto's promise of a *Rechtsstaat* as sufficiently reformist, while only a tiny group of liberals, typified by the Riabushinsky brothers, S. I. Chetverikov, and A. I. Konovalov, embraced the democratic political formulas of the Kadets.

Special attention has been paid to the political ideology of the capitalist merchants. The nature of their ideology in the 1855–1900 period has previously remained obscure, owing to the paucity of sources and to the disinclination of both Soviet and Western scholars to abandon the familiar concept of a "liberal bourgeoisie." Yet the reactionary ideology that took shape between 1855 and 1860 influenced virtually all the economic, political, and cultural activities of the Moscow merchant leaders in the following half-century. The slogans preached by the merchant-Slavophile alliance resounded not only in the halls of the Moscow Stock Exchange and the industrialists' various consultative bodies, but also in the Moscow City Duma, the Pan-Slav movement, journalism, and the world of art.

The merchants' reactionary ideology had two primary sources: their cultural heritage and their desire for economic security. The traditional merchants' faith in Orthodox Christianity, maintained in its fundamentalist, pre-Petrine version by the Old Believers, persisted among the capitalist merchants as well. The Slavophiles' philosophical and historical arguments further buttressed the merchants' religious faith, devotion to autocracy, and fervent Russian nationalism. Because the older merchant leaders of the late nineteenth century had received a strict religious upbringing in the 1840s and 1850s, and because active collaboration continued in later decades between merchants and church officials (notably the Moscow metropolitans and K. P. Pobedonostsev), religious feelings remained strong long after the merchants' most devout nationalist and Slavophile allies – Pogodin, Chizhov, Aksakov, and the Shipovs – had died.

Economic issues, which directly affected the capitalist merchants' prosperity, also exerted an indelible influence on their political outlook. Although governmental intrusions into their business affairs occasionally provoked the merchants' resentment, the great international issues of the 1855–1905 period – tariff protection, railroad development, control of Central Asian and Transcaucasian raw materials, and access to Persian, Central Asian, and Chinese markets – strengthened their long-standing dependence on the tsarist state. Because of its technological inferiority, Russian industry relied directly on state aid to repel the mortal threat of European competition, even in the case of textiles and other kinds of light manufacturing in the Central Region, which were less directly dependent on governmental purchases and subsidies than were the railroad and armaments industries of St. Petersburg. The violently xenophobic polemics of the merchant-Slavophile alliance helped to overcome the Finance Ministry's predilection in the 1850s and 1860s for freer trade and to win governmental favors for industry and commerce: railroads, credit facilities, and moderate taxation. It was not before the early twentieth century that the bureaucracy's perennial regulation and interference would finally combine with its labor legislation and military incompetence to make several merchant spokesmen repudiate their erstwhile patron, the tsarist state.

Given the mutual reinforcement of these economic and cultural factors, it appeared highly unlikely that a liberal political consciousness would develop within this social group. In the absence of a strong and well-established antiautocratic tradition in Russia, such liberal concepts as institutional checks on executive power, popular representation, and the right of free expression for citizens of all social and ethnic groups were accessible to the merchants only from Western Europe. Exposure to European ideas thus may be considered a necessary prerequisite for the development of an antiautocratic consciousness among the Moscow merchants. Yet even direct contact with parliamentary forms of government failed to transform the few wealthy merchants who traveled to Western Europe. By itself, it was not sufficient to bring them into the Russian liberal movement of the late nineteenth century. The superficial Anglophiles, Lanin and Iakunchikov, proved incapable of applying the English achievement of self-government to Moscow. Even the most cosmopolitan capitalist merchants – Kokorev, the Botkins, Morozovs, Tretiakovs, Mamontovs, Alekseevs, Shchukins, and Krestovnikovs – remained "*kvas* patriots."[1] Armed with their vigorously proautocratic political ideology, they eagerly supported the Pan-Slav crusade, the Holy Host, and the antiliberal periodicals of Aksakov and Sharapov. Finally, whatever inclination existed toward bourgeois class-consciousness and liberalism among the German, Alsatian, and French manufacturers in the Moscow merchant leadership (Knoop, Wogau, Kolli, Hübner, Zindel, and Goujon) remained invisible before 1900.

Those few merchants who expressed antiautocratic ideas apparently did so only because of their close contacts with Russian liberals – intellectuals, zemstvo leaders, and proponents of self-government in the Moscow Duma – or as a result of prolonged study in European universities. Soldatenkov received history lessons from Granovsky; S. I. Chetverikov, S. T. Morozov, and the Guchkov brothers held relatively scientific and rationalist views as a result of their university education; V. A. Morozova "first learned about constitutionalism" from the liberal professor V. A. Golt-sev;[2] and Professor A. S. Alekseev (born into the eminent merchant family in 1851) based his strong condemnation of Kokorev's hero, Bismarck, on the legal theories he had absorbed in Heidelberg and Paris.[3] Moreover, such liberal influences proved weak and transitory. Even the devotion of their political allies, the Slavophiles, to the esoteric principle of free speech within the autocratic system made no impression on the merchant leaders before 1904; and the reformist rhetoric of the Guchkov brothers soon faded in the revolutionary tumult of late 1905.

The Moscow merchants' political activities in the final prerevolutionary decade (1907–17) can best be understood, then, in terms of the tension between the new but very weak liberal strivings that first became evident in 1904–5 and the powerful merchant ideology of the previous half-century. Several daring protests by the young bourgeoisie of Moscow punctuated the decade. For the first time, Moscow manufacturers established their own newspapers to defend their economic interests and to articulate reformist political views. Both P. P. Riabushinsky's *Utro Rossii (The Russian Morn)*[4] and the Guchkovs' more conservative *Golos Moskvy (The Voice of Moscow)*[5] spoke confidently of the new importance in Russian society of the "bourgeoisie" and (shades of 1789!) "the third estate."[6] The Moderate Progressives, together with Shipov, Stakhovich, and Heiden, soon grew disillusioned with the Octobrists' accommodation with Stolypin's dictatorship and, in the summer of 1906, left that party to form the Party of Peaceful Renewal *(Partiia mirnogo obnovleniia)*,[7] the forerunner of the Progressive Party of 1912–17.[8] S. I. Chetverikov even ran for the State Duma as a Kadet in 1907.[9] As president of the Third State Duma in 1910–11, A. I. Guchkov himself lost patience with the incompetence and high-handedness of the tsarist ministers. He resigned his post in 1911 and spoke out with increasing indignation against the policies of Empress Alexandra and Rasputin.[10] In 1912, P. P. Riabushinsky publicly denounced "the degenerate Russian gentry"[11] and accused Prime Minister Kokovtsov of neglecting "the Russian people."[12] To the horror of MSEC President G. A. Krestovnikov, sixty-six Moscow merchants that year signed Chetverikov's appeal for academic freedom at Moscow University.[13] Several years later, Mikhail P. Riabushinsky published a full-fledged bourgeoise critique of the outworn bureaucratic-gentry regime and called for sweeping political and economic reforms.[14] Speaking freely in April 1917 after the collapse of tsarism, A. I. Konovalov bitterly castigated "the economic and political fetters" of "the old hateful order."[15]

And yet such protests appear somehow pathetic, for these same spokesmen for change remained committed to key elements of the old merchant ideology. Morozov's and Riabushinsky's defense of "the people" against the bureaucratic state smacked of Old-Believer and Slavophile nostalgia for the allegedly organic society of medieval Muscovy.[16] Likewise, Aksakov's aggressive nationalism echoed clearly in the Riabushinsky brothers' appeal for Russian commercial and strategic control of northern Persia,[17] their demand in 1910–11 for a huge armaments program,[18] and their proud claims to revive the merchants' "eternal historical mission" as zealots of victory in "the second patriotic [*otechestvennaia*] war"[19] against the Central Powers. Mikhail Riabushinsky's "plan" to base his family's industrial enterprises on such domestic raw materials as flax and timber[20] explicitly reiterated the autarchic conceptions of Kokorev and the Shipovs fifty years before. Finally, the manufacturers continued to regard the Ministry of Trade and Industry as a patron that, despite its bureaucratic inefficiency and penchant for interference in labor disputes, appeared relatively sympathetic to their economic needs.[21] Well into the final decade of the tsarist period, the Moscow manufacturers remained unconvinced of the benefits of parliamentary government, especially since they encountered in the State Duma the traditional anticapitalist prejudices of the liberal rhetoricians from the professions and the zemstvos.[22] On the very eve of the February Revolution of 1917, AIT put forth no political demands, but merely complained that excessive state involvement in certain sectors of the Russian economy constrained private enterprise.[23]

The eight-month interlude of liberal democracy between the February Revolution and the Bolshevik coup of October 1917 brought to power the Moscow merchant leaders A. I. Guchkov (minister of war until May), A. I. Konovalov (minister of trade and industry in the spring and fall),[24] and S. N. Tretiakov (president of the Supreme Economic Council).[25] The bourgeoisie hardly constituted a "ruling class," however. (Buryshkin bitterly bestowed that title on the Menshevik and Socialist-Revolutionary intelligentsia!)[26] The persistence of elements of the old merchant ideology well into the revolutionary period may be illustrated by the dramatic experience in early 1918 of S. I. Chetverikov, who as a prisoner of the Bolsheviks was sweeping snow from the tracks of the Moscow-Bogorodsk Railroad. A lone figure approaching on foot turned out to be one of Chetverikov's former schoolmates, Arseni I. Morozov. The last president of the Morozov family's huge Glukhovsk textile complex, Arseni had fled Bogorodsk after the workers seized control of his house and factory. "Since we were both eminent representatives of the Moscow merchants," Chetverikov observed wryly in his memoirs, "this meeting was not devoid of significance as a symptom of that period." In his arms, Morozov carried the single object of greatest value to him: the family icon, symbol of the religious faith that had sustained and strengthened the proautocratic Moscow merchant ideology of the preceding six decades.[27]

It might be argued that the religious and xenophobic tenor of the Moscow merchant ideology of the 1855–1905 period should not be considered unusual, since (apart from its purely economic components) it scarcely differed from the reactionary nationalism of the Russian gentry, bureaucracy, army, and Orthodox clergy. On the other hand, because capitalism has flourished most freely under rational, predictable forms of government in other countries and because Russian businessmen eventually did seek political power commensurate with their economic influence, the high degree of compatibility between the autocratic state and the commercial-industrial leadership must be seen as a historical fact that requires explanation. The present study has suggested that the nationalist arguments put forth by the merchant-Slavophile alliance provided a common ground for cooperation between the tsarist bureaucracy and the industrialists of the Central Region in the early years of Russian capitalist development. The Finance Ministry, although often impatient with what it perceived as timidity and lack of entrepreneurial talent among industrialists, actively fostered economic expansion, while the manufacturers endured with few complaints what they often viewed as wasteful bureaucratic tutelage,[28] and forsook the struggle for constitutional liberalism. In the difficult transition from a traditional agricultural society to a modern industrial one, Russian nationalism, articulated persuasively by the prophets of Slavophilism and Official Nationality, outweighed the desire for economic and political freedom. Here was located the basis of the merchants' crucial contribution to the salvation of the autocracy in its moment of greatest weakness, the Revolution of 1905.

The profound contrast between the ideologies of the Moscow merchants and their West-European counterparts should therefore call into question any optimistic assessment of Russia's political evolution toward liberal democracy under the last three tsars.[29] On the other hand, to assert that the social and political differences separating Russia from Western

Europe meant that liberalism was "never" a possibility, "before and after 1917,"[30] is to accept the inevitability of a twentieth-century dictatorship from at least Peter's time onward. Moreover, the fact of the Bolshevik victory neither demonstrates its inevitability nor precludes an eventual resurgence of liberalism in the post-Stalin era, however weak the liberal dissident movement may have been in the 1970s. Although in retrospect the chances of liberalism's victory seemed dim in early 1917, Bolshevik power was not consolidated until the end of the Civil War in 1920. Whether liberalism or radicalism or even a third alternative, such as that of a military dictatorship or protofascist regime of the right,[31] would prevail in the early twentieth century depended on the ways in which economic changes and cultural developments had affected all social groups during the preceding decades.

Only a series of detailed investigations into the social and ideological evolution of all strata of Russian society during the nineteenth century can supply the factual materials for an impartial and conclusive analysis of the prospects for constitutional democracy in Russia. Furthermore, among the industrialists alone, major regional variations have yet to be considered by historians. In the meantime, any discussion of the social basis of Russian liberalism must reckon with the vehement nationalism and hatred for constitutionalism that constituted the principal elements of the Moscow merchant ideology between 1855 and 1905.

Appendix

The following tables identify the major figures in the Moscow merchant leadership and the specific organizations to which they belonged. Table I consists of twenty organizations that existed between 1856 and 1892. Table II includes four of these, plus six additional groups, for a total of ten that existed between 1870 and 1906. Each individual listed in Table I participated in at least two organizations.

Asterisks (*) signify probable identifications, as when incomplete names appeared in the sources; plus signs (+) indicate definite membership.

Full titles of the organizations listed, and references consulted, are as follows:

1. Eighteen of 70 proponents of a "Society to Encourage Manufacturing and Trade" *(Obshchestvo pooshchreniia manufaktur i torgovli)*, whose creation was refused by the government. Petitions of Sept. 14, 1856, and Feb. 4, 1857, TsGIAM F 16.228.226, 8r.-9r. and 38v.; and an undated letter to Governor-General S. G. Stroganov (who replaced Zakrevsky in February 1859), GIM F 146.12, 18r.-19r.

2. Eight of 10 opponents of free trade in 1857, who called themselves "The Plenipotentiary Representatives of Russian Manufacturers and Domestic Traders" *(Upolnomochennye ot rossiiskikh manufakturistov i vnutrennikh torgovtsev)*. Sobolev, *Tamozhennaia politika*, 150.

3. Seven of 15 members of the Moscow section of the Manufacturing Council in 1858. FBON, "Zhurnal zasedanii Moskovskogo otdeleniia manufakturnogo soveta" for 1858.

4. Seventeen of 84 persons on the guest list for Kokorev's proposed banquet of February 19, 1858. Popelnitsky, "Banket," 208–9.

5. Twelve of 112 owners of fifty or more stocks in the Moscow-Iaroslavl Railroad, early 1860s. GBL-OR F 332.74.6.

6. Thirty-six of 43 full and alternate members of the Permanent Depu-

213

tation of Merchant Congresses (*Postoiannaia deputatsiia kupecheskikh s"ezdov*), 1865–7. *Birzha*, 35, and *Moskva*, Feb. 2, 1867, 3.

7. Eight of 11 members of the MSMC in 1865. FBON, "Zhurnal," 1865.

8. Twenty-six of 37 founders and officers of the Moscow Merchant Bank, 1865–71. TsGIAM F 253.1.2.

9. Thirty-five of 88 participants in the campaign to buy the Nikolaev Railroad, 1867–8. GBL-OR F 332.73.6, 1r.-2r.; *Sankt-Peterburgskie vedomosti*, Mar. 2/14, 1868, 1–2; *Moskva*, April 17, 1868, 3.

10. Twenty-eight of 34 members of the Moscow Section of RIS, 1868. *Moskvich*, Feb. 13, 1868, 3.

11. Fourteen of 19 members of the MSMC in 1869. FBON, "Zhurnal," 1869.

12. Twenty-five of 29 founders and officers of the Moscow Merchant Mutual Credit Society, 1869. Moskovskoe . . . kredita, *Ocherk*, 89–91, 93.

13. Nine of 16 founders and officers of the Moscow Discount Bank, 1869. TsGIAM F 271.2.343, 32r., 46r.

14. Fourteen of 15 founders and officers of the Moscow Trading Bank, 1871. Naidenov, *Vospominaniia*, vol. 2, 119–120; *PSZ-2*, no. 49,732.

15. Three of 4 officers of the Moscow Stock Exchange Committee, 1870–3. *Birzha*, 21–2.

16. Fourteen of 16 members of the campaign to buy the Moscow-Kursk Railroad, 1869–71. Delvig, *Polveka*, vol. 2, 469n.; *PSZ-2*, no. 49,634.

17. Seventy of 254 members elected at least twice to the Moscow Stock Exchange Society between 1870 and 1888. *Birzha*, 75–86.

18. Twelve of 96 members of the Moscow Section of the Holy Host, 1881–2. Senchakova, " 'Druzhina,' " 74–83; Fedorova, "Otdel," 170.

19. Thirteen of 257 participants in the Commercial-Industrial Congress of 1882 held by RIS. *Trudy . . . 1882*, xi–xvii.

20. Nineteen of 295 members of MIS, 1892. Obshchestvo dlia sodeistviia uluchsheniiu i razvitiiu manufakturnoi promyshlennosti, *Otchet . . . za 1892 g.* (Moscow, 1893).

21. Five of 1,013 persons invited to the Commercial-Industrial Congress of 1896. *Trudy . . . 1896*, vol. 1, 1–43 (separate pagination).

22. Three of 24 members of the council and board of the Moscow Discount Bank, 1903; also included were three men listed in Table I: A. I. Abrikosov, D. P. Botkin, and N. A. Naidenov. *Vsia Moskva*, 1903, col. 1071.

23. Five of 24 members of the council and board of the Moscow Merchant Bank, 1905. V. A. Dmitriev-Mamonov, *Ukazatel' deistvuiushchikh v imperii aktsionernykh predpriiatii i torgovykh domov* (St. Petersburg, 1905), 1805.

24. Nine of 39 signatories of the open letter from the MSES minority and their supporters, July 1905. *RVed*, July 26, 1905, 4; July 29, 3.

25. Twenty of 87 members of the Commercial-Industrial Party, 1905. Ivanovich, *Partii*, 77.

26. Four of 23 members of the Central Committee of the Octobrist Party, January 1906. "'Soiuz 17 oktiabria,'" 157.

Table 1. *Moscow merchant leaders and their organizations (1856–1892)*

	Ind. Soc. 1856–7 1	Reps. 1857 2	MSMC 1858 3	Banquet list 1858 4	Mos.-Iar. RR 1860s 5	Mcht. Dep. 1865–7 6	MSMC 1865 7	Mcht. Bank 1866–71 8
A. I. Abrikosov								
A. A. Alekseev				+				
S. A. Alekseev	+	*	+	+				
I. S. Aksakov								
V. D. Aksenov						+		
I. S. Ananov								+
I. K. Babst						+		+
I. K. Baklanov								
N. K. Baklanov								
A. I. Baranov						+		
V. M. Bostandzhoglo						+		
D. P. Botkin	+			+				
P. P. Botkin	+							
D. I. Chetverikov	+							
I. I. Chetverikov	+	*		+		+	+	
F. V. Chizhov					+	+		+
I. V. Ganeshin								
I. N. Geer				+				+
M. A. Gorbov					+	+		
E. F. Guchkov	+	*	+	+				
V. I. Iakunchikov				+		+		+
K. I. Katuar								
A. I. Khludov	+					+	+	
G. I. Khludov	+					+	+	
K. V. Kokushkin						+		+
V. A. Kokorev	+			+				+
V. D. Konshin								
N. N. Konshin								
A. A. Kolli						+		
A. I. Koshelev				+				
A. K. Krestovnikov	+					+		*
V. K. Krestovnikov						+		+
A. V. Lepeshkin	+							
D. S. Lepeshkin	+					+		
N. V. Lepeshkin	+		+			+		
V. S. Lepeshkin		+	+					
I. A. Liamin	+					+		+
L. V. Losev								
M. V. Losev								
S. P. Maliutin						+		+
A. N. Mamontov								
I. F. Mamontov				+	+			+
S. I. Mamontov					+	+		
V. S. Maretsky					+			
G. A. Medyntsev								+
F. S. Mikhailov						+		

Nikolaev RR 1867–8 9	MSRIS 1868 10	MSMC 1869 11	Cr. Soc. 1869 12	Disc. Bank 1869 13	Trad. Bank 1871 14	MSEC 1870–3 15	Kursk RR 1869–71 16	MSES 1870–88 17	Holy Host 1881–2 18	Congress 1882 19	MIS 1892 20
			+	+				+			
								+			
	+		+								
			+		+			+			
+								+		+	
+	+							+			
			+					+			
					+			+			
								+			
								+			
+		+	+				+	+			
+							+	+			
+				+			+	+			
	+	+									
+	+		+				+	+			
					+			+			
+			+		+		+	+			
+			+		+			+			+
				+				+			
								+			
		+						+			
+	+		+								
+			+					+			
								+		+	
+								+		+	
+											
+	+		+		+			+			
+	+				+			+		+	
								+			
+								+			
		+						+		*	
+	+		+			+		+			+
	+							+			
	+							+			
+	+		+					+			+
+	+	+					+	+			
+	+										
+							+	+			
			+				+	+			
	+										
								+			

Table 1 *(cont.)*

	Ind. Soc. 1856–7 1	Reps. 1857 2	MSMC 1858 3	Banquet list 1858 4	Mos.-Iar. RR 1860s 5	Mcht. Dep. 1865–7 6	MSMC 1865 7	Mcht. Bank 1866–71 8
T. S. Morozov						+	+	+
V. P. Moshnin								
N. A. Naidenov						+		
V. V. Pegov					+			+
I. A. Pervushin					+			
P. O. Pirling								
K. A. Popov						+		
M. E. Popov						+		+
A. Ia. Prokhorov								
K. V. Prokhorov	+	+	+				+	
F. F. Rezanov						+	+	+
P. M. Riabushinsky						+		
N. G. Riumin				+	+			
V. N. Rukavishnikov								
P. I. Sanin								
A. G. Sapozhnikov								
S. I. Sazikov				+				
I. V. Shchukin				+		+		
A. P. Shipov	+	+	+	+	+	+		
D. P. Shipov	+			+	+	+		
S. P. Shipov				+	+			
S. D. Shiriaev						+	+	+
N. F. Shubin								+
V. A. Sirotinin								
D. P. Skuratov	+	+	+		+			
K. T. Soldatenkov				+		+	+	
P. P. Sorokoumovsky						+		+
N. I. Strukov								+
I. O. Sushkin								+
P. D. Syreishchikov								
A. P. Tiuliaev						+		
A. K. Trapeznikov						+		+
P. M. Tretiakov								+
S. M. Tretiakov								
S. P. Vishniakov								
A. E. Voinov								+
P. G. Volkov								
K. M. Wogau						+		
M. M. Wogau								
E. I. Zindel		+				+		
A. Ia. Zhuravlev								+

Nikolaev RR 1867–8	MSRIS 1868	MSMC 1869	Cr. Soc. 1869	Disc. Bank 1869	Trad. Bank 1871	MSEC 1870–3	Kursk RR 1869–71	MSES 1870–88	Holy Host 1881–2	Congress 1882	MIS 1892
9	10	11	12	13	14	15	16	17	18	19	20
+	+	+	+		+	+	+	+		+	
+	+							+			
			+		+	+		+			+
+											
+											
	+			+				+			
			+	+							
			+			+		+			
								+	+		
+		+									
+	+	+									
	+				+			+			
+											
+	+						+				
	+							+	+		
		+						+			
			+	+				+			
				+				+			
	+										
+	+	+						+			
		+	+					+			
								+			
					+			+			
	+										
+	+	+	+	+			+	+			
			+					+			
					+						
			+					+			
	+										
+	+				+			+			
+			+				+	+			
+	+	+	+				+	+	+	+	
					+			+			
									+		
+								+			
											*
				+				+			
		+						+			
+											

Table 2. Moscow merchant leaders and their organizations (1870–1906)

	MSES 1870–88 (17)	Holy Host 1881–2 (18)	Congress 1882 (19)	MIS 1892 (20)	Congress 1896 (21)	Discount Bank, 1905 (22)	Merchant Bank, 1905 (23)	July 1905 letters (24)	Com.-Ind. Party (25)	Octobrist Cent. Com. (26)
V. S. Alekseev								+		
N.P. Bakhrushin	+								+	
V. A. Bakhrushin								+		
P. D. Botkin								+		
N. I. Botkin		+								
S. I. Chetverikov	+				+	+		+		+
J. P. Goujon	+				+	+				
A. I. Guchkov										+
I. E. Guchkov	+	+	+	+			+			
N. I. Guchkov					+			+		
V. V. Iakunchikov				+					+	
K.A. Iasiuninsky							+		+	
N. N. Konshin, Jr.									+	
S. N. Konshin									+	
G. A. Krestovnikov	+								+	
V. V. Krestovnikov									+	

A. L. Knoop
F. L. Knoop
Ia. A. Kolli
A. I. Konovalov
V. N. Lepeshkin
S. I. Liamin
A. L. Losev
A. I. Morozov
E. V. Morozov
I. A. Morozov
I. V. Morozov
S. T. Morozov
F. K. Prokhorov
I. I. Prokhorov
S. V. Prokhorov
S. I. Prokhorov
M. P. Riabushinsky
P. P. Riabushinsky
V. P. Riabushinsky
I. P. Sanin
V. G. Sapozhnikov
A. A. Shipov
A. S. Vishniakov

Table 3. *Genealogies of leading merchant families (showing links of intermarriage)*

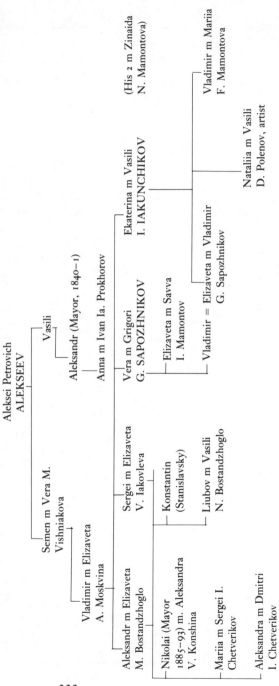

Mikhail Ivanovich
BOSTANDZHOGLO

Vasili (Merchant
Society *starshina*)

Aleksandra m Vasili
A. IAKOVLEV

(His two daughters by
a previous marriage)

Elizaveta m Sergei
V. Alekseev

Elizaveta m Aleksandr
V. Alekseev

Nikolai m Mariia   =   Mariia m Nikolai
V. Iakovleva   M. Bostandzhoglo
Vasili m Liubov
S. Alekseeva

Petr Kononvich
BOTKIN

Vasili
(writer)

Dmitri m Sofiia
S. Mazurina

Petr m Nadezhda
K. Shaposhnikova

Vera m Nikolai
I. Guchkov

Sergei

Aleksandr m Mariia
P. Tretiakova

Vladimir m
Anna E. Guchkova

Sergei m Aleksandra
P. Tretiakova

Mariia m
A. A. Fet

Ekaterina m
Ivan V. Shchukin

Evgeni   Petr
             (diplomat)
Gleb
(writer)

Fedor Alekseevich
GUCHKOV

Efim (Mayor 1856–8)

Ivan

Anna m Vladimir
P. Botkin

Nikolai (Mayor 1905–13)
m Vera P. Botkina

Nadezhda m Ivan
N. Prokhorov

Ivan

Aleksandr m
Mariia I. Ziloti

Dmitri
KONSHIN

Nikolai

Nikolai

Vladimir m Elizaveta
M. Tretiakova

Aleksandra m Nikolai
A. Alekseev

Praskovia m Anatoli
I. Chaikovsky

Ivan Vasilevich
CHETVERIKOV

Ivan

Aleksandra m Nikolai
P. Krestovnikov

Sergei m Mariia
A. Alekseeva

Dmitri m Aleksandra
A. Alekseeva

Table 3 (cont.)

224

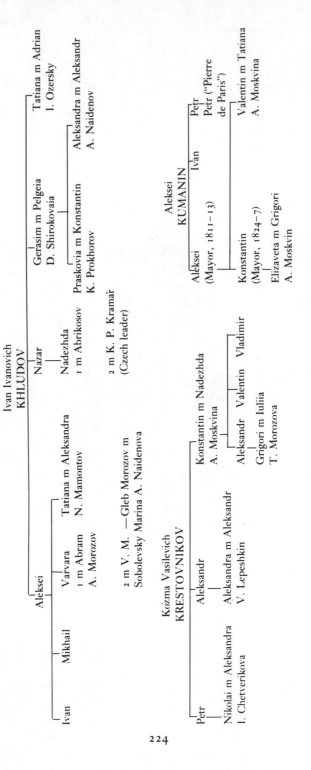

Ivan Ivanovich
KHLUDOV

Ivan Mikhail Aleksei Nazar Gerasim m Pelgeia Tatiana m Adrian
                                D. Shirokovaia   I. Ozersky

Varvara   Tatiana m Aleksandra   Nadezhda   Praskovia m Konstantin   Aleksandra m Aleksandr
1 m Abram   N. Mamontov   1 m Abrikosov   K. Prokhorov   A. Naidenov
A. Morozov
                                       2 m K. P. Kramař
2 m V. M. — Gleb Morozov m   (Czech leader)
Sobolevsky Marina A. Naidenova

Kozma Vasilevich
KRESTOVNIKOV

Petr   Aleksandr   Aleksandra m Aleksandr
                         V. Lepeshkin

Nikolai m Aleksandra   Konstantin m Nadezhda
I. Chetverikova   A. Moskvina

                        Aleksandr Valentin Vladimir
                        Grigori m Iulia
                        T. Morozova

Aleksei
KUMANIN

Aleksei   Konstantin   Elizaveta m Grigori   Ivan   Petr
(Mayor, 1811–13) (Mayor, 1824–7) A. Moskvin   Petr ("Pierre
                                                              de Paris")
                                                              Valentin m Tatiana
                                                              A. Moskvina

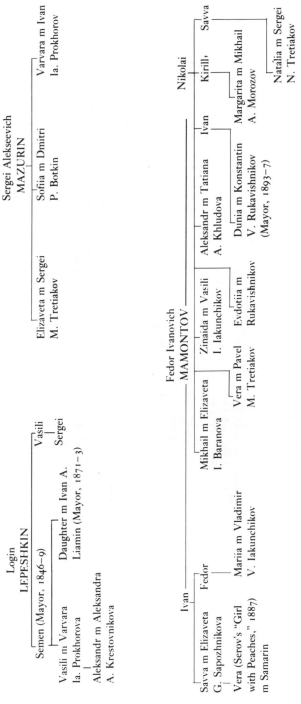

Login
LEPESHKIN

Semen (Mayor, 1846–9)   Daughter m Ivan A.   Vasili   Sergei
                          Liamin (Mayor, 1871–3)

Vasili m Varvara
Ia. Prokhorova

Aleksandr m Aleksandra
A. Krestovnikova

Sergei Alekseevich
MAZURIN

Elizaveta m Sergei   Sofiia m Dmitri   Varvara m Ivan
M. Tretiakov   P. Botkin   Ia. Prokhorov

Fedor Ivanovich
MAMONTOV

Ivan   Mikhail m Elizaveta   Zinaida m Vasili   Aleksandr m Tatiana   Nikolai
                        I. Baranova   I. Iakunchikov   A. Khludova

Savva m Elizaveta   Fedor   Mariia m Vladimir   Vera m Pavel   Evdotiia m   Dunia m Konstantin   Ivan   Kirill,   Savva
G. Sapozhnikova   V. Iakunchikov   M. Tretiakov   Rukavishnikov V. Rukavishnikov
                                                                                (Mayor, 1893–7)

Vera (Serov's "Girl   Margarita m Mikhail   Natalia m Sergei
with Peaches," 1887)   A. Morozov   N. Tretiakov
m Samarin

225

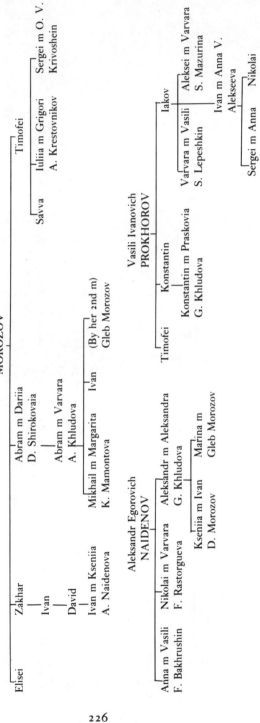

Table 3 (cont.)

Aleksandr
MOSKVIN

Grigori m Elizaveta
K. Kumanina

Tatiana m Valentin
A. Kumanin

Elizaveta m Vladimir
S. Alekseev

Nadezhda m Konstantin
K. Krestovnikov

Savva Vasilevich
MOROZOV

Elisei
- Zakhar
- Ivan
- David
  - Ivan m Kseniia
    A. Naidenova

Abram m Dariia
D. Shirokovaia
- Abram m Varvara
  A. Khludova
  - Mikhail m Margarita
    K. Mamontova
  - Ivan
  - (By her 2nd m)
    Gleb Morozov

Timofei
- Savva
- Iuliia m Grigori
  A. Krestovnikov
- Sergei m O. V.
  Krivoshein

Aleksandr Egorovich
NAIDENOV

Anna m Vasili
F. Bakhrushin

Nikolai m Varvara
F. Rastorgueva

Aleksandr m Aleksandra
G. Khludova
- Kseniia m Ivan
  D. Morozov
- Marina m
  Gleb Morozov

Vasili Ivanovich
PROKHOROV

Timofei

Konstantin
- Konstantin m Praskovia
  G. Khludova

Iakov
- Varvara m Vasili
  S. Lepeshkin
- Aleksei m Varvara
  S. Mazurina
  - Ivan m Anna V.
    Alekseeva
  - Sergei m Anna
    S. Alekseeva
  - Nikolai
    (gentry 1912)
  - Ivan m Nadezhda
    N. Guchkova

226

Ivan Vasilevich SHCHUKIN
m Ekaterina P. Botkina
- Petr (collector)
- Sergei (art patron)

Mikhail Zakharevich
TRETIAKOV
- Pavel (art patron) m Vera N. Mamontova
  - Vera m Aleksandr I. Ziloti
  - Aleksandra m Sergei S. Botkin
  - Mariia m Aleksandr S. Botkin
- Sergei (Mayor, 1876–82) m Elizaveta S. Mazurina
  - Nikolai
  - Sergei m Natalia S. Mamontova
- Elizaveta m Vladimir D. Konshin

Mikhail Ivanovich
VISHNIAKOV
- Vera m Semen A. Alekseev
- Petr
  - Ivan
    - Anna m Volkov (memoirs)
  - Semen
    - Aleksei
    - Vladimir
  - Nikolai

Abbreviations of sources

The following abbreviations are used in the Notes and Selected Bibliography

Moscow Archives

FBON   Fundamental'naia biblioteka obshchestvennykh nauk
GBL-OR   Gosudarstvennaia biblioteka SSSR imeni V. I. Lenina, otdel rukopisei
GIM   Gosudarstvennyi istoricheskii muzei, otdel pismennykh istochnikov
GTsTM   Gosudarstvennyi tsentral'nyi teatral'nyi muzei
MMKhAT   Muzei Moskovskogo khudozhestvennogo akademicheskogo teatra
TsGALI   Tsentral'nyi gosudarstvennyi arkhiv literatury i iskusstva
TsGIAM   Tsentral'nyi gosudarstvennyi istoricheskii arkhiv goroda Moskvy
TsGAOR   Tsentral'nyi gosudarstvennyi arkhiv oktiabr'skoi revoliutsii

Publications

BE   *Entsiklopedicheskii slovar' Brokgauza-Efrona.* 41 vols. in 82. Leipzig and St. Petersburg, 1890–1904. Supplement: 2 vols. in 4. 1905–7.
Birzha   Moscow. Birzha. *Moskovskaia birzha, 1839–1889.* Moscow, 1889.
CdMRS   *Cahiers du monde russe et soviétique.*
GM   *Golos minuvshego.*
IM   Akademiia nauk SSSR. Institut istorii. *Istoriia Moskvy.* 6 vols. Moscow, 1952–9.
IMKO   Storozhev, V. N., ed. *Istoriia moskovskogo kupecheskogo obshchestva, 1863–1913.* 5 vols. (incomplete). Moscow, 1913–16.
IV   *Istoricheskii vestnik.*
JfGO   *Jahrbücher für Geschichte Osteuropas.*
KA   *Krasnyi arkhiv.*
LN   *Literaturnoe nasledstvo.*
MIMK   *Materialy dlia istorii moskovskogo kupechestva.* 9 vols. Moscow, 1883–1909.
MIMKOP   *Materialy dlia istorii moskovskogo kupechestva. Obshchestvennye prigovory.* 11 vols. Moscow, 1892–1911.
MV   *Moskovskie vedomosti.*
ODR   Martov, L., P. Maslov, and A. Potresov, eds. *Obshchestvennoe dvizhenie v Rossii v nachale XX-go veka.* 4 vols. St. Petersburg, 1909–14. Reprinted, The Hague, 1968.
PSZ-2   *Polnoe sobranie zakonov Rossiiskoi imperii. Sobranie 2.* 55 vols. St. Petersburg, 1830–84.

PSZ-3	*Polnoe sobranie zakonov Rossiiskoi imperii. Sobranie 3.* 33 vols. St. Petersburg, 1882–1916.
RA	*Russkie arkhiv.*
RBS	*Russkii biograficheskii slovar'.* 25 vols. (incomplete). St. Petersburg, 1896–1918.
RPP	Dementiev, A. G., A. V. Zapadov, and M. S. Cherepakhov, eds. *Russkaia periodicheskaia pechat' (1702–1894).* Moscow, 1959.
RS	*Russkaia starina.*
RVed	*Russkie vedomosti.*
RVes	*Russkii vestnik.*
VE	*Vestnik Evropy.*
VMU-9	*Vestnik Moskovskogo universiteta, seriia 9: istoriia.*

Notes

━●━ ● ━●━●━ ● ━ ●━●━ ● ━ ● ━●━●━ ● ━ ● ━●━●━●━ ● ━ ●━●━● ● ━ ● ━●━●━ ● ━ ● ━●━●━ ● ━ ● ━●━━━●━ ● ━ ● ━●━●━●━ ● ━●━●━ ●

Preface

1 *BE*, vol. 27, 94, 106–11; vol. 36, 552. The respective populations were 10.6 and 38.5 million persons in 1897 and 1896. The central industrial provinces were Moscow, Kaluga, Tver, Iaroslavl, Vladimir, and Kostroma. Nizhny Novgorod, also included in this account, is sometimes excluded by Russian scholars.

2 *IMKO*, for example, overwhelms the historian with details of the merchants' philanthropic undertakings. Soviet art historians have likewise published profusely on the merchants' activities as patrons of culture, so that we can trace the development of Savva I. Mamontov's many-faceted career as an impresario and peruse Pavel M. Tretiakov's own letters to various Russian painters. See Mark I. Kopshitser, *Savva Mamontov* (Moscow, 1972) and the bibliography in Elizabeth Valkenier, *Russian Realist Art, the State and Society: The Peredvizhniki and Their Tradition* (Ann Arbor, 1977). At the same time, the Moscow merchants' attitudes and actions in many crucial political episodes, such as Sergei M. Tretiakov's term as mayor of Moscow (1876–82) remain almost a taboo subject; little information on the Moscow City Duma is available outside the control of the archivists at TsGIAM. Soviet scholarship on Russian labor in the prerevolutionary period is, of course, extensive.

3 Late in 1977, after the present study had been written, Alfred J. Rieber's sketch on the "Moscow entrepreneurial group" appeared, subtitled "The Emergence of a New Form in Autocratic Politics," *JfGO*, vol. 25, no. 1 (Mar. 1977), 1–20 and no. 2 (June 1977), 174–99. It contained pertinent information drawn from various sources, including the enormous Chizhov archive in the manuscript division of Lenin Library, Moscow. While this article supplements with numerous interesting facts the interpretation offered here, it does not alter any of the main conclusions. Without modifying my text, I have added several footnotes to point out what appear to me as somewhat dubious assertions of fact or interpretation in Rieber's generally well-informed article. Much interesting factual material on the merchants and their Slavophile allies also appears in Nikolai I. Tsimbaev, *I. S. Aksakov v obshchestvennoi zhizni poreformennoi Rossii* (Moscow, 1978).

4 Besides the monographs and reference works cited in Thomas C. Owen, "The Moscow Merchants and the Public Press, 1858–1868," *JfGO*, vol. 23, no. 1 (Mar. 1975), 38n. and those by Bergier, Cobban, Greenlaw, Laski, Moore, O'Boyle, and Stoianovich cited in Chapter 2, see general studies such as Guido de Ruggiero, *The History of European Liberalism*, trans. by R. G. Collingwood (Boston, 1959) and Felix Ponteil, *Les Classes bourgeoises et l'avènement de la démocratie, 1815–1914* (Paris, 1968), and specialized works, e.g., Bert F. Hozelitz, "Entrepreneurship and Capi― Formation in France and Britain since 1700," in Malcom E. Falkus, ed., *Readings in ―e History of Economic Growth* (New

York, 1968), 95–133; Elinor G. Barber, *The Bourgeoisie in Eighteenth-Century France* (Princeton, 1955); Adeline Daumard, *La bourgeoisie parisienne, 1815–1848* (Paris, 1963); Theodore S. Hamerow, *The Social Foundations of German Unification, 1858–1871: Ideas and Institutions* (Princeton, 1969); James J. Sheehan, *German Liberalism in the Nineteenth Century* (Chicago, 1978); George Fischer, *Russian Liberalism: From Gentry to Intelligentsia* (Cambridge, Mass., 1958); and Victor Leontovitsch, *Geschichte des Liberalismus in Russland* (Frankfurt, 1957).

1. The Moscow merchant estate before 1855

1 Jacqueline Kaufmann-Rochard, *Origines d'une bourgeoisie russe (XVIe et XVIIe siecles): Marchands de Muscovie* (Paris, 1969); quotations from Samuel H. Baron, "Who Were the Gosti?" *California Slavic Studies*, vol. 7 (1973), 15, 12. The essential features of the occidental city, out of which the modern European bourgeoisie emerged, were lacking in Russia after the fall of Novgorod to Muscovy in the late fifteenth century. Max Weber, *The City*, trans. and ed. by Don Martindale and Gertrud Neuwirth (Glencoe, Illinois, 1958), 81, 91–120; Samuel H. Baron, "The Weber Thesis and the Failure of Capitalist Development in 'Early Modern' Russia," *JfGO*, vol. 18, no. 3 (Sept. 1970), 321–36; Vatro Murvar, "Max Weber's Urban Typology and Russia," *Sociological Quarterly*, vol. 8, no. 4 (Autumn 1967), 481–94. Although Paul Bushkovitch, in his informative study, *The Merchants of Moscow, 1580–1650* (Cambridge, 1980), stressed that "the absence of a legally enshrined system of political rights and privileges did not prevent the merchant from exercising such power as his wealth gave him," he noted that the autocracy's monopoly on political power "may go far in explaining [the merchants'] political passivity in the ensuing centuries" (173).

2 William L. Blackwell, *The Beginnings of Russian Industrialization, 1800–1860* (Princeton, 1968), 428.

3 Pavel G. Ryndziunsky, "Gorodskoe naselenie," in M. K. Rozhkova, ed., *Ocherki ekonomicheskoi istorii Rossii pervoi poloviny XIX v.* (Moscow, 1959), 319. Gilbert Rozman has recently asserted that by 1800 the urban population of Russia comprised a far larger proportion of the total (above 8 percent) than previously believed. He found also that the pattern of settlement in Russia represented "a complete pre-modern urban network," comparable to those of Ch'ing China and Tokugawa Japan; "Comparative Approaches to Modernization: Russia, 1750–1800," in Michael F. Hamm, ed., *The City in Russian History* (Lexington, Kentucky, 1976), especially 78, 80 (quoted). These conclusions do not, however, invalidate the general proposition that the Russian autocracy denied to its urban population free economic activity and political self-government, the foundations of modern bourgeois culture.

4 I. Ia. Gorlov, *Obozrenie ekonomicheskoi statistiki Rossii* (St. Petersburg, 1849), 44–7.

5 Ryndziunsky, "Naselenie," 319.

6 Petr Keppen [Köppen], *Deviataia reviziia* (St. Petersburg, 1857), 181–5. He excluded Nizhny Novgorod province from the region.

7 This total included honorary citizens, defined later. The increase was in fact greater, since the third guild was abolished in 1863. Third-guild merchants outnumbered second-guild and first-guild merchants by wide margins of 3,453 to 330 and 137 in 1849. Vasili N. Iakovtsevsky, *Kupecheskii kapital v feodal'no-krepostnicheskoi Rossii* (Moscow, 1953), 173.

8 On the merchants' loss of their economic monopoly in the eighteenth century, see Michael J. Hittle, "Catherinean Reforms, Social Change, and the Decline of the *Posad* Commune," in Don Karl Rowney and G. Edward Orchard, eds., *Russian and Slavic*

History (Columbus, 1977), especially 281. Robert E. Jones, "Jacob Sievers, Enlightened Reform and the Development of a 'Third Estate' in Russia," *Russian Review*, vol. 36, no. 4 (Oct. 1977), 433–5, explicitly blamed the bureaucracy for hindering the development of a vigorous "third estate."

9   I. I. Ditiatin, *Ustroistvo i upravlenie gorodov Rossii*, 2 vols. (St. Petersburg, 1875 and Iaroslavl, 1877), vol. 2, 328.

10 Pavel G. Ryndziunsky, *Gorodskoe grazhdanstvo doreformennoi Rossii* (Moscow, 1958), 127; Ryndziunsky, "Naselenie," 293; Efgraf F. Kolokolov, *Ukazatel' zakonov Rossiiskoi imperii dlia kupechestva* (Moscow, 1847), 100–5; I. Ia. Rudchenko, *Istoricheskii ocherk oblozheniia torgovli i promyslov v Rossii* (St. Petersburg, 1893), 138–44.

11 *BE*, vol. 8, 679.

12 Details in Kolokolov, 54–5. On the *poverennye*, see Ditiatin, vol. 2, 257–8.

13 A. Leroy-Beaulieu, *L'Empire des tsars et des Russes*, 3 vols. (Paris, 1881–9), vol. 1, 304–5.

14 Kolokolov, 44. In 1845, the state began to limit access to the hereditary gentry by granting only personal gentry status to those who received medals of lesser value: *BE*, vol. 22, 118. On the quest for bureaucratic careers, see E. F. Korsh, "Byt kupechestva i meshchanstva," in Moscow, Gosudarstvennyi istoricheskii muzei, *Iz epokhi krepostnogo khoziaistva XVIII i XIX vv.: stat'i i putvoditel' po vystavke*, ed. Iu. Gote and N. B. Baklanov (Moscow, 1926), 32.

15 Cited in I. G. Bliumin, *Ocherki ekonomicheskoi mysli v Rossii v pervoi polovine XIX v.* (Moscow-Leningrad, 1940), 159.

16 Simone Blanc, "Aux origines de la bourgeoisie russe," *CdMRS*, vol. 5, no. 3 (July–Sept. 1964), 294–310.

17 Iakovtsevsky, 133–4.

18 City residents from any estate who completed a course of study at a university, a commercial academy, or an ecclesiastical seminary could become honorary citizens, as could the most notable of a given city's artists and dramatic actors. *BE*, vol. 9, 532; Kolokolov, 50–1.

19 Iakovtsevsky, 135–8.

20 TsGAOR F IIIe Otdelenie 198, 1r.–5r.

21 Nikolai A. Naidenov, *Vospominaniia o vidennom, slyshannom i ispytannom*, 2 vols. (Moscow, 1903–5; reprinted, Newtonville, Mass., 1976), vol. 1, 56; Pavel A. Buryshkin, *Moskva kupecheskaia* (Moscow, 1954), 88. *MIMK*, vol. 8, lists new enrollees as of 1850, most of whom are labeled former *meshchane*. On the basis of very fragmentary evidence, Ksana S. Kuibysheva, "Krupnaia moskovskaia burzhuaziia v period revoliutsionnoi situatsii v 1859–1861 gg.," in M. V. Nechkina, ed., *Revoliutsionnaia situatsiia v Rossii v 1859–1861 gg.* (Moscow, 1965), 316–18, asserted that new manufacturers from the *meshchanstvo* and the peasantry had displaced the older trading merchants as guild leaders by 1861.

22 See *IM*, vol. 3, ch. 6.

23 Blackwell, 46.

24 Merchants had long appreciated the need for tariffs; see Sergei Kozhukov's memorandum of 1801, "Patrioticheskoe rassuzhdenie moskovskogo kommersanta o vneshnei rossiiskoi torgovle," *RA*, 1907, vol. 2, no. 8, 527–49.

25 On Kankrin's views, K. Lodyzhensky, *Istoriia russkogo tamozhennogo tarifa* (St. Petersburg, 1886), 201–27; Blackwell, 140–4; Walter M. Pintner, *Russian Economic Policy under Nicholas I* (Ithaca, 1967), 91–111; Nina S. Kiniapina, *Politika russkogo samoderzhaviia v oblasti promyshlennosti 20-50e gody XIX v.* (Moscow, 1968), ch. 2; and V. K. Iatsunsky, "Krupnaia promyshlennost' Rossii v 1790–1860 gg.," in M. K. Rozhkova, ed., *Ocherki ekonomicheskoi istorii Rossii pervoi poloviny XIX veka* (Moscow, 1959), 176.

26 Iatsunsky, 177; Gerhart von Schulze-Gävernitz, *Volkswirtschaftliche Studien aus Russland* (Leipzig, 1899), 90–107.

27 On the phenomenon of serf entrepreneurs, see J. Kulischer, "Die Kapitalistischen Unternehmer in Russland (insbesondere die Bauern als Unternehmer) in den Anfangsstadien des Kapitalismus," *Archiv für Sozialwissenschaft und Sozialpolitik*, vol. 65 (1931), 301–55.

28 Morozov had paid 17,000 rubles in 1820 to purchase his freedom and that of his four eldest sons; his landlord held the fifth son, Timofei, for a later redemption at an unspecified "fantastic" sum. Chedomir M. Ioksimovich, *Manufakturnaia promyshlennost' v proshlom i nastoiashchem*, vol. 1 (Moscow, 1915), 3.

29 Iatsunsky, 181–2.

30 Iosif F. Gindin, *Gosudarstvennyi bank i ekonomicheskaia politika tsarskogo pravitel'stva, 1861–1892 gg.* (Moscow, 1960), 132–6.

31 Kiniapina, ch. 4; Blackwell, 153–5.

32 FBON, "Zhurnal Moskovskogo otdeleniia Manufakturnogo soveta," e.g., 1843, 51r.–54r.; E. S. Lure, *Organizatsiia i organizatsii torgovo-promyshlennykh interesov v Rossii* (St. Petersburg, 1913), 39.

33 Buryskin, 233. See Appendix, Table I. On MSEC members, *Birzha*, 19–23.

34 *Birzha*, 1, 45, 29 (quoted).

35 Kolokolov, 125.

36 Vladimir P. Riabushinsky, "Kupechestvo moskovskoe," *Den' russkogo rebenka* (San Francisco), vol. 18 (April 1951), 189; emphasis in original.

37 *Nashe kupechestvo i torgovlia s ser'eznoi i karikaturnoi storony*, 3 vols. (Moscow, 1865–7), vol. 3, 4–5. Ushakov is identified as the author in *BE*, vol. 69, 125.

38 Valentine Bill, *The Forgotten Class: The Russian Bourgeoisie from the Earliest Beginnings to 1900* (New York, 1959), 137–46; Belinsky quoted in *IM*, vol. 3, 170.

39 Blackwell, 112–13.

40 Naidenov, vol. 2, 11. P. Vistengof, "Ocherki Moskovskoi zhizni," in *Moskva v ee proshlom i nastoiashchem*, 12 vols. (Moscow, 1910–12), vol. 10, 24, noted these women's "round, bluish faces, thick hands, fatty legs, puffed lips, and black teeth."

41 Nikolai P. Vishniakov, *Svedeniia o kupecheskom rode Vishniakovykh*, 3 vols. (Moscow, 1903–11), vol. 2, 147, 148, 150. See also Vladimir Polunin, *Three Generations: Family Life in Russia, 1845–1902*, trans. by A. F. Birch-Jones (London, 1957), 1–2, and Leningrad, Russkii muzei, *Kupecheskii bytovoi portret XVIII–XX vv.* (Leningrad, 1925).

42 August von Haxthausen, *Studien über die innern Zustände, das Volksleben and insbesondere die ländlichen Einrichtungen Russlands*, 3 vols. (Hannover, 1847–52), vol. 2, 518.

43 See Sergei I. Chetverikov's anecdotes about the "Old-Testament" merchant family, *Bezvozvratno ushedshaia Rossiia* (Berlin, 192-), 95–102.

44 Blackwell, 213. According to the computations of Anton S. Beliajeff, "The Rise of the Old Orthodox Merchants of Moscow, 1771–1894," unpublished doctoral dissertation, Syracuse University, 1975, 23–8, in 1850 Old-Believer merchants comprised at least 16 percent of the guild members and produced at least 12.7 percent of the total industrial output and 14.3 percent of all textile goods in Moscow.

45 On the holiday festivities, Vera P. Ziloti, *V dome Tretiakova* (New York, 1954), 25–7, 41–4.

46 Haxthausen, vol. 2, 517.

47 Korsh, 28. Old Believers, of course, shunned the modern script introduced by Peter the Great.

48 Vishniakov, vol. 2, 80–1.

49 Vishniakov, vol. 2, 93–4. One wonders whether this story inspired the argument

between the tyrannical merchant and the educated student over the efficacy of lightning rods in Act IV of Ostrovsky's *Thunderstorm* (1860). In his comedy *Your Drink, My
Hangover* (1856), Ostrovsky applied his neologism *samodur* ("self-made fool") to a traditional merchant named Tit Titych. The word and the name (sometimes modified to
Kit Kitych) have ever since connoted the stereotype of the cruel, greedy, and ignorant
merchant patriarch.

50 *Studien*, vol. 2, 517, corroborated in Buryshkin, 58–9.

51 *Nashe kupechestvo*, vol. 3, 6.

52 Victor Hehn, *De Moribus Ruthenorum: Zur Charakteristik der russischen Volksseele*, ed. by
Theodor Schiemann (Stuttgart, 1892), 94.

53 The family archives of the Bakhrushins (GIM F 1), the Botkins (TsGALI F 54), and
the Guchkovs (GIM F 122), for example, contain such neat account books.

54 V. Zeltser, "Prokhorovy; i 'prokhorovka' v 30–40 gg. XIX v.," *Uchenye Zapiski Instituta
istorii*, vol. 5 (1928), 413, cites records of expenditures for theater tickets and for donations to priests in the account books of the Prokhorov family's Trimount (*Trekhgornaia*)
factory.

55 Forty percent of the goods were sold for cash; the rest were bartered or given on credit
(often without written promissory notes). Gorlov, 273–4.

56 GIM F 122.497, 58r.–59r.

57 Hehn, 94–5. The word "German" (*nemets*) was applied to all North-European foreigners. On trade in taverns, see Vistengof, 51, 60.

58 FBON, "Zhurnal," 1846, 148r., 158v. On the importance of religious solidarity in the
maintenance of informal credit networks, see Blackwell, chs. 9–10. Traditional Russian terms attributing greed and dishonesty to the merchants, like *arshinnik, arkhiplut,
protobestia, naduvala*, and *kanal'ia* ("swindler," "knave," "rogue," "robber," and "crook")
may be savored in Gogol's *Inspector General* (1836). Even the gypsies sang: "Greedy
merchant of Moscow,/ Dishonest and rich,/ Not a true Russian son,/ Just a son of a
bitch." (From the Russian version in Buryshkin, 47.)

59 Ivan S. Aksakov, *Issledovanie o torgovle na ukrainskikh iarmarkakh* (St. Petersburg, 1858),
14–17.

60 FBON, "Zhurnal," 1846, 162v.

61 On these measures, Kiniapina, chs. 4–6.

62 FBON, "Zhurnal," 1843, 53r.–54r.

63 *Birzha*, 12–13. For the next twenty years (1839–59), they stood on the steps in all
weather: Naidenov, vol. 2, 63.

64 Based on the accounts in Chetverikov, 108–9 and Hehn, 95.

65 I. N. Rybnikov, "Rossiiskoe kupechestvo na obede u Imperatora Nikolaia Pavlovicha
(1833 g.)," *RA*, 1891, vol. 3, no. 12, 565–7.

66 Vishniakov, vol. 2, 80, 82.

67 Vishniakov, vol. 3, 92–3.

68 FBON, "Zhurnal," 1846, 165v.

69 Ditiatin, vol. 2, 245. He was writing in 1877.

70 Ditiatin, vol. 2, 246.

71 Vishniakov, vol. 2, 83.

72 Roger Portal, "Du servage à la bourgeoisie: la famille Konovalov," *Mélanges Pierre Pascal, Revue des études slaves*, 1961, 148.

73 GIM F 146.1, 170r.

74 *MIMKOP*, vol. 8, 283–4.

75 Kolokolov, 43. They did not necessarily serve on the sections of the Manufacturing
and Commercial Councils.

76 N . P. Chulkov, "Moskovskoe kupechestvo XVIII i XIX vv.," *RA*, 1907, vol. 3, no. 12, 500.

77 *Russkie liudi*, 2 vols. (Moscow-St. Petersburg, 1866), vol. 1, 41–53. On the extensive religious philanthropy of Ivan I. Chetverikov (1819–71) and Davyd I. Khludov (1822–86), see *RBS*, vol. 22, 361 and vol. 21, 342.

78 Buryshkin, 149–50; Chulkov, 497.

79 *RBS*, vol. 23, 243.

80 "Z," "Po povodu stat'i 'Gorodskie golovy v Moskve,'" *MV*, Jan. 16, 1863, 3; Vishniakov, vol. 1, 140.

81 *Nekotorye cherti iz zhizni Aleksandrovskogo 1-i gil'dii kuptsa i pochetnogo grazhdanina Ivana Fedorovicha Baranova* (Moscow, 1849), 22.

82 Henri Chambre, "Pososkov et le mercantilisme," *CdMRS*, vol. 4, no. 4 (Dec. 1963), especially 342–3.

83 Mikhail Tugan-Baranovsky, *Russkaia fabrika v proshlom i nastoiashchem*, reprinted from 3rd ed. (Moscow, 1926), 32–40; *RBS*, vol. 17, 435; Wallace Lee Daniel, Jr., "Russian Attitudes toward Modernization: The Merchant-Nobility Conflict in the Legislative Commission, 1767–1774," unpublished doctoral dissertation, University of North Carolina, 1973; Jack Moore Lauber, "The Merchant-Gentry Conflict in Eighteenth-Century Russia," unpublished doctoral dissertation, University of Iowa, 1967.

84 Polevoi, *Rech' o kupecheskom zvanii* . . . (Moscow, 1832), 20, 9.

85 *Rech'*, 4, 9.

86 Strong echoes of Hegel's *Grundlinien der Philosophie des Rechts* (1821), especially paragraphs 201–5, may be discerned in Polevoi's speech. Twenty-seven years later, in 1859, the historian and ideologist of tsarist autocracy, Mikhail P. Pogodin, expressed precisely the same idea: "Each estate has its own role to play in the state: the clergy prays; the gentry serves in war and peace; the peasants till the land and feed the people; and the merchants are the mediators who provide what is necessary to each person." Nikolai Barsukov, *Zhizn' i trudy M. P. Pogodina*, 22 vols. (St. Petersburg, 1888–1910), vol. 16, 591. Like Pogodin, in denying the existence of a conflict of interest among social groups in Russia, Polevoi reiterated the familiar themes of official nationality, described in Nicholas V. Riasanovsky, *Nicholas I and Official Nationality in Russia, 1825–1855* (Berkeley, 1967), especially ch. 3. The most intelligent treatment of Polevoi's political views is N. R. Malcom, "Ideology and Intrigue in Russian Journalism under Nicholas I: 'Moskovskii Telegraf' and 'Severnaya Pchela,'" unpublished doctoral dissertation, Oxford University, 1974. This exhaustive study clearly explains how the publisher of *Moskovskii telegraf*, while admiring French progressive journalism and applauding national liberation movements in Europe and the New World, upheld autocracy as the ideal political form for Russia. See especially 265–300 on Polevoi's defense of Russian autocracy; 301–6 for his Herderian glorification of the merchants as "true representatives and the true bearers" of the national culture (302), who were therefore entitled to industrial protectionism (303); and 308–14, which explains his enthusiasm for the French Revolution of 1830 in terms of a personal aversion toward aristocratic exclusiveness, whether social, political, or literary. The crude attempts of Soviet historians (e.g., Bliumin, ch. 6) to portray Polevoi as the spokesman of a rising "bourgeoisie" opposed to autocracy therefore do violence to the facts.

87 Tugan-Baranovsky, 137–9.

88 Kuibysheva, 320.

89 M. N. Sobolev, *Tamozhennaia politika Rossii vo vtoroi polovine XIX veka* (Tomsk, 1911), 35ff. (58 quoted); Lodyzhensky, 284, 290; *IMKO*, vol. 2, part 1, 480–504; Pintner, 237–49.

90 Mariia K. Rozhkova, *Ekonomicheskaia politika tsarskogo pravitel'stva na Srednem Vostoke vo vtoroi chetverti XIX v. i russkaia burzhuaziia* (Moscow, 1949), 294–9, 348, 359–66; Mariia K. Rozhkova, "Torgovlia," in Rozhkova, ed., *Ocherki*, 274–5; Mariia K. Rozhkova, "Iz istorii torgovli Rossii so Srednei Aziei vo 60-kh godakh XIX v.," *Istoricheskie zapiski*, vol. 67 (1960), 203.
91 Blackwell, 169, 272–3; Kiniapina, 383–5; Tugan-Baranovsky, 238–9.
92 Kiniapina, 388, 407–9.
93 Tugan-Baranovsky, 145.
94 Kiniapina, 414–15. Pintner, 235, doubted that this decree demonstrated the government's hostility to industrialism.
95 Vasili A. Kokorev, "Vospominaniia davnoproshedshego," *RA*, 1885, vol. 3, no. 9, 154.
96 Quoted in A. V. Figner, "Vospominaniia o grafe A. A. Zakrevskom (1807–1846 gg.)," *IV*, 1885, vol. 20, 666.
97 Naidenov, vol. 1, 95–7, 98.
98 Undated letter from Petr P. Botkin to his brother Vladimir, TsGALI F 54.1.82, 3v. On Zakrevsky's career, see *RBS*, vol. 7, 195–9.
99 *General Economic History*, trans. by Frank H. Knight (New York, 1927), 276–8.
100 The cultural changes described later affected the first- and second-guild merchants, a minority of the entire merchant estate. Merchant certificate holders numbered approximately 3,000 in 1835; by 1849, they increased slightly to 3,920 (first guild, 137; second, 330; third, 3,453). In 1853, the total reached 4,334; the three guilds contained 144, 400, and 3,794 members, respectively. Iakovtsevsky, 135–8, 173; *IM*,, vol. 3, 749.
101 V. G. Belinsky's letter to V. P. Botkin, December 1847, quoted by Alexander Gerschenkron, *Economic Backwardness in Historical Perspective* (Cambridge, Mass., 1966), 166.
102 Leroy-Beaulieu, vol. 1, 307–8; Naidenov, vol. 2, 11–12.
103 P. I. Shchukin, quoted in Buryshkin, 62.
104 Jeremiah Curtin, *Memoirs of Jeremiah Curtin*, ed. by Joseph Schafer (Madison, 1940), 89–92; quotation from 92. On the tsar's visit in 1863, *IMKO*, vol. 5, part 1, 23.
105 Comte P. Vasili [pseud.], *La Sainte Russie: La cour, l'armée, le clergé, la bourgeoisie, et le peuple* (Paris, 1890), 322.
106 Ioksimovich, 42; P. N. Terentiev, *Materialy k istorii Prokhorovskoi Trekhgornoi Manufaktury i torgovo-promyshlennoi deiatel'nosti sem'i Prokhorovykh, gody 1799–1915* (Moscow, 1915), 105, 101.
107 Letter from Hamburg, 1846, quoted in Terentiev, 102.
108 April 5, 1846, GIM F 146.1, 35v., 35r. His brother Konstantin provided workers with religious books, and condemned "the pernicious spirit of the times." Sima M. Lapitskaia, *Byt rabochikh Trekhgornoi manufaktury* (Moscow, 1935), 19.
109 Letter of Aug. 20, 1846, to an older brother, GIM F 146.1, 38r.–39r.
110 Nikolai K. Krestovnikov, *Semeinaia khronika Krestovnikovykh i rodstvennykh im familii (Pis'ma i vospominaniia)*, 3 vols. (Moscow, 1903–4), vol. 2, 11–12; quotation from a letter home, 21.
111 V. A. Kokorev, letter to Iakunchikov, "Pis'ma," *RA*, 1910, vol. 3, no. 11, 528.
112 On Tretiakov, Aleksandra P. Botkina, *Pavel Mikhailovich Tretiakov v zhizni i iskusstve*, 2nd ed. (Moscow, 1960); on Botkin, Kuibysheva, 327, and Afanasi A. Fet, *Moi vospominaniia*, 2 parts in 1 vol. (Moscow, 1890), vol. 1, 218–19, 408.
113 Stuart R. Grover, "Savva Mamontov and the Mamontov Circle, 1870–1905: Art Patronage and the Rise of Nationalism in Russian Art," unpublished doctoral dissertation, University of Wisconsin, 1971.

114 Buryshkin, 149.
115 Georgi Shteker, "Svedeniia o kupecheskom rode Alekseevykh," Moscow, 1940, type-written manuscript in MMKhAT, 70.
116 Shteker, 76.
117 Ushakov, vol. 1, 16–17.
118 Pavel G. Ryndziunsky, "Staroobriadcheskaia organizatsiia v usloviiakh razvitiia pro-myshlennogo kapitalizma," *Voprosy istorii religii i ateizma*, vol. 1 (1950), 199.
119 Ryndziunsky, "Organizatsiia," 246.
120 *Torgovoe i promyshlennoe delo Riabushinskikh* (Moscow, 1913), 32–3; on the 1863 decree, Frederick C. Conybeare, *Russian Dissenters* (New York, 1962), 234.
121 In Edinoverie, Old Believers recognized the Orthodox priestly hierarchy, but re-mained free to practice their distinctive ritual, which dated from before the church reforms of 1666–7.
122 *Ocherk torgovoi i obshchestvennoi deiatel'nosti manufaktur-sovetnika, pochetnogo grazhdanina i kavalera I. F. Guchkova*, appendix to *Narodnaia gazeta* (St. Petersburg, 1867), 12; Belia-jeff, 156–65.
123 I. Iuzov [I. I.Kablits], "Politicheskie vozzreniia Staroveriia," *Russkaia mysl'*, 1882, no. 5, 190; *Ocherk torgovoi i obshchestvennoi deiatel'nosti manufaktur-sovetnika, pochetnogo grazhdanina i kavalera E. F. Guchkova*, appendix to *Narodnaia gazeta* (St. Petersburg, 1867), 13–15.
124 Quoted in Vasili I. Kelsiev, " 'Ispoved' ' V. I. Kelsieva," ed. by E. Kingisepp, *LN*, vols. 41–2, (1941), 331.
125 Naidenov, vol. 2, 50; *Birzha*, 21–3; Buryshkin, 246.
126 GBL-OR F 332.75.33. A synopsis of his two essays, *On Wealth* and *On Poverty*, is in Terentiev, 108–9.

2. The formation of a merchant ideology, 1855–1860

1   Vishniakov, *Svedeniia*, vol. 3, 3–4.
2   Naidenov, *Vospominaniia*, vol. 1, 106.
3   *IM*, vol. 3, 758–9. It never saw combat.
4   *IM*, vol. 3, 747.
5   A. S. Nifontov, "Vneshniaia torgovlia Rossii vo vremia vostochnoi voiny 1853–1856 gg.," in L. M. Ivanov, ed., *Problemy sotsial'no-ekonomicheskoi istorii Rossii: sbornik statei* (Moscow, 1971), especially 88–90. Raw cotton imports from the United States via the European border fell in value from 12 to 5 million rubles between 1853 and 1855, but in terms of weight declined only from 1.8 to 1.3 million puds. Imports from Central Asia almost doubled in the same period, rising from 120,000 to 224,000 puds.
6   Anna I. Volkova, *Vospominaniia, dnevnik i stat'i*, ed. by Ch. Vetrinsky (V. E. Cheshikhin) (Nizhny Novgorod, 1913), 21.
7   Ivan F. Gorbunov, "Otryvki iz vospominanii," in his *Polnoe sobranie sochinenii*, ed. by A. F. Koni, 2 vols., 3rd. ed. (St. Petersburg, 1904), vol. 2, 393; *RBS*, vol. 3, 298.
8   Naidenov, vol. 1, 105–6.
9   Quoted in *IM*, vol. 3, 770.
10 Feb. 23, 1856, *Ivan Sergeevich Aksakov v ego pis'makh*, 4 vols. (St. Petersburg, 1888–96), vol. 3, 231–2n.
11 Barsukov, *Zhizn'*, vol. 14, 515–16.
12 Aksakov, *V pis'makh*, vol. 3, 232n.
13 Blackwell, *Beginnings*, 192.
14 Aleksei S. Khomiakov, Konstantin and Ivan S. Aksakov, Ivan and Petr V. Kireevsky,

and Iuri F. Samarin are considered the original formulators of the Slavophile doctrines. Nicholas V. Riasanovsky, *Russia and the West in the Teachings of the Slavophiles* (Cambridge, Mass., 1952), 29.

15 Many educated Russians shared the Slavophiles' outlook, called themselves "Slavophiles," and were regarded as such by society. Among the most notable were A. I. Koshelev, the journalist and tax concessionaire; P. M. Sadovsky, A. N. Ostrovsky, and I. F. Gorbunov, the actors and playwrights; F. V. Chizhov, a former mathematics teacher and art historian who had turned to silkworm cultivation; the Shipov brothers, Dmitri (a Colonel), Aleksandr, and Sergei, all gentry industrialists; and at least two princes in the imperial bureaucracy, V. A. Cherkassky and D. A. Obolensky. The term is extended in this study to include them.

16 This point is argued cogently by Barrington Moore, Jr., *Social Origins of Dictatorship and Democracy: Lord and Peasant in the Making of the Modern World* (Boston 1966), ch. 1.

17 Stephen Lukashevich, *Ivan Aksakov, 1823–1886: A Study in Russian Thought and Politics* (Cambridge, Mass., 1965), 33.

18 Mar. 22, 1857, GBL-OR F 332.2.9, 2r.

19 See the Slavophile argument for cottage industry, "so backward in the technical sense, but so preferable in the moral sense to the foreign [factory system]." "O manufakturnoi promyshlennosti Rossii v otnosheniiakh ee k obshchei proizvoditel'nosti i k bytu nizshikh klassov naroda," *Moskvitianin*, vol. 2 (1845), 62.

20 Gorbunov, 382–3, 392.

21 Gorbunov, 393. Another scion of this tea family, Vasili P. Botkin, had attained fame as a writer of aesthetic and travel literature in the 1840s; on his repudiation of the westerner ideals of his youth, see Chapter 4, first section.

22 Kokorev's idea for an elaborate celebration in honor of the common sailors may have originated with the Slavophiles' festive welcome for S. A. Khrulev, the commander at Sevastopol two months before. *IM*, vol. 3, 770.

23 Barsukov, vol. 13, 85–114.

24 Aksaskov, *V pis'makh*, vol. 3, 231–2n.

25 Barsukov, vol. 14, 515. As early as 1849, Pogodin had praised the Old-Believer merchant Ivan N. Tsarsky for spending his fortune on rare old books and manuscripts, "on the nation's history, to the glory of the Fatherland," instead of on luxuries. *RBS*, vol. 21, 453.

26 Aksakov, *V pis'makh*, vol. 3, 232n.

27 Barsukov, vol. 15, 51–7; quotation from 57.

28 S. I. Mamontov's diary, Jan. 1, 1858, TsGALI F 799.1.11, 2r.

29 "Liubopytnye pokazaniia o nekotorykh predstaviteliakh moskovskogo obrazovannogo obshchestva v nachale proshlogo tsarstvovaniia," *RA*, 1885, vol. 2, no. 7, 447–9.

30 Aksakov, *Sochineniia I. S. Aksakova*, 7 vols. (Moscow, 1886–7), vol. 3, 468; Michael B. Petrovich, *The Emergence of Russian Panslavism, 1856–1870* (New York, 1956), 114–15.

31 Boris B. Glinsky, *Bor'ba za konstitutsiiu 1612–1861 gg.* (St. Petersburg, 1908), 544–5.

32 Glinsky, 544–8. These speeches, and the merchants' reactions to them, are analyzed later.

33 Kuibysheva, "Burzhuaziia," 324. Quotation from Fet, *Vospominaniia*, vol. 1, 225, Fet was married to Mariia P. Botkina.

34 See Appendix, Table I; Kuibysheva, 325–9; and *IM*, vol. 4, 23. Full list in Aleksei A. Popelnitsky, "Zapreshchennyi po vysochaishemu poveleniiu banket v Moskve 19 fevralia 1858 goda," *GM*, 1914, no. 2 (Feb.), 208–9.

35 Sobolev, *Politika*, 150. See Appendix, Table I for names.

36 Skuratov, a titular councilor in 1857–8, owned the "Resurrection" cotton mill in 1835.

37 Shipov's role in the merchant-Slavophile alliance is discussed in detail later in this chapter.

38 Sobolev, 155.

39 Quoted in Sobolev, 151, without reference.

40 *RBS*, vol. 23, 293.

41 On the letters, Terentiev, *Materialy*, 182–8; on the bribe attempt, for which Prokhorov was fined 5,000 rubles and briefly imprisoned, TsGAOR F III Otdelenie 486, 1r.–8v. and Naidenov, vol. 2, 71: on the society, TsGAM F 16.228.226 and Appendix, Table 1.

42 Ivan S. Aksakov, "Fedor Vasilevich Chizhov," *RA*, 1878, no. 1, 9–13; A. A. Liberman, ed., *Sbornik v pamiat' stoletiia so dnia rozhdeniia Fedora Vasilevicha Chizhova* (Kostroma, 1911), 20–30.

43 *Aktsioner*, Jan. 5, 1863, lead editorial.

44 Liberman, 45, quoting Chizhov in *Vestnik promyshlennosti*, without reference. Italics in Liberman.

45 Vladimir S. Mamontov, "Chastnaia opera S. I. Mamontova," typewritten manuscript in GTsTM F 155, 12.

46 Arkadi Cherokov, *Fedor Vasilevich Chizhov i ego sviazi s N. V. Gogolem* (Moscow, 1902), 31 4. Cherokov was Chizhov's secretary.

47 The address was published in *Russkii vestnik* (Aug. 1857) and as a pamphlet printed by N. M. Shchepkin and K. T. Soldatenkov: *O nekotorykh usloviiakh, sposobstvuiushchikh umnozheniiu narodnogo kapitala* (Kazan, 1856).

48 "Russkie protektsionisty," *Atenei*, 1858, part 2, 479. This slap at Old Believers perhaps indicated Babst's scorn for the old-fashioned merchants.

49 Babst's long, favorable review of *Die Grundlagen der Nationalökonomie* (Stuttgart, 1854, the first book in Roscher's multivolume *System der Volkswirtschaft*), in *Russkii vestnik* (Mar. 1856) is cited by Rozental, "Programma," 207. Ivan Aksakov wrote in 1860 that Babst "was enthusiastic about Roscher's theory" and that "it did a lot to lead him to nationalism in general." Aksakov, *V pis'makh*, vol. 3, 352. Chizhov, for his part, considered Roscher the foremost German economist: diary, Feb. 17, 1858, GBL-OR F 332.2.9, 16v.

50 GIM F 440.784, 45r.

51 Rieber, "Group," 15, appears mistaken in calling Babst a convert to "militant Slavophilism . . ." On Babst, see *Russkie vedomosti, 1863–1913: sbornik statei* (Moscow, 1913), vol. 2, 19.

52 *Ocherk deiatel'nosti A. P. Shipova, predsedatelia birzhevogo i iarmochnogo Komiteta v Nizhnem-Novgorode*, appendix to *Narodnaia gazeta* (St. Petersburg, 1866), 5.

53 FBON, "Zhurnal Moskovskogo otdeleniia manufakturnogo soveta," 1858, 35v.–36r.

54 *Ocherk . . . Shipova*, 7.

55 *RBS*, vol. 23, 293.

56 GBL-OR F 332.5.16, 1r. No donations from merchants were listed in this accounting of the journal's income for 1857-8.

57 E. A. Tseitlin, *Tekhnicheskii perevorot v l'nopriadenii i nachalo mashinnogo proizvodstva l'niannoi priazhi v Rossii* (Moscow and Leningrad, 1936), 205.

58 *Ocherk . . . Shipova*, 5.

59 His works are listed in *RBS*, vol. 23, 293, and Vladimir Ia. Laverychev, *Krupnaia burzhuaziia v poreformennoi Rossii (1861–1900 gg.)* (Moscow, 1974), 175–9.

60 *Vestnik promyshlennosti*, 1858, no. 1, 18.

61 *Vestnik promyshlennosti*, 1858, no. 2, 106–7.

62 L. B. Genkin, "Obshchestvenno-politicheskaia programma russkoi burzhuazii v gody

pervoi revoliutsionnoi situatsii (1859–1861 gg.) (po materialam zhurnala 'Vestnik promyshlennosti')," in L. M. Ivanov, ed., *Problemy sotsial'no-ekonomicheskoi istorii Rossii: sbornik statei* (Moscow, 1971), 98–9, noted that *Vestnik promyshlennosti* in 1860 roundly condemned officials' graft taking for its harmful effects on trade in an article entitled "Indirect Taxes" (*Kosvennye nalogi*).

63 *Vestnik promyshlennosti*, 1858, no. 3, section II, 177.

64 *Aktsioner*, Jan. 5, 1863, lead editorial.

65 See Alfred J. Rieber, "The Formation of La Grande Société des Chemins de Fer Russes," *JfGO*, vol. 21, no. 3 (Sept. 1973), 382.

66 Cherokov, 38, 39 (quoted). His diary skipped almost two years after July 1858, when *Vestnik promyshlennosti* and the organization of the railroad began. GBL-OR F 332.2.9, 23v.

67 Nikitenko, diary entry of Dec. 2, 1863, *Zapiski i dnevnik, 1826–1877*, 3 vols. (St. Petersburg, 1893), vol. 2, 415.

68 *Polveka russkoi zhizni, vospominaniia A. I. Delviga*, ed. S. Ia. Shtraikh, 2 vols. (Moscow and Leningrad, 1930), vol. 2, 87–9.

69 Cherokov, 38.

70 1858, no. 2, section I, 130–1.

71 *Vestnik promyshlennosti*, 1858, no. 2, section I, 131. Likewise, A. S. Khomiakov had invented a rotary steam engine and mined coal on his estate in Tula province: Blackwell, 147; *Aktsioner*, Sept. 30, 1860, 153. M. P. Pogodin approved of the Trinity line and proposed a railroad from Russia to India in order to facilitate the movement of military troops: Barsukov, vol. 16, 521 and vol. 15, 43–4.

72 Vol. 2, 110. On the Moscow Merchant Bank (1866), the Moscow Discount Bank (1869), the Moscow Merchant Mutual Credit Society (1869), and Naidenov's own Trading Bank (1871), see Naidenov, vol. 2, 108–26 and Appendix, Table I.

73 *Polveka*, vol. 2, 93, editor's note without reference. Chizhov once accused Kokorev and Putilov of relying on "bribery" and "lies." "In a word, there is not a trace here of any moral sense . . ." Quoted in Laverychev, *Burzhuaziia*, 74 (no date given).

74 Jan. 2, 1858, TsGALI F 799.1.11, 2v. Although Mamontov "consciously and admittedly patterned himself after Chizhov," he was by nature too "impetuous" for his "methodical" mentor. They quarreled seriously in 1872. Grover, "Mamontov," 40–1.

75 Quoted in Barsukov, vol. 15, 58.

76 Letter to Chizhov, Nov. 10, 1862, GBL-OR F 332.22.33, 1r.

77 Quoted in Sergei A. Nikitin, *Slavianskie komitety v Rossii v 1858–1876 godakh* (Moscow, 1960), 78.

78 GBL-OR F 332.75.31. This law, *PSZ-2*, no. 39118 of Jan. 1, 1863, weakened only slightly the traditional system under which each social estate performed specific economic roles. Except for landlords and peasants who sold the products of their own land – grain, cattle, wood, etc. (Art. 4) – every person engaged in wholesale or retail trade or in manufacturing was required to purchase an annual certificate. A new business certificate (*promyslovoe svidetel'stvo*) now went into effect, which granted no special personal advantages whatsoever except the right to engage in petty trade and peddling (Art. 13, 15). Another innovation was the reduction in the number of merchant guilds from three to two. Wholesale traders and large-scale manufacturers were to purchase a first-guild merchant certificate (*kupecheskoe svidetel'stvo*), and retail traders and small-scale manufacturers a second-guild one. The purchase of a merchant certificate still carried, in most cases, the title (*zvanie*) of "merchant," the obligation to serve in the various elective offices of the merchant estate, and the personal advantages of the title such as exemption from the poll tax and from military conscription (Art. 13; 34, note 2;

83). Russians of both sexes and "of all ranks" (*sostoianii*) who desired simply to engage in economic activity could, however, purchase a merchant or business certificate, either "keeping their present title or enrolling in the merchant estate," as they chose: Art. 21, 22 (quoted), 82. Each large corporation (joint-stock company, share partnership, bank, insurance company, etc.), but not its executives, must purchase a first-guild merchant certificate, and every brokerage office must obtain a second-guild one (Art. 36, 65, note 2).

Two key provisions prevented members of other estates from encroaching on the merchants' traditional role as the primary economic actors. First, a holder of a merchant certificate was required to enter the local merchant estate in his locality if he ceased to belong to another estate, as in the case of peasants who had paid all debts owed to their communes (Art. 24, 82). Furthermore, lest the gentry be attracted en masse into economic enterprise, the law specified that no public official, appointed or elected, could act as a contractor for the office in which he worked; and, more importantly, that any bureaucrat or elected official who went bankrupt must be dismissed from his governmental position (Art. 23). Two years later (*PSZ*–2, no. 41779 of Feb. 9, 1865), clergy and military men on active service in lower ranks were denied the right to purchase either merchant or business certificates (Art. 20), and the management of a manufacturing or wholesale commercial enterprise was made contingent not only on the purchase of a merchant certificate but also on entrance into the merchant estate, with or without concurrent membership in another estate (Art. 21; Grigori Voltke, *Pravo torgovli i promyshlennosti v Rossii v istoricheskom razuitii (XIX vek)*, 2nd ed., rev. (St. Petersburg, 1905), 20–1). (Jews remained under special restrictions regarding travel and residence outside the Pale of Settlement: Voltke, 21–30.)

79 Sobolev's caustic phrase, 173.

80 Chizhov's guidelines were very strict; he set annual depreciation for brick and wooden buildings at 1 and 2 percent, respectively. Cherokov, 40.

81 Cherokov, 34.

82 Letter of Dec. 28, 1861 to Chizhov, GBL-OR F 332.58.8.

83 Letter of Oct. 31, 1862, GBL-OR F 332.10.67. In contrast, Khludov spared no expense in amassing a huge collection of rare religious books and manuscripts and in publishing his brother-in-law's two-volume tract against the Old Believers: *RBS*, vol. 21, 341–2; P. S. Smirnov, *Istoriia russkogo raskola staroobriadstva* (Riazan, 1893), 230.

84 *Nekotorye cherty . . . Baranova*, 11.

85 Vasili A. Kokorev, "Ekonomicheskie provaly po vospominaniiam s 1837 goda," *RA*, 1887, vol. 1, part 2, 251.

86 "Provaly," vol. 2, part 6, 288.

87 "Provaly," vol. 1, part 2, 256 and vol. 2, part 7, 398–400.

88 Knoop, the importer of textile machines, received credit from the de Jersey Company and other firms in England and in turn extended credit to the Russian industrialists. His access to plentiful credit allowed him to maintain a complete monopoly for decades on the importation of English textile machines. Schulze-Gävernitz, *Studien*, 90–106.

89 For decades afterwards, Kokorev advocated that flax be processed into linen in Russian factories, and that the spinning and weaving of raw cotton imported from America be curtailed. "Provaly," vol. 1, part 2, 252–3. He approvingly cited M. P. Pogodin's xenophobic credo: "Here at home is our salvation, in our own land." "Provaly," vol. 1, part 3, 370.

90 Buryshkin, 207, called it "Slavophilish polemics."

91 This ideology of industrialization, drawn from Friedrich List and Wilhelm Roscher,

preceded that of the Marxist intellectuals, which Alexander Gerschenkron cited as typical of prerevolutionary Russia, in *Backwardness*, 25–6.

92 "Provaly," vol. 1, part 3, 382; vol. 1, part 2, 259; vol. 2, part 6, 267; vol. 1, part 2, 258; vol. 2, part 6, 269. Emphasis in original. Kokorev's resentment owed much to the fact that, as a tax concessionaire himself, he had suffered economic reverses as a result of this change.

93 "Provaly," vol. 1, part 3, 370–2.

94 Marc Raeff, "Some Reflections on Russian Liberalism," *Russian Review*, vol. 18 (July 1959), 220.

95 Harold J. Laski, *The Rise of Liberalism: The Philosophy of a Business Civilization* (New York, 1936), especially chs. 1 and 2; J.-B. Bergier, "The Industrial Bourgeoisie and the Rise of the Working Class, 1700–1914," in Carlo M. Cipolla, ed., *The Fontana Economic History of Europe*, 4 vols. (New York, 1976), vol. 3, 397–451. Even the Orthodox merchants in the Balkans had an active political role: Traian Stoianovich, "The Conquering Balkan Orthodox Merchant," *Journal of Economic History*, vol. 20, no. 2 (June 1960), 235, 312. The Marxist notion of an "ascendant bourgeoisie" that toppled the Old Regime in France is untenable, however, for it overlooks the crucial role of the urban masses and peasants in the violence of 1789–94; see Moore, 108–10, 428–9. On the other hand, several non-Marxist historians have tried to deny the entire concept of "bourgeois liberalism" (in the sense of parliamentary institutions serving capitalists' interests) by stressing the aristocratic leadership of the liberal movement in 1789; see the arguments on both sides in Ralph W. Greenlaw, ed., *The Social Origins of the French Revolution: The Debate on the Role of the Middle Classes* (Lexington, Mass., 1975). They also point to the important role of landowners, professional men, and government officials, as well as businessmen, in the political elite of nineteenth-century Europe: Alfred Cobban, "The Middle Class in France, 1815–1848," *French Historical Studies*, vol. 5, no. 1 (Spring 1967), 41–52. A balanced view is that of Lenore O'Boyle, "The Middle Class in Western Europe, 1815–1848," *American Historical Review*, vol. 71, no. 3 (April 1966), 826–45. She counters Cobban's objections by positing the existence of a class united by a common political ideology: "an amalgam of nobility and new men, of landlord, business, professional, and official interests, all more or less accepting the political and social changes arising from the Revolution," that is, the parliamentary republic and capitalism. "The 'Middle Class' Reconsidered: A Reply to Professor Cobban," *French Historical Studies*, vol. 5, no. 1 (Spring 1967), 55. The divergence of the Russian pattern from the English and the French rests on the fact that the various social groups that constituted O'Boyle's "middle class" remained distinct in Russia, estranged by enormous differences in politics and culture. Among them only the professional men and a few enlightened landowners inclined toward liberalism; and the Moscow manufacturers, unlike their West-European counterparts, were so poorly educated that they proved incapable of publishing their own newspapers and journals (see Owen, "Merchants," especially n. 60).

96 *IM*, vol. 4, 25.

97 Kokorev, "Vospominaniia," vol. 3, part 9, 155. Although Khomiakov demonstrated his allegiance to Old Russia, not Western Europe, by this action, the mere fact of nonconformity appeared to Zakrevsky as a critique of the government, hence a "liberal" manifestation.

98 "Liubopytnye pokazaniia," 449.

99 Kokorev had hung a sign advertising his "Collection of Folk Handicrafts" (*khranilishche narodnogo rukodeliia*); but Zakrevsky considered "this mention of the people to be liberal" and had the sign destroyed. Naidenov, vol. 1, 101. Ziloti, 65, called Kokorev and I. F. Mamontov "great liberals and Westerners" because they loved to visit Europe!

See also *RBS*, vol. 15, 628.

100 "Provaly," vol. 2, part 403. This word expressed ridicule by virtue of its joining a "neutral-terminological stem" with an "expressive-colloquial suffix." Iuri S. Sorokin, *Razvitie slovarnogo sostava russkogo literaturnogo iazyka, 30-90-e gody XIX veka* (Leningrad, 1965), 178, 182.

101 Kokorev, "Vzgliad," 38; "Obed 28-go dekabria," *RVes*, 1857, vol. 12, book 2, section "Sovremenaia letopis'," 208.

102 "Obed," 208–9.

103 On his article of January, 1859, "Milliard v tumane," which also called for the sale of state lands to raise a total of a billion rubles, see Kuibysheva, 331–5 and Barsukov, vol. 16, 82–4.

104 "Obed," 213.

105 Letter of Feb. 5, 1858, TsGALI F 54.1.81, 11v.

106 "Obed," 206.

107 Genkin, 100. Naidenov, whose family owned a small textile-dyeing shop, recalled, "Since it did not directly concern the group to which I belonged, I can say nothing about the most important reform of that time, the abolition of serfdom; my group knew little of what other strata of the society were doing about it." Vol. 2, 3.

108 Kuibysheva, 332–6; quotation from 333.

109 "Vzgliad russkogo na evropeiskuiu torgovliu," *RVes*, vol. 14, no. 5 (Mar. 1858), 37.

110 He advised Finance Minister Vronchenko on matters of state economic policy in the late 1840s: "Provaly," vol. 1, part 2, 252; with Khrulev, the commander at Sevastopol, he discussed war contingency plans in 1859: "Liubopytnye pokazaniia," 452; and he commiserated with Finance Minister Kniazhevich in 1859 about the pernicious influence of the liberal economists ("Them, Inc.") on Russia's economic fate: "Provaly," vol. 1, part 2, 258.

111 Mitrofan P. Shchepkin, "Nadgrobnoe slovo: K. T. Soldatenkov," *RVed*, May 22, 1901, 2; *T. N. Granovsky i ego perepiska*, 2 vols. (Moscow, 1897), vol. 2, 302, 433, 436. Granovsky lived in the Botkins' house shortly before his death in 1855: *RBS*, vol. 3, 296.

112 *RBS*, vol. 21, 83; *IV*, July 1901, 378. In his dissertation, "Izdatel'skaia deiatel'nost' K. T. Soldatenkova," (Moscow State University, 1973), 71–73, 83–85, and 194, A. P. Tolstiakov noted that Soldatenkov depended on Granovsky, Shchepkin, and N. Kh. Ketcher for advice on which books to publish.

113 *BE*, vol. 30, 749; N. A. Alekseev, ed., "Pis'ma N. G. Chernyshevskogo k Soldatenkovu," *Katorga i ssylka*, vol. 47 (1928), 62–79.

114 As claimed by Kelsiev, " 'Ispoved'," " 343–4. Tolstiakov, 55–9, expressed doubt that Soldatenkov actually gave to *Obshchee veche* the money that Kelsiev requested.

115 On tariffs, see Chapter 3; on Pan-Slavism, Chapter 4. His ties to Pogodin were satirized in an epigram composed by an anti-Slavophile wit, possibly relating to one of the dinners of 1856–8: "*Obed nam byl ves'ma negoden,/ Nemnogo bylo i uma:/ Nam rechi govoril Pogodin,/ A den'gi zaplatil Kuz'ma.*" ("The banquet seemed to us all wrong,/ There was too little sparkling wit;/ Pogodin gave us speeches long,/ And stingy Kuzma paid for it.") Gorbunov, vol. 2, 384.

116 Franco Venturi, *Roots of Revolution*, trans. by Francis Haskell (New York, 1966), 117.

117 Eugene Piziur, "Some Problems of Russian Constitutional Doctrine of the 'Sixties,' " unpublished doctoral dissertation, University of Notre Dame, 1961, 166–89. Dolgorukov's notion that the merchants would support a constitutional regime proved how little he knew of their real political attitudes.

3. *Economic challenges and accommodation with the state, 1855–1877*

1 Blackwell, *Beginnings*, chs. 11–12; statistics from 319.
2 GIM F 208.21, 1r.
3 Cherniaev, Shipov, and Vyshnegradsky were all on the board of the Rybinsk-Kostroma Railroad, begun in 1872. The other founders were Commercial Councilor Abram Moisevich Varshavsky and Actual State Councilor Nikolai P. Skripitsyn. GIM F 208.21, 45r.
4 Hehn, *De Moribus Ruthenorum*, 183–5.
5 On the company, see Rieber, "Formation," and Aida M. Solovieva, *Zheleznodorozhnyi transport Rossii vo vtoroi polovine XIX v.* (Moscow, 1975), 61–80. The company's charter appears in *PSZ*–2, no. 31448, Jan. 26, 1857. The "Main French Railroad Company," as Kokorev liked to call it, actually represented broad international financial cooperation. Besides the St. Petersburg banker Baron Stieglitz, financiers of the company included S. A. Frenkel (Warsaw), Baring Brothers (London), Gope (Amsterdam), Isaac and Emile Pereire (Paris), and Mendelsohn (Berlin).
6 On Chizhov's views see Chapter 2, note 64. On Aksakov's, *Moskva* editorial, July 3, 1868, 1–2. Kokorev considered the construction of Russian railroads with foreign capital and management proof of what he called bureaucratic "liberalism": "it was clear that we were playing the liberal [*liberal'nichaem*] before Europe and for Europe, and stifling at home any undertaking which sought to express Russian distinctiveness." "Provaly," vol. 2, part 403.
7 In comparison, the Moscow-Riazan road cost 76,000 rubles per verst; Chizhov's Moscow-Iaroslavl road, 64,000; and Kokorev's Volga-Don road, 61,000. Aksakov, *Moskva* editorial, July 3, 1868, 2.
8 Aksakov in *Moskva*, July 3, 1868, 1. In fact, Russian control has been reasserted in 1861: Rieber, "Formation," 389.
9 This has long been Chizhov's "hope, or perhaps dream": diary, June 19, 1864, GBL-OR F 332.2.10, 7v.
10 In the early 1860s, the stockholders owning fifty or more shares included 36 persons with civil rank, 23 military officers, 3 barons, 4 counts, and 2 princes. The 18 honorary citizens and 14 merchants or merchants' sons represented a significant contingent from the traditionally cautious mercantile estate. GBL-OR F 332.74.6. Pogodin himself bought shares from I. F.Mamontov in 1862: GBL-OR F 231.Pog/II.20.22, 5r.
11 *Moskva*, July 3, 1868, 2.
12 *Moskvich*, Jan. 28, 1868, lead editorial. On Winan's role in building the Nikolaev Railroad, see Blackwell, 312–314.
13 Cherokov's phrase, in his *Chizhov*, 39.
14 GBL-OR F 332.73.6, 1r.
15 "Dva pis'ma M. G. Cherniaeva, 1867 goda," *Shchukinskii sbornik*, 10 vols. (Moscow, 1902–12), vol. 10, 242.
16 *Moskvich*, Feb. 4, 1868, editorial, 1–2.
17 The latter, a coowner of the Nevsky arms and locomotive plant, also edited *Birzhevye vedomosti (Stock Exchange News)* in St. Petersburg: Gindin, *Bank*, 208; *RBS*, vol. 22, 379.
18 Kokorev, "Provaly," vol. 2, part 7, 401–3.
19 "Provaly," vol. 2, part 7, 402; Russia, *finansov, 1802–1902*, 2 vols. (St. Petersburg, 1902), *Ministerstvo*, vol. 1, 580.
20 Cherokov, 39.
21 Although a founder of this bank, Kokorev held no office in it: Moskovskoe kupecheskoe obshchestvo vzaimnogo kredita, *Ocherk deiatel'nosti Moskovskogo kupecheskogo obshchestva vzaimnogo kredita za dvadtsatipiatiletie (1869–1894)* (Moscow, 1895), 90–2.

22   *Polveka*, vol. 2, 469.
23   GBL-OR F 332.4.7, 1r.–2v.
24   Russia . . . *Ministerstvo*, vol. 1, 580; Naidenov, *Vospominaniia*, vol. 2, 99; Cherokov, 41 (quoted); *PSZ–2*, no. 49,634 of May 21, 1871.
25   Cherokov, 41–2; Boris N. Chicherin, *Vospominaniia*, 4 vols. (Moscow, 1929–34; reprinted, Cambridge, England, 1973), vol. 4, 88.
26   Annenkov, the literary critic, to the novelist Turgenev, in November 1856, quoted in V. N. Rozental, "Obshchestvenno-politicheskaia programma russkogo liberalizma v seredine 50-kh godov XIX v. (Po materialam *Russkogo vestnika* za 1856–1857 gg.)," *Istoricheskie zapiski*, vol. 67 (1960), 213. Two famous economists, Vladimir P. Bezobrazov (1828–89) and Ivan V. Vernadsky (1821–84), wrote antiprotectionist articles in *Russkii vestnik;* Vernadsky also published his own free-trade journals in St. Petersburg: *Ukazatel' ekonomicheskii, politicheskii i promyshlennyi* (1857), *Ukazatel' politiko-ekonomicheskii* (1858–61), and *Ekonomist: politiko-ekonomicheskii zhurnal* (1858–65, issued as a supplement to *Ukazatel'*, 1858–60). On Bezobrazov, see V. N. Rosental, "Ideinye tsentry liberal'nogo dvizheniia v Rossii nakanune revoliutsionnoi situatsii," in M. V. Nechkina, ed., *Revoliutsionnaia situatsiia v Rossii v 1859–1861 gg.* (Moscow, 1963), 384–90; and Gindin, *Bank*, 179–80. On Vernadsky, see Rozental, "Programma," 121–13; and *BE*, vol. 6, 38–9. Free trade was also propounded by the journals *Sovremennik (The Contemporary)*, *Otechestvennye zapiski (Notes of the Fatherland)*, *Golos (The Voice)*, and *Moskovskie vedomosti (The Moscow News)*. See the survey of the polemical literature in Sobolev, *Politika*, 360–81.
27   *Birzha*, 17.
28   Naidenov, vol. 2, 65; GBL-OR F 332.43.7.
29   *Birzha*, 17.
30   Naidenov, vol. 2, 66; *Birzha*, 35.
31   Naidenov, vol. 2, 67. Morozov was known as "the Englishman" for his cosmopolitan, luxurious style of living: Beliajeff, "Merchants," 193n.
32   Naidenov, vol. 2, 66–7.
33   Letter of Nov. 26, [1864], GIM F 44.1.107r.
34   *Mnenie Postoiannoi Deputatsii Moskovskikh Kupecheskikh S"ezdov. . . .* (Moscow, 1865). Babst's introduction was 40 pages long, and the statistics filled 300 pages.
35   v–vi. Subsequent Roman numerals refer to the introduction of the *Mnenie*.
36   xliii, xix.
37   xvii.
38   xiii.
39   xvi.
40   xxv.
41   iv.
42   xl–xli.
43   Naidenov, vol. 2, 68.
44   *Ministerstvo*, vol. 1, 544, stressed that "the main goal" of reducing duties on inexpensive goods was to increase revenues and combat smuggling.
45   *Birzha*, 36.
46   The Tariff Commission under Nebolsin was made up of eleven bureaucrats and twelve traders and manufacturers from various cities; all are named in Sobolev, 222.
47   Sobolev, 271. Morozov was obliged to apologize to Prince Obolensky for his outbursts: Naidenov, vol. 2, 81.
48   *Birzha*, 37; Naidenov, vol. 2, 84.
49   *Birzha*, 37.
50   *Ministerstvo*, vol. 1, 545.

51 Chizhov managed the economic section in these papers; see Owen, "Merchants," 34–8.
52 Laverychev, *Burzhuaziia*, 179. Katkov had also left the free–trade camp by 1867: Martin Katz, *Mikhail N. Katkov: A Political Biography, 1818–1887* (The Hague, 1966), 111–12.
53 Naidenov, vol. 2, 86.
54 Naidenov, vol. 2, 88.
55 Sobolev, 290–4n. By this means they offset the influence of merchants in Odessa and factory owners in western areas, whose interests lay in lower import tariffs. Sobolev, 325n.
56 Naidenov, vol. 2, 83–4.
57 Naidenov, vol. 2, 87, 90; Laverychev, *Burzhuaziia*, 180.
58 Sobolev, 240–1, 270, 277; *Ministerstvo* vol. 1, 544–5; Michael O. Gately, "The Development of the Russian Cotton Textile Industry in the Pre-Revolutionary Years, 1861–1914," unpublished doctoral dissertation, University of Kansas, 1968, 58–9. In 1857, 60 percent of all duties had been lowered and only 2.4 raised, whereas in 1868 only 46 percent were lowered and 30.7 raised. Sobolev, 302.
59 Lodyzhensky, *Istoriia*, 289.
60 Cherokov, 41; Sobolev, 417–19; *Ministerstvo*, vol. 1, 546.
61 *Moskva*, Feb. 14, 1867, 3; Laverychev, *Burzhuaziia*, 176–7; *RBS*, vol. 14, 319–20 on Poletika; and Reginald E. Zelnik, *Labor and Society in Tsarist Russia: The Factory Workers of St. Petersburg, 1855–1870* (Stanford, 1971), 287–8.
62 Pavel A. Berlin, *Russkaia burzhuaziia v staroe i novoe vremia*, 2nd ed. (Moscow-Leningrad, 1925), 163, quoting without reference.
63 *Nashi gosudarstvennye i obshchestvennye deiateli*, 2 vols. (St. Petersburg, 1890), vol. 1, 101.
64 Kiniapina, *Politika*, 206–12.
65 Permission to form a Society to Encourage Manufacturing and Trade had been denied in 1857; see Chapter 2, first section. A Society for the Promotion of the Prosperity of National Industry, approved in 1861 (*PSZ–2*, no. 37,283), apparently remained still-born.
66 *Moskva*, Feb. 13, 1868, 3, reprinting an article from Poletika's *Birzhevye vedomosti*.
67 Its secretary, Aleksandr A. Shavrov, contributed to the free-trade St. Petersburg newspaper *Golos: RBS*, vol. 22, 466–7.
68 On Shipov, see Chapter 2, first section; on Poletika, note 17. Skalkovsky later in the century became a leading bureaucrat, business executive, and journalist in St. Petersburg: *IV*, June 1906, 971–80.
69 *Vospominaniia o Vasilie Feduloviche Gromove* (St. Petersburg, 1870), 73.
70 Gindin, *Bank*, 73–4. The protectionist newspaper *Torgovyi sbornik (The Commercial Reporter)* became the "permanent organ" of RIS in 1868: Obshchestvo dlia sodeistviia russkoi promyshlennosti i torgovle, *Otchet o deiatel'nosti vysochaishe utverzhdennogo Obshchestva dlia sodeistviia russkoi promyshlennosti i torgovle* (St. Petersburg, 1869), 13.
71 *Otchet*, 1869, 15–32.
72 On the proposals of 1869, *Otchet*, 1869, 18–39; quotations from 24, 26 (emphasis in original).
73 See Vserossiiskii s"ezd fabrikantov, zavodchikov i lits, interesuiushchikhsia otechestvennoiu promyshlennost'iu, *Stenograficheskii otchet zasedanii l-go [etc.] otdeleniia pervogo vserossiiskogo s"ezda . . . promyshlennosti'iu* (St. Petersburg, 1872).
74 *BE*, vol. 5, 129–30.
75 The resolutions approved by the plenary session are in Russkoe tekhnicheskoe obshchestvo, *Zapiski*, 1872, no. 4, 119–26.
76 Vserossiiskii s"ezd, *Otchet*, 1/54.
77 Vserossiiskii s"ezd, *Otchet*, 1/82–3.

78 Vserossiiskii s"ezd, *Otchet*, 5/53–4.

79 Vserossiiskii s"ezd, *Otchet*, 5/12.

80 Vserossiiskii s"ezd, *Otchet*, 5/14. It was clear to both merchants and bureaucrats that the expansion of Russian trade with Central Asia depended on military conquest. Thus, trade with Khiva grew substantially only after its subjection in 1873–4: Rozhkova, "Iz istorii," 203.

81 Naidenov, vol. 2, 94–5; *Zapiski*, 121. Since 1829, members of the Commercial Council sections (but not their presidents) had been elected by local merchants; in sections of the Manufacturing Council, members and presidents had been appointed by the minister since 1828. In 1868, in response to complaints that the council sections had failed to express the merchants' views in the tariff struggle, the finance minister removed from the MSMC six persons whose combined ages totaled 475 years. Naidenov, vol. 2, 90.

82 Chizhov diary, Nov. 4, 1870, GBL-OR F 332.2.10, 24v.

83 Lure, *Organizatsiia*, 45–7; quotation from 47.

84 Naidenov's petition, dated Mar. 14, 1869, is in TsGIAM F 143.1.19, 7r.–7v. Naidenov, vol. 2, 93; *Birzha*, 54.

85 *MIMKOP*, vol. 9, 42. Railroads, banks, and technical schools were specifically mentioned.

86 Between 1866 and 1879, the number of workers in Russian factories rose from 231,700 to 390,400, and the value of total output in the cotton and woolen industries increased from 107 million to 196 million rubles between 1860 and 1876. Peter I. Lyashchenko, *History of the National Economy of Russia to the 1917 Revolution*, trans. by L. M. Herman (New York, 1949), 486–7.

87 In 1871 sixty-three factories, predominantly in Moscow and Vladimir provinces, were producing cotton goods for sale in Bukhara and Tashkent. These included the largest factories, owned by Zindel, the Prokhorovs, Rabenek, the Tretiakovs, Lepeshkin, Garelin, Baranov, Zubov, and one of the four branches of the Morozov family. Rozhkova, "Iz istorii," 208–10.

88 Vserossiiskii s"ezd, *Otchet*, 1/16.

89 *Birzha*, 73.

4. The political impact of the reactionary ideology, 1860–1890

1 Letters of Mar. 24 and 26, 1863, in Fet, *Vospominaniia*, vol. 1, 416. Fet recalled the horror which he, Botkin, and Katkov felt upon reading Chernyshevsky's radical novel, *What Is to Be Done?* (1862). Botkin angrily attacked the radical journals *Sovremennik* and *Russkoe slovo*, and damned the moderate *Vestnik Evropy* as "a center of various corrupting doctrines under the mask of liberalism" (Fet, vol. 2, 92, 86).

2 Kelsiev, " 'Ispoved',' " 318.

3 Kelsiev, 328.

4 Statistics in Beliajeff, "Merchants," 168.

5 See Chapter 1, notes 121–122.

6 Petr A. Valuev, *Dnevnik P. A. Valueva*, ed., introd., and commentary P. A. Zaion-chkovsky, 2 vols. (Moscow, 1961), vol. 1, 219; *RA*, 1889, vol. 2, part 5, 159; *Obshchee veche*, June 1863, 82–3. This periodical, Ogarev's journal of Old-Believer revolutionary agitation, appealed to peasants and *meshchane*, criticizing the merchant's advantages in trade: July 15, 2. It was characteristic of Soldatenkov's ambivalent role that he, the probable financial supporter of *Obshchee veche* (see Chapter 2, note 114), was vilified by that paper for his loyalty in 1863.

7 Kelsiev, 320–1.

8   *MV*, April 14, 1866, 2; *MV*, April 16, 1866, 2; entry of April 18, 1866, in Nikitenko, *Zapiski*, vol.2, 380. Pogodin may have been instrumental in drafting the latter statement, as it is held in his archive: GBL-OR F 231, Pog/IV.8.17, 3r.–4r.

9   A Russian translation of Carey's *Letters to the President on the Foreign and Domestic Policy of the Union* (Philadelphia, 1858) appeared in Moscow in 1860, and was advertised in Chizhov's paper *Aktsioner* (Dec. 30, 1860). Apparently, the tariff struggle of 1857 prompted this translation.

10 On the banquet, United States, Department of State, *List of Papers Relating to Foreign Affairs for 1866* (Washington, D. C., 1867), part 1, 393–401. This is Curtin's translation of Katkov's article in *MV*, Jan. 9.

11 Curtin, *Memoirs*, 93–4; quotations from 94. Curtin evidently considered Chizhov to be a merchant!

12 *Vospominaniia*, vol. 2, 69. Naidenov himself disdained such actions, feeling that they showed "blindness on the one hand and a desire to play a role in political questions on the other. . . . " For banquet speeches by Kokorev and Shipov, see Joseph F. Loubat, *Gustavus Fox's Mission to Russia in 1866* (New York, 1873), 255–60.

13 GBL-OR F 231, Pog/IV.8.3, 1r.; see also Loubat, 161.

14 On the Moscow City Duma's limited activities and the merchants' subordinate role within it under the Municipal Reform of 1862, during the terms of the gentry Mayors Prince A. A. Shcherbatov (1863–9) and Prince V. A. Cherkassky (1869–71), see Ditiatin, *Ustroistvo*, vol. 2, 525–35; Naidenov, vol. 2, 4–31; Ushakov, *Nashe kupechestvo*, vol. 2, 65, 70, 83; and *IM*, vol. 4, 485–93.

15 S. M. Sukhotin, "Iz pamiatnykh tetradei," *RA*, 1894, vol. 2, no. 6, 248n., gives the full text of the address.

16 Sukhotin, 248n., stated that 110 duma members signed it. Iu. F. Samarin specified that almost 150 signed, while Aksakov's wife, A. F. Tiutcheva, recorded in her diary that 107 did so. *IM*, vol. 4, 492; Tiutcheva, *Pri dvore dvukh imperatorov*, trans. by E. V. Gere, 2 vols. (Moscow, 1928–9), vol. 2, 210. The most detailed account of this episode, based on extensive archival research, is V. A. Nardova, "Adres Moskovskoi gorodskoi dumy 1870 g.," *Istoricheskie zapiski*, vol. 98 (1977), 294–312, who counted 104 signatures.

17 The number of merchant signers was not specified in printed sources, and the document, presumably held in the archive of the Moscow City Duma (TsGIAM F 179), was not available when requested. Laverychev's reference to GBL-OR F 327.I.53.5 (*Burzhuaziia*, 146, n. 29) is spurious.

18 Nardova, 299, categorically stated that these four merchants were the only ones who refused to sign. According to Naidenov, vol. 2, 29, these four refused in the chambers of the Duma; this statement contradicts the assertion of Samarin and Sukhotin that the signing was unanimous. Kartsev had written an intelligent criticism of the unruly merchant election of duma members in 1863 (*MV*, Jan. 25, 1863, 3). Naidenov, a capable stalwart in the tariff battles of 1864–8, became the leading merchant spokesman of the late nineteenth century. Popov, a former serf, ran one of the largest *sukno* factories in Europe and served on the MSEC and the Council of the Merchant Bank (see Appendix, Table I). Konshin, a former salesman for the Tretiakov firm, was the treasurer of the Commercial School (1865–8) and became an important linen manufacturer whose partners included S. Shipov, I. Liamin, and his brothers-in-law, S. M. and P. M. Tretiakov: *Spravochnaia kniga o litsakh, poluchivshikh na 1869 g. kupecheskie svidetel'stva po 1-i i 2-i gil'diiam v Moskve* (Moscow, 1869), 50.

19 Naidenov, vol. 2, 28.

20 Sukhotin, 249, and editor Bartenev's footnote, 249n.

21 Sukhotin, 249.
22 V. M. Golitsyn, "Moskva v semidesiatykh godakh," *GM*, 1919, no. 5–12 (May–Dec.), 137. The document cited by Laverychev (see note 17) is the letter signed by numerous duma members urging Cherkassky to stay on as mayor.
23 Tiutcheva, vol. 2, 210.
24 Sukhotin, 248. Tretiakov and Krestovnikov were willing to give up this privilege. There is no evidence that any other merchants besides the six mentioned here took part in the discussion of the address.
25 Tiutcheva, vol. 2, 210.
26 *PSZ-2*, no. 48,498; Walter S. Hanchett, "Moscow in the Late Nineteenth Century: A Study in Municipal Self-Government," unpublished doctoral dissertation, University of Chicago, 1964, 60. Hanchett's is the best study in any language of the Moscow municipal political system from 1870 to 1893.
27 *IM*, vol. 4, 496 (Art. 5 of the law).
28 *IM*, vol. 4, 495. In 1888, only 2.7 percent of the inhabitants enjoyed the franchise: vol. 4, 512.
29 *IM*, vol. 4, 494; Art. 17, 18. Male taxpayers aged 21 to 25 and female property owners voted through a qualified male relative. All companies, societies, institutions, and organizations which paid city taxes on their property also cast votes through proxies. Lester T. Hutton, "The Reform of City Government in Russia, 1860–1870," unpublished doctoral dissertation, University of Illinois, 1972, 106; and Art. 20–23.
30 Hutton, 117, n.6. Hanchett, "Moscow," 84, 119, 130 gives a meticulous analysis of the elections of 1884 and 1888–9, based on the *Izvestiia Moskovskoi gorodskoi dumy* and other contemporary published materials, which he consulted at Helsinki.
31 Proponents of vigorous self-government often complained that the old "estate principle" continued to dominate Moscow's system even after 1870; see, for example, Chicherin, *Vospominaniia*, vol. 4, 177; and "Trekhrazriadnaia izbiratel'naia sistema – bol'noe mesto gorodovogo polozheniia 1870 g.," *VE*, Dec. 1890, "Vnutrenee obozrenie," 822–39.
32 *IM*, vol. 4, 498.
33 *IM*, vol. 4, 502.
34 Hutton, 106; Hanchett, "Moscow," 100.
35 See "Obshchestvennoe khoziaistvo goroda Moskvy za 25 let: 1863–1887 gg.," *VE*, Aug. 1888, 874–8. One particularly perverse rule channelled the existing apartment tax revenues to the central government instead of to the city, thereby keeping apartment-dwellers of moderate means off the municipal tax rolls and depriving them of the franchise. Dmitri D. Semenov, *Gorodskoe samoupravlenie* (St. Petersburg, 1901), 55.
36 Hutton, 105–9; *IM*, vol. 4, 496–7; Art. 5.
37 Golitsyn, 112.
38 Naidenov, vol. 2, 31.
39 Golitsyn, 138, 126. Liamin resigned in March 1873: Laverychev, *Burzhuaziia*, 147.
40 Naidenov, vol. 2, 33. Quotations from Chicherin, vol. 4, 178, 176. The second version seems more accurate than Golitsyn's. For a speech by Liamin, see Loubat, 245.
41 Naidenov, vol. 2, 34; Chicherin, vol. 2, 178. On the crash and the crisis it caused, see Isaak I. Levin, *Aktsionernye kommercheskie banki v Rossii* (Petrograd, 1917), 213–21.
42 Chicherin, vol. 4, 179–82; quotations from 179.
43 *IM*, vol. 4, 508–10; Chicherin, vol. 4, 235ff.
44 Quoted from Aksakov's newspaper *Rus'*, in Krestovnikov, *Khronika*, vol. 3, 65. A. K. Krestovnikov died on June 14, 1881.
45 Golitsyn, 142.

46 Golitsyn, 143. Ziloti, *V dome*, 74, noted that he was called a "Westerner" and "Anglophile," but whether Iakunchikov's respect for English institutions made him an advocate of liberal political development in Russia remains an interesting empirical question.

47 Golitsyn, 143. On *Russkii kur'er (The Russian Courier)*, Lanin's daily Moscow newspaper (1880–91), see *RPP*, 603; D. Anuchin, "Iz vospominanii," *Russkie vedomosti, 1863–1913*, 2 vols. (Moscow, 1913), vol. 1, 73–4; Laverychev, *Burzhuaziia*, 129–31; and Berlin, *Burzhuaziia*, 124–5. Lanin's reputation as a "bourgeois liberal" rests on his career as publisher of this paper, and of all the Moscow merchants he certainly comes closest to filling this role. Yet the antipathy shown to Lanin by such powerful merchant leaders as Naidenov and Alekseev should guard the historian against the notion that Lanin spoke for his fellow merchants in the Duma. Mayor Chicherin simply considered him "a pest . . . who capitalized on loud liberal phrases [and] babbled at meetings" of the Duma: vol. 4, 184. See Lanin's obituary in *IV*, vol. 60 (April–June 1895), 664.

48 Golitsyn, 143.

49 Golitsyn, 142–3.

50 *IMKO*, vol. 5, part 2, 403–806, contains extensive information on nine large-scale charitable projects of the Moscow Merchant Board, acquired between 1834 and 1903. The Solodovnikov school for poor *meshchane* commemorated Alexander II's escape from Karakozov's assassination attempt in 1866 (vol. 5, part 1, 91–154).

51 Golitsyn, 142; see also Ziloti, 109.

52 Golitsyn, 142.

53 Buryshkin, *Moskva*, 132.

54 Chicherin, vol. 4, 180–1.

55 Chicherin, vol. 4, 180.

56 Golitsyn, 146; Valuev, vol. 2, 527.

57 Naidenov, vol. 2, 35 (quoted); "Obshchestvennoe khoziaistvo," 877–8. See also "Finansy goroda Moskvy za 1863–1894 gg.," in Moscow (City), Gorodskoe obshchestvennoe upravlenie, *Sbornik ocherkov po gorodu Moskve* (Moscow, 1897), section 5 (separate pagination), 3–4 and 47.

58 Chicherin, vol. 4, 197–8.

59 *RBS*, vol. 9, 292–3.

60 Chicherin, vol. 4, 188–90.

61 Pobedonostsev acted in response to an urgent telegram from Dolgorukov dated Oct. 13, 1882: *K. P. Pobedonostsev i ego korrespondenty*, 2 half-vols. (Moscow, 1923), vol. 1, 267, document 235. On Pobedonostsev's support for the idea of parish schools, see Edward C. Thaden, *Conservative Nationalism in Nineteenth-Century Russia* (Seattle, 1964), 189–95. The clash in 1881–2 between supporters of zemstvo schools (Baron Korf, A. I. Koshelev, and others) and proponents of parish schools (S. A. Rachinsky in Aksakov's *Rus'*, and others) is discussed in B. Veselovsky, *Istoriia zemstva za sorok let*, 4 vols. (St. Petersburg, 1909–11; reprinted Cambridge, England, 1973), vol. 3, 292–5.

62 Chicherin, vol. 4, 192.

63 Pobedonostsev, *Korrespondenty*, vol. 1, 295, document 265. Italics in original.

64 Chicherin, vol. 4, 191.

65 Chicherin, vol. 4, 248.

66 Chicherin, vol. 4, 251.

67 Aksenov's statement, repeated by Chicherin, vol. 4, 252, from a letter of an eyewitness, was remarkably self-confident: "I am about eighty years old, and I am saying what seems to me to be true. . . . "

68 Chicherin, vol. 4, 255.

69 Chicherin, vol. 4, 259.

70 Chicherin, vol. 4, 258. Although Chicherin did not make this point, the merchants clearly bore a special responsibility because of their numerical preponderance in the Duma from 1873 onward. Hanchett's sophisticated analysis, "Moscow," 100–3 and 130–3, shows, for example, that the merchants and honorary citizens occupied more than half of the 180 seats from 1885 to 1893 and that many were related to one another by blood or marriage.

71 Chicherin, vol. 4, 258.

72 Chicherin, vol. 4, 184. This last element was the boisterous group of *meshchane* and artisans elected from the third and largest assembly. Hanchett, "Moscow," 116–17, noted that their elections were sometimes marred by heavy drinking, arguments, and frivolity (including the placing of pickled cucumbers in the ballot boxes).

73 U. G. Ivask, "Moskovskie gorodskie golovy, i zamestiteli ikh," *RA*, 1912, vol. 2, no. 6, 81.

74 Pobedonostsev, *Korrespondenty*, vol. 1, 295–6.

75 Naidenov, vol. 2, 132.

76 Chicherin, vol. 4, 258. In 1889 he won reelection by a vote of 134 yeas and 18 nays: Hanchett, "Moscow," 192.

77 Naidenov himself, together with his friends, had appeared dangerously progressive to the merchant patriarchs who opposed the new municipal government system in 1862–3: Naidenov, vol. 2, 12–13.

78 Golitsyn, 146.

79 Chicherin, vol. 4, 192–6. Budget figures for 1863–94 in "Finansy," 3. Representative totals show a steady increase in municipal spending in millions of rubles: 1863, 1.7; 1873, 3.2; 1875, 3.4; 1880, 5.0; 1890, 7.5; 1895, 8.8.

80 Golitsyn, 153. G. Iaroslavsky, "Gorodskoe samoupravlenie Moskvy," in *Moskva v ee proshlom i nastoiashchem*, 12 vols. (Moscow, 1910–12), vol 12, 33, praised Alekseev for making other improvements as well: municipal laundries and a city fire insurance program. See Hanchett, "Moscow," chs. 7–15 on various municipal undertakings. Semenov, 55–9, noted that in 1886–7 Alekseev sponsored a plan to divert apartment tax revenues to the municipal treasury and thereby increase the budget and enfranchise renters (as N. P. Lanin and M. P. Shchepkin had urged in the 1870s, only to have the Duma reject the idea in 1878), but the Duma did not petition the Imperial government to implement this reform. See n. 35.

81 Chetverikov, *Ushedshaia Rossiia*, 83–4. He died on March 11, 1893.

82 This version is based on the eyewitness account by Chetverikov (Alekseev's brother-in-law), 90–2. Riabushinsky, "Kupechestvo," 182 (and Buryshkin, 148, apparently following him) cited the legendary figure of one million rubles in this incident; according to them, the rich merchant initiated the scene in order to satisfy his pride by humbling the mayor in public. Iaroslavsky, 36, credited Alekseev with raising 800,000 rubles in private donations for the hospital.

83 Chicherin, vol. 4, 183.

84 Chicherin, vol. 4, 259.

85 Veselovsky, vol. 4, 529. Except for Semenov (n. 80), various other sources, including available obituaries, provide no details on this vital question of the mayor's defense of municipal government. See, for example, "Tragicheskaia smert' N. A. Alekseeva," *VE*, April 1893, 868–73; and "N. A. Alekseev (nekrolog)," *MV*, Mar. 12, 1893, 3.

86 Golitsyn, 153, explained that Alekseev had been raised by indulgent parents as "a pet in the full sense of the word" since childhood. Chicherin, vol. 4, 182, described Alek-

seev's volatile character in terms of ethnic stereotypes: "His mother was a Greek, née Bostandzhoglo, and he combined in himself the cunning and evasiveness of a Greek with the expansive unruliness of the Russian nature."

87 See the well-argued case against Alekseev's impetuosity in "Moskovskoe zemstvo i N. A. Alekseev," *VE*, Jan. 1891, 473–6. One staff member recalled that the mayor, in the presence of some municipal employees just before the grand opening of the new duma building, said contemptuously of them: "We'll have to fill up this dirty scum with champagne." Quoted in Nikolai I Astrov, *Vospominaniia* (Paris, 1941), 255.

88 Golitsyn, 153. Disgusted by Alekseev's petty tyranny, one of the country's finest municipal statisticians, M. P. Shchepkin (1832–1908), quit his post as duma financial expert in 1891 and turned to zemstvo activities (1891–1906) before becoming a founding member of the Kadet Party in 1905. *Russkie vedomosti*, vol.2, 207; Hanchett, "Moscow," 177.

89 "Alekseev (nekrolog)," 3. Quotation from *Izvestiia Moskovskoi gorodskoi dumy*, 1887, vol. 23 (special session of July 23), cols. 615–16; the importance of this speech was noted by Hanchett, "Moscow," 207n.

90 *IM*, vol. 4, 505–6. This Soviet survey ignores the role of gentry progressives in the crucial Korf episode; fails to mention the intense personal rivalry between the merchant leaders Naidenov and Alekseev; and provides no factual details to support the concept of a gentry-merchant political struggle. Far more convincing is Hanchett's interest-group analysis, "Moscow," 103–6, which notes a certain tension on budgetary questions between the merchants (who favored hospitals for their staffs and workers) and the *meshchane*-artisan delegates (who preferred to increase educational spending for the benefit of their own children). This struggle carried no implications of political principle, however.

91 Nikitin, *Komitety*, 39–41, presents an informative list.

92 Nikitin, 62.

93 Nikitin, 64–7. Named were T. S. Morozov, P. M. Tretiakov, A. K. Krestovnikov, I. I. Chetverikov, the brothers Vishniakov and Lepeshkin, M. Liamin, a Bostandzhoglo, and an Alekseev.

94 Nikitin, 67. In the 1860s and 1870s the Moscow merchants refused to challenge foreign economic control of Slavic lands, despite the urging of committee leaders: Nikitin, 77–9.

95 Naidenov, vol. 2, 70.

96 GIM F 169.2, 85r., 89r., 94r.

97 *Moskva*, Jan. 8, 1867, 4.

98 Kokorev, "Provaly," vol. 1, part 4, 511.

99 Financial backing was provided by the firms of V. Aksenov; P. and S. Tretiakov and V. Konshin; I. Chetverikov; and E. Nikolaeva: Nikitin, 109.

100 The Moscow Merchant Society provided several thousand rubles for this purpose in 1872–4: Nikitin, 73. It also donated 2,000 rubles to aid Balkan Christians in November 1875: *MIMKOP*, vol. 9, 196.

101 Konshin, N. A. Alekseev, and others received medals from the Montenegrin government for their gifts: Nikitin, 74–5; "Alekseev (nekrolog)," 3.

102 Petr I. Shchukin, "Vospominaniia," *Shchukinskii sbornik*, 10 vols. (Moscow, 1902–12), vol. 10, 372; *RBS*, vol. 21, 342–3. On the abortive "Central Asian Steamship and Trade Company" proposed by Cherniaev, M. A. Khludov, and two other merchants in 1870, see David MacKenzie, *The Lion of Tashkent: The Career of General M. G. Cherniaev* (Athens, Georgia, 1974), 107–8.

103 MacKenzie, *Lion*, 105.

104 Nikitin, 272; Laverychev, *Burzhuaziia*, 123–4; *RPP*, 539–40.

105 Nikitin, 292; MacKenzie, *Lion*, ch. 8.

106 Nikitin, 302; *MIMKOP*, vol. 9, 230–1.

107 Naidenov, vol. 2, 156.

108 Nikitin, 307.

109 Nikitin, 312, 314; Valuev, vol. 2, 385. See Porokhovshchikov's own account of this period, when "Moscow, true to its heritage, became the center of the movement of all Orthodox Russia [*Rusi*]." He considered himself a follower of the Slavophile doctrine since 1856, and praised Ivan Aksakov for leading the Pan-Slav crusade. "Iz zapisok moskovskogo starozhila," *IV*, vol. 67 (Feb. 1897), 541, 539.

110 Porokhovshchikov, 552. Later that month Porokhovshchikov bragged about his meeting with the tsar, claiming that the monarch had not only expressed friendly sentiments but had even cried several times. This story disgusted leading bureaucrats in St. Petersburg, who regarded the Serbian adventure as pure folly. Valuev called Porokhovshchikov a "fop," and D. A. Miliutin, who refused to believe the Livadia story, characterized the garrulous merchant as "a colossally conceited windbag." Quoted in Valuev, vol. 2, 392, 527. Porokhovshchikov ran for mayor of Moscow in the 1880s, but made a poor impression on both Chicherin and Pobedonostsev: Chicherin, vol. 4, 168, 256, 330.

111 MacKenzie, *Lion*, 166, 182–90; Valuev, vol. 2, 527.

112 On his extreme political views, Thaden, 146–63.

113 Nikitin, 337–8, 340. Naidenov, vol. 2, 158, included in "our circle" S. M. Tretiakov, V. D. Aksenov, P. I. Sanin, and T. S. Morozov. On July 1, 1876, the Merchant Society resolved to aid the Bulgarian Christians against "their age-old enemies, the Moslem fanatics": *MIMKOP*, vol. 9, 247.

114 Nikitin, 338–41.

115 Nikitin, 342; *MIMKOP*, vol. 9, 298, 329–30. "About 265,000 rubles" was actually collected: *Birzha*, 68.

116 Cherkassky, *Kniaz' Vladimir Aleksandrovich Cherkassky: ego stat'i, ego rechi i vospominaniia o nem* (Moscow, 1879), 315.

117 Laverychev, *Burzhuaziia*, 150–1; Naidenov, vol. 2, 159. On donations, *MIMKOP*, vol. 9, 230–1.

118 Lukashevich, *Aksakov*, 141; Laverychev, *Burzhuaziia*, 133; and Aksakov, *V pis'makh*, vol. 4, 286.

119 He alleged that the Ministry of Internal Affairs "can only administer literature from the police point of view": *Rus'*, Dec. 6, 1885, quoted in Richard Pipes, *Struve: Liberal on the Left, 1870–1905* (Cambridge, Mass., 1970), 21.

120 Lukashevich, 142, 151.

121 Cherniaev wanted the Russian capital returned to Moscow, and had even "opposed the emancipation of the Russian serfs" in 1861: David MacKenzie, "Panslavism in Practice: Cherniaev in Serbia," *Journal of Modern History*, vol. 36, no. 2 (June 1964), 285, 281.

122 MacKenzie, *Lion*, 176, 191–2.

123 Richard A. Pierce, *Russian Central Asia, 1867–1917: A Study in Colonial Rule* (Berkeley, 1960), 41–2; Hugh Seton-Watson, *The Russian Empire, 1801–1917* (Oxford, 1967), 444.

124 Quoted in Laverychev, *Burzhuaziia*, 205–6. On Skobelev's ideology, Lukashevich, 158–60; *RBS*, vol. 18, 581–2; and various biographies. Gaëtan Combes de Lestrade, *L'Empire russe en 1885* (Paris, n.d.), 80, explicitly emphasized the merchants' sincere devotion to Skobelev.

125 Robert F. Byrnes, *Pobedonostsev: His Life and Thought* (Bloomington, 1968), 132.

126 *PSZ-2*, no. 58,585 of May 30, 1878. The florid Russian title, *Dobrovol'noe morskoe opol-*

chenie, recalled the great popular "militia" that liberated Moscow from Polish occupation in 1612. (The simple term *dobrovol'nyi flot* soon became its offical name.) On the Moscow Merchant Society's donation of 400,000 rubles, *MIMKOP,* vol. 9, 356 and vol. 10, 15. According to Naidenov, vol. 2, 160–1, the elderly M. M. Wogau contributed 10,000 rubles and then fainted.

127 Byrnes, 133–4. As late as 1895 the fleet linked Odessa, St. Petersburg, and Vladivostok: *RVed,* Jan. 6, 1895, 6.

128 Letter of Dec. 18, 1882, *Pis'ma K. P. Pobedonostseva k Aleksandru III,* 2 vols. (Moscow, 1925–6), vol. 1, 399. On one merchant's pride in knowing him, Naidenov, vol. 2, 153.

129 On the Zemstvo Statute of January 1, 1864, see Timberlake and Malloy, introduction to Veselovsky, *Istoriia,* vol. 1, 6.

130 L. G. Mamulova, "Sotsial'nyi sostav uezdnykh zemskikh sobranii v 1865–1886 godakh," *VMU-9,* vol. 17, no. 6 (Nov.–Dec. 1962), 35.

131 Mamulova, 35; these figures are for the entire 1865–90 period, in 33 provinces.

132 These figures are for the first elections, held in 1865. Merchants made up almost 80 percent of the urban delegates: Mamulova, 40. First-college figures from Mamulova, 35.

133 In Vladimir province, 39.3 percent gentry compared to 16.3 percent urban estates; Pskov, 47.4 and 15.3; Moscow, 36.5 and 14.9; Novgorod, 42.3 and 14.3; Iaroslavl, 34.2 and 13.8; Kaluga, 42.4 and 13.1; and Tver, 44.8 and 12.3: Mamulova, 47.

134 S. Ia. Tseitlin, "Zemskoe samoupravlenie i reforma 1890 g. (1865–1890)," in *Istoriia Rossii v XIX veke,* 9 vols. (St. Petersburg, 1907–11), vol. 5, 84, noted hardly any change in average figures between 1865 and 1890 when totaling memberships of district assemblies and boards; out of 13,196 delegates in 34 provinces, gentry and bureaucrats comprised 42.4 percent; peasants, 38.5 percent; merchants and *meshchane,* 16.1 percent; clergy, 2.3 percent; and other, 0.7 percent.

135 Donald Mackenzie Wallace, *Russia on the Eve of War and Revolution,* ed. Cyril E. Black (New York, 1961), 31.

136 Clergy and other estates held 0.4 percent and 0.2 percent of the assembly seats and no board posts: Tseitlin, 89–90. Unfortunately, there is no study of the separate provincial assemblies comparable even to Mamulova's of the district assemblies in the two elections of 1865 and 1883.

137 Veselovsky, vol. 1, 106–7.

138 Naidenov, vol. 2, 44–6.

139 Nikolai I. Iordansky, *Zemskii liberalizm,* 2nd ed. (St. Petersburg, 1906), 24.

140 Veselovsky, vol. 1, 107.

141 Veselovsky, vol. 1, 225.

142 Naidenov, vol. 2, 46, 45. Cases of merchants' complaints against the Zemstvos were common; on those of the Torzhok grain traders in the 1860s, see Gdb, "Vnutrenee obozrenie," *Delo,* July 1868, second pagination, 51; of the manufacturers Morozov and Borisovsky in Pokrovsk district, Vladimir province, in the 1870s, S. Sh., "Zemskoe chinovnichestvo i gg. fabrikanty," *Slovo,* 1879, no. 8, 14; and of the mine owners of southern Russia at every one of their annual meetings, [Osip] A. Ermansky, "Krupnaia burzhuaziia do 1905 goda," *ODR,* vol. 1, 335. For cases of zemstvo complaints against industrialists, see Veselovsky, vol. 1, 109–11.

143 Wallace, 40; Pavel N. Miliukov, *Russia and its Crisis* (New York, 1962), 218.

144 Wallace, 39.

145 Tseitlin, 88. In 1887 merchants paid seven million rubles, compared to 9.3 from private landowners and 18 from peasant communities: Tseitlin, 96–7. The same point is made with other statistics by Veselovsky, vol. 1, 109–24.

146 Veselovsky, vol. 3.
147 Naidenov, vol. 2, 46.
148 S. Sh., 10.
149 S. Sh., 10; 4–9, 19–20; 15; and 16–17, 26.
150 Mamulova, 43, n. 34.
151 Mamulova, 47.
152 Veselovsky, vol. 4, 202.
153 *RPP*, 160. Quotation from Tseitlin, 88.
154 Veselovsky, vol. 3, 311.
155 Skalon (1846–1907) then turned to liberal journalism, and served as coeditor of *RVed* from 1899 to his death. *Russkie vedomosti*, vol. 2, 160.
156 Ia. Abramov, "Khludovshchina," *Otechestvennye zapiski*, 1882, no. 5, 35–7.
157 Iordansky, 34–5 (quoted); Veselovsky, vol. 3, 311.
158 Mamulova, 43.
159 Quoted from *Russkii kur'er*, 1884, nos. 131 and 134, in Mamulova, evidently following Veselovsky, vol. 3, 311.
160 Chetverikov, 88–90. Alekseev continued to be elected to the provincial zemstvo assembly until his death in 1893: "Moskovskoe zemstvo" and "Alekseev (nekrolog)," 3.
161 Venturi, *Roots*, 616.
162 *Russkie vedomosti*, vol. 1, 30–3.
163 The Moscow Merchant Society had warmly congratulated the tsar on his escape from terrorist attacks in April 1879 and February 1880. In March 1881, after his assassination, the Moscow Duma appropriated 100,000 rubles for a monument to him in Moscow, to which the Merchant Society, moved by "feelings of infinite grief," added 25,000 rubles and a contribution of 100,000 rubles to renovate churches in the tsar's memory. *MIMKOP*, vol. 9, 408–9, 467, 508–9.
164 L. T. Senchakova, " 'Sviashchennaia druzhina' i ee sostav," *VMU-9*, 1967, no. 2 (Mar.–April), 74–83, lists all the members more or less alphabetically.
165 M. E. Fedorova, "Moskovskii otdel 'Sviashchennoi druzhiny,' " *GM*, vol. 6, nos. 1–3 (Jan.–Mar. 1918), 170. A. N. Maklakov (1838–1905), an M.D., duma member, and professor at Moscow University, hardly qualified as a merchant spokesman, but Fedorova's other generalizations appear sound. In Senchakova's list, P. I. Sanin was not named, and Semen I. Lialin *(sic)* was probably former Mayor I. A. Liamin's son, mentioned by Fedorova. See Appendix, Tables I and II. Other important merchant names from Senchakova's list are: Vasili N. Lepeshkin, Arseni I. Morozov, Aleksandr A. Sapozhnikov, Nikolai I. Shchukin, the Nizhny Novgorod Mayor Vasili A. Sobolev, and the nephew and business partner of K. T. Soldatenkov, court councilor Vasili I. Soldatenkov.
166 Ziloti, 162–4.
167 On the decline of the Holy Host, Senchakova, 70. An auxiliary antirevolutionary organization created in October 1881 for the specific purpose of protecting the new emperor and his family from terrorist attacks also received the enthusiastic support of the Moscow merchants. This "Volunteer Guard" *(Dobrovol'naia okhrana)*, whose council, according to Senchakova, 63–4, was composed of members of the "Holy Host" Executive Committee, included 200 Moscow merchants who acted as the honorary bodyguard at the coronation of Alexander III in the Kremlin. Laverychev, *Burzhuaziia*, 154, named "Alekseevs, Aksenovs, Bakhrushins, Botkins, Wogaus, Guchkovs, Naidenovs, S. M. and P. M. Tretiakov, I. A. Liamin, and others."
168 Lanin of course embraced this cause unequivocally: "Religious toleration is guaranteed

in our time by special laws in every well-ordered European state." Quoted from *Russkii kur'er*, Dec. 28, 1886 by Laverychev, *Burzhuaziia*, 153.

169 As does Serge A. Zenkovsky, "The Russian Church Schism," in Thomas Riha, ed., *Readings in Russian Civilization*, 2nd ed., 3 vols. (Chicago, 1969), vol. 1, 152.

170 Byrnes, 251; Thaden, 195–7; and Laverychev, *Burzhuaziia*, 128, on Pobedonostsev's need to be convinced that T. S. Morozov's paper *Golos Moskvy* (The Voice of Moscow) would not propagate Old-Believer ideas.

171 Iu. G. Oksman, ed., "Otkliki Moskovskikh promyshlennikov na antievreiskie besporiadki 1881 g.," *KA*, 1926, vol. 1 (14), 259.

172 Laverychev, *Burzhuaziia*, 61.

173 Laverychev, *Burzhuaziia*, 133; *MIMKOP*, vol. 10, 102. In 1885 the blatantly antisemitic Sergei F. Sharapov, then MSRIS Secretary, proposed banning Jews and foreigners from commerce and industry in Poland and West Russia: "Rech' o promyshlennoi konkurentsii Lodzi i Sosnovits s Moskovoiu," and "Po russkoi Germanii," in his *Sochineniia*, 2 vols. (St. Petersburg, 1892), vol. 1, 70–94 and 226–76.

174 See the critical comments on "Ekonomicheskie provaly" by V. A Poletika, D. D. Golokhvastov, and D. V. Kanshin, followed by Kokorev's rejoinders in *RA*, 1887, vols. 2–3, nos. 8–12. On the other hand, Skalkovsky, *Deiateli*, vol. 1, 178, opined that "Kokorev would have made an excellent Minister of Russian Trade and Industry" because of his economic knowledge and his practical approach to problems.

175 "Provaly," vol. 1, part 2, 245. Kokorev's emphasis in this and subsequent quotations.

176 "Provaly," vol. 2, part 6, 272.

177 "Provaly," vol. 2, part 7, 416, the final sentence of his memoirs. He particularly condemned "the hasty constitution written for Bulgaria" by Russians in 1878: vol. 1, part 4, 514.

178 *Nuzhno khotia-by vos'mushku Bismarka:* vol. 2, part 6, 272.

179 *Studien*, 173.

180 The shrewd Pobedonostsev considered the latter tendency more dangerous than socialism because its evils were not so readily apparent: *Studien*, 175, 199–200.

181 *Studien*, 106.

182 *Studien*, 168–9.

183 *Ocherki obshchestvennogo khoziaistva i ekonomicheskoi politiki Rossii*, trans. by B. V. Avilov and P. P. Rumiantsev (St. Petersburg, 1900), x–xi.

184 *Ocherki*, xiv–xv.

5. Industrial growth and the challenge of the labor movement,
1880–1900

1 The Russian Technical Society also held a congress in Moscow in the summer of 1882. The resolutions of this smaller gathering (mainly of southern mine owners and oil producers) paralleled those of RIS: Ermansky, "Do 1905," 342–3. The Technical Society's secretary declared (Sobolev, *Politika*, 433, n. 1), "The protectionist system has always saved our country from economic jolts and led it onto the path of prosperity."

2 *Trudy vysochaishe razreshennogo torgovo–promyshlennogo s"ezda, sozvannogo Obshchestvom dlia sodeistviia russkoi promyshlennosti i torgovle, v Moskve, v iiule 1882 g.*, 2 vols. (St. Petersburg, 1883), viii–xviii. This and subsequent references are to vol. 1.

3 Aksakov, Pogodin, Koshelev, and Chizhov had proposed this idea without success in 1863 (Barsukov, *Zhizn'*, vol. 21, 80), and the merchants' own petition to this effect had been ignored: Naidenov, *Vospominaniia*, vol. 2, 95 and G. M. Gorfein, "Iz istorii obrazovaniia Ministerstva torgovli i promyshlennosti," in S. N. Valk, ed., *Ocherki po istorii*

ekonomiki i klassovykh otnoshenii v Rossii kontsa XIX–nachala XX v.: sbornik statei (Moscow–Leningrad, 1964), 162–5.

4 *Trudy*, 21. Ermansky, "Do 1905," 326, incorrectly identified the speaker as T. S. Morozov's son, Savva. On Mendeleev's role as a proponent of industry, see the doctoral dissertations by Beverly S. Almgren, "Mendeleev: The Third Service," Brown University, 1968, and Francis M. Stackenwalt, "The Thought and Work of Dmitrii Ivanovich Mendeleev on the Industrialization of Russia, 1867–1907," University of Illinois, 1976.

5 Lure, *Organizatsiia*, 54–5, and "Preobrazovanie kommercheskogo i manufakturnogo sovetov," *VE*, Nov. 1872, 332–4.

6 *Trudy*, 21. Although only 27 years old, he spoke with great authority and presided over the first section in Mendeleev's absence: Torgovo-promyshlennyi s"ezd, Moscow, 1882, *Rezoliutsii* . . . (St. Petersburg, 1883), part 1, 5. He received a degree in physics and mathematics at Moscow University: Buryshkin, *Moskva*, 181.

7 *Trudy*, 260.

8 The liberal Goltsev favored tariff reductions as a means of lowering retail prices. He contributed articles to *RVed* and *Zemstvo;* edited the propeasant *Russkaia mysl'* from 1885 until his death in 1905; and supported labor legislation on the West-European model. *RPP*, 445, 610, 616; Boris P. Baluev, *Politicheskaia reaksiia 80-kh godov XIX veka i russkaia zhurnalistika* (Moscow, 1971), 184, 293.

9 *Trudy*, 264–9.

10 *Trudy*, 141, 143.

11 *Trudy*, 302–7; 327–8; 330–6; 342–54. V. K. Krestovnikov stressed that Siberian agricultural products could not compete in West-European markets without an extensive rail network to reduce transport costs: 272.

12 *Trudy*, 302.

13 *Rezoliutsii*, part 1, 5-13; quotations from 11 (emphasis in original). These demands went far beyond the policy recommendations advanced by the leading protectionist economists of the nineteenth century. Friedrich List's influential treatise, *The National System of Political Economy* (1841–6) opposed all duties on raw materials, and advised protective tariffs only for large countries with a "far advanced agriculture" and "a high degree of civilization and political development"; duties should never exceed 60 percent, even for the most essential infant industries, and if "continued protection" of 20 to 30 percent failed to maintain a given industry, then "the fundamental conditions of manufacturing power are lacking . . . " Trans. by Sampson S. Lloyd (New York, 1928), 247, 251. Likewise, in 1877 Wilhelm Roscher, whom Babst and Chizhov had regarded as the foremost economist of his time, explicitly labeled "absurd" the "equal extension of 'protection' to all the branches of a nation's economy," including iron and machines. Because smuggling and economic stagnation posed constant dangers, "prohibition proper operates, as a rule, very disastrously." Roscher, *Principles of Political Economy*, trans. by John J. Lalor, 2 vols. (Chicago, 1882), vol. 2, 426, 452, 455.

14 Thus, when the merchants spoke of the need to sell their own manufactured goods abroad, they suddenly dropped their protectionist rhetoric and became partisans of lower tariffs, especially in Turkey, Persia, and China.

15 *Rezoliutsii*, part 1, 28-33.

16 RIS issued a 215-page discussion of the Siberian railroad route twenty-one years before construction was finally begun: *O napravlenii Sibirskoi zheleznoi dorogi* (St. Petersburg, 1870).

17 Only two resolutions contradicted the Moscow merchants' wishes, so that Buryshkin's assertion (71) that they had little influence at the congress appears unfounded. Section

four called "extremely harmful" the payment of wages in the form of coupons from state bonds that had to be held to maturity *(dosrochnye kupony)*, used to keep workers from quitting. Section five refused to condemn foreign ownership of Russian railroads. *Rezoliutsii*, part 1, 13-28, 33-53. (Section two discussed handicrafts.)

18 Theodore H. Von Laue, *Sergei Witte and the Industrialization of Russia* (New York, 1963), 56–62. He stressed the influence of F. List, but see note 13 on the divergence between List's theory and the Russian practice.

19 Laverychev, *Burzhuaziia*, 97.

20 Obshchestvo dlia sodeistviia russkoi promyshlennosti i torgovle, *Protokol torzhestvennogo sobraniia . . . Obshchestva* (St. Petersburg, 1892), 3-4. Among the speakers at RIS's twenty-fifth anniversary celebration was its president, Count N. P. Ignatiev, the former ambassador to Constantinople and interior minister renowned for his Pan-Slav views; see his speech, 12–13.

21 *Protokol*, 17.

22 Ermansky, "Do 1905," 334–8.

23 *Obshchestvo dlia sodeistviia uluchsheniiu i razvitiiu fabrichno-zavodskoi promyshlennosti;* in 1907 it merged with a recently created employers' union, *Peterburgskoe obshchestvo zavodchikov i fabrikantov.* Both organizations represented the major commercial-industrial firms of the Petersburg region and had several leaders in common. It is therefore convenient to follow the example of Victoria King, a graduate student at the University of California, Berkeley, who is currently writing a doctoral dissertation on them, and assign to them the single name PSM. See also A. Gushka [pseud. of Osip A. Ermansky], *Predstavitel'nye organizatsii torgovo–promyshlennogo klassa v Rossii* (St. Petersburg, 1912), 15; and Lure, 81, 165.

24 *Obshchestvo dlia sodeistviia uluchsheniiu i razvitiiu manufakturnoi promyshlennosti.* It published *Izvestiia (News)* in 1890–4, cited by G. F. Semeniuk, "Bor'ba moskovskoi 'tekstil'noi' burzhuaziia za rynki sbyta i ekonomicheskaia politika tsarizma v kontse XIX v.," in *Nekotorye voprosy istorii Moskvy i Moskovskoi gubernii v XIX–XX vv.* (Moscow, 1964), 105.

25 Buryshkin, 88, 233; Lure, 48–51, 64.

26 Gushka, 65, 69, 70 (quoted); Ermansky, "Do 1905," 333 (quoted).

27 Gushka, 194.

28 *Birzha*, 73.

29 Finance Minister V. N. Kokovtsov (1904–5), quoted in Buryshkin, 281; see also Berlin, *Burzhuaziia*, 301.

30 The number of merchants registered in the exchange surpassed 400 in 1863, and reached 1,048 in 1870; after peaking at 1,499 in 1880, it declined to 1,058 in the following nine years. *Birzha*, 72.

31 Riabushinsky, "Kupechestvo," 173 (quoted); Buryshkin, 235.

32 See *Birzha*, 75–86, and Appendix, Tables I and II.

33 Berlin, 151 and 330. Plekhanov's gill-and-lung analogy, in his pamphlet *Our Differences* (1885), in fact buttressed the classical Marxist argument that "the employer class as a whole" required "political self-government" and "political freedom." Quoted in Leopold H. Haimson, *The Russian Marxists and the Origins of Bolshevism* (Cambridge, Mass., 1967), 21. See also note 129.

34 Schulze-Gävernitz, *Studien*, 260, 264. On the tariff levels and the resultant prosperity of protected industries, see Sobolev, 429–31, 451, 506, and 741; and Gately, "Cotton," 56, 118–19, 138–9, 146–8, and 151–2.

35 Arcadius Kahan, "Government Policies and the Industrialization of Russia," *Journal of Economic History*, vol. 27, no. 4 (Dec. 1967), 470–1.

36 Schulze-Gavernitz, 273. However, Russian profit rates are notoriously difficult to measure; see note 116.

37 Sobolev, 448, n. 1; 450–1.

38 Laverychev, *Burzhuaziia*, 185, citing a document in the family archive. On 183–90 he surveys the tariff debates of 1879–91.

39 Sobolev, 703, n. 1. On 791 he ridiculed this "protection on credit," which placed duties on cacao and palm oil products, surgical instruments, eyeglasses, binoculars, etc. See the extended discussion in Semeniuk, "Bor'ba," 109–19. Henceforth S. T. Morozov denotes Savva (1861–1905), not his brother Sergei.

40 "Voprosy tranzitnyi i o gorodskikh obshchestvennykh bankakh," *RVes*, Dec. 1882, 1010-13; quotation from 1013. (Reprinted from *MV*, nos. 330, 333, 344, and 354 of 1882.)

41 Naidenov's letter of Dec. 2, 1882 in Pobedonostsev, *Korrespondenty*, vol. 1, 296–7; quotation from Pobedonostsev's letter of Dec. 18, *Pis'ma*, vol. 1, 399.

42 A. T. Makarov, "Zakavkaz'e v torgovom otnoshenii," *RVes*, vol. 169, no. 1 (Jan. 1884), 151–84.

43 Firuz Kazemzadeh, *Russia and Britain in Persia, 1864–1914: A Study in Imperialism* (New Haven, 1968), 171. U. A. Shuster, "Ekonomicheskaia bor'ba Moskvy s Lodz'iu (iz istorii russko-pol'skikh ekonomicheskikh otnoshenii v 8o-kh godakh proshlogo veka," *Istoricheskie zapiski*, vol. 5 (1939), 203–6, explicitly noted the MSEC's crucial role in winning this battle. In 1892, the Finance Ministry finally granted a major demand of the merchants at the 1882 Congress: the payment of rebates of duties on imported yarn to Russian textile manufacturers who exported to Persia finished goods made with such yarn. Moreover, a Discount and Loan Bank in Persia founded in 1900 began to facilitate commerce there: Serafim A. Pokrovsky, *Vneshniaia torgovlia i vneshniaia torgovaia politika Rossii* (Moscow, 1947), 334. Semeniuk, "Bor'ba," 128–41, includes many details.

44 Details in Vladislav I. Massalsky, *Khlopkovoe delo v Srednei Azii i ego budushchee* (St. Petersburg, 1892), chs. 2–3; Laverychev, *Burzhuaziia*, 201–2; Lyashchenko, *History*, 610–11, 615, 851, 853, 855; and Gately, 140. In 1884, a Moscow cotton-importing and textile-exporting company began operations in Central Asia; its major shareholders included T. S. Morozov, N. N. Konshin, A. L. Losev, D. I. Morozov, M. A. Khludov, A. A. Baranov, and N. P. Kudrin. Vladimir Ia. Laverychev, "Moskovskie fabrikanty i sredneaziatskii khlopok," *VMU–9*, vol. 25, no. 1 (Jan.–Feb. 1970), 56.

45 Michael T. Florinsky, *Russia: A History and an Interpretation*, 2 vols. (New York, 1953), vol. 2, 1108.

46 *Birzha*, 65, specified that I. E. Guchkov's committee of stock exchange delegates drew up four complaints regarding railroad rates and services between 1879 and 1886.

47 Details in Grover, "Mamontov," 343–58.

48 The stability of the entire private banking system, for example, depended on the generous solicitude of the State Bank, which rescued many a failing bank in this period, including those of Kokorev and Naidenov. Details in Gindin, *Bank*, 322–7, 353, 369–70; and Levin, *Banki*, 231–5, 252–6, 280–9.

49 Chetverikov, *Ushedshaia Rossiia*, 102–4; quotations from 104.

50 Quoted in Richard Pipes, *Social Democracy and the St. Petersburg Labor Movement, 1885–1897* (Cambridge, Mass., 1963), 3n. As in German (*Arbeitgeber*), the Russian word for employer (*rabotodatel'*) meant "work giver," thus connoting benevolence.

51 E. M. Dementiev, *Fabrika, chto ona daet naseleniiu i chto ona u nego beret*, 2nd ed. (Moscow, 1897), 2.

52 Ziloti, *V dome*, 63.

53 Tugan-Baranovsky, *Fabrika*, 311, citing the detailed study of working conditions in Moscow province (1884) by the factory inspector Professor Ivan I. Ianzhul.

54 K. A. Pazhitnov, *Ocherki istorii tekstil'noi promyshlennosti dorevoliutsionnoi Rossii*, 2 vols. (Moscow, 1955–8), vol. 2, 72–3; A. M. Pankratova and V. M. Sokolov, "Predshestvenitsa Morozovskoi stachki," *Istoricheskii arkhiv*, vol. 7 (1951), 122–9, 142–5, 168–70, 185.

55 Zelnik, *Labor*, 135–6; Frederick C. Giffin, "In Quest of an Effective Program of Factory Legislation in Russia: The Years of Preparation, 1859–1880," *The Historian*, vol. 29 (1967), 176–8.

56 Tugan-Baranovsky on 1860, 298 (quoted); Zelnik, 155–7.

57 Tugan-Baranovsky, 303–4; quotations from 304.

58 Tugan-Baranovsky, 305–7; Valuev, *Dnevnik*, vol. 2, 507–508; Vladimir Ia. Laverychev, *Tsarizm i rabochii vopros v Rossi (1861–1917 gg.)* (Moscow, 1972), 44.

59 See Zelnik's persuasive case against Tugan-Baranovsky and Kiniapina on this point, 151–7.

60 Laverychev, *Tsarizm*, 54.

61 On the unreliability of such figures, however, see note 116.

62 "Fabrika kuptsa Khludova," *Nedelia*, Sept. 28, 1880, 1238–41.

63 "Fabrika," 1242; "Khludovskoe delo," *Nedelia*, July 5, 1881, 901–11; Gately, 88. Laverychev, *Tsarizm*, 55, put the number of strikers at 2,600.

64 N. Subbotin, *V pamiati ob A. I. Khludove* (Moscow, 1882), 4–11; quotations from 11, 6. The fire killed several workers because the foreman locked the doors from the outside in an effort to contain the blaze: Abramov, "Khludovshchina," 41.

65 Moscow Governor-General Dolgorukov worried in 1880 about labor disorders caused by the manufacturers' unjust fines and "cruel" treatment of workers: Laverychev, *Tsarizm*, 55.

66 Laverychev, *Tsarizm*, 59. At the same time, Chetverikov told the State Council how he had abolished night work for children and reduced the work shift from twelve to nine hours in his own woolens factory: *Rossiia*, 41–2.

67 Tugan-Baranovsky, 308–9; Laverychev, *Tsarizm*, 61.

68 Five hundred spinners had struck to protest exorbitant fines that year: Lev Martov, "Razvitie krupnoi promyshlennosti i rabochee dvizhenie do 1892 g.," *Istoriia Rossii v XIX v.*, 9 vols. (St. Petersburg, 1907–11) vol. 6, 122.

69 Ch. M. Ioksimovich, *Manufakturnaia promyshlennost'* (Moscow, 1915), vol. 1, 7.

70 An Old-Believer worker related this story to Riabushinsky: "Kupechestvo," 184.

71 The trial records filled thirteen volumes: Vladimir I. Nevsky, ed., *Morozovskaia stachka 1885 g.* (Moscow, 1925), 15–17. Other bibliographical information in Petr I. Kabanov and R. K. Erman, *Morozovskaia stachka 1885 goda: posobie dlia uchitelei* (Moscow, 1963).

72 Martov, 118.

73 Kabanov and Erman, 48 (quoting Moiseenko's memoirs); Nevsky, 234; Tugan-Baranovsky, 314. On Moiseenko's contacts with the radical socialists Plekhanov and Khalturin, Nevsky, 6.

74 Kabanov and Erman, 49, 56 (quoted).

75 Tsar Alexander and Interior Minister Tolstoi supported this policy of not capitulating to the workers: Kabanov and Erman, 71.

76 Morozov also fired a hated foreman, refunded some fines, and henceforth kept fine monies separate from the company's income. Kabanov and Erman, 76–7; Nevsky, 17.

77 Nevsky, documents no. 41–2 and 45–6. Three merchants served on the twelve-man jury: 230.

78 Quoted in Kabanov and Erman, 85. "Opravdatel'nyi prigovor," *VE*, July 1886, 373–8.

79 Tolstoi blamed manufacturers for driving workers to violence by fines, low wages, high prices in factory stores, and vague conditions of employment. Tugan-Baranovsky, 315.

80 Laverychev, *Tsarizm*, 63–6; quotation from 66.

81 Laverychev, *Tsarizm*, 65, 67.

82 Tugan-Baranovsky, 315–16; Gately, 96–100; and I. I. Ianzhul, *Iz vospominanii i perepiski fabrichnogo inspektora pervogo prizyva* (St. Petersburg, 1907), 68–71, give useful analyses of this complex law. Its major provisions included: detailed work contracts which forbade quitting or firing except in cases of mutual agreement; firing for cause only in cases of repeated absences, insolence, dangerous conduct; quitting for cause only in cases of the employer's breach of contract, assault and battery, unsafe working conditions, etc.; ban on wage reductions, with a penalty of 100–300 rubles; cash wages (no payment in coupons or in kind); regular paydays; no deductions for medical care, lighting, use of tools, etc.; strict limitations on infractions to be punishable by fines (absence, negligence, drunkenness, gambling, etc., and not accidents, sickness, or absence because of a death in the family); a maximum on fines as a percentage of wages (20 percent per month, 33 percent per pay period); mediation by factory inspectors in conflicts over fines; the placing of fines in a fund to benefit the workers; a ban on both lockouts and strikes; and prison terms for striking (3–16 months). A Provincial Factory Board *(prisutstvie)* composed of officials and manufacturers would ensure implementation. See also I. Kh. Ozerov, *Politika po rabochemu voprosu v Rossii za poslednie gody* (Moscow, 1906), 7–13, for a summary of Russian labor legislation passed in the late nineteenth century.

83 The commission conceded a few points to them, such as the use of punitive fines. Laverychev, *Tsarizm*, 68–9. On Alekseev's generally enlightened views, Ianzhul, 175–6.

84 Tugan-Baranovsky, 318.

85 *RPP*, 666, called it "a reactionary, chauvinist organ . . ." Manufacturers tried their hand at writing articles themselves, for example, in defense of night work: Laverychev, *Burzhuaziia*, 128–9.

86 Quoted in "Fabrichnye volneniia," *VE*, Feb. 1885, 896.

87 Laverychev, *Burzhuaziia*, 135; Ianzhul, 3, 180–3. Evidently unaware of the merchants' role, Baluev, 170, called it "just another reactionary gentry-monarchist" paper. Sharapov published it again in 1905–10: *RPP*, 672. David I. Morozov's brother Arseni, a Holy Host member, donated money to *Golos Moskvy*, *Russkoe delo*, and *Russkoe obozrenie*: D. A. Pokrovsky, "Ocherki Moskvy," *IV*, vol. 52 (1893), 122, and Buryshkin, 120.

88 Tugan-Baranovsky, 318. The paper's editor, Nikita P. Giliarov-Platonov (1824–87), apparently had no financial dealings with the merchants. See *RPP*, 501–2.

89 John L. Pesda, "N. K. Bunge and Russian Economic Development, 1881–1886," unpublished doctoral dissertation, Kent State University, 1971, 139; Berlin, 193, quoting one of Katkov's editorials of 1886.

90 Pesda, 139–42.

91 Berlin, 198.

92 Laverychev, *Tsarizm*, 79.

93 Tugan-Baranovsky, 319. Laverychev, *Tsarizm*, 78, summarized the twenty accusations against inspectors; these included almost all their assigned duties (see note 82).

94 Berlin's acid comment, 198; see also 128–9.

95 Tugan-Baranovsky, 319–20; Laverychev, *Tsarizm*, 77; Martov, 135; and Berlin, 199 (quoted).

96   Berlin, 194; S. Gvozdev, *Zapiski fabrichnogo inspektora, iz nabliudenii i praktiki v period 1894–1908 gg.*, 2nd ed. (Moscow-Leningrad, 1925), 16, 13.

97   Laverychev, *Tsarizm*, 58, 61, 77; Laverychev, *Burzhuaziia*, 131 (quoted); Ianzhul, 88–92.

98   Quotations from Schulze-Gavernitz, 137, 132. See his detailed statistical argument (111–18) and description of factory life in the first and second stages (147–55).

99   The latter schedule deprived the workers of adequate sleep and separated husbands and wives. In contrast, the new system of two shifts on a staggered two-day schedule left the machines idle, and the workers' families united, during the night (first day: on from 4 to 10 A.M., off until 4 P.M., on until 10 P.M., and off until 10 A.M.; second day: on from 10 A.M. to 4 P.M., and off until 4 A.M. the next day). Schulze-Gavernitz, 138–9.

100 Schulze-Gavernitz, 161–71; 116.

101 Tugan-Baranovsky, 322–5; Laverychev, *Tsarizm*, 93–5; Ermansky, "Do 1905," 324.

102 Martov, 93; Ozerov, 9; Tugan-Baranovsky, 328.

103 Schulze-Gavernitz, 161.

104 *IM*, vol. 5, 31–2.

105 Obshchestvo dlia sodeistviia uluchsheniiu i razvitiiu manufakturnoi promyshlennosti, *Pamiati Sergeia Ivanovicha Prokhorova* (Moscow, 1900), 4, 6, 19 (quoted), 5. See his obituary in *RVed*, Mar. 4, 1899, 2.

106 Lapitskaia, *Byt*, 40–9, 38 (quoted).

107 Riabushinsky, 184. The self-congratulatory history of his family's business, *Torgovoe . . . delo* (Moscow, 1913), 117, admitted that until 1897 the twelve-hour day had been standard in the Riabushinsky textile factory. Between 1901 and 1905, each shift lasted 11½ hours, and only in 1906 did the Riabushinskys implement the modern system of two shifts working 18 hours every two days, described here in note 99.

108 Gately, 104–7, 158–9; Martov, 82; Ozerov, 107 (quoted), 157; Laverychev, *Tsarizm*, 256.

109 Buryshkin, 278.

110 Ozerov, 25–7, 137 (quoted). See also Berlin, 201–2.

111 Iakov A. Novikov, *Protektsionizm* (St. Petersburg, 1890), especially book 1, ch. 1 and book 2, ch. 10. He attacked Sharapov by name (209–10) and ridiculed protectionists as "*kvas* patriots" (212). (On this epithet, see ch. 8, note 1.) On zemstvo opinions, Veselovsky, *Istoriia*, vol. 3, 371–2.

112 Pokrovsky, *Torgovlia*, 307–10; "Po povodu torgovogo dogovora Rossii s Germaniei," *RVes*, April 1894, 354–7; Florinsky, vol. 2, 1110.

113 *MV*, Aug. 16, 1893, 1; Laverychev, *Burzhuaziia*, 191.

114 Valentin (d. 1896) or Konstantin (d. 1899) K. Krestovnikov, quoted from *Novoe vremia*, 1893, without reference by Buryshkin, 180–1.

115 "Po povodu," 359–60 (quoted); Florinsky, vol. 2, 1110. Specific figures in Pokrovsky, *Torgovlia*, 310.

116 N. Annensky, "Vserossiiskii torgovo-promyshlennyi s"ezd," *Russkoe bogatstvo*, 1896, no. 9 (Sept., section "Khronika vnutrennei zhizni," 151. See, however, the argument of *MV* (Aug. 1, 1900, 4–5) that the conventional formula (annual profit divided by basic capital) ignored large investments of undistributed profits over the years and thus vastly overstated the profit rate in a given year. Bureaucratic difficulties allegedly kept the manufacturers from changing corporate charters to reflect gradual increases in basic capital.

117 Grover, 245 (quoted), 246, 272–6.

118 Quoted from *Volgar'* (July 6, 1896) in Annensky, 144–5, and Ermansky, "Do 1905," 343–4. See also Buryshkin, 65–6.

119 See the caustic accounts of two antiprotectionist observers, Annensky, 145–6 (from the Moscow University Juridical Society), and T— in, "Veserossiiskii torgovo-promyshlennyi s"ezd v Nizhnem Novgorode," *Novoe slovo*, 1896, books 1 and 2, 35–6. The merchants' credit troubles arose because the fair was held two months earlier than usual, to coincide with the Exhibition: Maksim Gorky, *Literaturnye portrety* (Moscow, 1959), 384–5.

120 Annensky, 166–7; Ermansky, "Do 1905," 344.

121 Twenty-nine resolutions on industry and trade, *Trudy vysochaishe uchrezhdennogo vserossiiskogo torgovo-promyshlennogo s"ezda 1896 g. v Nizhnem-Novgorode*, 8 vols. (St. Petersburg, 1897), vol. 1, 11–29. Debates of these sections in vol. 7, especially 204–17, 241–53, 424–9, 505–25.

122 *Trudy . . . 1896*, vol. 8, especially 21 and 90–4, recording Krestovnikov's exasperation and anger.

123 Between 1885 and 1894, it fluctuated between 50 and 85 kopecks a pud: Annensky, 152.

124 Annensky, 146–62. For the final debates in the general assembly, *Trudy . . . 1896*, vol. 1, third pagination, 1–62.

125 Quoted in Annensky, 163–4.

126 Annensky, 164–5, quoting *Nizhegorodskii listok*, Aug. 17, 1896.

127 Von Laue, *Witte*, 137 and 305, is explicit on this point.

128 Ermansky, "Do 1905," 315.

129 Riabushinsky, 179, recalled: "The relationship of Moscow to all government offices may be illustrated by the following. I was once preparing to go to Petersburg for some reason . . . My face was angry and discontented. My younger brothers and sisters laughed, 'Volodia is going to the Horde' [Muscovy's medieval suzerain] . . . In any case, when we arrived home from Petersburg we would say, 'Ugh!' To us freedom-loving Muscovites, it was hard to breathe in the offices of Petersburg." Witte, for his part, caustically dismissed in 1899 an MSEC complaint against large foreign capital investments with the remark that Russian manufacturers reaped "monopolistic profits" under the 1891 tariff; Sergei Iu. Witte, "Report of the Minister of Finance to His Majesty . . .,"trans. by Theodore Von Laue, in Riha, *Readings*, vol. 3, 424. At the same time, however, the manufacturers directed far fewer complaints against Witte's policies than did various spokesmen for landlords' and peasants' interests: Von Laue, *Witte*, ch. 8.

130 Von Laue, *Witte*, 101, noted that the finance minister preferred to burden the peasantry with excise taxes; as a partisan of capitalism "he was very loath to touch industrial and commercial profits." On the extremely complex question of taxes, see Rudchenko, *Ocherk*, especially 357 for statistics on the declining percentage of state revenues from commercial and industrial taxes in 1885–91; G. F. Semeniuk, "Moskovskaia tekstil'naia burzhuaziia i vopros o promyslovom naloge v 90-kh godov XIX veka," *Uchenye zapiski Moskovskogo oblastnogo pedagogicheskogo instituta im. N. K. Krupskoi*, vol. 127, *Istoriia SSSR*, vyp. 7 (1963), 141–74; and Laverychev, *Burzhuaziia*, 36, who noted that commerce and industry generated 45 percent of the national income but only 3.2 of the total tax revenues in 1895.

131 Ermansky, "Do 1905," 326.

132 Buryshkin, 246.

133 Buryshkin, 246–7.

134 Semeniuk, "Bor'ba," 106.

135 This tiny party, established in Moscow mainly by wealthy aristocrats, announced its entire program in its title: "The Union of Russians (*Soiuz russkikh liudei*) of All Estates and Ranks Who Believe Firmly that the Holy Church, the Autocratic Tsar, and the Russian People Shall, in Indivisible Unity, Create a Great and Mighty Russia." B.

Veselovsky, "Dvizhenie zemlevladel'tsev," *ODR*, vol. 2, part 2, 11. Although primarily a
defender of gentry interests and a critic of Witte's financial policies, Sharapov in the
1890s continued, in his paper *Russkii trud (Russian Labor)*, to denounce factory inspectors as creators of enmity between bosses and workers: Von Laue, *Witte*, 285.

6. *Toward a bourgeois consciousness: culture and politics,*
1880–1904

1   Louis Menashe, "Alexander Guchkov and the Origins of the Octobrist Party: The
    Russian Bourgeoisie in Politics, 1905," unpublished doctoral dissertation, New York
    University, 1966, 35.
2   Laverychev, *Burzhuaziia*, 70.
3   A. S. Nifontov, "Formirovanie klassov burzhuaznogo obshchestva v russkom gorode
    vo vtoroi polovine XIX v.," *Istoricheskie zapiski*, vol. 54 (1955), 244–5; G. A. Pozniakov,
    "Ploshchad' i naselenie goroda Moskvy," in Moscow, *Sbornik*, section 2, 2.
4   A. G. Rashin, "Dinamika chislennosti i protsessy formirovaniia gorodskogo naseleniia
    Rossii v XIX-nachale XX vv." *Istoricheskie zapiski*, vol. 34 (1950), 62, 65; Ernst Birth,
    Die Oktobristen (1905–1913): Zielvorstellungen und Struktur (Stuttgart, 1974), 55; Nifon-
    tov, "Formirovanie," 244.
5   Laverychev, *Burzhuaziia*, 65.
6   M. L. Gavlin, "Sotsial'nyi sostav krupnoi moskovskoi burzhuazii vo vtoroi polovine
    XIX v.," *Problemy otechestvennoi istorii*, vol. 1 (Moscow, 1973), 166 n. 2, 169, 172, 180.
7   Despite the crucial importance of these institutions in Russian economic life after
    1855, they have received little scholarly attention. Two preliminary statistical studies
    are Leonid E. Shepelev, *Aktsionernye kompanii v Rossii* (Leningrad, 1973), and Whitney
    A. Coulon III, "The Structure of Enterprise in the Russian Empire, 1855–1880,"
    unpublished M.A. thesis, Louisiana State University, 1979.
8   *IMKO*, vol. 5, part 1, 10 (Storozhev's emphasis). See Genealogies. On the Botkins' tea
    firm, Buryshkin, *Moskva*, 160–6; on the cotton textile dynasties, Ioksimovich, *Pro-
    myshlennost'*. See also JoAnn S. Ruckman, "The Business Elite of Moscow: A Social
    Inquiry," unpublished doctoral dissertation, University of Northern Illinois, 1975, ch.
    2. A tax law of June 3, 1898, allowed almost any person, whatever his estate, to engage
    in all kinds of trade and industry simply by purchasing a business certificate. The main
    exceptions were for Cossacks on active duty; foreigners; and, in provinces outside the
    Pale of Settlement, Jews who were not entitled to live in such provinces. Other restric-
    tions were implemented in the 1890s and early 1900s: no customs official could carry
    on wholesale or retail trade; bureaucrats must not act as contractors to the state except
    through their wives or other persons in their place of residence; certain bureaucrats
    could not establish corporations or serve as managers; and elected zemstvo and munici-
    pal officials could not engage in certain kinds of commerce. From 1898 onward, mem-
    bership in the merchant estate was contingent on the purchase of both a merchant
    certificate and a business certificate for manufacturing or wholesale commerce. Voltke,
    Pravo, 30–4; on special restrictions for Jews, Voltke, 37–48.
9   Nemirovich-Danchenko, *Life*, 124, 123, 131 (modified translations).
10 Riabushinsky, "Kupechestvo," 175, 186.
11 Quoted without reference in Buryshkin, 81–2.
12 Riabushinsky, 176.
13 "Vospominaniia," vol. 10, 273 (quoted); Riabushinsky, 176, 172.
14 Riabushinsky, 180.
15 *MIMKOP*, vol. 10, 388, 434; *IMKO*, vol. 5, part 1, 48–9, vol. 5, part 2, 319–402.

Notes to pp. 150–5   265

16 Riabushinsky, 169; also Buryshkin, 214.
17 Nikolai M. Chukmaldin, *Zapiski o moei zhizni*, ed. by S. F. Sharapov (Moscow, 1902), vi.
18 "Moskva i ee 'khoziaeva' (vremeni do pervoi mirovoi voiny 1914 g.)," *Vozrozhdenie* (Paris), vol. 105 (Sept. 1960), 101–4 and "Moskva vremeni do pervoi mirovoi voiny – Kitai-gorod," *Vozrozhdenie*, vol. 107 (Nov. 1960), 101–12.
19 Buryshkin, 100 (quoted), 101, 103.
20 Riabushinsky, quotations from 176–8, 187. Emphasis in original.
21 Riabushinsky, 174, 171 (quoted).
22 Riabushinsky, 172–3.
23 Buryshkin, 102, 101.
24 Quoted from GBL-OR by Laverychev, *Burzhuaziia*, 84.
25 Riabushinsky, 182. See also M. A. Plotnikov's sketch of the merchants' foibles, "K kharakteristike nashego kupechestva," *Russkoe bogatstvo*, 1898, no. 11 (Nov.), 199–204.
26 Michael Ginsburg, "Art Collectors of Old Russia: The Morosovs and the Shchukins," *Apollo*, N. S., vol. 98, no. 142 (Dec. 1973), 472; Buryshkin, 124. On his expenses, N. Zhuravlev, ed., "Iz rospisi lichnykh raskhodov fabrikanta M. A. Morozova," *KA*, vol. 83 (1937), 225–7.
27 Quoted in Laverychev, *Burzhuaziia*, 86. See also I. A. Belousov, "Ushedshaia Moskva," in N. S. Ashukin, ed., *Ushedshaia Moskvu* (Moscow, 1964), 326–7.
28 Shchukin, vol. 10, 249–50; Riabushinsky, 172; Buryshkin, 193; Ziloti, *V dome*, 143–4, 183–4.
29 Aleksandr Odintsov, ed., *Moskovskaia gorodskaia duma, 1897–1900* (Moscow, 1897), 73.
30 Buryshkin, 93 (quoted), 95.
31 Polunin, *Generations*, 347–8, 363–6, 353.
32 Riabushinsky, 173.
33 *MIMKOP*, vol. 10, 59, 71; *IMKO*, vol. 5, part 2, introduction, 73–7; Riabushinsky, 173.
34 Riabushinsky, 181; Buryshkin, 127, 131, 140, 223–4; Ginsburg, 476–7. Bakhrushin's library of 15,626 titles contained all the Slavophile and Pan-Slav authors; see *Katalog knig biblioteki Alekseia Petrovicha Bakhrushina*, 3 vols. (Moscow, 1911–12).
35 Buryshkin, 124, 222; Riabushinsky, 175, 182; Konstantin S. Stanislavsky, *Sobranie sochinenii*, ed. by M. N. Kedrov and others, 8 vols. (Moscow, 1954–61), vol. 1 (his autobiography); Vladimir I. Nemirovich-Danchenko, *My Life in the Russian Theater*, trans. by John Cournos (Boston, 1936), 24.
36 Vladimir V. Stasov, "Pavel Mikhailovich Tretiakov i ego kartinnaia gallereia," in *Stat'i i zametki, ne voshedshie v sobraniia sochinenii*, 2 vols. (Moscow, 1954), vol. 2, 389 (quoted), 388, 404–5; Buryshkin, 135–6; Botkina, *Tretiakov*; Ziloti, 139, 95–6.
37 Grover, "Mamontov," especially 38–42, 154, 213, 293–5, 357–9. On Mamontov's greatest discovery, the legendary bass Chaliapin, see Stanislavsky, vol. 6, 389–90. Although she used the term "bourgeoisie" too loosely, failed to consult Grover's dissertation on Mamontov, and misread Naidenov's *Vospominaniia* (204, n. 36 and 40), Valkenier, *Realist Art*, accurately described the relations between the *peredvizhniki* and their merchant patrons. She correctly characterized P. M. Tretiakov as "a conservative and deeply religious man with strong Slavophile sympathies." For example, Tretiakov insisted on hanging portraits of Dostoevsky, Ivan Aksakov, and Katkov, and he commissioned numerous paintings on religious and, during the late 1870s, Pan-Slavic themes: Valkenier, *Realist Art*, 65–8 (quotation from 66). On other art collectors, see Ginsburg, 472–5 and Buryshkin, 140–1, 165–6. Rieber's discussion of these art patrons ("Group," 10–12) is marred only by the assertion that the painter A. A. Ivanov advised

K. T. Soldatenkov on his trips to Italian art galleries in 1872. Ivanov, of course, died in 1858. Vasili E. Raev (1808–69), who was for many years the artist-in-residence in Soldatenkov's mansion and his traveling companion in Italy, left a "Kratkaia avtobiografiia": GBL-ORF 92.6498.1.

38 Faubion Bowers, *Scriabin: A Biography of the Russian Composer, 1871–1915,* 2 vols. (Tokyo and Palo Alto, 1969), especially vol. 2, 186.

39 Ginsburg, 472.

40 *Revelations of a Russian Diplomat: The Memoirs of Dmitrii I. Abrikossow,* ed. by George Alexander Lensen (Seattle, 1964), 41, 3.

41 Petr S. Botkin, *Kartinki diplomaticheskoi zhizni* (Paris, 1930), 171–8; Pierre Botkin, "A Voice for Russia," *The Century Magazine,* vol. 45 (Nov. 1892–April 1893), 612.

42 *RPP,* vol. 1, 706–7; Buryshkin, 120. An article of September 1896 on the Commercial-Industrial Congress praised Morozov and Witte and castigated the merchants' opponents, "the so-called intelligentsia," who did nothing but "talk and show their radicalism before the public." Al. P. Elishev [Bukeevsky], "Vnutrenee obozrenie," *Russkoe obozrenie,* 1896, vol. 5 (Sept.), 452–4, 458 (quoted).

43 Laverychev, *Burzhuaziia,* 136.

44 Laverychev, *Burzhuaziia,* 137.

45 Buryshkin, 286 (quoted); A. N. Bokhanov, "Russkie gazety i krupnyi kapital," *Voprosy istorii,* 1977, no. 3 (Mar.), 118–19.

46 Buryshkin, 287; *RPP,* vol. 1, 626–7. Its circulation, 30,000 to 40,000 copies, equalled that of *Novoe vremia,* far surpassing the 8,000 of *Moskovskie vedomosti:* Baluev, *Reaktsiia,* 171. See also note 68. One journalist who wrote humorous sketches devoted to merchant life left an enormous quantity of plays, stories, and novels, e.g., *Manufaktur-sovetnik* (Moscow, 1903, all of 525 pages long). The illegitimate son of Kuzma T. Soldatenkov, he was christened with an entirely fictitious name (Ivan Ilich Baryshev, 1854–1911), and used the pen name I. I. Miasnitsky. His relationship to Soldatenkov, with whom he worked closely, was a well-kept secret. Tolstiakov, "Soldatenkov," 85.

47 Polunin, 288.

48 Laverychev, *Burzhuaziia,* 132, 158–9. Sobolevsky remained her common-law husband because under her first husband's will she and her children would have lost their inheritance if she remarried. Thus she kept her first married name, and her children by Sobolevsky took the name Morozov. Buryshkin, 122.

49 Vladimir Nemirovich-Danchenko, quoted without reference in Buryshkin, 123. See also Aleksandr A. Kizevetter, *Na rubezhe dvukh stoletii: vospominaniia 1881–1914* (Prague, 1929), 233–4.

50 Buryshkin, 122; see also Ginsburg, 471–2.

51 Buryshkin, 122, 286.

52 Several are listed in *Russkie vedomosti,* vol. 2, 53, 120, 170, 189, 192.

53 *Russkie vedomosti,* vol. 2, 20.

54 G. I. Shreider, "Gorodskaia kontr-reforma 11 iiunia 1892 g.," *Istoriia Rossii v XIX veke,* 9 vols. (St. Petersburg, 1907–11), vol. 5, 194–5; N. Karzhansky, *Kak izbiralas' i rabotala Moskovskaia gorodskaia duma,* 2nd ed. (Moscow, 1950), 12; figures from *IM,* vol. 4,512–13.

55 Shreider, 202 (quoted); *IM,* vol. 4, 513; M. Tagansky [pseud. of Mikhail A. Silvin], "Moskovskaia Gorodskaia Duma i ee obshchestvennaia rol' v sobytiiakh poslednego vremeni," *Tekushchii moment,* 1906, 5 (separate pagination).

56 Shreider, 196, 197 (quoted); Astrov, *Vospominaniia,* 134–5; Karzhansky, 14; Walter S. Hanchett, "Tsarist Statutory Regulation of Municipal Government in the Nineteenth Century," in Michael F. Hamm, ed., *The City in Russian History* (Lexington, Kentucky, 1976), 112.

57 Shreider, 198 (quoted), 199; Astrov, 142–3, 141 (quoted). Astrov managed the city's administration from January 1913 to late 1914 in the absence of an elected mayor: *IM*, vol. 5, 686–7.

58 Shreider, 222. He argued that municipal enterprises, lighting, and transport systems, which were paid for by indirect taxation on the poorer strata, particularly benefited the rich: 216–21.

59 Shreider, 223–4 (quoted); *IM*, vol. 4, 515 (quoted). The new Art Theater's request for funds reached the board over a year after the theater had opened with private support! Nemirovich-Danchenko, 117.

60 Shreider, 226.

61 Chicherin, *Vospominaniia*, vol. 4, 183–4.

62 T. Tolycheva, *Nikolai Vasilevich Rukavishnikov*, 2nd ed. (Moscow, 1878); *RBS*, vol. 17, 434. At the same time, a relative of the mayor, Ivan S. Rukavishnikov (1877–1930), left uncomplimentary literary portrayals of merchant family life (Buryshkin, 188), as did one of Mayor Alekseev's relatives, Sergei A. Alekseev (1869–1922), who used the pseudonym Naidenov.

63 Odintsov, 118.

64 Astrov, 248–50.

65 Buryshkin, 232.

66 *IM*, vol. 4, 514.

67 Buryshkin, 232–3.

68 Figures based on Odintsov's text; quotation from 103. See A. M. Pazukhin's humorous story about a merchant duma member's unsuccessful attempt to learn the art of public speaking from a defense lawyer: "Rech' gotovit," in *Na rubezhe veka: sto ocherkov, rasskazov i stsenov iz sovremennoi zhizni* (Moscow, 1900), 9–13. This book contains dozens of satirical sketches about many traditional aspects of Moscow merchant life, from bride shows to ridiculous pretensions to aristocratic manners (e.g., 39–42, 45–7).

69 Astrov, 251, 264 (quoted), 265.

70 *RVed*, May 6, 1893, 3; Chicherin, vol. 4, 184.

71 Astrov, 250.

72 Menashe, 64–6, 68 (quoted).

73 Although the Guchkov textile firm had gone out of business by 1900, the brothers maintained close business ties with their relatives and friends on the Moscow Discount Bank. See Appendix, Table II.

74 Astrov, 251.

75 Chicherin, vol. 4 184; Odintsov, 37; Hanchett, "Moscow," 175–6.

76 Astrov, 250–1.

77 *MIMKOP*, vol. 10, 330.

78 *MV*, Dec. 19, 1896, 3.

79 Martov, "Razvitie," 145; Berlin, *Burzhuaziia*, 210–11.

80 Martov, 144; quotation from Berlin, 211. See also Ruckman, 403–7.

81 Martov, 144–5.

82 Quotations from Martov, 146. Laverychev, *Tsarizm*, 156; Shmuel Galai, *The Liberation Movement in Russia, 1900–1905* (Cambridge, England, 1973), 184; and Jeremiah Schneiderman, *Sergei Zubatov and Revolutionary Marxism: The Struggle for the Working Class in Tsarist Russia* (Ithaca, 1976), ch. 5.

83 Martov, 154–5; Ermansky, "Do 1905," 328.

84 Quoted by Ermansky, "Do 1905," 328 and Martov, 156.

85 Ruckman, 425.

86 See Evgeni D. Chermensky, *Burzhuaziia i tsarizm v revoliutsii 1905–1907 gg.* (Moscow, 1939), 21–3, for the views of southern coal and iron producers.

87 Buryshkin, 231.

88 Astrov, 274.

89 Astrov, 272 (quoted); Odintsov, 50, 46, 37, 123, 107 (quoted), 8, 11.

90 Alekseev's obituary, *MV*, Mar. 12, 1893, 3; Simon Karlinsky, ed., *Letters of Anton Chekhov*, trans. by Michael H. Heim and S. Karlinsky (New York, 1973), 211–13; Odintsov, 89; Menashe, 68; Galai, 24 (quoted). Although a recent study of the famine concluded that the tsarist government's measures compared favorably to other famine relief campaigns in Ireland, India, and the Soviet Union, and the nongovernmental efforts had little positive effect, the basic shortcomings of the tsarist system itself could not escape blame: insufficient concern for agricultural development; poor planning for emergency food transport and distribution; and the lack of zemstvo units at the local level. Thus the famine and the government's subsequent hostility toward agricultural reform and local self-government produced "growing alienation between the rulers and the ruled" that foreshadowed the Revolution of 1905. Richard G. Robbins, *Famine in Russia, 1891–1892: The Imperial Government Responds to a Crisis* (New York, 1975), 24–7, 157–61 (on A. I. Guchkov's activities), 168–83; quotation from 182.

91 *RVed*, Dec. 21, 1899, 3. On Sergei T. Morozov, see also Buryshkin, 114; Ziloti, 100; and Ruckman, 362, n. 39. S. V. Lepeshkin likewise studied folk arts and established a *kustar* (handicrafts) museum (Odintsov, 37), as did S. I. Mamontov's wife and niece (Grover, 218ff.).

92 Terence Emmons, "The Beseda Circle, 1899–1905," *Slavic Review*, vol. 33 no. 3 (Sept. 1973), 465–6; *RVed*, April 22, 1904, 3; Buryshkin, 286; Milan M. Boiovich, *Chleny Gosudarstvennoi Dumy (portrety i biografii), Chetvertyi sozyv, 1910–1915 gg.* (Moscow, 1913), 182.

93 Florinsky, *Russia*, vol. 2, 1167; B. Veselovsky, "Dvizhenie zemlevladel'tsev," *ODR*, vol. 1, 306.

94 Astrov, 275.

95 "Po povodu konflikta v Moskovskom zemstve," *RVed*, Oct. 15, 1904, 3. By 1903, he had achieved gentry status, but he continued to manage the Danilovsk worsted factory: *Vsia Moskva* (Moscow, 1903), 1085.

96 Astrov, 279.

97 Astrov, 280. The Riabushinsky firm donated "eight bales of warm clothing for the Far East": *RVed*, Nov. 18, 1904, 3.

98 *MIMKOP*, vol. 10, 490. So many icons were donated that a pun was coined: "Kuropatkin does not know how/with which icon [*kakim obrazom*] he will beat the Japanese." Astrov, 281.

99 Menashe, 69–71, 73 (quoted). His brother Fedor (1860–1913) "had a predominantly military career" and, after 1905, helped edit Guchkov's newspaper, *Golos Moskvy (The Voice of Moscow)*, besides serving as treasurer of the Octobrist party: Menashe, 23, 61n.

100 Although war-related industries prospered, consumer-oriented production, especially textiles, declined sharply. M. Balabanov, "Promyshlennost' Rossii v nachale XX veka," *ODR*, vol. 1, 33–9. See also Ruckman, 411.

101 Emmons, 469, n. 26, n. 25 (quoted). Certain prominent members of the Union of Liberation also headed the Zemstvo Constitutionalists.

102 Pipes, *Struve*, 335–6.

103 *Gorky i Leonid Andreev: neizdannaia perepiska*, ed. I. I. Anisimov and others, *LN*, vol. 72 (1963), 231–2, n. 1–2; Gorky, *Portrety*, 305–8, 386–8; Pipes, *Struve*, 372. Professor Khodsky, the principal opponent of industrial protectionism at the Commercial-Industrial Congress of 1896, edited *Nasha zhizn'*: S. I. Stykalin, "Russkoe samoderzhavie i legal'naia pechat' v 1905 godu," in B. I. Esin, ed., *Iz istorii russkoi zhurnalistiki kontsa XIX-nachala XX v.* (Moscow, 1973), 97.

104 A. Egorov, "Zarozhdenie politicheskikh partii i ikh deiatel'nost',"*ODR*, vol. 1, part 2, 395–6. S. T. Morozov, V. P. Riabushinsky, N. I. Guchkov, and M. V. Chelnokov participated in the congress: Evgeni D. Chermensky, *Burzhuaziia i tsarizm v pervoi russkoi revoliutsii*, 2nd, rev. ed. (Moscow, 1970), 38.

105 Astrov, 285–7; Chermensky, 1970, 38; Gorky-Andreev, 247, n. 4; [Osip] A. Er-mansky, "Krupnaia burzhuaziia v 1905–1907 g.," *ODR*, vol. 2, part 2, 63–4. Astrov, 288, and Tagansky, 8, specified 74 members, whereas other sources' figures ranged from 65 to 82. Vladimir Ia. Laverychev, *Po tu storonu barrikad: iz istorii bor'by moskovskoi burzhuazii s revoliutsiei* (Moscow, 1967), 26, listed among the sponsors N. I. and K. I. Guchkov, V. S. Bakhrushin, A. S. Vishniakov, and M. V. Chelnokov.

106 Andreev to Gorky, Dec. 4, 1904, 274.

107 Kizevetter, 374–5. The Provincial Board duly abrogated the resolution: *RVed*, Dec. 19, 1904, 3.

108 Buryshkin, 274.

109 *RVed*, Dec. 1, 1904, 4.

110 *RVed*, Nov. 4, 1904, 3 and Nov. 24, 1904, 3.

111 Astrov, 288–9; Buryshkin, 310–11. Merchants and honorary citizens made up about half of the membership of the 1905–8 Moscow Duma; complete figures in *RVed*, Dec. 18, 1904, 3.

7. The failure of the bourgeois revolution, 1905

1   "Bourgeois revolution" denotes the destruction of an old regime by a liberal movement, with the aid of violent uprisings of peasants and urban crowds. It ends in the repression of radical groups and the political triumph of the bourgeoisie. The concept is borrowed from Moore, *Social Origins*, xv, 109–10, 427–9.

2   Bergier, "Bourgeoisie," 418, perceived this latter factor as being crucial to the political consciousness of the European industrialists of the mid-nineteenth century: "Faced with this challenge [the labor movement], the industrial bourgeoisie in its turn finally became conscious of itself [and thus] became a 'class' in the full meaning of the word to resist the growing pressure of the working class." The words "bourgeoisie" and "class" are used here in this sense. See also note 105.

3   Vladimir Ia. Laverychev, "Moskovskie promyshlenniki v gody pervoi russkoi revoliut-sii," *VMU-9*, vol. 19, no. 3 (May–June 1964), 39; Chermensky, *Burzhuaziia*, 1970, 51; Galai, *Movement*, 71.

4   Generally included are the four already mentioned, plus V. P., D. P., and S. P. Riabushinsky, Savva T. and N. D. Morozov, S. V. Lepeshkin, A. S. Vishniakov, A. I. Konovalov, and S. I. Chetverikov. "Young" is a relative term, however. Chetverikov was born in 1850, S. T. Morozov in 1861, and P. P. Riabushinsky in 1871. N. A. Naidenov (1834–1905) was, of course, well cast in the role of the old reactionary, but his capable lieutenant and successor as MSEC president, G. A. Krestovnikov, was only six years older than his brother-in-law S. T. Morozov.

5   "Zapiska Moskovskikh zavodchikov i fabrikantov," *Pravo*, 1905, no. 4, cols. 260–1. An abridged version appeared in *RVed*, Jan. 28, 1905, 3.

6   "Zapiska," 261–2.

7   "Zapiska," 263.

8   "Zapiska," 261.

9   "Zapiska," 264–5.

10 "Zapiska," 265.

11 "Zapiska," 265; the two hundred industrialists were from St. Petersburg, according to

this account. However, *Gorno-zavodskii listok,* the organ of the mine owners and metal-lurgists of South Russia, reprinted this memorandum in vol. 18, no. 15–16 (April 9–16, 1905), 7697–8, without specifying the location of that meeting, and thereby implied that it occurred in Moscow. Laverychev, *Po tu storonu,* 31, listed S. T. Morozov, P. P. Riabushinsky, and S. I. Chetverikov as among the "eminent factory owners" who "participated actively" in writing the memorandum. (See note 90.) In early February, representatives from forty-seven of the largest firms in the Central Region, which employed together more than 125,000 workers, signed a similar statement: Ermansky, "1905–07," 31. On this statement, see Ruckman, "Elite," 416–25, who stressed its similarity to the January 27 memorandum. Among the signers were S. T., I. A., and N. D. Morozov, P. P. and V. P. Riabushinsky, I. S. and S. S. Prokhorov, and A. I. Konovalov.

12 S. T. Morozov had favored the workers' right to strike in 1900, but throughout the Zubatov episode all other manufacturers had opposed it. Ruckman, 421–2.

13 Ermansky, "1905–07" 30, and Berlin, *Burzhuaziia,* 226, in their otherwise excellent analyses, ignore all noneconomic sources of these and other statements by manufacturers.

14 Menashe, "Guchkov," 103, correctly noted this strange blending of "*Kupechestvo-slavophilism*" with "bourgeois liberalism; the resulting ideological credo was a typically Russian mixed-grill of indigenous-traditionalist and Western-modern components. It was a historic breakthrough for the Russian bourgeoisie for it signalled the end of cooperation with an *unreformed* autocracy" (emphasis in original).

15 James L. West, "The Moscow Progressists: Russian Industrialists in Liberal Politics, 1905–1914," unpublished doctoral dissertation, Princeton University, 1975, 125–6, 128. Naidenov wrote to the tsar that the Duma's petition must not be considered "as the opinion of the industrial estate": cited in Ruth A. Roosa, "Russian Industrialists, Politics, and the Labor Reform in 1905," *Russian History,* vol. 2 (1975), no. 2, 129.

16 Laverychev, *Burzhuaziia,* 165; committee telegram cited in D. Iu. Elkina, "Moskovskaia burzhuaziia i rabochii vopros v gody pervoi russkoi revoliutsii (1905–1907)," *Uchenye zapiski Moskovskogo gosudarstvennogo pedagogicheskogo instituta im. Lenina,* vol. 35, vyp. 2 (1946), 119. The tsar welcomed the MSEC's expression of sympathy on the assassination, by a revolutionary, of Grand Duke Sergei, governor-general of Moscow, in early February. Lev V. Nikulin, ed., *V staroi Moskve: kak khoziainichali kuptsy i fabrikanty, materialy i dokumenty* (Moscow, 1939), 153.

17 Chermensky, 1970, 56–9. According to Galai, 242, the old reactionary Pobedonostsev drafted the document.

18 Meeting of Feb. 23, 1905, *MIMKOP,* vol. 10, 509.

19 Quoted in Laverychev, *Burzhuaziia,* 165.

20 Telegram to Kokovtsov, quoted in Elkina, 119.

21 Quoted in Chermensky, 1970, 59.

22 Astrov, *Vospominaniia,* 295.

23 Further details on the Kokovtsov Commission in Ermansky, "1905–1907," 46–7; Menashe, 93, 105; Roosa, "1905," 135–8, 146.

24 A. Katts and Iu. Milonov, eds., *Professional'noe dvizhenie,* vol. 4 of *1905: Materialy i dokumenty,* 8 vols. (Moscow-Leningrad, 1926), 152–5; Ermansky, "1905–1907," 45; S. E. Sef, *Burzhuaziia v 1905 godu po neizdannym arkhivnym materialam* (Moscow-Leningrad, 1926), 117–18. S. T. Morozov and P. P. Riabushinsky convinced the commission on February 18 of the need for unions, arguing, "It is better to deal with some organization than with an uncontrollable crowd." Quoted in Chermensky, 1970, 77.

25 On the drafting commission were K. A. Iasiuninsky of Kostroma and four Muscovites:

S. T. Morozov, G. A. Krestovnikov, A. I. Konovalov, and V. S. Barshev. Chermensky, 1970, 72–4 (quoted); V. V. Reikhardt, "Partiinye gruppirovki i 'predstavitel'stvo interesov' krupnogo kapitala v 1905–06 godakh," *Krasnaia letopis'*, vol. 6 (39) (1930), 10–11.

26 Chermensky, 1939, 98–9.

27 The twenty-seven signers included, besides the three bearers of the petition, S. I. Chetverikov, G. A. Krestovnikov, A. I. Konovalov, and P. P. Riabushinsky of Moscow and the main speakers at the March 10–11 conference. Ermansky, "1905–1907," 50–1; Buryshkin, *Moskva*, 312; Reikhardt, 11.

28 Laverychev, *Burzhuaziia*, 34; Sef, 118–20; Ermansky, "1905–1907," 51.

29 *RVed*, Mar. 9, 1905, 4.

30 Gorky, *Portrety*, 301–8 (quotations from 307, 308, 301, 303); Buryshkin, 114–15; A. A. Serebrov [pseud. of Tikhonov], "O Chekhove," in S. N. Golubov and others, eds., *A. P. Chekhov v vospominaniiakh sovremennikov* (Moscow, 1960), 653, 790n.

31 Ioksimovich, *Promyshlennost'*, 9; *Gorky i sovetskie pisateli: neizdannaia perepiska*, ed. I. I. Anisimov and others, *LN*, vol. 70 (1963), 264, n. 1.

32 Galai, 251. By an overwhelming majority, the Moscow Duma approved on May 24 the radical proposal for the convocation of a Constituent Assembly to create an entirely new system of government: Chermensky, 1970, 89.

33 Quotations from Chermensky, 1970, 67 (Guchkov's words); Menashe, 85 (his emphasis); and Chermensky, 1970, 68 (citing Guchkov's memoir in TsGAOR F 5856 [*sic*].

34 Petitions dated June 11 and June 14: Sef, 120–1.

35 Reikhardt, 15. At least twice in the preceding five weeks the MSES "young group" had endorsed a legislative Duma. Ermansky, "1905–07," 52, dated this clash on June 2, and listed P. Riabushinsky, I. Morozov, and V. Bakhrushin among the minority of fourteen. West, 140, also mentioned a June meeting, but listed fifteen dissenters, including the three above, A. I. Konovalov, S. I. Chetverikov, S. N. Tretiakov, and A. S. Vishniakov. He cited their open letter in *RVed*, July 26, which, however, dated the meeting July 2, and lacked Konovalov's and Tretiakov's signatures. Laverychev, "Promyshlenniki," 43, specified that a meeting of June 14 discussed the same issue, and listed N. D. Morozov among the minority.

36 Roosa, "1905," 144; Reikhardt, 20; quotations from Sef, 57, and Laverychev, "Promyshlenniki," 44. The version of these events in *IM*, vol. 5, 127–8 is riddled with factual errors. Counted among the "young" leaders, for example, was Savva Morozov, who had committed suicide almost two months before.

37 Quoted in Chermensky, 1939, 97–8.

38 Sef, 58; Reikhardt, 20.

39 Chermensky, 1939, 178–9.

40 Sef, 66; Laverychev, "Promyshlenniki," 44–5; quotation from Chermensky, 1970, 87.

41 Laverychev, "Promyshlenniki," 45.

42 West, 142.

43 *RVed*, July 26, 4 and July 29, 3. Italics in original. See also Chermensky, 1939, 99.

44 West, 148.

45 The Moscow Merchant Society expressed to Nicholas its "unlimited loyal gratitude for the new favor": *MIMKOP*, vol. 10, 516.

46 K. V. Sivkov, "Gorodskaia burzhuaziia 10 let tomu nazad," *GM*, vol. 3, no. 12 (Dec. 1915), 97–8; Chermensky, 1939, 121–3 (quoted).

47 Sef, 67; Laverychev, "Promyshlenniki," 45–6.

48 Quotations from Astrov, 313–14 and Fedor Dan, "Ocherk politicheskoi evoliutsii

burzhuaznykh elementov gorodskogo naselenlia," *ODR*, vol. 2, part 2, 118; Ermansky, "1905–07," 67 and 56; Chermensky, 1939, 130.

49 Laverychev, "Promyshlenniki," 46. The newspaper *Narodnyi trud* had never appeared. Equally ineffective in quelling labor unrest was a "conservative paper for workers," *Russkaia zemlia (The Russian Land)*, funded by "an organization of Moscow industrialists" and published in 1905 by two sons of the reactionary publisher A. S. Suvorin: Effie Ambler, *Russian Journalism and Politics, 1861–1881: The Career of Aleksei S. Suvorin* (Detroit, 1972), 181.

50 *RVed*, Oct. 15, 1905, 3.

51 Evgeni Maevsky, "Obshchaia kartina dvizheniia," *ODR*, vol. 2, part 1, 85–7; Astrov, 318–28 (a vivid eyewitness account). Dan, 124–6, noted that merchants actually led or participated in Black-Hundred pogroms in many Russian cities.

52 Chermensky, 1970, 129–30; Chetverikov, *Ushedshaia Rossiia*, 46 (quoted). See also *RVed*, Oct. 15, 3, on the drafting of this document.

53 Quoted by Chermensky, 1970, 130, who named J. P. Goujon, A. V. Bari, V. Iu. Geis, V. S. Alekseev, and Sh. A. Siu as being among the signers. Chetverikov, 47, paraphrased his speech rather differently: "the path to the resolution of this conflict of the government with the people lay only in the satisfaction of those minimal rights which the population was defending."

54 Chetverikov, 47.

55 Stenographic record in V. V. Simonenko and G. D. Kostomarov, comps., *Iz istorii revoliutsii 1905 goda v Moskve i Moskovskoi gubernii: materialy i dokumenty* (Moscow, 1931), 281–7; quotes from 283–4.

56 Berlin, 234–6; Maevsky, 113; Jacob Walkin, *The Rise of Democracy in Pre-Revolutionary Russia* (New York, 1962), 209–10; Galai, 263; Roosa, "1905," 144.

57 On the bankers' united resistance to strikes, *RVed*, Oct. 14, 3. N. I. Prokhorov shut down the Trimount factory on October 17 and 18 only to avoid bloodshed: Ioksimovich, 52d; Lapitskaia, *Byt*, 89.

58 Simonenko and Kostomarov, 286.

59 Astrov, 326.

60 Quotations from N. Nikolaev, *Moskva v ogne, 1905–1907 gg.* (Moscow, 1908), 30 and *RVed*, Oct. 19, 1905, 2. On the militia question, Nikolaev, 33–45.

61 Astrov, 330, 332 (quoted); Tagansky, "Duma," 19–21; Karzhansky, *Duma*, 23; Chermensky, 1939, 137. The assertion of *IM*, vol. 5, 681, that a protest by radical duma employees prevented A. I. Guchkov from running for mayor is contradicted by Astrov, 331 and Laverychev, "Promyshlenniki," 49.

62 Of course, subsequent political events "did not justify these words," but they "faithfully expressed the mood of Moscow at that time." Chetverikov, 47–8.

63 Quoted from the MSEC archive by Elkina, 128.

64 Quoted from the MSEC archive by Chermensky, 1939, 149. See also Sef, 54–5.

65 Gorfein, "Iz istorii," 165–8.

66 Astrov, 328–9; Guchkov quoted in Veselovsky, "Dvizhenie," vol. 2, 18, and Tagansky, 21; Struve quoted in Chermensky, 1970, 158–9. Menashe, 87–8, stressed the importance of the Polish issue in splitting the zemstvo movement.

67 See Reikhardt, 23–9 and Ermansky, "1905–07," 55–6.

68 Roosa, "1905," 145; Chermensky, 1939, 186; Birth, *Oktobristen*, 36; N. Vasin, *Politicheskie partii: sbornik programm sushchestvuiushchikh v Rossii politicheskikh partii* (Moscow, 1906), 64–7; Reikhardt, 31.

69 Vasin, 66–8.

70 Vasin, 63, 65, 67.

71   Pipes, *Struve*, 386; Miliukov quoted in Chermensky, 1970, 134.

72   Vasin, 191–4 (quoted); Roosa, "1905," 145–6.

73   The Germans worked between 2,880 and 3,292 hours per year; and since the Russians observed many religious holidays, the latter would fall short under a universal eight-hour law, by 275 versus 288 days a year, or 2,200 versus 2,304 hours. Vasin, 200.

74   Vasin, 201–3 (quoted).

75   Quoted in Chermensky, 1939, 186, and Ermansky, "1905–07," 57. V. Ivanovich, ed., *Rossiiskie partii, soiuzy i ligi: sbornik programm, ustavov i spravochnykh svedenii* (St. Petersburg, 1906), 77. Last quotation from West, 158. According to Chermensky, 1939, 187, after the Sevastopol mutiny in November, the Moderate-Progressive Party moved to the right, and its leaders (Riabushinsky and Konovalov) signed, with Krestovnikov's party, a joint appeal to the voters in the State Duma elections.

76   Buryshkin, 177–8.

77   Even the sole merchant leader who joined the Kadets, M. V. Chelnokov, remained "spiritually and emotionally" under the influence of Shipov, "his living conscience." Petr B. Struve, "M. V. Chelnokov i D. N. Shipov, glava iz moikh vospominanii," *Novyi zhurnal*, vol. 22 (1949), 241–2, 245. According to the Soviet historian Kornei F. Shatsillo (letter to the author, June 19, 1980), Shipov's father was Nikolai Pavlovich; therefore, he was the nephew of Aleksandr P. and Dmitri P. Shipov, two of the key figures in the merchant-Slavophile alliance.

78   Quotations from Menashe, 75. Birth, 39–41, following Menashe, 78, emphasized that Guchkov was primarily a politician who used his business ties to further his political career, not the reverse. Ruckman's contention (444, n. 1) that the Guchkovs were politically untypical of the Moscow merchants is unconvincing.

79   Vasin, 74, 77.

80   Laverychev, "Promyshlenniki," 48–9; Astrov, 330. Because the Union of October 17 welcomed whole groups as well as individuals, several small business parties joined by January 1906. On such electoral alliances, see Birth, 37, 39.

81   Laverychev, "Promyshlenniki," 46; Chermensky, 1939, 190–6; Reikhardt, 30–1. On the Octobrists' abstention from anti-Jewish rhetoric, Birth, 173. Compare the reactionary program of the "Russian Assembly" *(Russkoe sobranie)* in Vasin, 227–32.

82   Witte, *Vospominaniia*, vol. 3, 68, 73, 102–11. The disdain was mutual. Witte characterized A. I. Guchkov as one who feared the "beast" of popular discontent and therefore wanted a Duma composed of "an insignificant minority of Russian gentry and bourgeois drapers [*burzhua-arshinniki*] . . .," vol. 3, 72.

83   Elkina, 130.

84   V. A. Kondratiev and V. I. Nevzorov, eds., *Iz istorii fabrik i zavodov Moskvy i Moskovskoi gubernii (konets XVIII–nachalo XX v.): obzor dokumentov* (Moscow, 1968), 263.

85   Elkina, 130.

86   Roosa, "1905," 143.

87   West, 153 (quoted); second quotation in Chermensky, 1939, 170. A week later, Goujon, V. S. Alekseev, V. V. Krestovnikov, and P. P. Riabushinsky warned that "the country is perishing" from the postal-telegraph strike: Simonenko and Kostomarov, 296–7. See also Sef, 79.

88   This *Obshchestvo zavodchikov i fabrikantov tsentral'nogo promyshlennogo raiona* was succeeded in early 1907 by the "Moscow Society of Manufacturers" *(Obshchestvo zavodchikov i fabrikantov moskovskogo promyshlennogo raiona):* Buryshkin, 255–8 and Johann H. Hartl, *Die Interessenvertretungen der Industriellen in Russland, 1905–1914* (Vienna, 1978), 97, 101. (Lure, 165; Sef, 81; Hartl, 97; and Buryshkin, 255 all contain minor errors of nomenclature and chronology regarding these two organizations.)

89   Lure, 165–175. Ermansky, "1905–07," 72, stressed the Russians' imitation of the exist-
     ing German *Arbeitgeberverbände*.

90   Katts and Milonov, 162–3. It appeared first in *Russkoe slovo*, Sept. 20, 1905: Elkina,
     127. *Gorno-zavodskii listok* reprinted it on Oct. 29: Sef, 81. Chetverikov's use of the
     words "prerogative" and "struggle" in this sense supports Laverychev's contention that
     he helped write the anonymous memorandum of January 27, 1905 (n. 11). See also his
     letter of March (note 29).

91   Lapitskaia, 90–101; Henry W. Nevinson, *The Dawn in Russia, or Scenes in the Russian
     Revolution*, 2nd ed. (New York, 1906; reprinted New York, 1971), especially 176–95
     (184 quoted). See also N. I. Prokhorov's own account, Ioksimovich, 52v–52zh.

92   Chetverikov, 48–52 (52 quoted).

93   Astrov, 334 (quoted); Dan, 123; Chermensky, 1970, 209–10 (quoted); *Moskva v dekabre
     1905 g.* (Moscow, 1906), 239; Elkina, 130–1; Ermansky, "1905–07," 69.

94   Ermansky, "1905–07," 69–70.

95   Naidenov died on Nov. 28, 1905: obituary, *IV*, vol. 103 (Jan. 1906), 365–6. In
     Naidenov's memory, the Merchant Society established a 10,000-ruble educational
     fund: *MIMKOP*, vol. 10, 529. Krestovnikov was elected after the universally respected
     Chetverikov refused the post: Buryshkin, 183.

96   Chermensky, 1970, 210. Meeting of Dec. 20, 1905: *MIMKOP*, vol. 10, 523. Shades of
     Kokorev's lavish welcome for the heroes of Sevastopol in 1856!

97   Quoted in Chermensky, 1939, 187.

98   Ermansky, "1905–07," 55, 73–4; *Moskva . . . 1905*, 239.

99   Chermensky, 1939, 239; Sef, 96; "Soiuz, 17 oktiabria' v 1906 g.," *KA*, 1929, vol. 4 (35),
     157.

100 Quoted in Sef, 98–9; figures from Chermensky, 1939, 254.

101 On AIT's first meeting in April, the confirmation of its charter in August, and the first
     congress in October 1906, see Carl A. Goldberg, "The Association of Industry and
     Trade, 1906–1917: The Successes and Failures of Russia's Organized Businessmen,"
     unpublished doctoral dissertation, University of Michigan, 1974, 21, 31–4, 69, 74, 98.

102 Ivanovich, 66–8, reprinted these resolutions without naming the authors. They were
     passed in late 1905 or early 1906.

103 On the support of some provincial manufacturers for the reactionary parties led by
     bureaucrats, landowners, and clergy, see V. Levitsky, "Pravye partii," *ODR*, vol. 3,
     349, 383, 393–4, and Dan, 103–5, 115, 124–6.

104 Ruth A. Roosa, "Russian Industrialists and 'State Socialism,' 1906–1917," *Soviet
     Studies*, vol. 23, no. 3 (Jan. 1972), 395–417; and the chapters in Goldberg on labor,
     taxes, tariffs, pollution control, chambers of commerce, etc.

105 Stanislaw Ossowski, *Class Structure in the Social Consciousness*, trans. by Sheila Patterson
     (New York, 1963), quoting Marx and Engels in *The German Ideology*. Vladimir P.
     Riabushinsky actually used the phrase "class consciousness" in a speech to the first
     national congress of the Commercial-Industrial Party on February 5, 1906. Members
     of "our class," he said, must learn to feel proud of their work in the office and the
     warehouse, and must actively resist the "intelligentsia socialism" propounded by the
     lawyers and bureaucrats of the Kadet and socialist parties. Echoing the polemics of the
     1850s, Grigori A. Krestovnikov denounced from the same podium the "theoreticians"
     who, despite their superior education, had ruled Russia badly in the past. *Pervyi vseros-
     siiskii s"ezd chlenov torgovo-promyshlennoi partii, 1906 g.* (Moscow, 1906), 22, 23 (quoted),
     9 (quoted).

106 Howard D. Mehlinger and John M. Thompson, *Count Witte and the Tsarist Government
     in the 1905 Revolution* (Bloomington, 1972), 153. On the large French loan of early
     April, which Witte claimed "saved" Russia, ch. 7.

8. The fateful legacy of reactionary nationalism

1 This term, which alleged a narrow-minded worship of all things Russian, was applied by Interior Minister Valuev to F. V. Chizhov in April 1866 (*Dnevnik*, vol. 2, 118) and to the Muscovite protectionists by a St. Petersburg industrialist twenty-five years later (see Chapter 5, note 111).

2 So she told him on October 17, 1905: Kizevetter, *Vospominaniia*, 233–4.

3 *Russkie vedomosti*, vol. 2, 6 and 218; see his proconstitutionalist article of 1915, "Manifest 17 oktiabria 1905 g. i politicheskoe dvizhenie, ego vyzvavshee," *Iuridicheskii vestnik*, 1915, book 11 (3), 19–42. His son Grigori was Prince G. E. Lvov's assistant in the zemstvo union: Buryshkin, *Moskva*, 148. The French citizen Jules P. Goujon, owner of a silk factory and metallurgical plant in Moscow, led his fellow manufacturers in protests during the Zubatov episode and in 1905. A. I. Konovalov's effort to bridge the cultural gap between merchants and liberal intellectuals at "economic discussions" in 1910 owed much to the fact that he had "lived a long time in England." Boiovich, *IV Duma*, 140 (quoted); Buryshkin, 292. See also West, "Progressists," 233–9.

4 Buryshkin, 284–5, 288–92; West, 216–18, 239–40.

5 Laverychev, "Promyshlenniki," 52–3; Buryshkin, 284–5; West, 217. It bore the same title as T. S. Morozov's short-lived paper of the 1880s. A mere coincidence?

6 Berlin, *Burzhuaziia*, 292, 284. This bourgeois consciousness included a grim determination to apply massive violence against rebellious workers and peasants. The views of V. P. Riabushinsky, in emigration a religious writer on Old-Believer themes, were paraphrased thus by V. Ia. Briusov in 1907: "The bourgeoisie will do everything. The proletarians must be slaves. If someone rebels, kill him . . . Shoot those who attack . . . and the peasants will understand that you have the right to the land." Quoted in Laverychev, "Promyshlenniki," 52.

7 Chermensky, *Burzhuaziia*, 1970, 333–7. Birth, *Oktobristen*, 67–8, named S. I. Chetverikov, A. S. Vishniakov, P. P. Riabushinsky, and A. I. Konovalov. See also West, 209–13.

8 West, chs. 5–6.

9 Birth, 68.

10 Birth, 129; West, 260–2.

11 Buryshkin, 305, 306 (quoted), 332.

12 Berlin, 301–2.

13 Chetverikov, *Ushedshaia Rossiia*, 53–5; Buryshkin, 296–300.

14 M. L. Lavigne, "Le plan de Mihajl Rjabušinskij: un projet de concentration industrielle en 1916," *CdMRS*, vol. 5, no. 1 (Jan. –Mar. 1964), especially 101–2.

15 Arkady Joseph Sack, *The Birth of Russian Democracy* (New York, 1918), 267, 258.

16 On the Riabushinsky brothers' efforts to create a national Old-Believer political organization in 1906, see West, 204–6.

17 Riabushinsky, "Kupechestvo," 179–80; Kazemzadeh, *Russia*, 506–8, 594–5; and the article on the railroad question by "P. A. T." in Vladimir P. Riabushinsky, ed., *Velikaia Rossiia*, 2 vols. (Moscow, 1910–11), vol. 2, 243–81.

18 Riabushinsky, ed., *Velikaia Rossiia*.

19 Vasili N. Storozhev, *Voina i Moskovskoe kupechestvo* (Moscow, 1914), ii. The Riabushinsky press published this paean to the merchants' generous war donations of 1812 and 1914. Lewis H. Siegelbaum, "Moscow Industrialists and the War-Industries Committees During World War I," *Russian History*, vol. 5, no. 1 (1978), 64–83, describes the tendency of the Moscow War Industries Committee (led by P. P. Riabushinsky, S. N. Tretiakov, and A. I. Guchkov) to cloak its opposition to the St. Petersburg monopolies and bureaucratic regulations in highly patriotic rhetoric.

20 Lavigne, 90–3, 102. *Torgovoe . . . delo Riabushinskikh*, 76–7, noted that the "Moscow Bank," founded in 1912, lent money as a matter of policy to linen and other credit-poor industries in the non-black-earth areas of the empire. The list of twenty-three founders (77–8) included not only six Riabushinsky brothers and their liberal associates (A. I. Konovalov and S. N. Tretiakov) but also the more conservative G. A. Krestovnikov, Ivan Abramovich Morozov, L. A. Rabenek, and A. G. Karpov (a son-in-law of T. S. Morozov).

21 Berlin, 244–5; Gorfein, "Iz istorii," 168–78. Gushka, *Organizatsii*, showed how passages from manufacturers' recommendations were incorporated directly into the ministry's final policy guidelines. However, the merchants' emphatic demand in 1906 for powerful representative bodies elected by businessmen themselves (*MIMKOP*, vol. 10, 530) met a negative response, as in the past. Goldberg, "Association," 28, stressed that "the Association depended entirely on the good will of the top government officials . . . Its only right with regard to government administration and legislation was the right of petition." On red tape generally, Goldberg, 29, and West, 273–85.

22 Berlin, 264–78; West, 285–92; Goldberg, 31; and Hartl, *Interessenvertretungen*, 36–40.

23 Roosa, "1906–17," 409–17. On the failure of AIT to unite businessmen in all sectors and regions in Russia, Goldberg, 37.

24 Buryshkin, 332, 344. The conservative and liberal bourgeois positions of 1905 persisted until 1917; see Guchkov's impassioned defense of the war effort in Sack, 292–7, and Konovalov's enlightened speech on the labor question, Sack, 258–71.

25 Buryshkin, 344.

26 Buryshkin, 83.

27 Chetverikov, 65, 66 (quoted).

28 The extent to which backwardness represented a problem to be overcome by state intervention or, conversely, itself resulted from the state's regimentation of society in previous centuries remains an interesting question. For opposing views, see Gerschenkron, *Backwardness*, ch. 1 and Olga Crisp, *Studies in the Russian Economy before 1914* (New York, 1976), ch. 1.

29 See, for example, the optimistic appraisal by Walkin, *Rise of Democracy*, especially chs. 6–9.

30 Theodore H. Von Laue, "The Prospects of Liberal Democracy in Tsarist Russia," in Charles E. Timberlake, ed., *Essays on Russian Liberalism* (Columbia, Missouri, 1972), 181.

31 Moore, *Social Origins*, 445, discusses the "fascist syndrome" in Russia after 1905; see also the extended discussion by Levitsky, "Pravye partii." Although Hans Rogger, in his informative article, "Was There a Russian Fascism?," *Journal of Modern History*, vol. 36, no. 3 (September, 1964), 398–415, argued against applying the term to Russia in the 1905–14 period, he noted the important role of merchants in the Union of the Russian People (*Soiuz russkogo naroda*), the major party of the reactionary right.

Selected bibliography

Each source cited in this study appears with full bibliographical information when first mentioned in the Notes. In the interest of brevity, this bibliography contains only the most pertinent sources, excluding both general works and those peripheral to the main themes. It is arranged in order of decreasing generality, beginning with books and articles to which nonspecialists might wish to refer and ending with archival collections.

1. Books

Soviet scholarship, besides being hampered by the Marxist notion that capitalists must function as bearers of liberalism, perpetuates an implausible duality with regard to "the Russian bourgeoisie": Insofar as the merchants oppressed the workers and extended their economic power geographically, they are vilified as class enemies and imperialists; but to the extent that they furthered the development of high culture (Tretiakov, Mamontov, Shchukin, Morozov, Bakhrushin, and Stanislavsky), they are respected as upright citizens of Mother Russia, particularly when they aided members of the "democratic intelligentsia." Within the constraints of this Leninist-Stalinist orthodoxy, the most that can be expected is a series of careful, empirical studies such as those of Gindin, Kopshitser, Kuibysheva, Laverychev, Semeniuk, and Tsimbaev. Numerous Russian industrialists deserve serious biographies on the order of Lukashevich's on Aksakov, MacKenzie's on Cherniaev, Pintner's on Kankrin, Pipes's on Struve, and Von Laue's on Witte, but to date none has appeared outside the field of cultural history.

Akademiia nauk SSSR. Institut istorii. *Istoriia Moskvy*. 6 vols. Moscow, 1952–9. (In notes: *IM.*)

Berlin, Pavel A. *Russkaia burzhuaziia v staroe i novoe vremia*. 2nd, rev. ed. Moscow-Leningrad, 1925.

Bill, Valentine. *The Forgotten Class: The Russian Bourgeoisie from the Earliest Beginnings to 1900*. New York, 1959.

Blackwell, William L. *The Beginnings of Russian Industrialization, 1800–1860*. Princeton, 1968.

Buryshkin, Pavel A. *Moskva kupecheskaia*. New York, 1954.

Chermensky, Evgeni Dmitrievich. *Burzhuaziia i tsarizm v pervoi russkoi revoliutsii*. 2nd, rev. ed. Moscow, 1970.

  Burzhuaziia i tsarizm v revoliutsii, 1905–1907 gg. Moscow, 1939.

Cherokov, Arkadi. *Fedor Vasilevich Chizhov i ego sviazi s N. V. Gogolem. Biograficheskii ocherk po povodu 25-i godovshchiny smerti ego*. Moscow, 1902.

Dementiev, E. M. *Fabrika, chto ona daet naseleniiu i chto ona u nego beret*. 2nd, rev. ed. Moscow, 1897.

Ditiatin, I. I. *Ustroistvo i upravlenie gorodov Rossii.* 2 vols. St. Petersburg, 1875 and Iaroslavl, 1877.

Gerschenkron, Alexander. *Economic Backwardness in Historical Perspective.* Cambridge, Mass., 1966.

Gindin, Iosif Frolovich. *Gosudarstvennyi bank i ekonomicheskaia politika tsarskogo pravitel'stva, 1861–1892 gg.* Moscow, 1960.

Gushka, A. [Pseud. of Osip Arkadevich Ermansky, né Kogan.] *Predstavitel'nye organizatsii torgovo-promyshlennogo klassa v Rossii.* St. Petersburg, 1912.

Iakovtsevsky, Vasili Nikolaevich. *Kupecheskii kapital v feodal'no-krepostnicheskoi Rossii.* Moscow, 1953.

Ioksimovich, Chedomir Miletevich. *Manufakturnaia promyshlennost' v proshlom i nastoiashchem.* Vol. I. Moscow, 1915.

Istoriia Rossii v XIX veke. 9 vols. St. Petersburg, 1907–11.

Karzhansky, N. *Kak izbiralas' i rabotala Moskovskaia gorodskaia duma.* 2nd ed. Moscow, 1950.

Kazemzadeh, Firuz. *Russia and Britain in Persia, 1864–1914: A Study in Imperialism.* New Haven, 1968.

Kopshitser, Mark I. *Savva Mamontov.* Moscow, 1972.

Lapitskaia, Sima Markovna. *Byt rabochikh Trekhgornoi manufaktury.* Moscow, 1935.

Laverychev, Vladimir Iakovlevich. *Krupnaia burzhuaziia v poreformennoi Rossii (1861–1900 gg.).* Moscow, 1974.

   Tsarizm i rabochii vopros v Rossii (1861–1917 gg.). Moscow, 1972.

Leningrad. Russkii muzei. Istoriko-bytovoi otdel. *Kupecheskii bytovoi portret, XVIII–XX vv.* Leningrad, 1925.

Levin, Isaak Ilich. *Aktsionernye kommercheskie banki v Rossii.* Vol. 1. Petrograd, 1917.

Liberman, A. A., ed. *Sbornik v pamiat' stoletiia so dnia rozhdeniia Fedora Vasilevicha Chizhova.* Kostroma, 1911.

Lodyzhensky, K. *Istoriia russkogo tamozhennogo tarifa.* St. Petersburg, 1886.

Lukashevich, Stephen. *Ivan Aksakov, 1823–1886: A Study in Russian Thought and Politics.* Cambridge, Massachusetts, 1965.

Lure, E. S. *Organizatsiia i organizatsii torgovo-promyshlennykh interesov v Rossii: Podgotovitel'nye materialy i etiudy dlia kharakteristiki predprinimatel'skogo dvizheniia.* St. Petersburg, 1913.

MacKenzie, David. *The Lion of Tashkent: The Career of General M. G. Cherniaev.* Athens, Georgia, 1974.

Martov, Lev, P. Maslov, and A. Potresov, eds. *Obshchestvennoe dvizhenie v Rossii v nachale XX-go veka.* 4 vols. St. Petersburg, 1909–14. Reprinted, The Hague, 1968. (In Bibliography: *ODR.*)

Moore, Barrington, Jr. *Social Origins of Dictatorship and Democracy: Lord and Peasant in the Making of the Modern World.* Boston, 1966.

Moscow. Birzha. *Moskovskaia birzha 1839–1889.* Moscow, 1889.

Nikitin, Sergei Aleksandrovich. *Slavianskie komitety v Rossii v 1858–1876 godakh.* Moscow, 1960.

Ocherk deiatel'nosti A. P. Shipova, predsedatelia birzhevogo i iarmochnogo Komiteta v Nizhnem-Novgorode. Appendix to *Narodnogo gazeta.* St. Petersburg, 1866.

Ocherk torgovoi i obshchestvennoi deiatel'nosti manufaktur-sovetnika, pochetnogo grazhdanina i kavalera E. F. Guchkova. Appendix to *Narodnaia gazeta.* St. Petersburg, 1867.

Ocherk torgovoi i obshchestvennoi deiatel'nosti manufaktur-sovetnika, pochetnogo grazhdanina i kavalera I. F. Guchkova. Appendix to *Narodnaia gazeta.* St. Petersburg, 1867.

Petrovich, Michael Boro. *The Emergence of Russian Panslavism, 1856–1870.* New York, 1956.

Pintner, Walter M. *Russian Economic Policy under Nicholas I*. Ithaca, 1967.
Pipes, Richard. *Struve: Liberal on the Left, 1870–1905*. Cambridge, Mass., 1970.
Pokrovsky, Serafim Aleksandrovich. *Vneshniaia torgovlia i vneshniaia torgovaia politika Rossii*. Moscow, 1947.
Riasanovsky, Nicholas V. *Russia and the West in the Teachings of the Slavophiles*. Cambridge, Mass., 1952.
Rudchenko, I. Ia. *Istoricheskii ocherk oblozheniia torgovli i promyslov v Rossii*. St. Petersburg, 1893.
Russia. Ministerstvo finansov. *Ministerstvo finansov, 1802–1902*. 2 vols. St. Petersburg, 1902.
Russkii biograficheskii slovar'. 25 vols. (incomplete). St. Petersburg, 1896–1918. (In notes: *RBS*.)
Ryndziunsky, Pavel Grigorevich. *Gorodskoe grazhdanstvo doreformennoi Rossii*. Moscow, 1958.
Schulze-Gävernitz, Gerhart von. *Volkswirtschaftliche Studien aus Russland*. Leipzig, 1899.
Skalkovsky, Konstantin Apollonovich. *Nashi gosudarstvennye i obshchestvennye deiateli*. 2 vols. St. Petersburg, 1890.
Sobolev, M. N. *Tamozhennaia politika Rossii vo vtoroi polovine XIX veka*. Tomsk, 1911.
Subbotin, N. *V pamiati ob A. I. Khludova*. Moscow, 1882.
Thaden, Edward C. *Conservative Nationalism in Nineteenth-Century Russia*. Seattle, 1964.
Tolycheva, T. *Nikolai Vasilevich Rukavishnikov*. 2nd ed. Moscow, 1878.
Tsimbaev, Nikolai I. *I. S. Aksakov v obshchestvennoi zhizni poreformennoi Rossii*. Moscow, 1978.
Tugan-Baranovsky, Mikhail. *Russkaia fabrika v proshlom i nastoiashchem*. Vol. 1: *Istoricheskoe razvitie russkoi fabriki v XIX veke*. Reprinted from 3rd ed., Moscow, 1926.
[Ushakov, Aleksandr Sergeevich.] *Nashe kupechestvo i torgovlia s ser'eznoi i karikaturnoi storony*. 3 vols. Moscow, 1865–7.
Veselovsky, B. *Istoriia zemstva za sorok let*. 4 vols. St. Petersburg, 1909–11. Reprinted, Cambridge, England, 1973.
Voltke, Grigori. *Pravo torgovli i promyshlennosti v Rossii v istoricheskom razvitii (XIX vek)*. 2nd ed., rev. St. Petersburg, 1905.
Von Laue, Theodore H. *Sergei Witte and the Industrialization of Russia*. New York, 1963.

2. Articles

Elkina, D. Iu. "Moskovskaia burzhuaziia i rabochii vopros v gody pervoi russkoi revoliutsii (1905–1907)," *Uchenye zapiski Moskovskogo gosudarstvennogo pedagogicheskogo instituta im. Lenina*, vol. 35, vyp. 2 (1946), 111–34.
Ermansky, [Osip] A [rkadevich, né Kogan]. "Krupnaia burzhuaziia do 1905 goda," *ODR*, I, 313–48.
"Krupnaia burzhuaziia v 1905–1907 g.," *ODR*, II/2, 30–100.
Fedorova, M. E. "Moskovskii otdel 'Sviashchennoi druzhiny,' " *GM*, vol. 6, nos. 1–3 (Jan.–Mar. 1918), 139–83.
Gavlin, M. L. "Sotsial'nyi sostav krupnoi moskovskoi burzhuazii vo vtoroi polovine XIX v.," in *Problemy otechestvennoi istorii*, part 1 (Moscow, 1973), 166–88.
Genkin, L. B. "Obshchestvenno-politicheskaia programma russkoi burzhuazii v gody pervoi revoliutsionnoi situatsii (1859–1861 gg.) (po materialam zhurnala 'Vestnik promyshlennosti')," in L. M. Ivanov, ed., *Problemy sotsial'no-ekonomicheskoi istorii Rossii: sbornik statei* (Moscow, 1971), 91–117.

Ginsburg, Michael. "Art Collectors of Old Russia: The Morosovs and the Shchukins," *Apollo*, N. S., vol. 98, no. 142 (Dec. 1973), 470–85.

Hanchett, Walter S. "Tsarist Statutory Regulation of Municipal Government in the Nineteenth Century," in Michael F. Hamm, ed., *The City in Russian History* (Lexington, Ky., 1976), 91–114.

Iaroslavsky, G. "Gorodskoe samoupravlenie Moskvy," in *Moskva v ee proshlom i nastoiashchem*, 12 vols. (Moscow, 1910–12), XII, 17–48.

Iuzov, I. [Kablits, I. I.] "Politicheskie vozzreniia Staroveriia," *Russkaia mysl'*, 1882, no. 5, 181–217.

Kahan, Arcadius. "Government Policies and the Industrialization of Russia," *Journal of Economic History*, vol. 27, no. 4 (Dec. 1967), 460–77.

Kuibysheva, Ksana Semenovna. "Krupnaia moskovskaia burzhuaziia v period revoliutsionnoi situatsii v 1859–1861 gg.," in M. V. Nechkina, ed., *Revoliutsionnaia situatsiia v Rossii v 1859–1861 gg.* (Moscow, 1965), 314–41.

Kulischer, J. "Die kapitalistischen Unternehmer in Russland (insbesondere die Bauern als Unternehmer) in den Anfangsstadien des Kapitalismus," *Archiv für Sozialwissenschaft und Sozialpolitik*, vol. 65 (1931), 301–55.

Laverychev, Vladimir Iakovlevich. "Moskovskie promyshlenniki v gody pervoi russkoi revoliutsii," *VMU-9*, vol. 19, no. 3 (May–June 1964), 37–53.

MacKenzie, David. "Panslavism in Practice: Cherniaev in Serbia," *Journal of Modern History*, vol. 36, no. 2 (June 1964), 279–97.

Mamulova [married name Zakharova], L. G. "Sotsial'nyi sostav uezdnykh zemskikh sobranii v 1865–1886 godakh," *VMU-9*, vol. 17, no. 6 (Nov.–Dec. 1962), 32–48.

Nifontov, A. S. "Formirovanie klassov burzhuaznogo obshchestva v russkom gorode vo vtoroi polovine XIX v.," *Istoricheskie zapiski*, vol. 54 (1955), 239–50.

Owen, Thomas C. "The Moscow Merchants and the Public Press, 1858–1868," *JfGO*, vol. 23, no. 1 (Mar. 1975), 26–38.

Portal, Roger. "Du servage à la Bourgeoisie: la famille Konovalov," *Mélanges Pierre Pascal*, *Revue des études slaves*, 1961, 141–50.

Raeff, Marc. "Some Reflections on Russian Liberalism," *Russian Review*, vol. 18, no. 3 (July 1959), 218–30.

Rashin, A. G. "Dinamika chislennosti i protsessy formirovaniia gorodskogo naseleniia Rossii v XIX-nachale XX vv.," *Istoricheskie zapiski*, vol. 34 (1950), 32–85.

Reikhardt, V. V. "Partiinye gruppirovki i 'predstavitel'stvo interesov' krupnogo kapitala v 1905–06 godakh," *Krasnaia letopis'*, 6 (39), 1930, 5–39.

Riabushinsky, Vladimir Pavlovich. "Kupechestvo moskovskoe," *Den' russkogo rebenka* (San Francisco), vol. 18 (April 1951), 168–89.

Rieber, Alfred J. "The Formation of La Grande Société des Chemins de Fer Russes," *JfGO*, vol. 21, no. 3 (Sept. 1973), 375–91.

"The Moscow Entrepreneurial Group: The Emergence of a New Form in Autocratic Politics," *JfGO*, vol. 25, no. 1 (Mar. 1977), 1–20 and no. 2 (June 1977), 174–99.

Roosa, Ruth Amende. "Russian Industrialists, Politics, and the Labor Reform in 1905," *Russian History*, vol. 2, (1975), no. 2, 124–48.

Ryndziunsky, Pavel Grigorevich. "Staroobriadcheskaia organizatsiia v usloviiakh razvitiia promyshlennogo kapitalizma," *Voprosy istorii religii i ateizma*, vol. 1 (1950), 188–248.

Semeniuk, G. F. "Bor'ba moskovskoi 'tekstil'noi' burzhuazii za rynki sbyta i ekonomicheskaia politika tsarizma v kontse XIX v.," in *Nekotorye voprosy istorii Moskvy i Moskovskoi gubernii v XIX–XX vv.* (Moscow, 1964), 95–144.

"Moskovskaia tekstil'naia burzhuaziia i vopros o promyslovom naloge v 90-kh godakh XIX veka," *Uchenye zapiski Moskovskogo oblastnogo pedagogicheskogo instituta im. N. K. Krupskoi*, vol. 127, *Istoriia SSSR*, vyp. 7 (1963), 141–74.

Senchakova, L. T. " 'Sviashchennaia druzhina' i ee sostav," *VMU-9*, vol. 22 no. 2 (Mar.–April, 1967), 62–83.

Sh., S. "Zemskoe chinovnichestvo i gg. fabrikanty," *Slovo*, 1879, no. 8, 1–26 (separate pagination).

Shuster, U. A. "Ekonomicheskaia bor'ba Moskvy s Lodz'iu (iz istorii russko-pol'skikh ekonomicheskikh otnoshenii v 80-kh godakh proshlogo veka)," *Istoricheskie zapiski*, vol. 5 (1939), 188–234.

Stasov, Vladimir Vasilevich. "Pavel Mikhailovich Tretiakov i ego kartinnaia gallereia," *RS*, vol. 80 (1893), no. 2, 569–608. Reprinted in *Stat'i i zametki, ne voshedshie v sobraniia sochinenii*, 2 vols. (Moscow, 1954), II, 376–416.

Von Laue, Theodore H. "The Prospects of Liberal Democracy in Tsarist Russia," in Charles E. Timberlake, ed., *Essays on Russian Liberalism* (Columbia, Mo., 1972), 164–81.

3. Dissertations

A number of recent doctoral dissertations written outside the Soviet Union contain both new factual material and important theoretical insights on Russian social history. In contrast, the typical Soviet dissertation simply drapes the orthodox interpretation in new facts. For example, Tolstiakov stresses Soldatenkov's ties to Chernyshevsky, while barely mentioning his crucial role as a leader in the economic, religious, and political life of the Moscow merchant estate.

Beliajeff, Anton S. "The Rise of the Old Orthodox Merchants of Moscow, 1771–1894." Syracuse University, 1975. University Microfilms #76-7631.

Gately, Michael Owen. "The Development of the Russian Cotton Textile Industry in the Pre-Revolutionary Years, 1861–1913." University of Kansas, 1968. #69-11216.

Grover, Stuart R. "Savva Mamontov and the Mamontov Circle, 1870–1905: Art Patronage and the Rise of Nationalism in Russian Art." University of Wisconsin, 1971. #71-25474.

Hanchett, Walter S. "Moscow in the Late Nineteenth Century: A Study in Municipal Self-Government." University of Chicago, 1964.

Hayward, Oliver S. "Official Russian Policies Concerning Industrialization During the Finance Ministry of M. Kh. Reutern, 1862–1878." University of Wisconsin, 1973. #73-21159.

Malcolm, N. R. "Ideology and Intrigue in Russian Journalism under Nicholas I: 'Moskovskii Telegraf' and 'Severnaya Pchela.' " Oxford University, 1974.

Menashe, Louis. "Alexander Guchkov and the Origins of the Octobrist Party: The Russian Bourgeoisie in Politics, 1905." New York University, 1966. #67-4831.

Pesda, John Lawrence. "N. K. Bunge and Russian Economic Development, 1881–1886." Kent State University, 1971. #72-09277.

Piziur, Eugene. "Some Problems of Russian Constitutional Doctrine of the 'Sixties.' " University of Notre Dame, 1961. #61-3733.

Ruckman, JoAnn Schrampfer. "The Business Elite of Moscow: A Social Inquiry." University of Northern Illinois, 1975. [Covers 1890–1905.] #76-4901.

Tolstiakov, A. P. "Izdatel'skaia deiatel'nost' K. T. Soldatenkova. (Iz istorii progressivno-demokraticheskogo knizhnogo dela v Rossii vtoroi poloviny XIX v.)" Moscow State University, 1973.

West, James L. "The Moscow Progressists: Russian Industrialists in Liberal Politics, 1905–1914." Princeton University, 1975. #75-23,252.

4. Published documents

Aksakov, Ivan Sergeevich. *Ivan Sergeevich Aksakov v ego pis'makh.* 4 vols. St Petersburg, 1888–96.

Sochineniia I. S. Aksakova. 7 vols. Moscow, 1886–7.

Barsukov, Nikolai. *Zhizn' i trudy M. P. Pogodina.* 22 vols. St. Petersburg, 1888–1910.

Katts, A., and Iu. Milonov, eds. *Professional'noe dvizhenie.* Vol. IV of 1905. *Materialy i dokumenty,* 8 vols. (Moscow-Leningrad, 1926).

"Liubopytnye pokazaniia o nekotorykh predstaviteliakh moskovskogo obrazovannogo obshchestva v nachale proshlogo tsarstvovaniia," *RA,* 1885, vol. II, no. 7, 447–52.

Materialy dlia istorii moskovskogo kupechestva. 9 vols. Moscow, 1883–9. (In notes: *MIMK.*)

Materialy dlia istorii moskovskogo kupechestva. Obshchestvennye prigovory. 11 vols. Moscow, 1892–1911. (In notes: *MIMKOP.*)

Nevsky, Vladimir Ivanovich, ed. *Morozovskaia stachka 1885 g.* Moscow, 1925.

Nikulin, Lev Veniaminovich, ed. *V staroi Moskve: kak khoziainichali kuptsy i fabrikanty, materialy i dokumenty.* Moscow, 1939.

Pobedonostsev, Konstantin Petrovich. *K. P. Pobedonostsev i ego korrespondenty. Pis'ma i zapiski.* Introduction, M. N. Pokrovsky. 2 half-vols. Moscow, 1923.

Pis'ma K. P. Pobedonostseva k Aleksandru III. Foreword M. N. Pokrovsky. 2 vols. Moscow, 1925–6.

Popelnitsky, Aleksei A. "Zapreshchennyi po vysochaishemu poveleniiu banket v Moskve 19 fevralia 1858 goda," *GM,* 1914, no. 2 (Feb.), 202–12.

Sef, S. E. *Burzhuaziia v 1905 godu po neizdannym arkhivnym materialam.* Moscow and Leningrad, 1926.

Simonenko, V. V., and G. D. Kostomarov, comps. *Iz istorii revoliutsii 1905 goda v Moskve i Moskovskoi gubernii: materialy i dokumenty.* Moscow, 1931.

Spravochnaia kniga o litsakh, poluchivshikh na 1869 g. kupecheskie svidetel'stva po 1-i i 2-i gil'diiam v Moskve. Moscow, 1869. [Issued annually, 1869–1916.]

Storozhev, Vasili Nikolaevich, ed. *Istoriia moskovskogo kupecheskogo obshchestva, 1863–1913.* 5 vols. (incomplete). Moscow, 1913–16. (In notes: *IMKO.*)

Terentiev, P. N. *Materialy k istorii Prokhorovskoi Trekhgornoi Manufaktury i torgovo-promyshlennoi deiatel'nosti sem'i Prokhorovykh, gody 1799–1915.* Moscow, 1915.

Torgovo-promyshlennyi s"ezd, Moscow, 1882. *Rezoliutsii vysochaishe razreshennogo torgovo-promyshlennogo s"ezda, sozvannogo Obshchestvom dlia sodeistviia russkoi promyshlennosti i torgovle.* St. Petersburg, 1883.

Trudy vysochaishe razreshennogo torgovo-promyshlennogo s"ezda, sozvannogo Obshchestvom dlia sodeistviia russkoi promyshlennosti i torgovle, v Moskve, v iiule 1882 g. 2 vols. St. Petersburg, 1883.

Trudy vysochaishe uchrezhdennogo vserossiiskogo torgovo-promyshlennogo s"ezda 1896 g. v Nizhnem-Novgorode. 8 vols. St. Petersburg, 1897.

Vserossiiskii s"ezd fabrikantov, zavodchikov i lits, interesuiushchikhsia otechestvennoiu promyshlennost'iu, 1st, Leningrad, 1870. *Stenograficheskii otchet zasedanii 1-go [etc.] otdeleniia pervogo vserossiiskogo s"ezda . . . promyshlennost'iu.* St. Petersburg, 1872.

"Zapiska Moskovskikh zavodchikov i fabrikantov," *Pravo,* 1905, no. 4, cols. 260–5.

5. Memoirs and family histories

Although used sparingly by Soviet historians, these sources remain especially valuable because they accurately reflect contemporary attitudes of merchant leaders and their close associates in the public life of Moscow.

Selected bibliography 283

A valuable Soviet reference work on published diaries and memoirs entitled *Istoriia dorevo-liutsionnoi Rossii v dnevnikakh i vospominaniiakh* (Moscow, 1976–present) is currently being produced by a large staff of bibliographers headed by that indefatigable empiricist, Petr A. Zaionchkovsky. Volume 3, in four parts, will cover the 1857–94 period; and part 1 of this volume (Moscow, 1979) is devoted to economics and culture.

Ashukin, N. S., ed. *Ushedshaia Moskva: Vospominaniia sovremennikov o Moskve vtoroi poloviny XIX veka.* Moscow, 1964.

Astrov, Nikolai Ivanovich. *Vospominaniia.* Paris, 1941.

Botkina, Aleksandra Pavlovna. *Pavel Mikhailovich Tretiakov v zhizni i iskusstve.* 2nd ed. Moscow, 1960.

Chetverikov, Sergei Ivanovich. *Bezvozvratno ushedshaia Rossiia: neskol'ko stranits iz knigi moei zhizni.* Berlin, 192-.

Chicherin, Boris Nikolaevich. *Vospominaniia.* 4 vols. Moscow, 1929–34. Reprinted, Cambridge, England, 1973.

Golitsyn, V. M. "Moskva v semidesiatykh godakh," *GM*, 1919, nos. 5–12 (May–Dec.), 111–62.

Gorbunov, Ivan Fedorovich. "Otryvki iz vospominanii," in his *Polnoe sobranie sochinenii*, ed. A. F. Koni, 2 vols., 3rd ed. (St. Petersburg, 1904), vol. II, 373–404.

Gorky, Maksim. *Literaturnye portrety.* Moscow, 1959.

Ianzhul, I. I. *Iz vospominanii i perepiski fabrichnogo inspektora pervogo prizyva.* St. Petersburg, 1907.

Kelsiev, Vasili Ivanovich. " 'Ispoved' ' V. I. Kelsieva." Ed. by E. Kingisepp. *LN*, vol. 41–2 (1941), 253–470.

Kokorev, Vasili Aleksandrovich. "Ekonomicheskie provaly po vospominaniiam s 1837 goda," *RA*, 1887, vol. I, no. 2, 245–79; no. 3, 369–82; no. 4, 503–14; vol. II, no. 5, 130–44; no. 6, 263–72; no. 7, 394–416.

"Vospominaniia davnoproshedshego," *RA*, 1885, vol. III, no. 9, 154–7; no. 10, 263–72.

Krestovnikov, Nikolai Konstantinovich. *Semeinaia khronika Krestovnikovykh i rodstvennykh im familii (Pis'ma i vospominaniia).* 3 vols. Moscow, 1903–4.

Naidenov, Nikolai Aleksandrovich. *Vospominaniia o vidennom, slyshannom i ispytannom.* 2 vols. Moscow, 1903–05. Reprinted, Newtonville, Mass., 1976.

Obshchestvo dlia sodeistviia uluchsheniiu i razvitiiu manufakturnoi promyshlennosti. *Pamiati Sergeia Ivanovicha Prokhorova.* Moscow, 1900.

Polveka russkoi zhizni. Vospominaniia A. I. Delviga. Ed. S. Ia. Shtraikh. 2 vols. Moscow-Leningrad, 1930.

Polunin, Vladimir. *Three Generations: Family Life in Russia, 1845–1902.* Trans. A. F. Birch-Jones. London, 1957.

Porokhovshchikov, Aleksandr Aleksandrovich. "Iz zapisok moskovskogo starozhila," *IV*, vol. 67 (Feb. 1897), 539–54.

Rabenek, Lev L. "Moskva i ee 'khoziaeva' (vremeni do pervoi mirovoi voiny 1914 g.)," *Vozrozhdenie* (Paris), vol. 105 (Sept. 1960), 101–04.

"Moskva vremeni do pervoi mirovoi voiny – Kitai-gorod," *Vozrozhdenie*, vol. 107 (Nov. 1960), 101–12.

Shchepkin, Mitrofan Pavlovich. "Nadgrobnoe slovo: K. T. Soldatenkov," *RVed*, May 22, 1901, 2.

Shchukin, Petr Ivanovich. "Vospominaniia," *Shchukinskii sbornik*, 10 vols. (Moscow, 1902–12), vol. X, 140–70; 245–71; 370–418; 418–26.

Torgovoe i promyshlennoe delo Riabushinskikh. Moscow, 1913.

Vishniakov, Nikolai Petrovich. *Svedeniia o kupecheskom rode Vishniakovykh.* 3 vols. Moscow, 1903–11.

284 *Selected bibliography*

Volkova, Anna Ivanovna. *Vospominaniia, dnevnik i stat'i.* Ed. by Ch. Vetrinsky (V. E. Cheshikhin). Nizhny Novgorod, 1913.
Witte, Sergei Iulevich. *Vospominaniia.* 3 vols. Moscow, 1960.
Ziloti [Siloti], Vera Pavlovna. *V dome Tretiakova.* New York, 1954.

6. Archives

Despite the assiduous help rendered by some Soviet archivists, visiting scholars often encounter delays and arbitrary refusals. In only a few archives may foreigners routinely see the inventories *(opisi)* from which to select specific documents.

The following archives contain some of the most promising material for future research. One encouraging sign is the useful guide to more than a thousand corporate archives recently compiled by the young Soviet specialist, Andrei G. Golikov: "Materialy rossiiskikh aktsionerno-paevykh torgovo-promyshlennykh predpriiatii," 2 vols, unpublished candidate's dissertation, Moscow State University, 1974.

Merchant papers at GBL-OR: Nikolai P. Vishniakov (F 54); K. T. Soldatenkov biography by N. P. Kiselev (F 128); Soldatenkov (F 577); the Botkins and Ivan K. Babst (F178); diary of Mariia N. Kalinina (née Shustova) and memoirs of Mayor Rukavishnikov's daughter, Evdokiia K. Dmitrieva (F218); and Khrisanf N. Abrikosov's family chronicle (F 369).

At GIM: Bakhrushins (F 1); Botkins and Guchkovs (F 122); Prokhorovs (F 146); S. M. Tretiakov (F 169); and Shchukins (F 265).
At TsGAOR: Aleksandr I. Guchkov (F 555); Nikolai P. Vishniakov (F 875); and Mikhail V. Chelnokov (F 810).
At TsGALI: Botkins (F 54); Nikolai P. Vishniakov (F 722); and Mamontovs (F 799).
At GTsTM: Mamontovs (F 155).
At TsGIAM: Vasili A. Kokorev (F 959); Moscow Stock Exchange Committee (F 143); and numerous companies and banks.

Other papers at GBL-OR: Memoirs of Vladimir I. Guerrier (Ger'e) (F 70); Mikhail P. Pogodin (F 231); and Fedor V. Chizhov (F 332).

At GIM: Mikhail G. Cherniaev (F 208); and Ivan K. Babst (F 440).
At TsGALI: Ivan S. Aksakov (F 54).
At TsGIAM: Moscow City Duma (F 179).

The standard reference work on personal archival collections is *Lichnye arkhivnye fondy v gosudarstvennykh khranilishchakh SSSR,* 2 vols. (Moscow, 1962).

Index

and Zubatov, 164
Wogau, K. M., 60, 208
Wogau, M. M., 254n126
wool textiles, 7, 21, 66
workers, *see* labor

Zakrevsky, Arseni A., 21, 30, 37, 48 − 9,
    51
Zamoskvoreche (Moscow merchant quarter),
    10, 23, 30
zemskii sobor (consultative assembly), 51, 72,
    170, 184, 198
zemstvo
    and capitalism, 140, 210
    and liberalism, 76, 82, 88, 95 − 6, 98, 163,
    208

congresses of, 169 − 70, 184, 186 − 7, 189,
    194
    Moscow, 88
    Tver, 162
    under counterreform of 1890, 100, 166
    Vladimir, 99
Zemstvo (journal), 99
Zemstvo Constitutionalists, 169 − 70
Zhitkov, Professor, 140
Zhukovsky, V. V., 181
Zhuravlev, N. M., 46
Zhurov, 61
Ziloti, Vera P. (née Tretiakova), 122
Zindel, Emile, 60, 133, 208
Zinoviev, I. A., 199
Zollverein, 59
Zubatov, Sergei V., 164 − 5, 176, 177